Etruscan Roman
Remains

Etruscan Roman Remains

Charles G. Leland

Phoenix Publishing Inc.

PHOENIX PUBLISHING, INC.
P.O. Box 3829
Blaine, Washington USA 98231
www.phoenixpublishing.com

Distributed in the U.K. by
ROBERT HALE LTD.
Clerkenwell House
45-47 Clerkenwell Green
London EC1R 0HT

ISBN 0-919345-29-8

Printed in the U.S.A.

CONTENTS

PART FIRST
GODS AND GOBLINS

PART SECOND

INCANTATIONS, DIVINATION, MEDICINE, AND AMULETS

LIST OF ILLUSTRATIONS

INTRODUCTION

HERE is in Northern Italy a mountain district known as La Romagna Toscana, the inhabitants of which speak a rude form of the Bolognese dialect. These Romagnoli are manifestly a very ancient race, and appear to have preserved traditions and observances little changed from an incredibly early time. It has been a question of late years whether the Bolognese are of Etrurian origin, and it seems to have been generally decided that they are not. With this I have nothing whatever to do. They were probably there before the Etruscans. But the latter at one time held all Italy, and it is very likely that they left in remote districts·those traces of their culture to which this book refers. The name Romagna is applied to their district because it once formed part of the Papal or Roman dominion, and it is not to be confounded with La Romagna proper. Roughly speaking, the region to which I refer may be described as lying between Forli and Ravenna. Among these people, *stregeria*, or witchcraft—or, as I have heard it called, "*la vecchia religione*" (or "the old religion")—exists to a degree which would even astonish many Italians. This *stregeria*, or old religion, is something more than a sorcery, and something less than a faith. It consists in remains of a mythology of spirits, the principal of whom preserve the names and attributes of the old Etruscan gods, such as *Tinia*, or Jupiter, *Faflon*, or Bacchus, and *Teramo* (in Etruscan *Turms*), or Mercury. With these there still exist, in a few memories, the most ancient Roman rural deities, such as Silvanus, Palus, Pan, and the Fauns. To all of these invocations or prayers in rude metrical form are still addressed, or are at least preserved, and there are many stories current regarding them. All of these names, with their attributes, descriptions of spirits or gods, invocations and legends, will be found in this work.

Closely allied to the belief in these old deities, is a vast mass of curious tradition, such as·that there is a spirit of every element or thing created, as for instance of every plant and mineral, and a guardian or leading spirit of all animals; or, as in the case of silkworms, two—one good and one evil. Also that sorcerers and witches are sometimes born again in their descendants; that all kinds of goblins, brownies, red-caps and three-inch mannikins, haunt forests, rocks, ruined towers, firesides and kitchens, or cellars, where they alternately madden or delight the maids—in short, all of that quaint company of familiar spirits which are boldly claimed as being of Northern birth by German archæologists, but which investigation indicates to have been thoroughly at home in Italy while Rome was as yet young, or, it may be, unbuilt. Whether this "lore" be Teutonic or Italian, or due to a common Aryan or Asian origin, or whether, as the new school teaches, it "growed" of itself, like Topsy, spontaneously and sporadically everywhere, I will not pretend to determine; suffice to say that I shall be satisfied should my collection prove to be of any value to those who take it on themselves to settle the higher question.

Connected in turn with these beliefs in *folletti*, or minor spirits, and their attendant observances and traditions, are vast numbers of magical cures with appropriate incantations, spells, and ceremonies, to attract love, to remove all evil influences or bring certain things to pass ; to win in gaming, to evoke spirits, to insure good crops or a traveller's happy return, and to effect divination or deviltry in many curious ways—all being ancient, as shown by allusions in classical writers to whom these spells were known. And I believe that in some cases what I have gathered and given will possibly be found to supply much that is missing in earlier authors—*sit verbo venia.*

Many peasants in the Romagna Toscana are familiar with scores of these spells, but the skilled repetition and execution of them is in the hands of certain cryptic witches, and a few obscure wizards who belong to mystic families, in which the occult art is preserved from generation to generation, under jealous fear of priests, cultured people, and all powers that be, just as gypsies and tramps deeply distrust everything that is not "on the road," or all "honest folk," so that it is no exaggeration to declare that "travellers " have no confidence or faith in the truth of any man, until they have caught him telling a few lies. As it indeed befell me myself once in Bath, where it was declared in a large gypsy encampment that I must be either Romany or of Romany blood, because I was the biggest liar they had ever met—the lie in this case having been an arrogant and boastful, yet true, assertion on my part, that though penniless at the moment to stand treat, I had, at home, twenty-four gold sovereigns, eighteen shillings in silver, and twopence in bronze. " And I don't believe," added the gypsy, " that he had a d——d sixpence to his name. *But he's all right.*" So these travellers on the darkened road of sorcery soon recognised in the holder of the Black Stone of the Voodoo, the pupil of the Red Indian *medaolin,* and the gypsy *rye* (and one who had, moreover, his pocket always full of fetishes in little red bags)—a man who was worthy of confidence—none the less so since he was not ungenerous of pounds of coffee, small bottles of rum, cigars, and other minor requisites which greatly promote conviviality and mutual understanding in wisdom. Among these priestesses of the hidden spell an elder dame has generally in hand some younger girl whom she instructs, firstly in the art of bewitching or injuring enemies, and secondly in the more important processes of annulling or unbinding the spells of others, or causing mutual love and conferring luck. And here I may observe that many of the items given in this book are so jealously guarded as secrets, that, as I was assured, unless one was in the confidence of those who possess such lore, he might seek it in vain. Also that a great portion has become so nearly extinct that it is now *in articulo mortis, vel in extremis,* while other details are however still generally known.

An interesting and very curious portion of my book consists of a number of occult remedies, still preserved from remote antiquity among the mountain peasantry. Marcellus Burdigalensis, court physician to the Emperor Honorius made a collection, in the fourth century, of one hundred magical cures for disorders, such as were current in his time among the rural classes. He gathered them, as he informs us in a work entitled *De Medicamentis Empiricis*, "*ab agrestibus et plebeis*" ("from rustics and common people"). The collection has been edited by Jacob Grimm in a work entitled *Über Marcellus Burdigalensis*, Berlin, 1849. These "charms" were very ancient even in the time of Marcellus, and, like most early Roman magic, were probably of Tuscan or Etrurian origin. Of these one hundred sorceries I have found about one-half still in current use, or at least known. As given by Marcellus they are often imperfect, many incantations being wanting. Some of these I have been able to supply, and I think that no critical reader, who will compare *all* that I have collected, will doubt that these Italian formulas contain at least the spirit of antique originals.

In addition to this I have included a number of curious tales, anecdotes, and instances, many of which are identical with, or allied to, much which is narrated by Ovid, Virgil, Pliny, Cato, Varro, and others—the result of it all being that a careful comparison of the *whole* can hardly fail to convince us that the peasantry of the Romagna Toscana, who have lived with little change since prehistoric times, have preserved, through Etruscan, Latin, and Christian rule, a primæval Shamanism or a rude animism—that is, worship of spirits—and a very simple system of sorcery which can hardly fail to deeply interest every student of ethnology.

The result of my researches has been the collection of such a number of magic formulas, tales, and poems as would have exceeded reasonable limits, both as to pages and my readers' patience, had I published them all. What I have given will, I believe, be of very great interest to all students of classical lore of every kind, and extremely curious as illustrating the survival to the present day of "the Gods in Exile" in a far more literal manner, and on a much more extensive scale than Heine ever dreamed of. And I think that it will be found to illustrate many minor questions. Thus, for example, Müller in his great work on the Etruscans could hardly have doubted that the *Lases* were the same as the *Lares*, had he known that the spirits of ancestors are still called in the Romagna, *Lasii, Lasi*, or *Ilasii.*

I must here express my great obligations and gratitude to my friend, Professor—now Senator—D. Comparetti, of Florence, who not only placed his admirable library at my disposal, but also aided me materially by "advice, cautions, and criticism." Also to his son-in-law, Professor Milani, the Director of the Archæological and Etruscan Museum, and who, as an Etruscan antiquary is, I believe, second to none. I would here direct attention to his great forthcoming work, *Le Divinite è la religione degli Etrusci* ("On the Deities and religion of the Etruscans"), which is a complete account of all which is known on the subject.

As regards truthfulness or authenticity, I must observe that the persons from whom these items were obtained were in every instance far too illiterate to comprehend my real object in collecting. They were ignorant of everything classical to a degree which is supposed to be quite unusual in Italy. I have read many times lists of the names of Roman deities without having one recognised, till all at once I would be called on to stop—generally at an Etruscan name—there would be a minute's reflection, and then the result given. It was the same with regard to accounts of superstitions, tales, or other lore—they were very often not recognised at all, or else they would be recalled with very material alterations. Had there been deceit in the case, there would have been of course a prompt "yes" to everything. But in most cases my informants gave me no answer at the time, but went to consult with other witches, or delayed to write to friends in La Romagna. Thus it often happened that I was from weeks to years in collecting certain items. The real pioneer in folk-lore like this, has always a most ungrateful task. He has to overcome difficulties of which few readers have any conception, and must struggle with the imperfect language, memories, and intelligences of ignorant old people who have half-forgotten traditions, or of more ignorant younger ones who have only half learned them. Now I have been, as regards all this, as exact as circumstances permitted, and should any urge that *nihil est, quod cura et diligentia perfici haud possit*, I can only reply that in this work I exhausted mine. And it is unfortunately true that in collecting folk-lore, as in translation, the feeblest critic can pick out no end of errors as he will, or show how *he* could have bettered it, in reviewing the very best books on the subject—which is one great cause in this our day why many of the best books are never written. For truly there is not much money to be made thereby, and if discredit be added thereunto, one can only say as the Scotch "meenister" did to his wife: "If ye have nae fortune, and nae *grace*, God knows I have got but a sair bairgain in ye."

It should be observed that *all* these superstitions, observances, legends, names, and attributes of spirits are at present *far* from being generally known. Much of the lore was originally confined to the *strege*, or witches—who are few and far between—as constituting secrets of their unlawful profession. Again, of late, the younger generation have ceased to take any interest in such matters, and as regards the names of certain spirits, it is with difficulty that a few old people, or even one here and there, can be found who remember them. Mindful of this, I took great pains to verify by every means in my power the authenticity of what I have given, especially the names and attributes of spirits or gods. My most intelligent collector did her best to aid by referring to more than one *vecchia*, or old woman. An intelligent young *contadino* was specially employed at this work. He went on market days when the peasantry came down in numbers from the mountains, and asked the old women and men from different places, if they knew this or that spirit. He was eminently successful in verifying nearly all the names which I have here given. But he declared that he found it very difficult as regarded some of them, firstly, because only a very few old people knew the names which I was *specially* desirous of confirming, such as those of Tinia, Faflon, and Téramó, and that, secondly, these people were very averse to communicating what they knew, because such subjects are *scongiurati*, or prohibited by the priests. Adhering closely to the letters of his instructions, he however not only obtained the verifications, but induced a number of old peasants to write certificates, or *fogliettini*, as to what they had affirmed. These, written on strips of writing-paper of different colours, have a curious effect, looking something like testimonials of character of the ancient deities, as if the latter were seeking situations or charity. The following are specimens of these documents :—

" The Lasii are spirits of our ancestors, and are known at Santa Sofia.
                                                                "AUGUSTO FIERRARI.
" *March*, 1891."

" Fafflond (*Faflon*) or Fardel is the spirit of wine. He is known at Politeo (*i.e.*, Portico).
                                                                "OTTAVIO MAGRINI."

" Tigna, the great spirit of lightning, has been generally known here in Dovadola from ancient times.
                                                                " V. DEL' VIVO."

"Teramo is the spirit of merchants, thieves and messengers. He is known at San Benedetto, where the deeds of this spirit have been related for many years.
                                                                "TITO FORCONI.
" *March*, 1891."

Enrico Rossi testifies of *Mania della Notte*—the nightmare—that, " She was remembered once by many, but now it is a long time since any one at Galeata has spoken of her." I have more of these certificates ; suffice it to say that the youth, aided by his father and friends, succeeded in abundantly verifying all the names, save three or four. I should say, however, that these agents were exceptionally well qualified for the task, there being a very wise woman—in fact two—in the family. In some few cases they varied the orthography of the names. Thus " Peppino " declares in a letter that the correct name of Faflon is *Faflo*, and that the *Lasii* are *Ilasie*. What I would say is that I took all the pains in my power to verify the truth as to the actual existence of the names and attributes of these spirits, as well as of the other subjects of folk-lore given in this work.

There is another difficulty or contradiction to be noted. Many superstitions and observances are recorded as if they were still in familiar current use, or well known, which are in reality almost forgotten ; while others again are tolerably familiar to the multitude. I have often spoken of things as living which are rapidly becoming obsolete because my informants did so, after the fashion of old people— *ut est à nobis pauloantè commemoratum.* I have been told that these stories and rites are perishing very rapidly, that twenty years ago an incredibly vast and curious collection of them could have been made, and that ten years hence it will probably be impossible to find the names of the old deities, or more than a mere fragment of what I have preserved, and that a great deal has perished or vanished from among the people even since I first began to collect it. For all of this I crave due allow-ance. I have also to request it for what may strike some readers as a defect. A great deal of this folk-lore came from persons who had learned it long ago, and who, consciously or unconsciously, had often only a dim recollection of a song or incantation, and so, voluntarily or involuntarily, repeated it, perhaps imperfectly, just as it would have been done among the *contadini,* who are by no means ac-curate in such matters, and yet are endowed with a great gift for improvising. That the *motive* or tradition existed in every case, and that its sense is preserved, I am sure. I simply urge that I have collected and published *as well as I could,* doing my best to select from a terribly mixed and confused mass of material, and that I can do no more. Further sifting must be done by those better qualified than I am.

What will seem strange to many readers is that so many of the incantations and other portions of narrative which I have given in measure or rhyme, are in the original quite devoid of both, and seem to be mere prose. I call special attention to this, because it has been to me a special difficulty. What I have heard sung to airs, so that it sounded melodiously, I have rendered in something like poetic form What is called *cantare alla contadinesca* ("singing country fashion") means to sing prose in a peculiar kind of chant. To illustrate this I may mention that there is one very popular little song :—

> " Ma guerda la Rusena
> A fazeda a la finestra,"

which has not either in Romagnolo nor in Italian a trace of rhyme or rhythm, and which, as it was given to me in writing, seemed much more prosaic than are the majority of the incantations, or poems, in this work.

I am indebted to Senator COMPARETTI, of Florence, for pointing out to me the fact that this would strike many readers as a fault, and I have therefore devoted to it a special explanation. But I also owe to his extensive knowledge the remark that it is not less true that in many countries, as for instance the Slavonian, we see popular incantations now passing rapidly from poetry into mere prose. For this is the first stage of decay, and it is natural enough that those who have acquired folk-lore in this uncertain, half-changed, shifting form should give it again imperfectly. When the next generation comes it will be altogether lost, and then perhaps antiquaries would be thankful for such books, even if they were as full of defects as this of mine. Of which it may be observed that those who insist that all which is collected and published shall be absolutely and unquestionably *faultless* as regards *every* detail, while they certainly secure for themselves the gold all smelted and certified for them to manufacture or coin, exclude from commerce all ore or alloyed metal from which more skilful metallurgists may extract .even greater values. I do not by saying this offer an apology for *carelessness*, or worse, but a hint that by exacting too much we may lose a great deal, as did the ancient Greeks who threw away as refuse from the mines of Laurium a vast amount of precious metal which modern science has turned to great profit.

But I have what I think is a good reason for giving translations of so many incantations and songs in measure and rhyme. There is a remark by Heine to the effect that many people think that when they have caught a butterfly, put a pin through it, and preserved it with some chemical, that they really have a perfect specimen ; and it is in this spirit that many study folk-lore. But that is not a butterfly at all. For to such a "flying flower," as the Chinese call it, there belongs the exquisite fluttering in sunshine, the living grace of its moving wings, and lines of flight—curves within curves, as in a living arabesque of motion—" from shade to sunlight among summer flowers." One of these *contadina* songs, as sung with melody and expression, is a living butterfly, but when written down—with a pen through it—it has lost its life. And as rhyme and measure to a degree restore this, I have thought that by giving these songs such form I have come somewhat nearer to the spirit of the originals. I could also have given in every instance the Romagnolo-Bolognese, but this my limits positively forbid. Many, perhaps most, of my readers will understand Italian, but very few Romagnolo or Bolognese. As regards the very bad quality of the Italian, every reader will understand that I have given it with very little correction.

I will not, however, be understood as going to the very extreme limits of humility and apology as regards these poems. A great many are in themselves

strikingly beautiful, original, and imbued with a classic and often delicately appropriate spirit—as in those to Pan and Faflon—and the women from whom they were
derived could absolutely have no more invented them than they could have
invented the flying-machine of the future or settled "the great national Italian
problem" of flaying peasants without hurting them, or eating a cake and having it.
This is simply true, and as not a line or letter of them came ever so indirectly from
me, the question is simply, how could women, so illiterate as to hardly understand
what they repeated, have invented it all—much more, how could they have woven
into them, as is done in most cases, the most classical and appropriate allusions,
characteristics, and colour? Of all of which I can truly say, that if my informants
really manufactured these incantations, the interest and value of my book is
thereby augmented a hundredfold, as being the most remarkable *piéce de manufacture* ever presented to the public.

What will strike many readers as strange is that there should have existed to
the present day—though it is now rapidly disappearing—in a Roman Catholic
country, an ancient heathen religion of sorcery, from earliest Tuscan times. That
such a survival under such a *stratum* is not without parallel, I have shown by
an incident, which is thus described in my *Gypsy Sorcery :*—

" It has been discovered of late years in India, that during thousands of years of Brahminic, Buddhistic
and Mahometan rule, there always existed among the people a rude Shamanism, or worship of spirits and
stones, eked out with coarse sorcery, which formed a distinct religion by itself, and which came to light as soon
as British government removed religious oppression. This religion consisted of placing small rocks after the
fashion of Stonehenge and other 'Druidic' monuments, and in other rites of the most primitive kind. And
it is very evident that the oldest religions everywhere are founded on such a faith."

But I was much more astonished to find that in Tuscany, the most enlightened
portion of Italy, under all Roman rule an old pagan faith, or something like it, has
existed to a most extraordinary degree. For it is really not a mere chance survival of superstitions here and there, as in England or France, but a complete
system, as this work will abundantly prove. A few years ago Count ANGELO DE
GUBERNATIS informed Mr. GLADSTONE, in conversation, that there was actually
among the Tuscan peasantry ten times as much heathenism as Catholicism. I
repeated this remark to a woman whom I employed to collect folk-lore, and her
reply was : " Certainly, there is ten times more faith in *la vecchia religione* " (" the old
religion "). " For the peasants have recourse to the priests and the saints on great
occasions, but they use magic all the time for everything."

At another time when I expressed my astonishment that a certain girl who
had grown up in the country was utterly ignorant of the name of a single spirit,

and could recall nothing relating to witchcraft, she became scornful, and then excited, exclaiming :—

"And how should such a stupid fool, who is afraid of the priests and saints, know anything ? I call myself a Catholic—oh, yes—and I wear a medal to prove it "—here she, in excitement, pulled from her bosom a saint's medal—" but I believe in none of it all. *You* know what I believe."

"*Si ; la vecchia religione*" (" the old faith "), I answered, by which faith I meant that strange, diluted old Etrusco-Roman sorcery which is set forth in this book. Magic was her real religion.

Much of this magic is mixed up with Catholic rites and saints, but these in their turn were very often of heathen origin. Some saints such as Antony, Simeon, and Elisha, appear as absolutely sorcerers or goblins, and are addressed with ancient heathen ceremonies in cellars with magical incantations. The belief in *folletti*, a generic term for goblins, and other familiar spirits, has not sunk as yet to the "fairy-tale" level of beings only mentioned for entertainment—as in Grimm's Tales—they enter into popular belief as a part of the religion, and are invoked in good faith. There is actually in Tuscany a culture or worship of *fetishes* which are not Catholic, *i.e.*, of strange stones and many curious relics.

But there is, withal, as I have remarked, a great deal of mystery and secrecy observed in all this cult. It has its professors : men, but mostly women, who collect charms and spells, and teach them to one another, and hold meetings ; that is, there is a kind of college of witches and wizards, which, for many good reasons, eludes observation. It was my chance to become acquainted in Florence with the fortune-teller referred to, who was initiated in these secrets, and whose memory was stocked to an extraordinary and exceptional degree with not only magical formulas but songs and tales. Such familiarity with folk-lore and sorcery as I possess, resulted in confidence—the end being that I succeeded in penetrating this obscure and strange forest inhabited by witches and shadows, faded gods and forgotten goblins of the olden time, where folk-lore of every kind abounded to such excess that, as this book shows, I in time had more thereof than I could publish. To do this I went to strange places and made strange acquaintance, so that if the reader will kindly imagine something much out of common life, and often wild and really *weird*—*i.e.*, prophetic—when fortune-telling was on the cards, as the dramatic accompaniment of every charm and legend in this book, he will but do it justice. To collect volumes of folk-lore among very reticent Red Indians, and reserved Romanys is not unknown to me, but the extracting witch-craft from Italian *strege* far surpasses it. " I too was among the shadows."

There are many people, even Italians, who will say, " It is very remarkable that *we* never heard of any association of witches nor met with any of all this mythology or lore—we who know the people so well." Just the same might have been said of almost every respectable white native of Philadelphia when I was there a few years ago, as to the Voodoo sorcerers, who, silent and unseen, conjured and worked in darkness among the coloured people of that city. What did any of us know about even our own black servants in their homes? And the class which corresponds to the Voodoo acts in Tuscany, in opposition—unlike the American—to a powerful national religion which till of late ruled by the strong hand, and it fears everybody.

The extraordinary tenacity and earnestness with which the peasant Tuscans have clung to these fragments of their old faith is quite in accordance with their ancient character. LIVY said of them they were "a race which excelled all in devotion to religious rites and in the art of cultivating them" (v. 1. 6). But as KARL OTTFRIED MÜLLER remarks in *Die Etrusker*—a work which has been of great use to me—" while the Greeks expressed their religious feelings with boldness in varied forms . . . the Tusker (Tuscans) blended them in the most intimate manner with every domestic practical interest. Tuscan divination was consequently the most characteristic trait of the nation and the *Hauptpunkt*, or beginning of their intellectual action and education." And this spirit still survives. Among all the wars and convulsions of Italy the peasants of Tuscany have remained *the same race*. Englishmen and Frenchmen are the result of modern mixtures of peoples, but the Italians, like HAWTHORNE'S Marble Faun, are absolutely ancient, if not prehistoric. There are families in Italy who find their family names in Etrurian monuments on their estates. And CICERO, TACITUS, LIVY, VIRGIL, and many more, testify that all their divination and religious observances were drawn from and based on Etruscan authority. " This," says MÜLLER, "was shared *by the common people*. There were in Italy schools, like those of the Jewish prophets and Gallic Druids, in which the system was thoroughly taught." And there is the last relic of these still existing among the Tuscan " witches." In later times the Chaldæan sorcerers took the upper hand in Rome with their astrology, but the Etruscan *augures* were still authorities, so late as the fifth century, A.D., since they were consulted at the birth of CLAUDIUS. In 408, they protected Narnia by invoking lightning against the Goths (MÜLLER).

The Etruscan books of magic were common among the Romans. In Cicero's time (*Cic. de Div.* i. 33), there were many of them. I have been assured that there is in existence a manuscript collection of charms and spells such as are now in use —in fact it was promised me as a gift, but I have not succeeded in obtaining it. I have, however, a large MS. of this kind which was written for me from collection and memory, which I have used in writing this book. It is true that all I have is only the last sparks, or dead ashes, and coals of the ancient fire, but it is worth something.

I have freely illustrated my collection with instances drawn from reading, and have added to it certain tales, or stories, which have very curious connections with classic lore and superstitions. There are also a few records of certain plants, showing how the belief that many herbs and flowers have an indwelling fairy, and are in fact fairies themselves, still survives, with a degree of *personification* which has long since disappeared in most other European countries. There has been much collection of plant-lore of late years by many writers, but I am not aware that any one has observed this faith *in the plant itself* as a creature with a soul.

There is the same superstition as regards minerals, the reason being very curious. For there are in the earth deep mysteries; the earth-worm and mole are full of them because *the foot of the sorcerer* passes over them, and gives power, the *salagrana*, or stalagmite, and different metallic ores are really holy, from being subterranean, and yet sparkling with hidden occult light when broken they meet the sun; and plants which send their roots deep down into the earth draw from it mystic force which takes varied magic forms according to their nature when brought up into light and air. Owing to the inability of my informant to express herself clearly, I had difficulty for a long time in understanding this properly *chthonic* theory; when I did master it, I was struck by its Paracelsian character—this belief in a "geomantic force" which Chinese recognise as *Fengshui*.

Should the reader be astonished at the number of incantations which occur in this work, I would remind him that among the peasantry in Italy, but especially in the Tuscan Romagna there is, or has been, till of late years, some formula of the kind uttered for almost every conceivable event in life. And this is perhaps a proof of their antiquity. PRELLER, in his Roman Mythology, speaks as follows on this subject :—

" The belief in a *fate* in every form conceivable, such as Fortuna, the goddess of destiny, oracles, and all varieties of divination, was always very active in Italy, especially in divine omens, warnings, forebodings which developed themselves in the most varied phases and kinds, and it resulted in Rome in such a mass of marvels and superstitions running into every possible shape, as never was heard of in such a high stage of civilisation."

For every one of these fancies there was an incantation : if salt upset they said, "*Dii avertite omen !*" But the great source of it all was Etruria, from which the Romans derived the laws of their religion—that is to say, a divination which had a spell for almost everything which the heart of man could conceive. And it was from Etrurian Tuscany that I took these spells, which, by comparison with those which remain from Roman times, *all* bear unmistakable marks of antiquity.

I would also observe that though I have spoken of these sorceries and super-stitions as passing away rapidly, they are very far from having disappeared. While I was writing the foregoing, that is to say, on the second day of March, 1891, there was going on in Milan one of the most serious outbursts of a mob which had occurred for years. It being believed that a child had been bewitched by a certain woman, the populace in wrath pursued the sorceress with much abuse into a church. The details of this outrage, which occupy a column in the *Secolo* of April 3 and 4, 1891, will be given in the following pages. Milan, be it remem-bered, is "far away" the least superstitious city in Italy, and much in advance of Florence as regards such matters, while Florence is as light to darkness com-pared to the Romagna.

Since the manuscript of this work was put in my publisher's hands something has occurred which should properly have found an earlier place in this Preface. It is this : Some years ago I published a work on the Algonkin Legends of New England. Within a few months a contributor to the English *Folk-Lore Journal* has made a remark to the effect that he had always doubted the authenticity of these Legends, while another has said in *The American Folk-Lore Journal* that Mr. Leland is throughout inaccurate when reporting what Indians had told him. This last writer had gone to the same tribe, though probably to *other* Indians, and taken down with a *phonograph*, in the original Indian tongue, the same tales. His contribution consists in a measure of comments on my stories, which do not suffer in the least by his subsequent collection.

When I began to collect those Indian legends, all that I knew of them was that a Catholic missionary, who had lived many years among the Penobscot or Passamaquoddy tribes, had succeeded in getting only one story, so reticent were the Indians towards white men regarding their myths. During an entire summer I was very intimate and confidential with a very intelligent Abenaki, or Saint Francis, Indian, who, as he spoke and wrote well both French and English, might be supposed to have been superior to vulgar prejudice. I endeavoured constantly —sometimes by artful wiles or chance remarks—to draw from him something like a legend, but he constantly declared that he did not know one, or anything relating to old beliefs, and that all had long since perished. There was also a jolly old Indian woman, one of the same tribe, who told fortunes by cards, and she sang the same song. A year after I succeeded better with Tomah or Toma-quah, a Passamaquoddy, who not only related to and collected for me a vast number of remarkable legends, myths, and folk-lore items of all kinds, but who told me that my two Abenaki friends were noted repositories or living chronicles of such learning. As for the authenticity of the legends, there is hardly one which has not its close parallel, in some particulars at least, in the MS. folio of Mic Mac legends, collected by Rev. S. Rand, or among the cognate Chippeway records of Schoolcraft and Kohl. As for accuracy, the pioneer who first makes his way into such a jungle, or cane-brake, has enough to do to keep the twigs out of his eyes and clear away the brush, without thinking of leaving a macadamised road for his followers.

After I had made a beginning, the Indians, finding that one or another had let out a cat, or told a legend, and also that the telling thereof was productive of dollars and tobacco and pounds of tea, did somewhat abate their ancient reticence, and the path having been cleared, several followers walked in it—among others the gentleman with the phonograph, who, as is usual, grumbled at the road. It was easy enough to collect stories *then*, and to detect inaccuracies in the first reported.

But the difficulties which I had in collecting Red Indian legends were but an inch of pin-wire compared to a crowbar with what I had to encounter in gathering these Italian relics. Very recently, as I write, I told my chief authority that I expected to publish all these accounts of spirits, tales, and conjurations in a book, and that if there was aught in it *not perfectly authentic* that I should incur *un gran' disgrazia.* To which she with some excitement replied :—

"Signore, you know very well how difficult it has been for you to gather all this. I do not believe that any other signore in Italy could collect it among the people. For all the strange things of antiquity which you seek are mostly known only in a very few families, or to some old people or witches who are mortally afraid of the priests, and who are very timid, and conceal everything from their betters. And then there is the much greater number of those who really believe that when a learned man asks them for such things that he himself is a *stregone,* or wizard—oh, the people are *very* superstitious and fearful as to *that !* And you must remember that, as regards what I have told you, I have had to go about among old people, and question many, and have been often seeking for weeks and months before I could answer many of your questions."

To which she might have added that much was only half-recollected or jumbled up, or, worse than all, restored by lively Italian minds gifted with the fatal gift of improvisation, as, for instance, when a sorceress retains only the idea or general features of an incantation, but proceeds to utter it boldly, believing that it is "about the thing." And bearing in mind what has been said in reputable journals of my work on Algonkin Legends, every fraction of which was honestly given from good authorities, every one of which I named, I would here declare that I received everything in this book from Italians who declared that all had been derived from tradition, and that where it was possible—which was often not the case—I verified this as well as I could. But as regards possible imposture, or error, or lies, or mistakes, I hold myself responsible for nothing whatever, limiting everything to this simple fact—that I very accurately recorded what was told me by others. I believe that the names of the old Etruscan gods, as I have given them, still exist, because " Peppino " actually, with much trouble, verified them from the memories of old people, and if he, a *contadino*, and one of themselves, had to complain that he elicited this information with great trouble, because it was forbidden knowledge, and " accursed by the priests," it may be inferred how hard it would be for a superior to obtain it. As for the incantations, or aught else— bearing in mind the criticisms which I have received—I utterly disclaim all responsibility, and wash my hands clear of the whole concern, saving and except this, that I myself believe—unconscious errors excepted—that it is all honest, earnest, and true. In the main I propose it as a guide to be followed by other and more learned or better qualified scholars and seekers, who may correct its errors, only begging them to do so in civil language, and not accuse me directly or indirectly of recklessness or untruthfulness or carelessness.

And a nice time they will have of it if they walk the ways which I have walked, in the paths which I have trod. I have just heard that one old woman who is several times cited as authority in this book has died in a den of infamy, and that on the day of her decease [1] her son, who had been doing three years for a murder, " in the heat of passion," left prison. There has always been a dread sense of the existence of a Prefect and the police hovering like a dark shadow over me while pursuing my researches among my Etruscan friends; to them, unfortunately, these powers that be occasionally assumed a far more tangible form, and even the best and most respectable among them was once cited before the former, only escaping durance vile by a fine, which is recorded in my diary as " Expenses in collecting Folk-Lore." *Feliciter evasit*—and to this escape the recovery of three lost Etruscan gods is truly due ! There are records of several great works written in consequence of their authors having been in prison—this portion of my book is ; I

---

[1] The manner of her death was characteristic, as described to me by another. "She was all her life a very wicked old woman, believing nothing, and she died in extreme sin because she would hear nothing of priest or prayer ; and what was more, had all my *biancheria* (underclothing), which I had asked her to keep, but which she would not return, and so I lost it utterly. And the night she died there was another old woman watching by her, and the other one fell asleep. After a while she was awakened by Something on her chest, and thinking it was the little dog, grasped it and cast it from her, and slept again. And it came again, and this time, still thinking it was the old woman's little dog, searched all the room closely for it, but found nothing. And going to the bed she found that the old woman was dead. And it was her soul which had awakened the one sleeping." " *Did she die a witch ?* " " *Sicuro*—certainly."

believe the only literary labour described which was due to the author's keeping *out* of the penitentiary, which—it must be candidly admitted—is a much cleverer and far more difficult feat.

That there are a few decent Italians who know something of this witch-lore is proved, for instance, by the shoemaker to whom I owe the legends of Ra and Bovo. But the sorceries, and all relating to them, are chiefly in the hands of "witches," who tell fortunes and prepare spells and charms, and who, far from being desirous of fame, or "greedy for glory as authority," rather shrink from celebrity, albeit from no marked sense of modest merit, but rather from a vivid sense of justice—that is, of the manner in which it may be meted out unto them. Therefore I, in this book, have made no great parade of my authorities. Something of this may be due to the fact that, as chief of the English gypsies—or at least as President of the English Gypsy-Lore Society, which amounts to the same thing—I have a natural proclivity for ways that are dark and low society, *et cetera ;* —it may be so, the spell was wrought by other hands than mine—but so far as I know, *this* manner of Folk-Lore cometh not from going among a poor but virtuous peasantry, or by collecting penny broadsides, or walking in the paths of grace according to the handbooks of criticism.

> I bring you not the metal, but rude ore ;
> I gathered as I knew—what would you more?

Now, to meet all queries from critics, I declare distinctly that, as regards all authenticity, I am one with the man of the tale told by Panurge in the Chronicles of Rabelais. This worthy, who was a beggar in Paris, went about with two little girls in panniers, one hung before and the other behind him. And he being asked if they were truly maids, replied, " As for the one whom I carry in front, I am not sure, but I incline to believe that she really is what you inquire ; but as for the one behind, of her I will assert nothing." So I declare that, as for the names of the Etruscan gods which I have given in front, I believe they are authentic, but do not swear to it ; while as for all the rest, I affirm nothing. If all the bishops in England had sworn to it, somebody would have denied it ; and those from whom I obtained it were not even bishops' daughters, albeit they may have been those of priests.

For there has sprung up of late years a decided tendency in critics to *utterly* condemn books, no matter how valuable they may be, for small faults or defects, just as a friend of mine treated all the vast mass of learning and ingenious observation in the works of De Gubernatis as worthless trash, because the Count has carried the Solar Myth too far. To all such I can only say that they need read no further in this work of mine, for it is not written for them, nor by their standard, nor to suit their ideas. It is simply the setting down of a quantity of strange lore as given by certain old women, living or dead (among which latter I class divers deceased antiquaries)—and further than this the deponent sayeth not.

The moral of all which is that if a work like the Algonkin Legends, which is very accurate in all save, perhaps, in a few *very* trivial details, and whose absolute truth is confirmed by a thunder-cloud of witnesses, can be openly accused in the two leading Folk-Lore journals of England and America of sinning in these respects, what may not be alleged or said of this, which was compiled, collected, and corrected under circumstances where I had, so to speak, to feel my way in the lurid fog of a sorcerers' *sabbat*, in a bewildering, strangely scented " witch-*aura*," misled ever and anon by goblins' mocking cries, the tittering cheeping of bats on the wing, the hoots of owls—yea, and the rocking of the earth itself—as the text abundantly witnesseth, seeing how often I in it go blindly feeling my way from the corner of one ruined conjecture to another, ever apprehending that I have found a mare's-nest—or, more properly, that of a *night*mare of the most evasive kind ? Now, as it is no light thing to be accused in high places before the world of folly and falsehood, when the author has done his work with very careful honesty, it may well be understood that as " the combusted infant manifests apprehension of the igneous element," so I, knowing very well that a crafty Italian is not in the same boat with an " honest Injun," naturally take precautions against the captious critic by admitting *all* possible imperfections. To which there will be others of these noble souls to cry, "*Qui s'excuse, s'accuse.*" Certainly there will be, as ever.

> Ah well, and let them cry it an they will !
> There never yet was castle built so fair,
> So strong, or deeply founded, but some thief
> Or petty spy did worm his way therein.

CHAPTER I

TINIA

"Tinia was the supreme deity of the Etruscans, analogous to the Zeus of the Greeks and the Jupiter; 'the centre of the Etruscan god-world, the power who speaks in the thunder and descends in the lightning.' He alone had three separate bolts to hurl."—*The Cities of Etruria*, by G. DENNIS.

T was a peasant-girl with a wheel-barrow, or small hand-cart, in the streets of Florence. Had she been in London she would have been peddling apples or nuts, but as it was in Italy she had a stock of ancient classics in parchment; also much theological rubbish of the most dismal kind, the fragment of a Roman *lituus*, and a paper of old bronze medals. Of these I took twelve, paying for them two or three pence each as I pleased—and as the price was accepted with smiles, I knew that the blue-eyed dealer had realised several hundred per cent. profit. On examination I found that I had bought :—

1. The bronze medal, which the brazen Pietro Aretino had struck in his own honour with the inscription, *Divus P. Aretinus flagellum Principum,* of which I had often read but never seen, and would have given twopence any day to behold.

2. A very good bronze of Julius Cæsar—the reverse utterly hammered flat, but the great man himself fine and bold.

3. Nero Claudius Cæsar. A gold-like bronze, in good preservation—the wicked eye and bull neck to perfection.

4. A strange old Greek medal in hard white bronze of *Luson Basileōs,* reverse, apparently three Graces, with the word *Apol,* and beneath *Dionuso Lares.* "Witch-money" so-called here.

5. A medal of 1544, perfect, representing a Cardinal who, reversed, is a jester with cap and bells, with the motto, *Et Stulti aliquando sapite.*

That will do; all were interesting and curious, but I do not propose to catalogue them. What struck me was the remarkable resemblance of the whole find, and the manner in which it was obtained, to the legends and other lore which I have got together in these pages. These, too, have come down from old Roman times ; some are sadly battered and worn, some, like the Nero, have been covered with a rich olive *patina,* which has again—more's the pity !—been scaled away to restore it, even as an English curate "restores" a Gothic church ; others, like the Julius, have only a slight *ærugo*-rust ; some are of the Catholic-Heathen Renaissance—one is a Leo I. ; in short, there are the same elements of society in the one as in the other, Christian and Heathen Lares turned to goblins, Dionysius-Faflon, witch-money, vulgarity, and Imperial grandeur.

And they were all picked up, the medley like the medals, both bearing legends, from poor peasant women who were in blessed ignorance as to their classical origin, save that there was something of sorcery in it all. I say this because there will be many to think that I have been over-keen to find antiquity and classic remains in these literary fragments ; but no native Italian scholar who knows the people would say this. For here in Italy, just as one may find a peasant girl selling old Decretals, and Dantes, and Roman lamps, and medals from a wheelbarrow, you may find in her mind, deeply rusted and battered remains corresponding to them—and, indeed, things far older. For if you will reflect a minute it will occur to you that the bronze of my Julius Cæsar medal may have come from melting some *other* coin or medal or object which was primævally old, ere ever he who bestrode the world, like a Colossus, was born. The ruder a bronze, the older it may be; so it may befall that these rough legends touch the night of time. True it is that there are rude things also of later date, and such

APLU   TINIA   TÉRAMÓ

often occur and are intermingled in this collection, and I also admit that with few books at my command, I have not been able to push the process of analysis and discovery very far. But there will be no lack of others to correct me where I have conjectured wrongly. I will now proceed to one of my first discoveries.

HEINE has shown in his Gods in Exile, how the old classic deities came down in the world after being dethroned. Had he been aware of the humble condition to which they have been reduced in Tuscany he could have added much curious confirmation of his view. Let us begin with Jupiter :—

"The Etruscans," writes OTTFRIED MÜLLER, "adored a god who was compared to the Roman Jupiter, the leading deity, and who was often called so, but who in Tuskish was known as Tina or Tinia. Tina was therefore the highest of their gods ; the central point of the whole world of deities. He was honoured in every Tuscan city, as in Rome—at least since the times of the Etruscan kings, with Juno and Minerva—in the temple of the citadel. Lightning was, in the Tuscan art, ever in his hands ; he is the god who speaks in it and descends in it to earth."

Do you know the name of *Tinia ?* " I asked of my witch authority, who knows not only the popular names of the current Tuscan mythology, but the more recondite terms preserved among the *strege*, or sorceresses.

" Tignia or Tinia ? Yes. It is a great *folletto* " (a spirit, or goblin) ; "but an evil one. He does much harm. *Si, e grande, ma cattivo.*"

And then bethinking herself, after a pause, awaiting the expected memory as one waits a moment for a child whom one has called, she resumed :—

" *Tinia* is the spirit of the thunder and lightning and hail. He is very great " (*i.e.*, powerful). "Should any peasant ever curse him, then when a *temporale*, or great storm, comes he appears in the lightning, and *bruccia tutta la raccolta*, spoils all the crop.

"Should the peasant understand why this happened and who ruined the fields he knows it was Tinia. Then he goes at midnight to the middle of the field or vineyard, and calls :—

> " 'Folletto Tinia, Tinia, Tinia !
> A ti mi raccomando
> Che tu mi voglia perdonare,
> Si ti ho maladetto,
> Non lo ho fatto
> Per cattiva intenzione,
> Lo ho fatto soltanto
> In atto di collera,
> Se tu mi farei
> Tornare una buona raccolta.
> Folletto Tigna !
> Sempre ti benedico ! ' "

> (" 'Spirit Tinia, Tinia, Tinia !
> Unto thee I commend me
> That thou wilt pardon me.

If I have cursed thee
I did not do it
With ill will.
I did it only
In act of anger :
If thou wilt give me a good harvest,
Spirit Tinia,
I will ever bless thee ! ' ")

This, I think, establishes the identity of the modern Tinea with the ancient god of thunder. According to MÜLLER the name occurs only once as *Tina*. His form is often found on mirrors. It is very interesting to learn that an invocation to the Etruscan Jove still exists as a real thing, and that, after a humble fashion, he is still worshipped.

There is another invocation to the thunder and lightning, but it is not connected with this deity. It is as follows :—

" When you see thunder and lightning you should say :—
" ' Santa Barbara, benedetta,
Liberateci dalla saetta,
E dal gran tuono !
Santa Barbara e San Simone,
San Simone e San Eustachio,
Sempre io mi ·raccomando ! ' "

Or in English freely rendered :—

"Saint Barbara, the blest, I pray,
Keep the shafts from me away !
And from thunder in the skies,
Simon—Barbara likewise—
Saint Eustace and Simon too
I commend myself to you ! '

For there are two distinct religions, " one good if the other fails," in La Romagna, and many still believe that that of the spirits, or ancient gods, is, on the whole, the most to be relied on. It is true that it is departing very rapidly, and that now only a few of the faithful still know the chief names and invocations, yet, after slender fashion, they still exist. Ten years hence some of the most important of these names of the gods will have utterly passed away ; as it is, they are only known to a few among the oldest peasants, or to a *strega*, who keeps the knowledge as a secret.

Strangely allied to Tinia is the herb or plant of the same name, which is popularly regarded with great respect from its superior magic qualities. It is, in fact, a spirit itself. A specimen of it was obtained in Rocca Casciano for me, and with it I received the following :—

"The plant Tigna should be held of great account, because when one is afflicted by the spirit Tigna (Tinia) this herb should be put in a little (red) bag and always worn, and specially on children's necks.

"When Tigna begins to vex a family it is terrible. Then with this plant we should make every morning the sign of the cross and say :—

> " 'Padre in pace se ne vada
> Per mezzo di questa erba,
> Quella testa in Tigna.
> Figlio in pace sene vada,
> Quello spirito maligno,
> Spirito in carna ed ossa,
> In pace te ne possa,
> Te ne possa andare ;
> Amenne per mezzo di questa erba
> In casa mia piu tu non possa entrare,
> E forza di farmi del male
> Piu non avrai ! ' "

This incantation, which was either imperfectly remembered, and is certainly in a somewhat broken form (as is the case with others which had not been recalled for many years), may be rendered in English as follows :—

> " Father, let depart in peace,
> By means of this herb,
> That witness (bears) Tigna !
> Son, let depart in peace
> That malignant spirit !
> Spirit, in flesh and bones
> In peace thou shalt not go,
> Until by means of this herb
> Thou shalt no longer enter my house,
> And no longer have power
> To do me harm ! "

"And never forget to bless yourself with this herb."

Tigna, as the reader may recall from the Preface, was testified to by V. Del Vivo as "The great folletto of lightning, who has been long in Dovadola, *e si conoscie tutt'ora*, is still known." His existence is well confirmed, but he is still one of the deities who are rapidly passing, and who are now known to very few. That he is on the whole far more feared than loved is manifest, and the Tinia of the Etruscans was altogether a deity who was, unlike Jupiter, one of horror and dread. Nearly all the deities of the Etruscans were—as compared to the Græco-

Roman—of a horrible or malevolent nature, and a number of them wielded thunder and dealt largely in storms and hail. All of which in due proportion the

TÉRAMÓ (TURUS; MERCURY)

reader will find to be the case with the spirits which exist in popular belief at the present day in *La Toscana Romagna*.

It is to be observed that the name of *Tinia*, or its equivalent, is found in Tuscan legends as that of a great and wealthy lord—*un milionario*—the richest in all the country. Thus in the tale of *La Golpe* in the *Novelle Popolare Toscane* of Pitré, the Marquis of Carabas in the Italian Puss and Boots is called " Il Sor Pasquale del Tigna." In both the English and Italian stories the mysterious and unseen, or hidden Marquis, like the Sor di Tigna, is a *deus ex machina*, or higher power, who is exploited for the benefit of the poor hero. I do not think it is forcing the question when we conjecture that we have in him a god in exile, or one come down in the world.

> " Fallen, fallen, fallen, fallen,
> Fallen from his high estate.

TÉRAMÓ

The following account of this spirit, which was obtained from several authorities, but especially from an old woman living not very far from Forli, is for several reasons very interesting :—

" Téramó is a spirit favourable to thieves and merchants. When a band of *ladri*, or robbers, meet in some secluded place to arrange a theft, Téramó is always present to aid, unless they intend murder (*se non ragionano di spargere sangue*). But if no violence of that kind be meant, he is always there, though they do not see him but only a shadow. Then he says, ' *Giovanetti*—boys, get to work, I will help you—*presto all' opera e io sono in vostro aiuto*—work in peace and do not be afraid, and you will not be discovered, but do not forget to help the poor who are in such great need. Do this and I will show you myself what to do ; but if you forget charity then you shall be found out, *e cosi non godrete niente*—and so you will enjoy nothing.'

" But if they intend spilling blood he will probably put their victims on guard, and cause their arrest.

" With merchants, or dealers, if one had cattle or anything of the kind to sell,[1] Téramó was always busy. And sometimes he played roguish tricks, as when one had a very pretty wife or daughter he would go to the house disguised as a very handsome young man, and so delude her that the affair ended by two in a bed. Or if a merchant agreed to deliver goods to a customer at a certain time, and broke his appointment, Téramó would make the goods disappear, and the man to whom they were promised would find them in his house, and be under no necessity of paying money. Or if he had paid he got the goods.

" Téramó is also a *spirito messagiero*, a spirit of messengers, one who carries notices or news from one city to another or from one part of the world to another very quickly. But to have his aid one must be one of his kind (*bastara pero à farsi prendere da lui o sinpatia*), such as a statesman or thief, or such as are his friends.

" When any one, say a thief or lover, wishes to send news to a friend, he must go into a cellar by night and pray to Téramó, and say : —

---

[1] Téramó, or Hermes, true to his first impulses, is always concerned with cattle.

> " The babe was born at the first peep of day ;
> He began playing on the lyre at noon,
> And the same evening he did steal away
> Apollo's herds."

" ' Téramó, Téramó, as it is true,
That you are my friend I pray to you,
And may this message which I send,
Quickly and safely reach its end ! '

" Then the one praying takes a pigeon, and fastens his note to its wing, or neck, and says :—

" ' Go fly afar for me !
And Téramó keep you company ! ' '

" But one should never forget the spirit Téramó !" (*Sempre pero rammentarsi dello spirito di Téramó*).

This last exhortation means that one should never forget to make the proper invocation or address to him at proper times.

We have here evidently enough Mercury, "the guardian deity of the *mercatores* and *collegii mercatorum*," as well as of thieves, who was the swift-footed messenger of the gods ; although those who told the tale knew nothing of such a name as Mercurio, let me twist it as I would. But it may be that we have here in Téramó the old Etruscan name for Mercury, very much changed. "In Etruria," writes PRELLER (*Rom. Myth.* p. 597,) "the Greek Hermes was called Turms, which is formed from the Greek name, just as Turan came from Urania." That is to say, Turms or Turmus would be Italianised to Turmo, which in the harshly accented Romagnolo, with its prolonged R, would naturally pass to *Turamo*.

The reader must not neglect to observe the pious adjuration at the end of the communication. It is a strange reflection that there are still people who cherish religious sentiments for the son of Jupiter and Maia.

As the name of Téramó was of importance, special pains were taken to verify the fact that what I have given is authentic. As the reader will have seen by the Preface, Tito Forconi testified that at San Benedetto the deeds of Téramó, as guardian spirit of merchants, thieves and messengers, " have been related for many years." And, since then, others have testified to knowing him. He is, however, one among those who are rapidly becoming unknown or forgotten, save by a few

¹ " Téramó, Téramó, Téramó !
Che tu ai le sinpatie
E credo fra questi esserci
Io pure e non mi vorrai abbandonare
Questa notizia nella tal citta,
Di farmi arrivare.

" E cosi si presentera un columbo, si lega a lui al collo un foglio scritto, a si dice :—

" ' Vai vola, lontan lontano !
Che lo spirito di Téramó
Ti accompagnia !' "

old people, as Peppino declared—being, I suppose, naturally obnoxious to the priests who love no rivals in granting pardons to thieves, camorrists, &c. " Fur ac nebulo Mercurius," says Lactantius, " quid ad famem sui reliquit, nisi memoriam fraudum suarum ? "

It is worth remarking that I had most trouble to collect evidence of the existence of the few special names such as Tignia, Faflon, and Téramó, which were, however, of the most importance. " It is well, since you care for such things, that you came when you did," said an informant, " because in a few years' time most of these names will have been forgotten by everybody." And I sincerely believe that ten years hence not a tenth part of it will survive.

And it was by a remarkable chance that I hit upon, in Florence, the one person of all others who had an innate love of sorcery, strange tales, and old songs, who was herself a fortune-teller, and had been taught the old names of spirits and innumerable incantations by a witch foster-mother. But for this "find " I might have sought in vain for the best part of what I have here given.

It is perhaps worth mentioning in connection with Téramó—once Teramus—that there was an old Scythian god, *Tharamis*, of whom Lucan (l. 1. Pharsal.) says :—

" Et Tharamis Scythicæ non mitior ara Dianæ."

He appears to have been a Celtic god, worshipped by the Britons. Selden gives an inscription connecting Tharamis *deabus matribus*, with the maternal deities, which would identify him, not with Jove, but Mercury. But of this Celtic god, and any possible connection with Téramó, there is really no proof whatever. On Etruscan mirrors, says Dennis, the name of this god is generally Turms or Thurms, in one case he is called Turms Aitas, or the infernal Mercury (Gerhard. Etrus. Spiegel. ii., plate 182). He was associated by Tarquin with the three great gods (Serv. ad Æn. ii., 296).

BUSCHET

This narrative was given as a conclusion to that of Téramó with which, however, it has very little connection :—

" The spirit *Buschet* was always a companion with Téramó in all his dealings. If a man had pretty daughters then all went well (with him), if there were none there was mischief.

" Now there was a merchant who had a very beautiful daughter, but Buschet could not prevail upon her, nor enter the house. For she had had a lover, and when he died, she had his body turned to stone, and put it in a chest, and kept it secretly under her bed. And Buschet could not enter a house in which there was a corpse. Then he thought he would sing a song which would alarm her ; but she was not to be frightened at anything, so great was the love which she had for the dead man.

" And he began to sing :—

> "Oh, rose, oh, lovely rose ! for so I call thee,
> Because thou art so fair that thou dost seem
> To be a rose indeed ; and since thou'rt fair,
> Oh, beauty, I would press thee to my lips,
> And fain would kiss thee sweet.[1]

> And yet it seems to me an evil thing
> That thou hast a dead lover 'neath thy bed,
> 'Tis not a fitting tomb, and if thy father
> Knew it was there, ah, then what would he say
> Tell me, poor girl !

> I warn thee now, and tell thee what to do :
> Take that dead lover from beneath thy bed ;
> Take him away. The devil else will come.
> Thou art in deadly danger ; so beware,
> Now thou art warned ! '

" But she paid no heed to this, nor was she at all frightened, but went to pray, as was her wont, over the body of her lover. Then Buschet went and sang under the window of her father :—

> " 'Oh, good merchant, 'neath thy window
> I will sing a small *stornello*,
> And I hope that you, with patience,
> Now will listen to my ditty ;
> Otherwise I ween that you'll repent it ![2]

> Well thou knowest that thy daughter
> For a year has kept her chamber ;
> Thou didst think she was so saint-like,
> Or perhaps a real angel,
> And did'st always speak so well of her !

> But instead of that, good merchant,
> Know that she betrays you—truly
> I am grieved that I must tell you—
> All her life is given to evil,
> And she covers you with great dishonour.

---

[1] " Rosa, o bella Rosa cosi ti chiamo,
Perche siei tanto bella mi sembri,
Un vero fior di rosa, e quanto siei
Bella vorrei posarti sopra i labbri miei,
E ti vorrei bacciar ! "

[2] " 'Sotto alla tua finestra,
O buon' mercanta, una piccola
Stornello vengo a cantare ;
Spero che mi vorrei ascoltare,
Altrimenti te ne vorrai pentire.'

Go into thy daughter's chamber;
Go at ten, and you'll not find her
Sleeping in her bed, but kneeling
O'er a chest which holds a dead man
Turned to stone ; oh, shame and sorrow for you !

Bear away at once that coffin,
Hide it quickly, for if Justice
Knew of it you'd come to trouble
As you know, and that full quickly,
All occasioned by your shameless daughter.'

Hearing this, the merchant, rising,
Sought the chamber of his daughter,
Oped the door and found her praying,
Praying o'er her stone-cold lover,
And he asked her how the dead man came there ?

And all wailing, thus she answered :
' This was he who loved me dearly—
Ah, too dearly !—here together
Every night we slept till morning,
But one night he died in my embraces.

And I did as God inspired me,
From my chamber he should never
More be borne, for I would have him
Here to pray for, ever loving,
Now he is dead it is no sin to kiss him.'

But the father would not listen
To her wailing nor entreaty ;
Little cared he for her sorrow,
So at once they bore the lover
Off and placed him in the *campo santo*.

So of course Buschet was happy.
Time passed on, in time she listened
For a pastime to his singing ;
Listening, she forgot her lover,
And the end was that the spirit triumphed."

This is a very close translation both as regards words and metre, though it wants the delicate grace of the original—which original recalls the Pot of Basil. The reader cannot fail to observe in it, however, the wild, uncanny spirit of witchcraft, the utter want of a proper *moral* or human feeling, and the extraordinary manner in which this " poor simple Isabel," after such exquisite devotion to the dead lover, forgets him for Buschet. But to the witch all of this suggests something so entirely different that it is almost impossible to explain it. Her feeling or sympathy is with the goblin or god; he is to her like the Indian deity and the bayadere, in Goethe's poem. The girl is supposed in the German ballad to pass through fire to rise to heaven ; so here she endures a penance to fit her for the spirit Buschet. It is the triumph of his unscrupulous sorcerer's *cunning* which pleases the Romagnolo poet, and which interested the woman who gave it to me.

Apropos of the *Dieu et la Bayadere*, or the plot of the Indian play *Vasan-tasena* which Heine declared was so immoral that it would be hissed off any stage in Paris. This suggested to some French manager an idea, and it was soon brought out, and had an immense success all over Europe and America. Perhaps some *impresario* would like to try Buschet. True, it is not so *very* improper, as I have given it here—but a vivid French imagination may make wonders of it. There is the midnight prayer over the dead lover, the demon's serenade, the Mephistophelean song to the father, and finally the great love scene. What an opportunity for a dramatic poet !

This incident of the girl who has kept in a coffin her dead lover, over whom she nightly mourns, bears a great resemblance to a tale in the *Arabian Nights' Entertainments*, " where a beautiful princess, who is also a sorceress, keeps the body of her negro lover, by her magic art, in a kind of apparent life, and covers it with the kisses of despair, and which she would fain, by the greater magic of love, wake from the twilight-dimmering half-death to the full truth of life." Of which Heine remarks : " Even as a boy I was struck, in reading the Arabian tale, with this picture of passionate and incomprehensible love." [1]

It only remains to be remarked that " Hermes and Apollo in the myths became fast friends " (*The Etruscans*, by John Fraser, B.A.). Buschet, as the ally of Téramó, would therefore be Aplu, Aplus, or Apollo ; but I cannot establish any identity between the names. *Schet* is a Romagnola termination, and Apluschet is quite possible, nor is it more remote from the original than Téramó from Hermes ; but guess-work like this is hardly philological. Apollo, like Buschet, had a great antipathy for corpses and pestilence.

IMPUSA DELLA MORTE

" Vidi un Fantasma, in disusato aspetto,
Che richiamò dal suo furor la mente,
Mirabil mostro, e mostruoso oggetto.
Donna giovin di viso, antica d' anni."

Satire di Salvator Rosa

The Impusa della Morte is probably the Empusa of the Greeks. She is a terrible sorceress, much dreaded. There is a short saying, or invocation,

[1] Heine's *Shakespeare's Maidens and Women : Desdemona*. Translated by Charles G. Leland. London : W. Heinemann. 1891

addressed to her: "*Impusa della Morte me destavo!* (or, *mi svegliavo!*)." She appears, as a wandering beggar, to be confused with Feronia of the Markets. Of her I learned :—

"*Impusa* (also called *Infrusa* and *Infusa*) was a witch, so wicked that she did all the harm she could, and was so avaricious that she would not give a *soldo* even to any one who had earned it. However, this old witch owned a fine castle, but would not suffer even one of her own relations to enter it, for fear lest they should carry something away. She died at last; and before she departed she concealed all her riches; but was scarcely dead before all the palace shook as if by an earthquake, and there was a rattling of chains as if all the devils from hell were around, and then the window was flung wide open, and there flew from her hand a crow (*cornacchia*), and this was her soul, which went to hell. They buried her in that corner of the churchyard which is kept for the unbaptised.

"The palace remained, with little furniture, unoccupied, though it was known that great treasure was buried in it. And some of those who entered it died of fright. Yet this witch had a nephew to whom she was attached. And to him she appeared one midnight, and said :—

> " ' Nipotino, bel nipotino,
>   Per il bene che ti ho voluto
>   Levami di queste pene,
>   Perchio no ho bene,
>   Fino che tu non avrai
>   Scoperto il mio tesoro,
>   Io sono la tua zia,
>   La tua zia *Infrusa*,
>   Cosi cosi mi chiamo
>   Essendo sempre la Infrusa,
>   Col mio danaro, ma se
>   Tu avrai tanto coraggio
>   Di scoprire il tesoro,
>   Che ho nascosto, io saro
>   Felice, e tu sarai
>   Ricco, ma ti raccomando,
>   Che tu abbia coraggio
>   E non sparventarvi, perche
>   Tutti quelli che son' morti,
>   Sono morti per la paura.'

> ' Little nephew, fair young nephew,
>   By the good I ever wished thee,
>   Free me from the pain I suffer!
>   And I must endure the torment,
>   Suffer till thou hast discovered
>   Where it was I hid my treasure;
>   For I am thy aunt *Infrusa*;
>   So I call me, being always
>   *La Infrusa* with my money
>   But if thou hast only courage
>   To discover all the treasure
>   Which I buried, then I truly

Shall be happy, and thou also
Wilt be rich ; but this I tell thee :
That thou'lt need thy utmost courage ;
In that search full many perished,
And they died from naught but terror.')

"Then the nephew of the Infrusa went to sleep in the palace, and he made a good fire and provided good wine and food, and sat by the fire and ate. But just at midnight he heard a voice howl down the chimney, '*Butto?*' ('Shall I throw?') And he replied, 'Throw away!' When there was thrown down first a man's leg, then a foot, an arm, a hand, and head, and so all the parts of twelve men. And when all were thrown they reunited and made twelve men, who all stood looking at him. But he, cool and calm, asked them if they would like to eat or drink.

"And they answered, 'Come with us!' But he replied, 'I have eaten and drunk, and do not wish to go.' Then they took him on their shoulders, and bore him far down into a vault, and took spades, and bade him choose one and dig. And he replied, 'I have eaten and drunk, and am willing.' Then they all dug together—when at last they came, indeed, to the treasure, and it was very great. Then one said to him :—

"'Va a letto, tu che sei
Il padrone del tesoro,
E di questo bel palazzo,
E di tutte queste richezze,
Per il tuo gran coraggio ;
E la tua zia *Infrusa ;*
Stara in pace, ma sara
Sempre un folletto, che verra
Tutte le notte a vedere
I suoi danari, essendo
Tanto egoista, ma tu
Sarei sempre il padrone.'"

("'Go to bed, now thou art master
Of the palace and the treasure ;
By thy courage thou hast won them,
And at last thy aunt Infrusa
Rests in peace, yet ever will be
Through all time a wandering spirit ;
Every night she'll come to look at
Her old treasure—'tis her nature—
But thou'lt ever be the master.'")

This is a variation of a well-known Italian "fairy tale," but it has some value in this connection as indicating the character of the *Impusa*. It is possible, from its rude poetry, that this may be a very ancient version of the tale.

There is a point to be observed that in this, as in all other Tuscan tales of the kind, the witch is freed from her sufferings as soon as she is relieved from the responsibility of her treasure. In other narratives she is at peace as soon as she can put off the witch-power on another.

It has been suggested to me that in all this, only the name is in common with the Greek account of *Empusa*, who had one leg of an ass and the other of brass. All of which should be carefully considered by the investigator. It is not remarkable that the name is Greek, since the Tusci had from the earliest times much intercourse with Greece, and, what is more to be considered, that the name became popular in Italy at a later date as that of a bug-bear spirit which was one of the minor faun-like gods. Thus in a very curious and rare work, entitled, *Idea del Giardino del Mondo*, by Tommaso Tomai of Ravenna (second edition), Venice, 1690, there is mention of "demons called incubi, succubi, or *empedusi*, and other *lemuri*, who are enamoured of men or women." What is indeed remarkable in these Tuscan names is that there has been on the whole so little change in them. It is of little matter that the *Impusa* does not appear in the modern account with one foot of brass or like that of an ass (alterum verò habeat æneum aut asininum —*Suidas*), since during the Middle Ages the word was often used as a synonym for Lamia, Lemur, or witch of any kind. If Italian writers could describe the Empusa as being the same with Lemures and Incubi, it is not remarkable that mere peasants should have applied the name quite as loosely.

SIERO

SIERO, in the modern Tuscan mythology, is a *folletto cattivo birbone*—a very mischievous evil spirit. There is also a feminine of the same name, or Siera. Of him I have the following account :—

" When *Siero* is angry with a peasant's family, and the head of it goes to milk the cattle, he draws what appears to be very fine milk ; but when it is to be used it turns to *green* water, for which reason it is so-called from the goblin. (Latin, *serum* ; Italian, *siero*—whey, buttermilk.)

" Then the peasant, to make matters right again in his house, implores *Siero* to be favourable. Upon which the goblin comes and knocks at the house-door, and if the *contadino* has a pretty daughter, cries, ' Yes, I will make you happy ; but you must let me sleep one night with your daughter.' But if he has a plain daughter, *Siero* laughs, and says, 'If you had a girl less ugly, and had mocked me less, I would have made you prosperous. But since your daughter is so plain, I cannot revenge myself for all the ill things you have said of me.' And if the peasant has girls neither pretty nor plain, then Siero calls, ' If you will remember to bless me every day, I will make you happy ; but should you forget it, you will be wretched while you live.' "

With Siero was associated *Chuculvia*, or *Ch'uch'ulvia* (with the strongly aspirated Tuscan *ch'*), of whom all I could learn that he was on earth a great sorcerer, now become an evil spirit. He is a kind of bugbear.

I do not pretend to suggest that these are descendants or forms of Etruscan deities, but I would point out a very singular coincidence of names in a passage in MÜLLER'S *Etrusker*, vol. ii., p. 110 note.

" On a vase there is a goddess of death, *Asira*, who flourishes an axe over the head of Amphiarus. A fury, Tuχuχla (Tuchulcha), with a bird's beak, lashes with snakes Theseus, condemned to the lower world, in a picture on a wall in the tomb dell' Orco, in Corneto."

There is probably nothing whatever in this similarity of names ; but it is worth noting.

NORCIA, THE GODDESS OF TRUFFLES

" Ye elves of hills, brooks, standing lakes and groves,
And ye that on the sands with printless foot
Do chase the ebbing Neptune, and do fly him
When he comes back ; you demi-puppets, that
By moonshine do the green-sour ringlets make
Whereof the ewe not bites ; and you whose pastime
Is to make *midnight mushrooms*."
The Tempest, Act v., s. I.

" Nortia was the goddess of destiny."—*History of Etruria*, THOS. HAMILTON GRAY.

HERE is a Tuscan rural sprite of whom I could learn little, save that she is disposed to be troublesome. One of her specialities is to distract and disturb dogs when hunting for truffles. It may be that she has more dignified work at other times. Her name is *Norcia*, or *Nortia*. Nortia was of yore a very great Etruscan goddess—a Fortuna, according to MÜLLER. Her temple was known to Roman antiquaries by the calendar nails driven in it. An inscription in hexameters from Volscinium (BURMANN, *Anthol. Lat.*, cl. I, cp. xix., p. 57) begins with " Nortia te veneror lare cretus Volsiniensi." But I find no truffles in all

NORTIA

From the Etruscan Museum of Gori (in which the head is wanting).
Another is given by Gerhard

this *paté*, only the reflection that the peasantry everywhere bring down great gods to small uses. True, we have two goddesses of the same name in the same country, and that is something.

Since writing the foregoing, I learn that when a truffle-hunter has no fortune in discovering the precious *tartufi*, he addresses his dog thus :—

> " O cane, cane chi da me siei tanto amato,
> La fortuna tu mi ai levato,
> Non trovandomi piu i tartufi,
> Dunque cane, o mio bel cane,
> A folletta di *Norcia* va ti à raccomodare
> Che i tartufi ti faccia ritrovare,
> E cosi io lo potro tanto ringraziare,
> Che la fortuna mi voglia ridare ! "

> (" Oh dog, my dog, so dear to me ;
> We're out of luck I plainly see !
> No truffles hast thou found to-day,
> So then to *Norcia* go and pray ;
> For if her favour we implore,
> She'll grant us truffles in such store,
> Fortune will smile for evermore.")

By an extraordinary coincidence truffles are also called nails, as their heads are round and small. And Norcia was identified with *nails* (PRELLER, *Myth.* p. 231).

"And, after all, it is altogether possible—or even probable—that this Norcia of the Truffles has nothing whatever to do with Nortia, but takes her name from the town of Norcia, or Norchia, famous for its pigs and its truffles." So a very learned friend suggests. However, all the principal Etruscan gods gave names to towns. Of which I find in DENNIS's *Etruria* (vol. i., p. 204) that " Orioli suggests that the town of ' Norchia' may be identical with Nyrtia, mentioned by the ancient scholiast on Juvenal (x. 74) as a town, the birthplace of Sejanus, giving its name to, or deriving it from, the goddess Nortia, or Fortuna." As I said, this goddess was identified with nails, because in her temple at Vulsinii every year the priest drove a nail into the door, to serve as a kind of register (PRELLER). It may seem ridiculous to connect this with the slang name for mushrooms and truffles ; but such similes are common among the people, and they never perish.

It may be remarked here that Saint Antony is invoked when seeking truffles by peasants of a Roman Catholic turn of mind. But Norcia, as a goddess of the earth, may be supposed to know better where they are to be found ; for she was unquestionably of the under-world, and a form of Persephone.

Nortia is still very generally known in La Romagna, as peasants certified.

Of one thing there can be no doubt—her specialty is to make "midnight mushrooms."

APLU

> " Sadly is gazing Phœbus Apollo,
> The youthful ; his lyre sounds no more
> Which once rang with joy at the feasts of the gods."
> *The Gods of Greece*, by H. HEINE.

"The name of the Greek God *Apollon* frequently occurs on Etruscan bronze mirrors as Aplun, Apulu, Aplu."—*Über die Sprache der Etrusker*, by W. CORSSEN, vol. i., p. 846.

When I returned to Florence in November, 1891, after some research I found my chief authority in ancient lore, installed in what had been, some three or four hundred years ago, a palace. It is true that its splendour had sadly departed. The vast and dismal rooms were either utterly unfurnished, or supplied with inferior *mobiglia*, placed at such distances from one another as to be hardly within call, unless they called very loudly. But there were frescoes on the walls which had been sketched by no mean hand—(they set forth charming scenes from Tasso)—and though the bare stone floors suggested a dreary cellar, there was a walled-up fireplace, over which rose a boldly arched and curved remainder of a fine Renaissance *focolare*. A single window badly lighted a great, grim apartment in which there was absolutely not a single article of furniture, save a small table and two chairs. From that window I sketched the fourteenth-century statue of a rain-worn saint on an opposite wall. Everything was in keeping with the lore which I had come to collect—very old, rubbed-down, and degraded from its high estate.

I asked the *strega* if she knew the name of Aplu. It *was* known to her, and it awoke some shadowy reminiscences ; but she said that she must consult a *vecchia*, an old woman of her acquaintance, regarding it. "It would come with talking." And this was the result of the consultation :—

" Aplu is a spirit who greatly loves hunters. But if they, when they have bad luck in the chase, speak evilly of him, then in the night he comes and pulls the bed-clothes from them, and gives them dreams of being in the cold open air, and having a prosperous hunt. Then he sits on them in nightmare, and the game seems lost. And they wake inspired with a desire to seek the woods, and if they express a wish to him (*i.e.*, invoke him) they will return that evening with much game." To which was added somewhat vaguely the words : "*E lo spirito d'Aplu sempre nella mente*" ("And with Aplu ever in their minds").

Then there was a pause, and I was told :—

" Aplu is the most beautiful of all the male spirits. He is also a spirit of music, and when any one would become a good hunter, or good musician, or a learned man—*un uomo dotto e di talento*—he should repeat this :—

> " Aplu, Aplu, Aplu !
> Tu che siei buono, tanto di sapienza !
> E siei dotto e di talento,
> Aplu, Aplu, Aplu !
> Tu che siei buono tanto,
> E da tutte le parti del mon (mondo) siei rammentato
> E da tutti si sente dire :
> Aplu, Aplu, Aplu !
> Anche lo spirito deve essere generosa
> E addatarci di fortuna e di talento
> Aplu, Aplu, Aplu !
> Io ti prego darmi
> Fortuna e talento ! "

This was given to me so irregularly and in such a confused state, owing to the imperfect memory of the narrator, that I had trouble to bring it to this form.   It is in English as follows :—

> " Aplu, Aplu, Aplu !
> Thou who art so good and wise,
> So learned and talented,
> Aplu, Aplu, Aplu !
> Thou who art so good
> And through all the world renowned ;
> And spoken of by all,
> Aplu, Aplu, Aplu !
> Even a spirit should be generous,
> Granting us fortune and talent.
> Aplu, Aplu, Aplu!
> I (therefore) pray thee give me
> Fortune and talent ! "

Aplu, as is recorded in detail by all writers on Etruscan mythology, was Apollo.   His is one of the commonest figures on vases and mirrors.

My informant had, as I learned from close questioning, never heard the name " Apollo."   I asked her if she had never seen his statue in Uffizi ?   But though she had lived many years in Florence she had never been in a gallery, so I gave her a franc and recommended her to invest it in a practical lesson in mythology. Neither did she remember to have heard of *Venere*, or Venus, whose name is very familiar to all middle and Southern Italians, though she knew all about Turana, her Etruscan original, as appears in another chapter.   *Ad alteram jam partem accedamus*, as Gladstone says.

TURANNA

" *Turan* is the Etruscan name of Venus, and it occurs so frequently with the most unmistakable representations of the goddess that it is time lost to seek its Etruscan origin, as Müller has done, in the Latin Venus *Fruti*, or to identify it, according to Schwenck, with Hera" (*Über die Gottheiten der Etrusker.* Ed. *Gerhard, Akademische Abhandlungen*, Erster Band, p. 324).

APLU (APOLLO) AND ARTEMISIA

It was a long time before I could find out this now almost forgotten name ; but one day it came forth as if by chance or inspiration, and then I was told the following details :—

" Turanna is a spirit who was when in life (or on earth) a fairy, and being very beautiful and good, she did good to all who were like her.

" There was in a land mother and son, who lived in great misery. This fairy with her magic wand caused this youth—all tattered and torn (*tutto stracciato*) to be transported to a distant place.

" The fairy was there, and she asked him how it was that he had come so far into a country where there were no herbs to nourish him?

" The youth replied that it was a spirit of kindly disposition who had borne him thither to make his fortune.

" The fairy answered, ' That spirit am I, and will make thee king.'

" The youth looked at her, marvelling, and said, ' Lady, it is impossible that one so miserable as I can ever become a king.'

" ' Go, youth, to that tree which thou seest. Go below that tree.

" ' There thou wilt find nuts to carry to the king.

" ' Thy fortune is sworn, and thy fortune will be when thou art under the tree—

" ' Tree which thou seest there below. Carry its nuts to the king.'

" He saw (found) himself dressed like a lord, and found a basket of nuts, all brilliant diamonds and precious pearls,

" And with a crown, on which they sang and danced.[1]

" ' Carry these things,' said the fairy, ' to the king, and tell him that thou desirest his daughter for wife. He will drive thee forth with ill-will.

" ' At that time by magic I will make it appear that the princess is with child, and she will say that thou wert its sire.

" ' Then the king, to avert scandal, will give her to thee. And the instant thou art married all that appearance of being with child will vanish.'

" So it came to pass. When the king was in a rage Turanna was in a dark forest, with the card of the king of hearts, which was the poor youth, and the king of spades, which was the king, and the queen of hearts, which was the princess.

" Her incantation (*i.e.*, what she sung to enchant the king) :—

> " ' Io sono Turanna la fate.
> Fino che vivro, la fata Turanna io saro.
> E quando morta io saro
> La spirito di Turanna che verro
> Sempre scongiurata, e chi lo meritera
> Molte grazie da me ricevera !
>
> Io, Turanna, bene e fortuna
> Per quel giovane io voglio fare,
> Tre diavoli benigne vengo a scongiurare :
> Uno per il re che lo faccio convertire,
> Uno per il povero che fortuna le faccia avere,
> Uno per la figlia che la faccia presentare
> Al padre incinta, e dire
> Che e incinta del giovane che a chiesto la sua mano.
> Questi tre diavoli scongiuro che piglino
> Il re per i capelli e lo trasinino

---

[1] Here there is manifestly something omitted. " *Colla corona sopra quali cantavano, ballavano.*" Perhaps " around which fairies sang and danced."

Forte, forte gli faccino
Le pene della morte che non possa vivere,
E non possa stare,
Fino che la figlia a quel giovane
Non a consento dare '

(" 'I am Turanna the fairy,
While I live that fairy I shall be.
And when I shall be dead
I shall become the spirit of Turanna,
Ever to be invoked, and those who merit it
Shall receive many favours from me.

I, Turanna, wish to bestow
Prosperity and fortune on that youth ;
I conjure three beneficent demons,
One for the king whom I will change,
One for the poor young man that he may succeed,
One for the daughter whom I will present
As with child to her sire, and say
That she is *enceinte* by the youth who sought her hand.
These three demons I conjure that they may take
The king and drag him by the hair !
Strongly, strongly they shall do so,
Cause him deathly pain that he may not live
Nor shall he be able to stand
Till he consents to give his daughter to the youth.')

"And so the king consented, and when he saw in an instant that his daughter was not with child,
he said, 'I have been deluded by the fairy Turanna, and it seemed to me that I was as if dying, and
were dragged by the hair of my head.'

" But his word having been given, he could not withdraw it, so they were married. and happy.
And so the poor youth, by the protection of Turanna, won a kingdom and a wife, and took care of his
mother, and in time had a fair son."

This whole narrative is properly a song. It appears to be very old, and
is evidently given in an abbreviated or almost mutilated form, for which the reader
must make allowance. Nor was it well remembered by the old woman who
repeated it.

And of Turanna I was further told that :—

" She is the spirit of lovers, of peace and of love, and the goddess of beauty. When a youth is
n love he should go into a wood and say :—

" 'Turanna, Turanna !
Che di beltà sei la regina !
Del cielo e della terra,
di felicita e di buon cuore !

Turanna ! Turanna !
In questo folto bosco
Mi vengo a inginnochiare
Per che tanto infelice
E sfortunato sono
Amo una donna e non sono cofrisposto.

Turanna ! Turanna !
A te mi vengo a raccommandare !
Le tue tre carte a volere
Scongiurare che quella
Giovane mi possa amare.

Turanna ! Turanna !
Fallo per il bene che ai sempre fatta,
Sei stata sempre tanta buona generosa,
Sei buona quanto e bella,
Che di belta siei la stella ! ' "

(" ' Turanna, Turanna !
Thou who art the queen of beauty !
Of heaven and of earth,
And of happiness and fortune !

Turanna, Turanna !
In this dark forest
I come to kneel to thee,
For I am unhappy and unfortunate ;
I love a girl and am not loved again.

Turanna, Turanna !
I commend me unto thee,
Enchant thy three cards at will,
Conjure that maid to love me !

Turanna, Turanna !
Do this. By the good which thou hast done !
Thou hast ever been so good and generous,
Thou are good as thou art fair,
For of beauty thou art the star ! ' ")

Ere I forget it, I would remark that Turanna performs her miracles and confers fortune by means of the three winning cards. Cards are the successors of *dice* in this modernised mythology, and it is significant that among the Romans the highest cast of dice, or three sixes, was known as the Venus-throw. Here again I regret not having by me my copy of *Pascasius Justus de Alea*—a little Elzevir which I well remember buying in my sixteenth year with my only shilling. But I might as well sigh for the lost work, *De Alea Lusu* (Of the Game of Dice), by the Emperor Claudian, of which Suetonius tells. But I learn from Pauly's

Real Encyclopædia that the *jactus Veneris*, or "Venus-throw," was three sixes, when thrown with three dice (Martial, 14, 14), or 1, 3, 4, 6 when with four dice. Hence Venus as Queen of Hearts, and also with three cards.

Turanna is therefore probably Turan, the Etruscan Venus. Of which Corssen says in *Sprache der Etrusker*, to which I have been greatly indebted for this subject, as well as to Gerhard, Inghirami, and Lanzi : " *Turan* is the name of a goddess often represented on Etruscan mirrors as a beautiful woman, fully naked, or naked to the hips, or in Greek female apparel, her hair flowing in ringlets, or artistically bound up, wearing much rich jewellery. She is evidently the Etruscan duplicate of the Greek Aphrodite."

It is very characteristic of the gambling Italian and fortune-teller that the dealing out the fate of mankind with cards should be characteristic of Turanna. The conception of her managing their destiny with dice is probably known to the reader, as it was to Rabelais, who made the old judge decide cases by it.

I have already, in the Introduction, expressed my great obligations to Professor, now the Senator Domenico Comparetti, of Florence, owing to whose friendly advice and suggestions my attention was first directed to these researches. I am again reminded of it by the aid which I have received from him, and also from Professor Milani, director of the Archæological and Etruscan Museum in Florence, in the chapters on Turanna, Aplu, and Pano.

"Remains to be said," that the ancients regarded dice as sacred things, mysteriously inspired and moved by the Spirit of Chance, or, when favourable, by Lady Venus in her gentlest mood ;—the great, good, and glorious Emperor Claudian having written a book in praise of dicing. (I extol him because he was the first who ever went heart and soul into raking up Etruscan antiquities and folk-lore—*eloquentissimus juxta et sapientissimus scriptor*.) But the later Christians abominated them—because the Roman soldiers gambled with them for Christ's garments ; and Bartolomeo Taegis, in his *Risposte*, or Essays (Novara, 1554), says that they were invented by the devil, and that "this game is a tempest of the soul, a fog of fame, a sudden shipwreck of fortune—as was shown by the king of the Parthians, who sent unto another monarch golden dice, all to remind him of his fickleness." That will do for to-day.

Apropos of Turanna and her cards I have something to say. It has been remarked of my *Gypsy Sorcery* that it does not deal sufficiently in the romantic element or minister unto the marvellous, looking rather for the sun by noon-light than with Dame Crowe at the night side of Nature in the dark. Now that the lovers of the incomprehensible may not be utterly disappointed, I give, on my honour as absolutely true, or as strictly " on the cards," the following :—

Several weeks before the failure and evasion of Emanuele Fenzi, the banker, in Florence, January, 1892, the woman specially referred to in these pages as a fortune-teller, was, more for her own pleasure than mine, consulting the cards to find out whether I would find the lost books of Livy, or the Annals of Claudian, or something else in the way of transcendental cartomancy, when she found that certain incidents or predictions not connected with the main inquiry kept forcing themselves forward, like unbidden guests, into the play : as often happens when the twenty-five demons who are always invoked at the beginning of such divination are more than usually friendly, and not only come in person but bring with them all their friends. The chief intruder on this occasion was a distinguished, great or rich, man, with whom I was to have, or about whom there would be, *un gran' disturbo*, that is, great trouble and rumour, noise or report. Through him I was to lose a small sum, but narrowly escape a great loss.

I had not forgotten, but I gave no heed to this suggestion by Turanna, when some weeks later the failure of Fenzi the banker made a tremendous *disturbo* in fair Florence. By which fraudulent bankruptcy I did indeed lose four hundred and sixty francs ; but as I had been on the point of depositing with Emanuel—who did but little credit to his name—a very much larger sum which would have caused me serious inconvenience, my culpable neglect of business in this instance saved me more money than I should have made all the winter by diligently attending to it. Then I was reminded of the prediction by my Sybil, and I give very accurately what I remember of it. On asking the divineress if she remembered what she had said, and how the cards had " come," she replied " Yes," and wrote me out these words :—

" When the cards were ' made '—*quando si fecero le carte*—they announced that you ought to have money from (or with) a great *signore*, and through this would be greatly troubled, but the trouble would come to no great loss (*veniva a essere non tanto grande*) ; and in this disturbance was involved a journey, between you and the other *signore*.

" And you will come well out of it, but there will be tears and great trouble for him."

Truly there was a voyage—a shooting of the moon, and a moving between two days—unto Corfu, as it is said, by the banker. The two accounts—mine and the witch's—are interesting as setting forth exactly the prediction as we both recalled it. Be it observed that, as the cards fell, the interpretation was perfectly correct. " Hæc ita clara, ita explorata sunt, ut frustra sit qui testium nubem in fidem vocaverit."

" 'Tis all so proved, explored, well tried, and plain,
That he who doubts it does so all in vain."

Manuscripts of the Middle Ages, such as the "Othea" of Christina de Pisa, establish Venus as dealing out hearts, and her connection with lucky cards. She became the Queen of Hearts at a very early period. It is worth noting in this connection that Friday, the *dies Veneris*, was always a lucky day, especially for marriage, till the priests spoiled it. The Turks still insist on this great truth, because, as they believe, it was on a Friday that Adam married Eve; Solomon, Balkis; Joseph, Zuleika (*i.e.*, Mrs. Potiphar); Moses, Sisera; and Mahomed, Chadidscha and Ayesha. For according to authentic records given by the Persian and Turkish poets, Joseph, it appears, after the little incident recorded in the Bible, subsequently "thought better of it," and Mrs. P——, as women always do, had her own way in the end. *Alors—vivè le Vendredi!*

PANO

"Pan! oh, Pan—we sing to thee!
Hail, thou king of Arcady!"
WILSON

' Eca súthi nésl Pan . . .
Hanc (cellam) mortale posuit Pan. . . . "
Über die Sprache der Etrusker, VON W. CORSSEN, 1874

Every reader of these pages will remember to have learned, long ago, that "great Pan is dead," and how the fact was revealed to Thamnus, an Egyptian, who proclaimed it to the midnight by command, whereupon there was heard-such a wailing of nymphs, satyrs, dryads oreads, and all the sprites who live in woods or streams, that it would seem as if all the fair humanities of olden time—*mortem obversari ante oculos*—did see grim death itself before their eyes, "since 'twas in Pan that they all held their life." All of which Eusebius, and in later times an exceeding sweet English poet, have discussed, while others have contended that he is not dead at all, but lives for ever on in all Nature. "This thing did often occupy my thought," therefore it was with a strange feeling, like that which was felt by him who, opening an Etruscan tomb, saw, for a minute only, an ancient warrior —perfect as in life, ere his face fell into ashes—that I discovered that in the Romagna Toscana there is a perfect solution of the question and a reconcilement of this difference of opinion. For there the great Pan did indeed once die—for the love, as it seems, of some beautiful nymph—but now lives as a spirit who is exceeding kind and gracious to all who approach him with the proper incantation or hymn in her name, the which *scongiurazione* I, to my great joy, succeeded in obtaining. What I was told of him was in these words—he being called *Pano* :—

"Pano is a spirit of the country, and benign—one of whom benefits are sought. (*E uno spirito benigno, per la campagna e per chi le chiede del bene.*)

"Pano when in this life had a love whom he indeed did very greatly love.

"Whoever would beg a favour of him must go in the evening, and kneel to him in a field by the light of the moon, and say :—

PAN

" ' Pano, Pano, Pano !
  Inginnochio in un' campo,
  Sono a lume della luna,
  In nome della tua bella

Che tanto amavi,
Che da un campo di sera via
Ti fu portata e ti fu uccisa,
Per il pene di quella ti prego
Di farmi questa grazia !'

("' Pano, Pano, Pano !
I am kneeling in a field,
I am here by the light of the moon
In the name of thy beautiful one
Whom thou didst so much love,
Who from a field one evening
Was rapt from thee and slain ;
By her sufferings, I adjure thee,
To grant me this favour ! ')

"Then one asks of him some favour, as that the country may become beautiful" (this, I take it, is a prayer for good crops), "or according to that which one requires."

From all which we may observe that even in the end of the tail of this great serpent-century Pan still lives. And of those who wail for, and sympathise with, and invoke him, it cannot be said with Salvator Rosa :—

"Non è con loro una voce Etrusca.

("There is not with them one Etruscan voice.")

Though indeed there are not many of them, for Pan is now one of the obscurest and least-known spirits.

It is significant of ancient Pan that he was noted for his loss of lady-loves. He mourned for Echo, and Syrinx turned to a reed to escape him, so he made of her pan-pipes on which he wailed her evanishment. She was really "rapt from him in a field at eventide," and it was her voice which he ever after awoke in the Pandean pipes, which in latter days became the church organ. But as a *loser* of loves Pan is alone among the deities.

Were the name wanting this circumstance would be a clue. Whether Pan was ever evoked in Latin times by memories of Syrinx or Echo, I do not know, but it is very significant that peasant tradition has preserved this very peculiar feature of his history. Pan, the great god of earth, made of his memory an endless tomb.

But though as god of the earth, fields, and crops, Pan is a benevolent spirit, yet as one who may be offended, and who has the power to destroy the harvest, he is also dreaded. From another authority in the Romagna Toscana, I learn by letter that " he is regarded by old men in Premilcuore as a *spirito maligno*, because when the corn is high he comes in roaring winds which beat it down. As it does not rise again, it cannot be sold, and for this the peasants curse him."

A certificate signed by C. Placidi, Dec. 12, 1891, now before me, attests that : " Here in Premilcuore much is remembered of the spirit Pano."

Pan, it may be observed, was, as a windy spirit, also feared of yore. Hence the panic terror (*Gazaus*, p. 174). And an ass was often sacrificed to him (Ovid, *Fasti*, i., 425).

I have given a great deal of cautious and fearful apology in this my book, as regards possible errors or improvisations in tradition and especially incantations. But I must remark of this one to Pan (and it may be said of nearly all of them), that any true scholar critic, and above all true poet, cannot fail to at once perceive that it is a composition far above the intellectual capacity of a woman who actually could not be made to take an interested comprehension of the fable of Pan, or to see how it agreed with her verses. That is, she did not actually understand what she repeated, which effectively disposes of the question as to whether she altogether invented it. That some and perhaps many of these incantations only set forth a shadowy or shifting form of what is said, or may be said, in calling certain *folletti*, I have already clearly declared, but that others are used as here given is also true. Thus in several cases those who were consulted, said there *were* incantations referring to this or that spirit which they could not recall. But in *all* cases they existed.

According to Friedrich, who has devoted a chapter to the subject (*Die Welt-körper*, &c., 1864), Pan and his seven reeds sets forth the music of the spheres, when this god is the chorus leader of the heavenly dances, who playing on his pipe inspires the Seven Spheres, and the divine harmony (Serv. to Virgil, Eclogues ii., 31). Hence Pan is invoked in an Orphic hymn (xi., 6) as :—

> " Inspired among the stars,
> Playing the harmonies of creation
> Upon the jesting flutes."

Which idea of the All-god of Nature and the seven planets suggested, as I think, a verse to Emerson :—

> " I am the ruler of the sphere :
> Of the Seven Stars and the solar year."

It was just at the time when he wrote this that my old schoolmaster, J. Bronson Alcott, published his Orphic Sayings in the *Dial*. And they were very intimate in those days.

CHAPTER II

MASO

"Omnia transformat sese in miracula rerum."—VIRGIL, *Georg.* l. 4.

"As to what became of the old god of war Mars since the victory of the Christians I can tell you but little. I am inclined to believe that during the Middle Ages he exercised the law of the strong hand. The nephew of the executioner of Münster once met him in Bologna."—HEINE, *Die Götter in Exil*

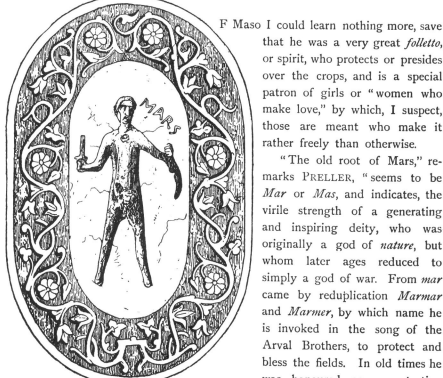

F Maso I could learn nothing more, save that he was a very great *folletto*, or spirit, who protects or presides over the crops, and is a special patron of girls or "women who make love," by which, I suspect, those are meant who make it rather freely than otherwise.

"The old root of Mars," remarks PRELLER, "seems to be *Mar* or *Mas*, and indicates, the virile strength of a generating and inspiring deity, who was originally a god of *nature*, but whom later ages reduced to simply a god of war. From *mar* came by reduplication *Marmar* and *Marmer*, by which name he is invoked in the song of the Arval Brothers, to protect and bless the fields. In old times he was honoured as a protecting deity of marriage and of married life. Here Martea is allied to Mars as the goddess of love and of desire."

49

If Maso be Mars, it is probable that we have him here known only by his first name and earliest attributes.   My informant positively denied that Maso was in this case only the diminutive of Tommaso, or Thomas—as was (of course)

WINGED MARS
Maso.   After Gerhard and Gori

promptly suggested by one of the learned.   And I am inclined to believe the former, because there is no apparent reason whatever, beyond mere resemblance of name, why a spirit of nature should be called Thomas after a saint, while that between the modern Maso and the ancient *Mas* is very great. A *single* coincidence, be it of name or attribute, or incident, gives basis for nothing more than an hypothesis, or supposition ; *two*, as of name and attribute, entitles us to form a theory ; *three*, as when both are borne out by established tradition and testimony, constitute authentic history. In this case the latter is wanting, but great allowance must be made for the fact that *Maso* appears in company with a number of others of whose authenticity there can be little doubt.

It is to be particularly observed that in the prayer to Mars given by Cato (*de re rustica, cap :* 141), which is of very great antiquity, this deity is, as Panzer (*Bayerische Sagen*, p. 525) observes, invoked solely as a god of crops, " *ist ganz als Ärntegott dargestellt*," and that all the offerings brought to him indicate that he was a god of harvests. This view of Mars, according to Panzer, is confirmed by passages in the Euguboean tablets, so far as they have been deciphered.

Elias Schedius (*De Dis Germanis*) has gathered together much learning to prove that *Mars autem nullus alius nisi Sol* (" Mars is none other than the Sun "), that is to say, the fructifying and vivifying principle of nature. And it is as such that he appears in old Etruscan mythology.

MANIA DELLA NOTTE

" The real god of the world below among the Tuscans, or Tusker," writes OTTFRIED MÜLLER, " was called Mantus, who was therefore compared with Dispater. In Etruscan histories the name of Mantua was derived from him. With him was worshipped a goddess of the lower realms—the *Mania*. . . . This was a truly Etruscan divinity. . . . To the strange and terrible gods to whom the Tuscan *libri fatales* give human sacrifices . . . belong Mantus and *Mania*. Terrible to the old Italians seemed Mania . . . who is inseparable from the Tuscan faith of the Lares, being allied to the Manes. She was an awful divinity to whom, under TARQUINIUS SUPERBUS, boys were offered. Her fearful image—afterwards a child's toy—was in early times hung on doors to avert contamination. This *Mania* was the mother or grandmother of the Manes, also the mother of the Lares." MÜLLER indulges in much speculation as to this chthonic goddess, or deity of darkness.

And she still lives in Tuscany, and is called *Mania della Notte* (Mania of the Night), but regarded simply as the Nightmare, and Succuba, and as a mysterious nocturnal spirit inspiring wanton dreams.

It has been suggested to me that " the Greek word *mania*, meaning insanity or madness, has nothing to do with the Latin *mania*," which to a degree weakens

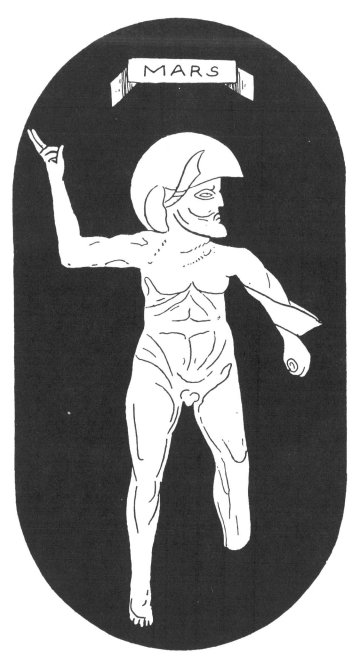

MARS

the connection between the nightmare and the spirit of the night. This I leave to others to discuss; it is enough for me to have shown that there was an Etruscan Mania of the Night of old, and that the nightmare is called by the same name now, in La Romagna Toscana.

It may be observed that both Mania of the Night and Martha of the Day, or her prototype Mater Matuta, were said to be the mothers of the Lares. This indicates the existence of a primal goddess of both night and day. "Mania," writes Mrs. Hamilton Gray (*Hist. of Etruria*), "was a most fearful spirit to the old Italians. Her frightful image used to be hung over the doors, like a scarecrow, to frighten away evil." This is quite identical with the old Assyrian observance recorded by Lenormant of placing the images of evil or dreaded deities in places to scare away the demons themselves.

I have mentioned in the Preface that Enrico Rossi testified of Mania della Notte that she was "remembered once by many, but it is now a long time since any one at Galeata has spoken of her." From which it may be inferred that the name is passing away rapidly, and but for my inquiries would soon have been among those

> "Of the gods who had their turn,
> And whose fires no longer burn."

CHAPTER III

FERONIA

" The Etruscan Feronia—the Dawn—is also the goddess of trade."—*The Etruscans*, by JOHN FRASER
" Vividi gaudens Feronia luco."—VIRGIL, *Æneid*, viii., 800.
" Ora manusque tua lavimus,
Feronia, lympha."—HORACE, *Sat.* i., v. 24

HERE is a kind of argument very much in vogue among historians of the Mommsen class. It consists in picking a small flaw in a legend or incident, or even offering an unproved conjecture of one's own, as Mommsen does, and then boldly assuming from it that all is false. No heed whatever is taken of the fact that this incident, or narrative, taken with others *as a whole*, may have a basis of truth— no—all must go at a guess.

I beg the reader to bear this in mind as regards several chapters, of which the following is a type, requiring a broader and more liberal method of judgment.

There is a goddess of whose identity with a modern spirit, or *folletto*, there can be very little question. *Feronia*, according to MÜLLER, was the ancient goddess of the market-place and fairs. This would, as a matter of course, identify her with, and make her the patron of, all strolling characters who frequent such places. MÜLLER expresses a doubt whether she was really a member of the Etruscan *Heiligthum*, or mythology, since VARRO claims her as Sabine. But as she had temples in Etruria, he deems it possible that she was common to both races. The ancients were at a loss where to place her among the deities ; she appears, however, to be a goddess of the earth, and allied to Mania, "which makes it intelligible how it was in her power to give to the Prænestic Herilus three souls from the lower world." But what is most important of all for my purpose is that she was feared, and that people brought her offerings.

Feronia is at the present day "a *strega-folletta*—a witch-spirit who goes wandering about the country begging alms in disguise. When the peasants are liberal to her all goes well with them ; but should they give her nothing then they suffer for it. She bewitches children, oxen, horses, and all the beasts *che tengono nella stalla*—which are kept in stables."

A wandering witch, who exacts offerings, and who is rather evil than good, is a very legitimate descendant from a goddess of the markets, and who, as a form of Mania, is prone to mischief and revenge. There can be no question but that the ancient Feronia was Persephonic or chthonic, or a queen of the realm below therefore a witch now, who, if not propitiated, inflicts on the peasants what they most dread—loss of children and cattle. Sabine or Etruscan, she still lives, and is much feared in Tuscany.

Since writing the last line I have learned that Feronia haunts market-places, specially "*Perche e lo spirito del mercato.*" I have, regarding her, also the following, which was attributed to *Impusa*, but which, I am quite sure, was an error of the copyist :—

"*Feronia* was an old woman who went about begging in the country, yet she always had a *gran pulitica*—that is, she was intelligent or shrewd or very cunning in manners—and, as one would have believed, she was a witch. All who gave her alms were very fortunate, and their affairs prospered. And if people could give her nothing because of their poverty, when they returned home after the sun rose (*dopo chiaro*) they found abundant gifts—enough to support all the family—so that henceforth all went well with them ; but if any who were rich gave her nothing, and had evil hearts, she cursed them thus :—

"'Siate maledetti
Da me che vi maladisco
Di vero cuore !
E cosi i vostr 'affari
Possono andare
A rotto di collo !
Fame e malattie !
Cosi non avrete,
Non avrete piu bene ! '

("' Be ye all accursed
By me who curse you
With my heart and soul !
May your lives for ever
Go to utter ruin ;
Illness and starvation
Be ever in your dwelling ! ')

" By this they knew she was a witch. But when she was dead she became terrible, and did much harm. However, when those who had wronged her, and knew it, went to her tomb and begged pardon they were always sure to obtain it."

The incident of the begging, and the elegant style and distinguished air indicate a character like that of Juno and Ceres combined. The curse attributed to her has a great strength, and may be of extreme antiquity. The connection of Feronia with Mania explains why she was feared as a witch. And it is very remarkable indeed that while MÜLLER lays stress on the fact that she had offerings brought to her, the modern Tuscan account makes it a main incident. Taking her altogether, Feronia appears to be exactly what such a goddess would naturally come to be in the minds of the people at a stage while they still believed in and feared her, and before she had sunk to a mere reminiscence in a *Mährchen*. And it is the *Mährchen*, or child's tale, alone which is chiefly sought by folk-lorists who have no conception of the extent to which the, as yet, living myth exists.

The Roman-Etruscan *Feronia* was very famous for the extent of the offerings made to her. " All who dwelt near brought her the first fruits, and many offerings, so that in time an immense quantity of gold and silver formed a treasure in her temple, which was all carried away by the soldiers of Hannibal " (Livy, xxvi., 11 ; Silius Italicus, *Pun.* xiii. ; Preller, *Rom. Myth.*, 377). This agrees with the modern story of her exacting tribute. Again, she was the special protectress of the freed slaves—that is a friend of the poor—and the *Libertini* in Rome made offerings to her (Livy, xxii., l.). This is curiously identical with the legend. If, as MÜLLER asserts, Feronia was a duplicate of Persephone, who was often a counterpart of the charitable Ceres, this would explain the very singular statement that the poor always received their gifts from her " after the sun rose," *i.e.*, they came, or were given, during the night. Her market and temple were also a great resort for merchants and traders, which seems to cast some light on the otherwise uncalled-for statement that she was of *gran pulitica*—very shrewd. The modern Feronia is also a great friend to the poor.

But there is yet another reason why Feronia may have retained a reputation as a witch or wonder-worker. She was of old especially identified with the great miracle, of which so much was made during the Middle Ages, of walking on red-hot ploughshares or glowing coals. As appears by the following passage from Strabo, Lib. 5 :—

> "Sub monte Soracte urbs est *Feronia*, quo nomine et Dea quædam nuncupatur, quam finitimi miro dignantur honore. Eodem in loco ipsius templum est, mirificum sacrigenus habens. Nam qui ejus numine afflantur, nudis pedibus prunas calcant. Eò ingens mortalium multitudo convenit, et celebritatis ipsius, quæ quotannis celebratur, gratia, paritur et spectaculi."

The ordeal of hot coals was very commonly applied to witches, and it is not improbable that the accused appealed to Feronia to protect them, owing to some tradition. One thing is apparent both in the ancient and modern Feronia, that she is, or was, a protector and friend of the poor, one of slaves and refugees, as now of paupers. The identification of the elder goddess with the ordeal indicates protection and benevolence. On which interesting subject the reader may consult : I. Roth, *De more quo apud plerosque Europæos populos per ferrum candens ardentes prunas rogumque probatur*, Ulm, 1676. Lescher, *De probatione rerum dubiarum per ignem facto*, Leipzig, 1695. Eckard, *De ritu antiquissimo per ignes et carbones candendes incedendi*, 1791, and Nork, *Sitten und Gebräuche der Deutschen.*

It will be seen, therefore, that the modern Feronia corresponds to the ancient character of the same name in many ways. And I would call attention to the fact that beyond the *name* itself (for which I indeed inquired) nothing was by me suggested or demanded.

According to Fraser (*The Etruscans*), "Feronia in Etruria held an honourable position, for not only was she goddess of Falerii, but she had a sanctuary also at the Etruscan town of Losna (Latin, *Luna*). The name of this town, Losna, is another proof that Feronia is the goddess of the Dawn, for it comes from the Greek *los* or *las*, light."

Monti has written a very beautiful, though rather feeble poem, called the *Feroniade*, in which the heroine, as a goddess, approaches much more closely to the same character as set forth in modern popular legend than to the stately goddess Feronia of classic tradition. For she is with him at first only a small sylvan Etruscan deity, the queen of the violets, who wanders through ravines and forests, or "a nymph."

> " Ella per fiere
> Balze e foreste erro gran tempo
> Una *ninfa* già fu delle propinque
> Selve leggiadra abitatrice, ed era
> Il suo nome Feronia."

This is altogether *our* Feronia, and not the great Goddess of the olden time, which she is subsequently represented as being—the reason for which very evidently was that Monti began with an inspiration derived from the popular Tuscan legend, and, as he wrote, by going back into classic lore for material, entirely changed the character of his heroine.   This is absolutely the only explanation which can be offered of this manifest blunder.

SILVIANO

"Silvanus" (the god of fields and cattle) "has still dominion in the land."—*The Cities of Etruria*, by GEORGE DENNIS, vol. i., p. 229.

"Quin et Silvanos Faunosque et deorum genera silvis ac sua numina tanquam et cœlo attributa credimus." —PLINY, *Hist. Nat.*, xii., 2.

"Fama est, Cyparissum puerum ab ipso fuisse amatum, quare ubi in arborem sui nominis mutatus fuisset, Cupressum manibus semper gestasse Sylvanus dictus fuit."—*De Hermaphroditorum, Monstrosorum, &c., Caspari Bauhini*, 1614.

Silviano was described to me, as " Lo spirito dei boschi " (" the spirit of the forests or woods "), and his peculiarities were set forth as follows :—

"Silviano is very fond of annoying the peasants who burn charcoal (*che fanno le cataste di carbone*— literally, who pile up the heaps and then ignite them).   And when all the sticks are piled, then comes Silviano and upsets them, and the *contadini* begin to quarrel among themselves, accusing one another of the deed.   So they have to begin their work over again.   Then Silviano roars with laughter, and the men begin to swear and perhaps to fight, every one thinking that the other is laughing at him.   And while all this is going on Silviano piles up the wood again—to their great amazement when they return to work.

"This happened once to two men, and they thought it must be a miracle worked by some saint.   So they went to the *parocco*, or parish priest, and told him of it.   So he went there and examined, but found nothing remarkable, and told them they were fools for their pains, and so returned with all his *precissione* (procession), persuaded that nothing wonderful had happened.

"But good-natured as Silviano is, he is *altrettanto vendiccativa*—tolerably revengeful.   And from that day, whether in wood or grove—*nella macchia o sia nel boscho*—nothing went well with them.   Other men found their work all done to hand for them, while theirs was spoiled.   And this time they went to an old witch who understood the business, and knew what to do.   And she said :—

> " ' E il folletto Silviano,
> Che l'avete contradito,
> E ora li vi fa tutti
> I dispetti, ma dell'erba
> Che vi daro vi fara tornare
> In la sua buona grazia.

> (" ' 'Tis the spirit Silviano,
> Unto him ye were ungracious,
> Therefore he has made these troubles
> For you—but I'll give you something,
> 'Tis an herb which will restore you
> Once again to his good graces.')

" Then she took the herb called *silvestra* and also *ginestra*, or broom, and made of it a small square, and said, putting it on their backs :—

SILVANUS (SILVIANO) AND NYMPH

" ' Questo e lo spirito
  Di Silviano che mi protegge !

(" ' This is in truth the spirit
  O Silviano who protects me ! ')

"So they returned again into his good graces, and never did anything more to offend him. And they learned from this a lesson not to go and call on priests when there had been a spirit present."

Silvianus is plainly enough the old Roman Silvanus, of whom Preller remarks : "He was like Faunus, a good spirit, but now and then a *spuk Geist* who frightened people. He was identified with everything beautiful, romantic, and rural. Planted pleasant fields, openings in the forest, wherever there was a cool shelter, a shady grotto, or where a murmuring brook attracted the shepherd in the mid-day heat, there was a spot always sacred to Silvanus." So he became very dear to all rural folk ; he was like one of themselves, and traces of this love are to be felt in this Tuscan tale.

For reasons, which I have not space to give, I would here say that the ancient identification of Sylvanus with the *cypress*-tree fully explains his connection with charcoal-burning and burners. And as a spirit who specially haunts such men Silviano is identical with Rubezahl of Germany. PRELLER declares that the Silvanæ, or Silviæ wood-nymphs, belong rather to the German, Celtic, and Slavic races, than to the Latin. But why ? May not Rubezahl himself be of Italian birth ? Silvanus was the son of a river-god and a she-goat, and everything related of him is far more suggestive of pastoral Italy than of wild Germany.

The utter heathenism of this story and its "moral" cannot have escaped the reader. The narrator was as absolutely a heathen herself as any who ever lived in the time of Tarquin, and never missed an opportunity to show that she considered the worship of the spirits of the olden time, and all its incantations and ceremonies, far superior to the Roman Catholic, for which latter she had a special aversion. With the old *strege* this religion of ancient times is not *folk-lore* but a living faith, and I was often as strangely moved by this reality as if I had been taken back two thousand years.

This chapter, and others, therefore suggest the possibility that the Northern mythology of goblins may have been originally of Italian origin, or from a common source.

PALÓ

This deity was described to me in the following words :—

"Palò is a spirit of the fields, vines, meadows, for all kinds of crops, and when men work, be it in planting maize, or in the vineyards, they must never forget to say :—

" ' Lo spirito Palò
Sara quello
Che mi fara
La buona fortuna ! '

("'The spirit Paló
He shall be
The one who brings
Good luck to me!')

"And thus the peasant will be sure to ever have good fortune.'

It is not difficult to recognise in Paló the Pales of the Romans, or the ancient deity of agriculture of all kinds. To him or to her—for *Pales* appears to have been recognised both as male and female—offerings were made by the peasants who also drank much, and leaped over flames. PRELLER writes that in the morning the shepherd uttered four times an invocation to Pales, then drank a mixture of milk and new wine, and then jumped over blazing straw. Therefore the invocation must have been very short, since it was so often repeated. It would be strange—and yet it is not impossible—that in the four lines here given there is an echo at least of the early invocation. There is so much which is unquestionably ancient in these Tuscan traditions that I find it almost impossible sometimes to believe that there is anything modern in them. Critics may very reasonably indicate many errors and inconsistencies in details, but a comparison of the whole must leave the impression of antiquity. A single negro would not absolutely prove the existence of a black race, but a number of them would render it extremely probable.

As was the case with most deities, Pales had a town named after him. It is the modern Palo, half way between Rome and Civita Vecchia. I mention this because it may be thought—as was indeed urged as to Norcia—that the modern Tuscan deity was so called after the town.

ESTA

"Nec tu aliud Vestam quam vivam intellige flammam,
Nataque de flammis corpora nulla vides."
OVID, *Fast.* 6

When a light is suddenly and mysteriously extinguished or goes out apparently of its own accord, especially when two lovers are sitting together, it is commonly said in jest that "Esta did it." Esta is supposed to be a spirit who pays particular attention to lights, but beyond this I could learn nothing of her.

Hestia was an ancient name for Vesta, and CICERO thought that Vesta was derived from Ἑστία. In any case the sudden extinguishment of a light or fire, and the satirical covert allusion to love in the dark, seems to indicate that the goddess of chastity and her light are here alluded to. However, this is a matter which those who are best able to determine must settle for themselves if they think it worth the while. I do but record the fact that Esta put out the light, and *then* put out the light which was extinguished over Evelyn's bower.

CARMENTA

When I asked if the name Carmenta was known it was promptly recognised as that of a spirit who gives, presides over, and loves children, who aids in birth, and who is dear to mothers. Then the following was repeated :—

" Carmenta, Carmenta !
Che tanta bella sei !
E inamorata sei
Tanto dei fanciulli !
Tante spose sono venute
A te a raccomandare
Che dei figli tu gli facesse fare,
E tu buona quanto e,
Bella i suoi voti tu ai,
Ascoltati ti prego pure
I miei di volere ascoltare
Perche sono molto infelice,
Il mio marito non mi ama più
Che tanto m'amava perche figli crear
Non so, ma date, o bella Carmenta,
Mi vengo a raccomandare
Che un figlio tu mi possa far fare,
E la pace con mio marito possa ritornare ! "

(" Carmenta, Carmenta !
Thou who art so fair,
Thou who truly lovest
Children, everywhere !
As I come to thee,
So have many others,
Knelt before thy shrine,
Seeking to be mothers !
Thou didst grant their wishes,
Thou as good as fair,
Listen unto me,
Grant my humble prayer !
Once my husband loved me,
Now he loves no more ;

Because I bear no children
All his love is o'er,
Make me once a mother,
He will love me as before ! ")

This corresponds in name and in every detail to the Latin Carmenta or Carmentis, who was another form of the Fauna or Bona Dea. Of her PRELLER says : " The Goddess of Birth, Carmenta, was so zealously worshipped near the Porta Carmentalis, which was named from her, that there was a *Flamen Carmentalis*, and two calendar days, the eleventh and the fifteenth of January, called the Carmentalia, devoted to her worship. These were among the most distinguished festivals of the Roman matrons. She was peculiarly the goddess of pregnancy.

IL SENTIERO

The boundary-stones which determine the limits of fields are believed in Tuscany to have in or attached to them spirits called *Spiriti dei sentieri*, which means, however, "spirits of the paths," or lines of demarcation. It was, however, distinctly asserted that they lived in the stones. "And if any one removes them the spirit will quite ruin him." The single spirit is a *sentiero*.

This spirit is exactly the *Terminus* of the Romans, or the divinity of the boundaries. Fearful penalties were attached to the removal of such landmarks. The inscription of a *terminus* reads : *Quisquis hoc sustulerit aut læserit, ultimus suorum moriatur* ("Should any one remove or injure this stone, may he die the last of his race ! "). There is indeed quite a litany of old Latin curses, almost equal to a Roman Catholic excommunication, extant, as applied to these "land-grabbers." That the memory of these has survived is evident from the only comment which my informant made—*Il spirito lo guasta* ("The spirit ruins them ").

Lactantius, heaping ridicule on the heathen for worshipping many deities of small duties, specifies Terminus as one because he was rough and rude.

" He was the stone which Saturn swallowed thinking it was Jupiter. When Tarquin wished to build the Capitol and found these shrines of many ancient gods, he consulted them by augury whether they would yield to Jupiter. All agree to go save *Terminus*, who was suffered to remain. Hence the poet calls him the immovable rock of the Capitol. And what can I say of people who worship such stocks and stones (*lapides et stipites*) save that they are stocks and stones themselves ? " (*Adversus Gentes*, book i., chap. xx.).

It is a pity that Lactantius could not have lived to the end of the nineteenth century, when he might have seen among Christians an array of saints of small

things, compared to whom all the heathen gods whom he mentions as laughable
are grave and respectable deities.   Terminus, a rock, as the emblem of stability
(for he was truly nothing more), is a sound and sensible image, but what shall we
think of Antony as the saint of pigs and truffles ; Simeon of lotteries, or the
Roco-co saint of dogs ; or why is the Latin Cunina, who presided over children
in the cradle, and whom Lactantius calls on us to laugh at, more ridiculous than
Santa Anna who does the same, or even the Madonna herself—the incarnation
of nursing motherhood ?   But the saints—and even the Virgin—had not "come
up" as yet in those days !   Taking them all through, the most crushing and
terrible condemnations of the later Catholic Church and its Hagiology are to be
found in the arguments of the Fathers against the Gentiles, and especially in the
vigorous satire of "the Christian Cicero."

CHAPTER IV

FAFLON

"Oh, Fufluns! Fufluns! awful deity!"—*Pumpus of Perusia* in the *Gaudeamus* of W. SCHEFFEL

"But it went better with Bacchus than it did with Mars or Apollo after the grand retreat of the gods."—HEINE, *The Gods in Exile*

HE Arno, which rushes roaring before the window where I am writing, swelled by much rain to a spring flood, is now a great river, very muddy and somewhat unmanageable. I have seen it in summer when it was limpid and clear, but then it was only a rivulet which went from one shining pool to another, like a silken thread scantily strung with sun-lit pearls, or a pilgrim wandering from shrine to shrine. It would have been easy then for a hundred people to carry it all away in barrels, or for all the population of the place to drink it up—as they would assuredly have done like "Macpherson," had it been wine. Now all the men in Tuscany, with all their buckets, could make no estimate of its water.

APLU, FUFLUNS, AND SEMELE

This reminds me of the task on which I am engaged. If it were only to gather, collate, and correct a collection of fairy tales, or proverbs, or parables, or games, or Exempla, it would be an easy, or at least a *defined* work. Such pools are not hard to fathom, or count, or measure, or exhaust. But this mass of old, obscure, unrecorded mythology, comes pouring and foaming down like the Arno from the mountains of La Romagna, in whose mysterious recesses still dwells

> "the dragon's ancient brood,
> And rocks fall over roaring in the flood."

Well, it is a strange country little known—we have Goethe's word for that—and it has sent me, all in a spring freshet, obscure deities of doubtful name and fame, sorceries, rhymes, legends—dirt and diamonds—*tutti confusi e misti.* What should I give? What should I suppress? As compared to anything which I have as yet met in folk-lore this has been more like counting Ossian's ghosts than aught else. Many a time have I almost despaired over it, and many a time been awed.

But hope springs eternal in the human breast, and so I will proceed to discuss my last discovery of a divinity who is generally supposed to have utterly died out nearly two thousand years ago, and yet who lives as a real *folletto* among a few old witches in La Romagna. I mean *Faflon.*

FUFLUNUS was the Etruscan Bacchus. "His name," writes MULLER (*Die Etrusker*, vol. ii., p. 79), "was sounded (*lautet*) Fuflunus, Fuflunu, Fufluns—generally Fufluns. GERHARDT, i., 83, 84, 87, 90, &c.; CORSSEN (i., p. 313-5). We find on goblets *Fufunl* (FAHR. P, Spl. n. 453) and Fuflunsl (CORSSEN, i., p. 430), according to CORSSEN from *poculum*, and *poculum Bacchi.* He derives the name of the god from the Indogennanic root *fu*, to beget, *ab. Gerhard* from Populonia "—which is very doubtful.

On inquiring from my best authority if there was in La Romagna Toscana a spirit of the vineyards, or of wine, I was promptly informed that there was such a being known as *Fardel*, or *Flavo*, but among the witches, or those better informed in such mysteries, as *Faflon.* And at once there was narrated to me a legend which was then written out:—

"*Faflon* is a spirit who lives in the vines, and when women or men have gathered grapes and filled the panniers, then comes this *Faflon* and scatters them all on the ground; but woe to the *contadini* should they be angered at it, for then *Faflon* knocks them right and left, and tramples (on the grapes), so that they get no profit. But if they take it good-naturedly, he gathers them again, and replaces them in the panniers.

"Now there was a peasant who greatly loved the spirits, and frequently blessed them. One year everything went wrong with him; his crop of grapes and all other fruit failed, yet for all this he still loved Faflon and blessed him.

"One morning he rose to gather what little there was on the vines, but found that even that little was gone. The poor peasant began to weep, and said: '*Non mi resta che morire.* All that remains for me now is to die, for I have lost what little crop I had in my little vineyard.' When all at once Faflon appeared, but beautiful with a beauty like enchantment—*ma tanto bello di una bellezza da fare incantare*—and said: 'Oh, peasant with great coarse shoes, but with a fine brain, thou hast loved me so well I will reward thee. Go to thy cellar, and there a great quantity

> " D'uva mastatata tu troverai
> E gran vino tu lo farai.

> (" Pressed grapes thou shalt see,
> And great thy store of wine will be.)

"Now what *Flaflon* had said seemed to be like a dream to the peasant, but he went to his cellar, and truly the wine which he had that year made him rich, *e non ebbe più biogna di fare il contadino*— he was no longer obliged to live as a peasant."

No one can doubt that this Faflon—it was written in the MS. sometimes *Flaflon*—is the Fufluns, or Fufunal, of the Etruscans. His appearance as a very beautiful being is perfectly in accordance with that of Bacchus. It is exactly in this manner that Bacchus flashes up in beauty from disguise in classic tales. Bacchus of old carried off mortal beauties for mistresses, and I now give word for word as related by a witch a story of a modern Ariadne :—

"There was a *contadino* who had several vineyards, yet all went so ill with them for several years that he had not wine enough to drink for his family.

"Now he had a daughter—*di una belleza da fare incantare*—of enchanting beauty. And one evening as he was sitting almost in despair, his daughter said: 'Father, dear, do you not know how all this came to pass? Have you forgotten that strange and beautiful youth who once came to you and begged for me—he was so much in love? And when you denied him what he asked, he replied: "If I cannot have her neither shall you have any vintage." '

"Then the peasant was very angry, and beat his daughter, so that she had to go to bed. Then he went into the cellar, but what a sight he saw! On all the barrels were devils frolicking; fire flashed from their eyes and flamed from their mouths, and as they danced they sang :—

> " ' Give Faflon that girl of thine,
> And henceforth thou shalt have wine :
> If the maiden you deny,
> As a beggar thou shalt die.'

"Then the man gave his daughter to Faflon, and lo! all the barrels were filled with the best, and from that time his vintages were abundant."

The picture of the cellar full of frisking Bacchanals and Fauns is good. I suspect that a Catholic influence made them "devils with fire coming out of their mouths." But perhaps it was only

" Il vino divino
Che fiammeggia nel Sansovir.o."

("The wine divine
Which flames so red in Sansovine.")

I should have been really sorry if, after all this fine Bacchic lore, I had not found a hymn to him. And here it is. When a peasant wants a good vintage he may possibly pray for it in church, but to make sure of it he repeats the following to the jovial god :—

" Faflon, Faflon, Faflon !
A vuoi mi raccomando !
Che l'uva nella mia vigna
E multa scarsa,
A vuoi mi raccomando,
Che mi fate avere
Buona vendemmia !

Faflon, Faflon, Faflon !
A vuoi mi raccomando !
Che il vino nella mia cantina
Me lo fate venire fondante,
E molto buono,
Faflon, Faflon, Faflon ! "

(" Faflon, Faflon, Faflon !
Oh, listen to my prayer.
I have a scanty vintage,
My vines this year are bare ;
Oh, listen to my prayer !
And put, since thou canst do so,
A better vintage there !

Faflon, Faflon, Faflon !
Oh, listen to my prayer !
May all the wine in my cellar
Prove to be strong and rare,
And good as any grown,
Faflon, Faflon, Faflon !")

There, reader, is the very last real and sincere hymn to Bacchus which was ever sung in Italy—probably the last truly Bacchanalian song which will ever be heard on earth. There have been whole libraries of such lyrics—Della Cruscan Redi wrote a *Bacco in Toscana ;* but that was art—this is religion. And what is stranger is that this Bacchic hymn was possibly, in some form, not much unlike it, also the first which was ever composed.

I should add that after the above was written my two *contadino* friends, who made a special business of going on market days to pick up the testimony of old peasants from all parts of La Romagna, fully confirmed the existence of this spirit, with this variation—that Ottavio Magrini wrote the name Faflond, while Peppino declares, " *Il nome legitimo di questo spirito e Faflo* " (" The legitimate name of this spirit is Faflo "). It was one of the gods who were specially inquired for or cried at the market-place and elsewhere with satisfactory result.

Fufluns was also anciently known as Vertumnus. " Allied to him," says Dennis, " probably more than in name, was Voltumna, the great goddess at whose shrine the confederate princes of Etruria held their councils " (*Cities, &c., of Etruria*, vol. i., p. lvii.).

Lo Spirito della Contentezza

The spirit of Content is certainly a very good one, and I wish with all my heart that it may dwell with my reader, not only as regards this book, but be in all his life in everything.   It is very creditable to the Italians that in such a terribly overtaxed country the idea of a spirit of content can be entertained, however, it is certain that they do invoke her when setting out on a journey to seek fortune. And it is uttered as follows :—

" When one is about to travel to seek fortune he says to his friends :—

" ' Vado in viaggio
Per fare fortuna.'

(" ' I am going on my way
To find a fortune if I may.')

" Then his friends reply :—

" ' Che lo spirito della contentezza
Ti possa guidare sempre ! '

(" ' May the spirit of content
Guide thy steps wherever bent !')

" Then the traveller may go his way joyous and at ease, sure that he will succeed, but he must never forget that it is due to the Spirit of Content."

There can be no question but that this Spirit of Content is the *Fortuna Redux*, " the goddess of happy journeys, and of prosperous returns, to whom, after the long absence of the Emperor AUGUSTUS, altars, temples, and sacrifices were ordained."   When Augustus (B.C. 19) returned, October 12th, from a long absence in Asia, this day was appointed for an annual celebration of the event, and an altar raised which was consecrated on the 15th of the following December.

It should not escape the notice of the reader that the Italian account of this goddess concludes with an exhortation never to forget that one's good fortune will be due to the spirit which has been invoked ; that is to say, it is to an old Roman deity under another name that you will owe success, and that the traveller is to be grateful to Fortuna Redux.   This is in truth a most naïf unconscious survival of heathenism.

" Still in our ashes glow the wonted fires."

Schedius gives in relation to this divinity the following inscription from a monument : —

" FORTUNÆ

REDUCI.   LARI

VIALI.   ROMÆ

AETERNÆ

Q.   AXIS.   AELIA.

NUS.   VE.   PROC.

AUG.

C."

CORREDOIO

T may be observed as a very singular fact, that all these Tuscan spirits of the forests and fields, the fireplace and vineyard, are of a perfectly fresh, unaffected simplicity, befitting the out-of-door nature from which they are derived. Herein they differ radically and entirely from every personification of the Roman Catholic Church, from the Trinity itself which is a "mystery," down to the Cupid-cherubim, gilt lightnings, hammers and nails, hearts on fire, Madonnas in silks with gold surroundings, jewelled shepherd's crooks, and the whole mass of mystical theatrical properties which indeed take hold of vulgar nature in part, but not of all. This natural simplicity was of yore heathen, and its existence in folk-lore is always a proof of certain elements, at least of antiquity.

I remarked in my *Gypsy Sorcery* that if the Pope and Cardinals of 1891 had lived in 1484 and dared to express what they all (with the exception perhaps of the Spaniards), now think of witchcraft, they would all have been tortured horribly, and then burned alive as heretics. So we may observe, that the whole modern machinery of the Church would have been utterly damned by the Fathers, from its immensely artificial, stagey character. Very revolting to many would have been its miserably affected, moping melancholy, its wretched ideal of life without laughter, and innocence without smiles. Apropos of which I come to the charming spirit Corredoio, who is purely heathen.

There is in the Romagna a spirit, fairy or goddess (male or female), who is of a gay and festive nature. She is called Curedoia or Corredoio, and loves dances and festivals. She is a *vera fanatica per la musica*—wild after music—and though you may not suspect her presence, she is sure to attend wherever there is a frolic or a ball. I offer with all modesty, or even distrust, the suggestion that we may have in her the *beau reste* or possible fragment of *Curitis* or *Quritis*—the *is* and *us* of Latin are very commonly changed to vowels in Italian, which would make Curitoio at once.

"Curitis," says MÜLLER, "was the name in Falerii, where she was zealously worshipped, of Juno." Magnificent festivals with every circumstance of splendour and gaiety were held in her honour. White cows were sacrificed, the streets laid with carpets (OVID, iii., 12, 13, 24), maidens wrapped, according to Greek custom, in white garments, bore as *cannephoroe*, the holy utensils on their heads. The Etruscans surpassed any race of antiquity in their passion for processions, festivals, and the intensity of their frolics. The Romans seem to have taken their *style* from Greece, but their keen relish for splendid pleasure from the *Tuski*. And if Curitis was the popular name for Juno, and if she was indeed above all others the goddess of the *pompa* and the festivals and of joyousness, it is not impossible that the name survives in the modern deity of the dance, and what most nearly corresponds to the grand displays of the olden time. Of Corredoio I have the following :—

"*Corredoio e uno spirito che va molto nelle feste da ballo,* Corredoio is a spirit who much frequents dances and who in every way diverts himself. (There are conflicting accounts as to the sex of Corredoio or Corredoia). He is delighted to come in like a *ventata*—a gust of wind—*e così si alza le sottane a quelle Signore*—and so raise the devil—or the skirts—among the ladies, then he (or she) bursts into loud laughter, so that the ladies blush. Then Corredoio flies up into the orchestra, and makes all the musicians whirl round, and then he makes all the instruments sound of themselves, and everybody is amazed to hear music and see no performers—at which he utters another roar of laughter—*e se ne va*—and flies away."

There is an incantation or invocation to Corredoio which is extremely curious :—

"Corredoio, Corredoio, Corredoio
Che siei tanto buono e gentile,
Che tu non ai fatto mai male
Quando viene del male in casa mia
O bel Corredoio vai e la discacci
Con una bella risata,

Tu o bel Corredoio sei un spirito
E vero, ma sei anche lo spirito
Dell' allegria ; tu vai nelle case
A mettere la buona armonia ;
Dunque bel Corredoio tu che sei
Tanto bello, viene qualche volta
In camera mia, e cosi
Mi aiuterai a stare allegro,
E non avere mai guai e cosi
Se qualche grazia ti chiedero,
Da te bel Corredoio, sono certo,
Che quella grazia di te io l'avro.

("Corredoio, Corredoio, Corredoio !
Thou who art so pleasant and benign,
Thou who never dids't do harm to any,
Should any sorrow come into my house
Oh, fair Corredoio, send it flying
With a ringing peal of merry laughter.
Thou, fair Corredoio, art a spirit,
Truly but thou also art a spirit
Of all merriment, thou enterest houses
To promote all loving peace and union,
And so, fair spirit, since thou art so kind,
Come now and then I pray thee to my room,
And help me to maintain a merry mind,
And never know a sorrow—and if thou
Can'st grant me some small grace which I may ask
Of thee, fair Corredoio, this is sure,
That when I ask that grace thou'lt grant it me.")

The reader who understands Italian, if he will make allowance for the fact that it is only that of a poor peasant woman, translated " as she went along," from Romagnola, may admit that this is a very remarkable and beautiful invocation with a ring as of Shakespeare in it. It is utterly out óf the pale of the Church and as heathen as can be. There is in the whole Catholic—I may say Christian— religion, no trace of such a glorious Robin Goodfellow as Corredoio—one who goes to all the balls, plays on all the instruments, whirls all the women in a wild waltz, then wends him laughing, ho, ho, ho ! and yet makes it his constant occu- pation to go into families and promote peace and harmony, or please and play with the children, and depart, leaving everybody jolly.

This invocation is as earnest a prayer in the Romagna as any in the Prayer Book, and it begs the deity to sometimes " look in on a fellow and cheer him up in a friendly way "—a deity who is very beautiful, graceful, accomplished ; it is only in Italy that one could find a god who can " do the whole orchestra," and who makes it the business of his life to make people happy. Truly I cannot but feel grateful that such a fragment of light-hearted Paganism has survived, if only to show to an astonished world that Piety and Jollity can go hand-in-hand. The priests in Italy have been teaching the people that religion and salvation and everything saintly is of tears, wails, fasting, blood, torture, and death—yet all the while under these ashes of misery, the old heathen Roman-Etruscan spirit of human nature and genial tenderness still survived. In all the religions current in all the world there is nothing so *real,* so touching, and so beautiful as this spirit of Corredoio. *Sancte Corredoio ride pro nobis!*

ORCO

" Cast up the account of Orcus, the account thereof cast up."--*Codex Nazaræus.*

It would hardly be worth while to mention Orco, the Italian form of Orcus, who has passed into innumerable fairy tales as the Ogre, and who is known to every Italian child, were it not for the peculiar description of him given by my chief authority. "Orco," she said, "is a terrible spirit who was once a great wizard." For this is all the world over the earliest conception of spirits, and especially of those who are feared. Among savage tribes in the early stages of Shamanism, like the Red Indians of America, every remarkable spirit was once a man, always a magician. We may say that the Latin Orcus was a personification of hell, or of the horrible, just as Jupiter was of lightning,[1] but, etymology to the contrary, it is a fact that rude races apply such names as hell and lightning to men. According to Euhemerus of Messina, who derived all gods from men, in which he appears to have been, to a certain degree, right, so far at least as rude races are concerned.

TESANA

Tesana is "the Spirit of the Dawn," one may say Aurora—"*lo spirito della alba.*" She is good, and while a *contadino* is sleeping when the morning red is first seen on the hills she comes to him in dreams and says :—

> " Svegliando li
> Pian piano,
> O buon uomo !
> Sveglia te,
> Che l'alba spunta :

---

[1] " Pluton Latiné est Diespiter : alii Orcum dicunt " (*Tertullian Div. Instit. Lib.*, i., chap. 14)

LALAE   LINTHUN   THESAN   MEMRUN

Sono un spirito
Consolatore,
Che vengo per aiutarti
Al buon coraggio,
Ed alla buona fortuna,
Ma pero sempre
Col tuo lavoro,
E cosi con la buona—
Buona volenta
Di lavorare
Avrai sempre
Buona salute
E volenta di lavorar,
Il ricco e nato ricco
Per aiutar il povero.
E il povero
Per aiutar il ricco,
Col suo lavoro
Perche il signore
Non sarebbe copare
Alle fatiche :
Lavora o buon contadino !
Che al momente
Spunta il sole,
Quando sei stanco
Chiamami
In tuo soccorso,
Ed io saro sempre
Il tuo angelo
Consolatore !

" Waking, awaking,
Softly and gently,
Thou truly good man,
Rise from thy sleep !
The day is dawning,
I am a spirit ;
One who brings comfort ;
I come to thy aid,
To give to thee courage,
To give thee fortune,
But it will come
Ever from labour ;
Thus thou shalt have
Always good health,
And good will to work.
The rich is born rich
To give aid to the poor man,

The poor man to aid
The rich by his labour,
For the rich is unequal
To such heavy labour ;
Work then, good peasant !
The sun is rising.
When thou art weary,
Call me to aid thee,
And I will be ever
An angel consoling.)

" And so the peasant awakes and goes to his work, contented and *allegro*—gay at heart—believing that he has seen in a dream and conversed with a saint—*santo, o una santa*—when instead of that he has been talking with a *spirit*."

This is absolutely heathen—witch-heathen—and a protest of "the old religion " against the new. For " a spirit *instead* of a saint " means here simply nothing but an old Romano-Etruscan or pure Etruscan deity. There are no such very beautiful incarnations of the Dawn in the Roman Catholic mythology with its wooden-plaster rococo saints who are all of the stage stagey, and of the shop shoppy, even here in Italy. This graceful Aurora—this *spirito della alba*—belongs to a purer and better race of beings. She comes out of true love to the peasant, asking neither tithes, prayers, or worship, fasting nor vigils, to please her vanity, but simply cheering him. This is very heathenish indeed, and quite in keeping with her simple old-time conservatism—that rich and poor must exist and observe mutual obligations one to the other.

A learned friend who has revised this work, remarks of Tesana, that Thesan, according to Corssen, is an Etruscan goddess of the dawn (*Die Sprache der Etrusker*, i., p. 259).

It cannot have escaped the reader that Tesana appears strangely in this legend as reflecting on stages of society, human laws, and relations. This is decidedly marked. And Gerhard (*Gottheiten d. Etrusker*, p. 39, and *Etrus. Spiegeln*, plate 76) remarks that there was an identity between Thesan and Themis. This if accidental is certainly extraordinary. Before I had met with this observation I had been deeply impressed with the remarkable character of the reflections as to social rights which are so prominent in the song, and which were far above the range of thought of the woman who sung it.

SPULVIERO

It is remarkable that as the ancient Tusci surpassed all other nations in the number of their gods of thunder and storm—having, indeed, one for every season—

so their descendants have also great fear not only of Tinia, or Jupiter, but also of *Spulviero*, the dreaded spirit of the wind and tempest, of whom there is an account which might have originated among the Algonkin Indians.

Spulviero, also Spolviero, is the Spirit of the Wind. His name literally is probably derived from *polvere*—" dust," referring to the eddies or whirls of dust caused by the wind—the Pau-pu-ke-wiss of the Chippeways. It may conceal, however, a derivation from *pluvio*—" rain." But this is the legend as recited to me and then written :—

" The Spirit of the Wind, called *Spulviero*, is an evil spirit—*spirito chattivo*—who in his lifetime was a wizard, one of those wizards so evil that he ruined many good families, people of good hearts—*bonquore*— who did good to all—even those who had done good to him. For he was so wicked that when any one had done him good, he at once did them harm ; nor could any one revenge himself on him, because he flew swift as the wind.

" But, evil as he was, his turn came and he died, but before dying he was in a hospital. And he commended himself to all there, patients and servants, and asked if any one would take the inheritance of his witchcraft ; but none replied, for they knew him well. But a servant took two brooms, and put them under his bed, and said : " Leave it to these," since but for this he could not die.

" So he died at once, but suddenly there arose a great, terrible wind so that the hospital was nearly blown over, and his spirit departed in the wind."

The legacy refers to the belief that a wizard or witch cannot die till his or her power is transferred to another. The broom is an old Latin charm against sorcery. What is very ancient and purely Shamanic in this legend is the faith that all spirits or deities were once sorcerers. The train of facts is intricate, but it may be followed out. The Etruscans had risen to polytheism, still retaining Shamanic forms—but the people have remained in an *earlier* stage, believing that every great spirit was once a man. So that they have here really led back a myth to its beginning. So Chuchulvia is declared to be a wizard, now become an evil spirit. But I doubt if this really be a relapse since it is not probable that the peasants of Romagna have ever really changed since the beginning. The Etruscan great and wise men developed gods, but the people while accepting them always believed in Euhemerism—that they were only developed magicians. And whether this legend be modern, or older than the earliest Tuscan records, one thing is self-evident—that the spirit of it is as old as anything recorded. Those who love the antique do not always reflect that a pebble may be older than anything man ever made.

URFIA

Of this spirit I know nothing save that I heard it remarked, " *E una donna che si presente nella casa* " (" It is a lady who manifests herself in houses.") I believe she is a benevolent spirit.

CHAPTER V

LARES, LASA, AND LASSI

" E nos Lases iuvate,
   Neve luerve Marmar sins incurrere in
      pleoris.
   Satur furere Mars limen sali, sta berber.
   Semunis alternei advocavit conctos
   E nos Marmo iuvato.
   Triumpe. Triumpe."
                    Song of the Arval Brothers

Y the Latin words *Lar* and *Lares* we generally understand domestic family spirits, on which subject MÜLLER (*die Etrusker*) gives much information and conjecture. He writes : " That the Lares belong to the Tuscan mythology is shown by the name, for as Larth and Laris were common surnames, they must have originated in an *Ehrennahme* (some common name of honour). But both among Tuscans and Romans it was a very comprehensive name. . . . There were

Lares coelopotentes, permarini, viales, vicorum, compitales, civitatum, rurales, grundules, and finally the *domestici* and *familiares,* the comprehension of which

LASA, OR GUARDIAN SPIRIT

in the course of time has become obscure, owing to confusion with the others. The rural Lares, on the other hand, are those which in the very ancient song of the Arval brothers are called on as *E nos Lases iuvate.*"

"*Lases* was certainly in Rome the oldest form of the word " (*Note* p. 93).

" Now it is very remarkable at first sight that under these extremely varied deities there are *human souls*." This is confirmed by MÜLLER with a mass of proofs. He then adds :—

" The *Lares familiares* must necessarily be included among these, as they were generally nothing else than souls of ancestors become gods, many of the ancients (APULEIUS, MARTIAN, and VARRO) having declared that *genius* and *lar*, referring especially to domestic lares, were one and the same."

Our author declares that the Lasa were generally female spirits occupied in adorning men and women, as depicted on vases, and that, "so far as Etruscan is concerned, it is doubtful whether *Lasa* and the *Lares* are connected."

Conversing one day with my best authority on Tuscan folk-lore, I asked if she knew such a word as *Lar, Lares,* or *Lare ?* " No, she had never heard it." " Did anything with a similar name haunt churchyards ? " " No ; but," reflecting a minute, " there are the *Lassi* or *Lassie*." " And what are they ? " The answer was as follows :—

" *Lassi* are spirits which are heard or seen in a house when one of the family dies. They are the *ghosts of the ancestors* of the family, who come at such a time."

This was conclusive, and I have no doubt that these *Lassi* or *Lasie* are the *Lasa* referred to in the song of the Arval brothers. Of course this is not absolutely proved, but when we consider that Tinia, Fufluns, Feronia, and Mania all exist with most of their ancient characteristics, it must be admitted that we have here an extremely strong probability. The *Lasa* were in the very oldest Latin in existence ghosts of ancestors, or domestic familiar spirits, and so are the *Lassi*. And MÜLLER gives no proof whatever that the Lasa, or " winged spirits on the vases, with a frontal band or cap and earrings, naked or in a short *chiton* with armlets, half boots or shoes," and holding a great variety of objects in their hands, were not *Lares* deified. It seems to me to be most natural that the spirits of the ancestors, revived in youth and beauty, should be the first to wait on and aid the descendant risen to paradise. MÜLLER himself says elsewhere, " In the *Lar* the *Genius* always comes to light." What are these *Lasa* if not the geniuses of the departed ? Unfortunately, MÜLLER, though gifted with perfectly German industry, and not deficient in sagacity, had not a gleam of intelligence as regarded the folk-lore of a race, or the immense value of minor matters. To write in an admirable and clear style, *en grand critique*, over the *great* events or subjects of a race is certainly very fine, but it is to be hoped that a time is coming when we shall have seen the last of these Mr. Dombeys of History, with their prize works crowned by Academies, in which there is not a gleam of intuition, nor a *nuance* of colour, and as little real knowledge of *life*.

There is a story of the Lasi or Lasii, also an invocation to them. I would say that, as regards the songs or metrical passages in all such accounts, I have not been able, with all care, to give them in the original or best form. In most cases my informant translated them from the original Romagnola dialect into Italian, and they were often manifestly imperfect or partly supplied. The tale is as follows :—

"There was once a great lord who was very rich, and he had a son who was a great prodigal—*che sciupeva tutto il danaro.* His father said to him, ' My son, I cannot live long, therefore I beg you to always behave well. Do not go on gambling, as you are wont to do, and waste all your patrimony. While I live I can take care of you, but I fear for you after my death.' After a little time the father died. And in a few days the son brought all to an end. Nothing remained but the palace, which he sold. But those who occupied it could not dwell there in peace, because at midnight there was heard a great clanking of chains and all the bells ringing. And they saw black figures like smoke passing about, and flames of fire. And they heard a voice saying :—

  "'Sono il *Lasio,*
  In compagnia
  Di tanti *Lasii,*
  E non avrete mai
  Bene, fino che
  Non prenderete
  Questo palazzo
  A mio figlio.' [1]

  ("'I am the *Lasio,*
  And there are with me
  Many more *Lasii.*
  No good shall come to you
  Till you restore
  This place to my son!')

"So they gave back the palace to the heir. But he too was greatly terrified with the apparitions, and there came to him a voice which said:—

  "'Sono il Lasio
  Di tutti Lasii,
  Son' tuo padre,
  Che vengo adesso
  In tuo soccorso
  Purche tu m'ubbedisca,
  Smetti il giuoco,
  Altrimenti non avro
  Mai pace—e tu

---

[1] In all cases where the text is in metre the original was chanted or intoned.

Ti troverai ancora
In miseria estrema ;
Ma se tu m'ubbedisca,
Io vivro in pace,
E sarai tanto ricco
Da non finire
Il tuo patrimonio ;
Anche divertendo te
E faccendo molto bene,
Ma prometté mi
Di non piu giuocare.'

(" 'I am the Lasio
Of all the Lasii.
I am thy father
Come to thy succour ;
If thou'lt obey me,
Cease gaming for ever,
Or thou shalt never
Know peace . . . and thou
Wilt again find thyself
Sunk deep in misery ;
But if thou obey'st me,
I shall have peace again,
And thou shalt be wealthy
Far beyond measure,
Living in pleasure ;
Only this promise me,
Never to play again.')

" Then the son answered :—

" ' Padre perdonatemi !
Non giuochero piu.'

(" ' Father, forgive me ;
I will ne'er play again.')

" Then the father replied :—

" ' Rompi quante trave
Che son' nel palazzo
E piene di danaro,
Le trovarei,
Cosi starei benme,
Ed io staro in pace,
Nelle require
E mettermi.   Amen ! ' "

(" ' Break down the beams
Which are in the palace ;
They are full of money,
As you will find.

FAUN AND FEMALE LASA OR FAIRY

> Then I shall be quiet
> In the rest of the dead.
> There I go. Amen ! ' ")

It was explained to me that by the beams meant breaking away the ceiling. Two things strike me in this strange semi-poem. One is that the story is very much like that of the Heir of Lynne in PERCY'S *Relics*. Secondly, that it is altogether more like an Icelandic narrative than anything Italian. It is grim, strong, and very simple—one may say almost archaic.

There is also an invocation of witchcraft to these spirits of ancestors which is not less curious :—

> " Lasii, Lasii, Lasii !
> Che tante buoni siete !
> D'una grazia io ne ho
> Gran bisogno ;
> E da vuoi spiriti
> Spiriti e Lasi,
> In mezzo a uno cantina,
> Mi vengo inginnochiare
> A vuoi altri
> Mi vengo a raccomandare
> Che questa grazia.
> Mi vorrete fare !
> Lasii, Lasii, Lasii !
> A vuoi vi presento,
> Con tre candele,
> Candele accese,
> Tre carte, l'asso di picche,
> Quello di fiori,
> E quello di quadri,
> Le buttero per l'aria,
> Che vuoi certo mi vedete ;
> Per cio le butto
> In vostra presenza
> Nell punto della mezza notte,
> Queste carte
> Per l'aria buttero,
> Se la grazia mi farete,
> L'asso di fiori scoperto,
> Trovare mi farete,
> Se scoperto l'asso di pique,
> Mi fate trovare,
> E segno che la grazia
> Non me volete fare ;
> Se mi farete trovare
> Quello di quadri
> Segno e che
> La grazia mi fate."

("Lasii, Lasii, Lasii!
Ye who are gracious!
There is a favour
Which I need greatly,
And of ye spirits,
Spirits and Lasii,
Here in a cellar
Now I am kneeling,
And I commend myself
Unto your graces,
That ye will grant me
This special favour!

Lasii, Lasii, Lasii!
Here I present myself,
Bearing three candles,
Three candles lighted,
Three cards—the ace of spades,
And that of clubs,
And that of diamonds.
I fling them in the air
That you may see them
Plainly before you,
Here just at midnight
In air I throw them;
If you grant me a favour,
Cause me to find
The ace of clubs plainly.
If 'tis the ace of spades
'Tis a sign that you will not
Grant me the favour;
But if you make me find
The ace of diamonds,
Then 'tis a sign
That my wish will be granted.")

"But," added the fortune-teller, in a prosaic voice, "it will not be until after a long time."

Games of chance and lotteries are such a serious element in Italian life that no one need be astonished at an invocation like this being addressed to the Lares. Perhaps the Romans did the same for luck at *alea*, or dice. I would that I had by me my copy of PASCHASIUS JUSTUS' *De Alea*. I might find it in that!

It may be remarked that in this account the *Lasii* appear as benevolent spirits, devoted to a family. Since recording this Tuscan story of the Lasio who gave the treasure, I have met with the following in the *Romische Mythologie* of L. PRELLER :—

TINIA AND LASA

" The *lar familiaris* is the *Schutzgeist*—guardian spirit of the family. Next to the *Lar familiaris*, who is simply called the *lar* or *lar pater* (the *father lasio*), there are many *lares familiares*. . . . It happens, perhaps, that the grandfather confided a treasure to him which he secretly hid . . . and he gives this to the only daughter of the house, a good girl who has always given him daily offerings such as incense or wine or garlands."

This is briefly the same story as that which I have related. The Lar or Lasio has a treasure in reserve which he gives to the heir. It was comfortable to think that there was in the house an attached family spirit who might do one a good turn, and therefore the belief lasted long among all rural people.

The young man Peppino, who went about much, at home and in the market-places, to collect evidence of knowledge of the spirits by me recorded, found that the Lasii were known, but gives the name as *Ilasii*. This is evidently only an addition of the plural article *i* (the) to *Lasii*.

Some time after I had written the foregoing relative to the Lasii, I heard the following, which I made the narrator repeat, and took down accurately :—

" When I was about twelve years of age something happened to me which I thought at the time was funny or queer (*mi trovai à un caso buffo—così io lo chiamai*), but I have since regarded it in a very different light. Once I went with some relations into the country. One day I was in a dark forest, and wandered about picking leaves and wood-flowers, and at last found myself in a very lonely place by a stream. I had a habit of talking aloud to myself, and I said, ' Oh, I would like to bathe there '—the weather was very hot—when all at once there stood before me an old woman, who said : ' Dear child, if thou wouldst like to bathe, undress without fear, I will protect thee.' There was something about her which pleased me greatly, a care and kindness and sweetness which I cannot describe. And when I had bathed and dressed myself she said : ' *Bimba*, thou hast had many troubles, and many more are before thee, but be not afraid (*non ti sgomentare*), for in thy old age thou wilt have good fortune,' and so she disappeared, and I never saw her again—and I still await the good fortune which has not as yet come to me.

" I believe this was indeed a *lasia*, a spirit of some ancestor long dead, who wishes me well."

What was best in this story I cannot relate, and that was the earnestness with which it was told, and the manner in which the narrator repeated the details, and the deep faith with which she expressed the conviction that this was really a *lasia*. Truly they are a strange race, these Etruscan mountaineers —their young folk see visions and their old men dream dreams.

Pictures of Lases abound on Etruscan vases. They are represented as beautiful spirits, young, and more frequently feminine than male. They are, I believe almost always, winged, and generally bear a bottle or large phial. The old Etruscan religion, which was distinctly Euhemeristic, regarded the becoming a Lar as the first step to becoming a god. On which subject the following is of interest :—

" Les Lares, ou Lases, qui jouent un rôle si important dans les anciennes religions de l'Italie, qui peuplent le monde romain, qu'on trouve partont, au foyer de la famille, dans la ville, à la campagne, sur les routes—Lares familiares, urbani, rurales, viales, &c. ; les *Lares* ont sans acun doute fait partie de la cosmogonie Etrusque. Leur nom seul semble le prouver, Larth ou Laris est un nom et un titre d'honneur que l'on rencontre fréquemment sur les inscriptions funéraires de l'Etrurie. On lisait, d'ailleurs, dans les Livres Achérontiens qui faisaient partie de la doctrine de Tagès, que les âmes humaines pouvaient, en vertu de certaines expiations, participer a l'essence des dieux, et sous le nom de *dii animales*, ou âmes divines, prendre place parmi les Pénates et les Lares " (Servius ad *Aen.*, iii., 168 ; cf. Fabretti, Gloss. Ital. s. v.). " Ainsi s'accomplissaient dans les croyances de l'Etrurie les mysterieuses destinées de l'âme humaine. Le *Genius jovialis*, après l'avoir recueille comme une émanation de la divinité, lui donnait entrée dans la vie ; puis quand la mort venait séparer de la matière ce souffle divin, l'âme, éprouvée par les sacrifices, ou l'expiation, pouvait retourner parmi les dieux, et comme pénate elle remontait au rang ou le *Genius jovialis*, ainsi que nous l'avons vu, était placé lui-meme " (*L'Etrurie et Les Etrusques, par A. Noël des Vergers*, Paris, 1862, vol. i., pp. 301, 302).

It will be seen by this extract that the still existing very singular belief that certain sorcerers' souls are sometimes reborn as mightier sorcerers than before, and from this proceed to be spirits, is exactly paralleled by the old Etruscan doctrine taught by Tages.

LOSNA

MÜLLER (*die Etrusker*, p. 81) says that CORSSEN (i., p. 346-7) " has erroneously attributed LOSNA, a goddess of the moon, to Etruria. She only occurs on a single mirror from Præneste (GERHARD, i., clxxi.), and is Latin (*Lucna, Luna*)."

" It is not for us to settle the question." But on asking my authority if she knew of such a being as *Losna*, I received the following reply, which I wrote down as uttered :—

" LOSNA is a spirit of the sun and moon—of *both*, not of the moon alone. When a brother debauches his sister it is always her doing. She loves to deride people gaily. When she has made her mischief she will appear at the table where a *contadino* is with his family, and laugh and say : ' Thou art a stupid fellow, thou knowest not that thy daughter is *incinta* (with child) by her brother, for thou didst once say, " *E un grande piacere à fare l'amore col proprio fratello.*" ' And when she has done this mischief she goes away singing, because she has caused discord in the family."

This startling myth has that in it which seems to prove great antiquity. The gypsies in the East of Europe have a legend that they are descended from the Sun and Moon ; the Sun having debauched his Moon sister was condemned to wander for ever, in consequence of which they also can never rest. The natives of Borneo and the old Irish believed that the Man in the Moon is imprisoned there for the same deed. Finally, the Esquimaux have a similar story. These coincidences are fortuitous, but in any case they are remarkable. As for its character, I have already remarked that if these tales are truly handed down from the olden time they ought to be replete with sensuality—as they are. In the spirit of collection, first established by GRIMM, nothing was preserved, much less sought for, which was not fit, I will not say for young ladies, but even for the nursery. In fact, fairy tales suggest nothing as yet, even to well-informed people, but innocent, sweet, pretty, and amusing *Mährchen*. But the old myths out of which these grew were nothing of the kind. However, it has come to pass that most collectors, influenced by fear of the Major-General Reader, quietly pass over this element which was, if not the great guiding influence in myths of what we may call the tertiary formation (or polytheism as it was passing into pantheism), was at least almost the chief. And if we wish to investigate the witchcraft of the first period, or this of the time when men had begun to regard Fertility and Reproduction, and such reviving influences as Light and Wine and gaiety as causes of life, we must turn over a vast amount of what is fearfully " shocking " to all who do not seek " *abditis rerum causis* "— into the hidden causes of things. For it was out of what could most terrify and revolt man that all primitive sorcery and much secondary Shamanism were formed, and if we would know Man's early history we must not, or cannot, avoid such study. Religious magic, at present, has dropped this portion of its first state, only retaining, or returning to, the early fear of infernal agency, or devils and hell, as the chief motive power in duty and incentive to worship. To fully understand all that now exists, and have a *clear* idea of what we really believe—which no living believer has—we must understand man in the past. Till we do we shall not comprehend the present nor clear the way for the future.

" *Losna*, that is *Louna*," says PRELLER, " appears on an Etruscan mirror with the half-moon associated with Pollux, on another monument as Lala, *i.e.*, Lara, Δέσποινα, with the sun-god Aplu." It is just possible that some tradition of such association with the sun may have given rise to the Tuscan story which is probably a mere fragment. In any case it is remarkable that in it there is an allusion to the sun and moon as an incestuous brother and sister.

I call the attention of the reader specially to the picture representing LOSNA. It is from a mirror which has for a century been frequently engraved in works on Etruscan art. This is now in my possession, and lies on my paper as I write. According to Corssen (*Sprache der Etrusker*, vol. i., p. 346), who refers to Gerhard's *Etruscan Mirrors*, iii., 165, Ritschl, Cavendoni, Schoene, Benndorff, Helbig, &c., as discussing it, it is from Praeneste, also that *Lusna* was the original name, and that *Losna* is a dialectical form peculiar to Praeneste.

This mirror had greatly interested me. I had purchased in London one book simply because it contained an engraving of it, and had made with great

LOSNA

(From the original Etruscan bronze mirror, now in possession of the Author.)

care three or four drawings of it from different works, with all of which I was dissatisfied, and when my publisher, Mr. Fisher Unwin, went over my illustrations with me here in Florence, March 5, 1892, I threw " Losna " out—very unwillingly.   I state simply the truth when I say that of all the mirrors ever made, it was this one in particular which I most desired to see, and I remember that it was much on my mind.   On the afternoon of the following day I went by chance, or led by my Socratic demon, into a shop for odds and ends, or " curiosities," and there in a glass case, and very much out of place, found an ancient Etruscan mirror—the *very one* which had been engraved, and which I so longed to see.   I need not say that I purchased it at once.   I should mention that the engraving here given is absolutely correct, having been made on a tracing or rubbing from the mirror itself, which is in a state of perfect preservation.

These mirrors were believed among the Etruscans to possess magic power. It is the same with the Chinese of the present day who make similar ones, the reason being this : The Chinese mirror, like the ancient, is polished on one side and has a picture, or more commonly an inscription, on the other.   If we let the sun shine on the mirror and reflect it on a smooth white surface, the picture on the other side is distinctly visible in the reflection.   I have heard explanations of this which did not satisfy me.   About the year 1856 a daguerrotypist in the United States having cut two lines in a cross on the *face* of a copper plate found that though the cross was not perceptible on the back, yet that when reflected in sunlight it could be distinctly seen in the reflection.   Hence I inferred that the pressure on the face hardened the metal throughout, which perfectly explains the phenomenon.   I suppose that the Etruscan mirrors when new had the same quality.   Of which invention there is no mention, not even by J. Baptista Porta in his many recipes for making marvellous " mirrors."   The same may be made of glass by *annealing* the picture.   That is, we take a pattern in hard glass, cast a bed of soft glass about it, and when cold grind off and polish the surface, which will seem uniform.   But the reflection against the sun will show the light from the soft glass as duller than that from the hard.

All mirrors are, according to ancient and modern superstition, repulsive to witches, or evil spirits, and good against the evil eye and its like.   Fascinators— like basilisks—had their own terrible glance turned against them if they saw themselves reflected, " Si on luy presente un miroir, par endardement reciproque, ces rayons retournent sur l'autheur d'iceux."   As a lunar-solar goddess, I believe that Losna was peculiarly associated with the mirror as a magic object.   Philostratus declares that if a mirror be held before a sleeping man during a hail or thunder-storm, the storm will cease.

LARONDA

Laronda in Tuscany is a very kind, benevolent spirit, who, strangely enough, is peculiar to, or who dwells in, *caserme*, or soldiers' barracks—"Sarebbe un spirito delle caserme dei militari. E molta buona."

She seems to be identified with the old Etruscan Larunda, or Lara, of whom Lactantius remarks : "Who can keep from laughter when he hears the silent goddess mentioned ? [1] This is she whom they call Lara, or Larunda" (i., 20, 35). OVID speaks of her as the *Dea muta*, or silent goddess. But from a passage in PRELLER'S Mythology, I infer that she was specially known as *good*, since in reference to a prayer to her he remarks : "Here we plainly understand *ein guter Geist—ein seliger*"—a good or happy spirit.

But what is certainly very remarkable is that Larunda was especially the mother of the *Lares compitales*. "*Compitum* is a point where several roads meet. At such a place the Romans erected large buildings with passages and rooms," literally corresponding to modern barracks. "In them all the people round about met to discuss business and hold festivals." Therefore the *Lares compitalium* were the guardian spirits of such large public buildings, where great bodies of men lived, or met. And Larunda was literally then, as Larunda is now, the chief spirit of what corresponds most accurately to the modern *caserme* which is now the only building in Italy which is quite like the ancient *compitum*. All of which PRELLER illustrates with much learning, and of all this I knew nothing when I first ascertained what I have written of the modern Tuscan spirit. And when we read that these ancient buildings were the resort of boxers, actors, gladiators, and of political clubs, we may well infer that soldiers also occupied them.

In the course of time stories grow up or are attached to names with which they have very little real connection. Such a legend relating to Laronda is the following :—

"Laronda is the *folletto* of the casernes. Once she was a *donna* named Rosa who, during her life, was devoted to soldiers. After a while the officers noticed it and forbade her frequenting the barracks, at which she was so much grieved that she fell ill, and was long confined to her bed. Then the soldiers themselves missed her sadly, and so arranged it that she could come secretly among them ; so for a time all went well.

"Among these soldiers was one who had a sweetheart who was a *zingara*, or gypsy, as well as witch. Now the witch discovered that Rosa visited the caserme, and that all the soldiers were devoted to her, and that less for her beauty than for her gaiety and goodness ; and with this the gypsy was ill-pleased and said to Rosa :—

---

[1] "Quis, quum audiat deam Mutam tenere risum queat ? Hanc esse dicunt, ex qua sint nati Lares, et ipsam Laram nominant, vel Larundam." Which is what an ancient heathen might have said at seeing a Spanish Virgin Mary in an old French bonnet, or even some of her similitudes here, in Italy, which are ten times sillier and more laughter-moving than the rudest works of Roman times.

" ' Rosa, oh, Rosa, oh, fair Rosa ! it is true that I am not so beautiful as thou art, for I am a gypsy. And thou art esteemed by all the soldiers and my own lover loves thee, so I beg thee not to frequent the barracks any more !

> " ' Per cio ti voglio pregare
> Nelle caserme di non più andare ! '

" Then Rosa replied frankly but resolutely, that she would yield nothing whatever to please her foolish jealousy, at which the other, in a rage, said : ' May my curse fall like lead upon thy head, nor wilt thou live long—but one year do I give thee.

> " ' E fin anno che tu camperai,
> Tu non avrai che pene e guai.

> " ' A year thou'lt live in pain and grief,
> Ere death will come to bring relief.

" ' And since thou lovest soldiers so well, thou shalt have no rest after death, but shalt become *il folletto della ronda* (the spirit of the patrol, or night-guard), and LA RONDA thou shalt be.'

" As she threatened so it all came to pass, and the soldiers grieved for her death. But while they were sorrowing they were suddenly amazed to see at a window the apparition of a lady of great beauty clad in white, who said :—

" Io sono la bella Rosa, I am the beautiful Rosa—but now I am dead I have become the *Folletto della Ronda* of the soldiers, and when night flees from the world of the eternals I will come to seek you, and when you hear me call, then open the windows to *La Ronda*."

There will be many to whom this adaptation of a modern pun to a word will quite suffice to destroy all connection with the classic Larunda. In this way we might utterly invalidate all and any tradition whatever, just as VOLTAIRE declared that the petrified shells found on mountain-tops had probably been scallop shells dropped by pilgrims from the Holy Land. But Laronda was from very ancient times the guardian spirit of the public building, while this story turns upon a mere resemblance of the word to a technical term with a very different meaning. I think it most probable that some ingenious but ignorant person, hearing of Laronda, adapted it to the word for patrol or "round."

I have since heard it asserted that Laronda may be, or is, the spirit of any large building frequented by many people, such as a hotel. This seems to be the old and generally entertained idea, while I have no guarantee whatever that the *story* is not a mere modern fabrication founded on a jest.

If Larunda be modern *because* there is a modern story fitted to the name, then of course any myth may be punned or conjectured out of existence.

LEMURI

On asking if such a word as Lemures was known, I was told that *Lemuri sono i spiriti dei campo-santi*—" Lemuri are the spirits of the churchyards." This clearly enough identifies them with the Latin *Lemures,* which were the same as the Larvæ, or the unhappy and terrifying ghosts of those who have died evil deaths, or under a ban, to which there are innumerable allusions in all Latin writers.[1]

Tago

Tago is a spirit whose name appears to be known only to a few old people. He is described as a *spirito bambino,* or appearing as a little boy. Of him Favi

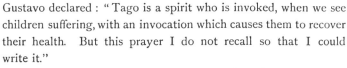

Gustavo declared : " Tago is a spirit who is invoked, when we see children suffering, with an invocation which causes them to recover their health. But this prayer I do not recall so that I could write it."

Another authority informed me that there is a *spirito bambino,* or spirit like a boy, who is, however, a wizard. His name is *Terieg'h* (harsh and guttural and uncertain). He comes up out of the ground, and predicts the future or tells fortunes. As these are the only spirits in such form I suppose them to be the same being.

The name Tago will naturally suggest to the scholar that of Tages, " the wise Etruscan child plowed from the earth," whose history is given in detail by Preller and many more, but by no one so succinctly or elegantly as by Petrarch in his Italian-Latin. This child, one day, as a peasant was ploughing—*Hetrusco quodam arante in agro Tarquiniensi*—leapt from the furrow, an infant in form but with an old man's head and wisdom—*puerili effigie sapientia senili*—and proceeded forthwith to astonish everybody by his prophesies and instructions in what was then religious wisdom, but what we should now call magic. And it was indeed from his books and teachings that all Roman divination and sacred observances were drawn. And as Etruscan lore began with him, it would be indeed deeply interesting if we could prove that he still lives in his Etrurian home as Tago or Terieg'h. Truly such survivals as these may not be of the fittest for the spirit of the age, but it is befitting that they be recorded, if only to show the extraordinary manner in which they are frozen up in popular tradition to be now and then

---

[1] " Verum illi manes, quoniam corporibus illo tempore tribuuntur quo fit prima conceptio, etiam post vitam iisdem corporibus delectantur, atque cum iis manentes appellantur Lemures" (MARTIAN, *Cap de Mess.,* ii., 9, p. 40 ; ap. MULLER). "Lemures larvæ nocturnæ et terrificationes imaginum et bestiarum" (AUGUSTIN, c. Dei. ix. 11 ; ap. PRELLER). "Lemures umbras vagantes hominum ante diem mortis mortuorum et ides metuendus" (PORPH. ; ap. PRELLER).

TAGES

(From the Etruscan Museum of Gori.)

thawed out to some seeker. But whether Tago or Terieg'h really be Tages I leave for others to settle. *Davus sum non Œdipus.* For, as Johannes Practorius says in his *Anthropodemus Plutonicus,* that "all this story of *Tages* may be a mere fable wherewith the devil, after his fashion, hath deluded and betrayed man with a wonder, that he might use the many superstitions which had their beginning in Tages, his fortune-telling and sorcery."

FANIO

> " Hæc loca capripedes, Satyros, nymphasque teneræ,
>   Finitimi fingunt et FAUNOS esse loquntur,
>   Quorum noctivago strepitu."
>   LUCRETIUS, iv., 584

To a person of humanity and tender feelings there is something very touching or indescribably pitiful in the manner in which the people in Europe clung to their old gods and resisted Christianity. For it is *not* true at all, as is generally mis-represented, that they gladly took to the mystical, abstract, Hebrew-Persian Roman Catholic religion of *professed* love, and priestly and feudal oppression which they did not understand. Nor did they find any attractions in its making a duty of obedience to cruel feudal tyrants, of asceticism, fasting, and dread of the devil. It was all forced on them, and they long resisted it. Despite cruel perse-cution (as Horst and Michelet observe), the peasants persisted in their devotion to the poor old forbidden gods, and every few years, so late as the fifteenth century, councils thundered at, colleges condemned, and priests burned people for heathen sacrifices. And they were not a few who thus clung to the ancient faith. They were all over Europe, and, as I have shown, there are some still left in the Toscana Romagna.

This old religion of nature was congenial to the people because they under-stood and deeply felt it. They had, as I hope the reader has, an impression that there is a spirit in the pathless woods, deep song in silent shade, life in the long-forgotten land of early days—homes of visions in the old grey rocks with possible portals through which elves or their own elfin thoughts may pass. They know the Voice of the Waterfall, and what the stone said when it was thrown at twilight into the well or silent pool " under the stars," and why the laurel crackled when it burned, and what words it said—these were all spirits, and they had learned the spirit-lan-guage from their fathers. There was an indescribably delightful, companionable sense in believing that there was a jolly, mischievous, *familiar* goblin who lived in the fire, or haunted the fireplace, who teased the girls and bothered the boys, and was " *so* sociable." All of these were like themselves, and within their natural comprehension, and they *would* believe in them because, as they *must* adopt some kind of supernaturalism, they took that which was most natural, sensible, and congenial to them. A haggard, bleeding, pallid spectre, everlasting goody-goodiness of

ETRUSCAN RURAL DEITIES

Madonnas, and the agony of tortured saints with no end of fasting and prayer, are *not* congenial to us, nor did healthy humanity ever accept them in loving earnest, as it did the old heathen gods. The whole history of the Middle Ages—or you may continue it later an you will—is one of mankind making believe that they believed in misery. And the proof of it, reader, is very plain, and it is simply this—that wherever and whenever Christianity has any " superstitions " or elements quite in common with the old heathenism, there people are most truly religious. " Man is properly the only object which interests man ; " he feels and lives in Humanity and Nature, and never truly cares for what is remote from or is forced into these.

You and I, reader, feel the true spirit of old heathen religion when we walk in the forest and skirt the line of " thus far—and then no more—the language of the sounding sea to the sands upon the shore," or are sitting by the fire in silent night. We do not make it into goblins, but our own thoughts and memories become to us quite the same as spirits, for we feel or see how we can give them life or expressed thought in act or words. Make this *literal*—not a mere figure of speech—and then, friend, you will be as happy as a heathen suckled in a creed outworn—yea, quite as well off—which was all that Wordsworth wished for, and was not unlike the desire of François Villon, who yearned for the ladies of the olden time.

It is a great pity, but pity 'tis 'tis true, that owing chiefly to the *affected-*sentimental, or false influences of mediæval religion and its resultant " art," we do not really know what we *ought* to admire or " feel beautiful " over, or enthuse about, till somebody has told us how. Then we go and " do it." We do it by going to see all the places prescribed by the hotel directions, " there and back, twenty-five francs for a party of four," and duly admiring them, and pass by without note a hundred spots even more beautiful. And verily such a doing thereof as I behold here among tourists in Italy to see what it is " the thing " to see (*i.e.*, everything, according to Ruskin, Bædeker, and Co.), might draw tears from a millstone. A child or a peasant is better off—it or he takes Nature as it comes—naturally. The tourist who goes by precept may *think* that he can feel nature as a child, but he does *not*. You cannot serve God and Mammon together.

This old spirit of unaffected feeling of nature without " culture " is deeply impressed in all this Tuscan-Etruscan folk-lore, and I would that my heart could utter the thoughts which it often inspires. It was all summed up for the ancients in the single word *Faunus*. Faunus and the Fauni were the incarnation of forests, streams and fields, fairy-life and flowers. Therefore I was glad to find that this deity, who is only another form of Pan, still lives in the Romagnola, as is set forth in the following passages.

" FÁNIO is a wizard who comes in the form of a spirit." This appears to be the Euhemeristic conception of all the spirits in this very primitive Tuscan mythology. First a wizard, or a man of power on earth, who is remembered after death, and then is supposed to still haunt the scenes of his former life. What Fánio does was narrated as follows :—

" Fánio frightens peasants in the woods. He appears as a man leaping up with his hands wide open, thrown forward, or looks like a devil, scattering fire, and then laughs at the fear which he has caused. And when there is a wedding he often anticipates the bridegroom in his kisses, and when the husband comes and would embrace his wife he feels invisible blows and cuffs, which put him in a rage, when Fánio bursts out laughing, and says :—

> " ' Vuoi sapere chi sono?
> Sono lo spirito *Fánio*,
> Che cio che m'e piacuto in vita,
> Mi piace al altro mondo ;
> Mi dovresti ringraziare,
> Che ti ho risparmiato tanta fatica ! '

> (" ' Who I am ?—if you would know,
> I'm the spirit Fánio !
> What in life once gave me bliss,
> Pleases me as much in this ;
> And I think that thanks are due
> Unto me for helping you ! ')

" Then if the husband is vexed at this, and if his wife is angry and curses the goblin, he only torments her the more and returns as a nightmare to disturb her sleep."

It is not difficult to recognise in this Fánio the Faunus of the Latins. All of the characteristics attributed to him in the account agree accurately with what PRELLER relates :—

" In some phases of popular belief Faunus appears as nearly allied to Silvanus, as a spirit of the forest, who lurks in deep shadows, in hidden caverns, or by rustling waterfalls, where he predicts fortunes or catches birds, and chases the nymphs. . . . The fauns as a class were much given to teasing and tormenting mortals in their sleep, so that they sometimes appear altogether as annoying imps—like the nightmare to us—against which attacks people used all kinds of roots and quackeries, especially the root of the forest-peony (*Wald-päonie*), which had to be dug by men by night, else the great wood-pecker would peck out their eyes. But, above all, the women had to be on their guard against the fauns and Silvani, for these lecherous wood-goblins readily slipped into their beds, whence the popular name of *Incubus* for them." " From their lechery they were called Faunificarii. ' Vel Incubones, vel Satyros, vel sylvestres quosdam homines quos nonulli *Faunos picarios* vocant ' " (*Hieron. in Isai*, v. 13, 21).

These fauns and silvani of Tuscan belief are very much allied to the mischievous household goblins. They all make naughty love to women, and act as incubi, or nightmares, and cause wild dreams. Quite the same spirits were known of old in Assyria. Lenormant says (*Magie Chaldaienne*) :—

"To the Incubus and Succubus was joined the Nightmare in the Accadian *Kiel-udda-karra*, in the Assyrian, *Ardat*. . . . It is probable, judging from its name, that it was one of those familiar spirits which

FAUN
(On a patera. (Etruscan) Museum, Florence.)

make the stables and the houses the scene of their malicious tricks ; spirits whose existence has been admitted by so many people, and which are still believed in by the peasants in many parts of Europe."

It may be remarked that nearly all the spirits which occur in this peasant mythology are of the nature of the fauns. Also that while the Romagnola *contadino* has retained old Etruscan names of gods, and those of the minor sylvan and rural deities, such as Sylvanio, Fano, and Paló, he has not the great Latin gods. Bacchus is commonly enough sworn by, but I could gather no information regarding him, save that he was "the god of wine, and therefore must be the same as Faflon." The best treatises which I have met on the Fauns, Satyrs, Silvani, Incubi, &c., form chapters in that strange work by C Bauhinus, 1667, entitled *De Hermaphroditis*, &c.

The peony was, on account of its red colour, regarded as great protection against the fauns as nightmares. PRÆTORIUS (*Anthropodemus Plutonicus ; Von Alpmännrigen*, 1666) mentions that people, to keep away the Incubus, wear round their necks, or hanging from them, "flints, corals, or peony roots."

It is worth observing that the *ceppo sacro*, a holy log of wood which is burned on Christmas Eve—the yule-log of the North—is taken with due observance and incantation to the fauns or other spirits of the forest. For, despite his immoral and mischievous conduct, Fánio is a general favourite, as was Faunus of old, for many reasons not too far to find, but not worth specifying.

In a work on Faunus, *Del Dio Fauno, e de suoi segnaci, di Odoard Gerhard* (Eduard Gerhard, Naples, 1825), the author declares that whatever deity he may have been, mixed and mingled as he was with others, is not difficult to determine. The truth is that all these minor spirits of forests and fields, firesides and bedrooms, were naturally familiar and mischievous creatures, as much alike as romping schoolboys, therefore all nightmares ; teasers of girls, therefore seducers, and consequently wanton and gay. They were in reality more distinguished by names than by natures.

QUERCIOLA

This word refers to an herb or small plant which, as in the case of rue, *rosalaccio*, and others, is by mysterious association also a fairy. *Querciuola* is properly, in Italian, a small oak-tree, but, as in many other instances, it has been transferred from one plant to another in Romagnolo. What I learned of it (given to me with specimens of the plant), is as follows :—

"When one has quarrelled with a lover, one should go and sit beside the plant called Querciola, wherever it is growing, because the fairy of that name is a great friend to lovers. So when one is distant, or separated, be it as to the heart or place, the other sits by the herb and sings :—

" ' Fata Querciola !
    Sei tanto bella quanto buona
    A ti mi vengo raccomandare,
    Che il mio bene
    A mi tu faccia ritornare.

    Fata Querciola !
    Ai fatto tanto bene
    A tante persone
    Anch' io voglio sperare
    Che di me non ti di me
    Vorrai dimenticare.

    Fata Querciola !
    Sei tanto bella e altra tanto buona
    Ti chiedo una grazia sola
    E spero non me la vorra negare,
    E lo mio amore
    Mi farai ritornare.

    Fata Querciola !
    Sofrirei tante pene ;
    Se da me non tornasse il mio bene,
    Ma da me le conviene si ritornare,
    Perche la fata me l'ha promesso,
    Di farlo ritornare sotto al mio tetto.

(" ' Fairy Querciola !
    Thou art good as fair ;
    Let me hope and not in vain,
    That thou wilt send happiness
    Unto me again !

    Fairy Querciola !
    Thou hast blest so many,
    Send a blessing unto me,
    Let me hope that I, though humble,
    May not forgotten be !

    Fairy Querciola !
    Fair as thou art good ;
    One favour I implore,
    Which I hope thou'lt not deny :
    Make him who was my lover
    Return to me once more.

    Fairy Querciola !
    I shall suffer sore
    Unless my love as' lover
    Comes back as once before.]
    But, fairy, thou hast promised me,
    And what thou sayst will surely be,
    He'll seek my roof once more.' ")

Querciola, or Querciuola, as the name of a nymph or sylvan spirit, is clearly enough closely connected with that of *Querquetulana*, an old Roman or Italian simile for *Vira* (which see), a wood-nymph ; though the term, like Querciola,

SETHLANS, VULCAN, AND THE TROJAN HORSE

refers especially to a dryad, or spirit of an oak. So FESTUS observes (PRELLER, *R. M.*, p. 89, second edition) : " *Querquetulanæ Viræ putantur significari nymphæ presidentes querqueto virescenti, quod genus silvæ indicant fuisse intra portam quæ ab eo dicta sit Querquetularia.*" Querciola is therefore clearly a dryad.

These Querquetulanæ have an apparent, or barely possible, survival in the spirits called *Querkeln* in Bavaria. They emigrated from that country, passing over the river Main by the village of Wiesen (*Bayerische Sagen von Fried. Panzer*, Munich, 1848).

Sethano

I am not sure whether this name is Sethano or Sethlrano or Settrano, nor have I been able to learn more than what is contained in these lines :—

" Settrano is the spirit of *fire*. He is remembered by all here. They know a proverb (*i.e.*, a saying, invocation, or spell) which is repeated. When they do not wish the fire to burn they invoke (*se voca*) that spirit."—Sette Tico.

Of all these spirits there are invocations and tales, but I have not in all instances been able to collect them.

Sethlans was the Etruscan Vulcan.

CHAPTER VI

CARRADORA

CARRADORA was in her life *una strega buona*—a good witch—who protected infants against other or evil witches. She appears to be well known. While the following story was being narrated, the one who told it paused, not remembering the name of the plant which was used, whereupon an old woman who was present—not from the Romagna, but a Florentine—gave it at once as *corbezzolo* (arbutus).

I infer from this that the story is widely spread.

" There was once in the country a lady who had a small baby. It was a pretty child, but day by day it began to weaken—*diminuire*—nor did the mother know what to do. Then she was advised to go to Carradora, who could explain it all, because she was a witch who did good as well as harm (*il male*).

" Then the lady went to the witch, who said : ' Go to thy home and put the babe to bed, and put a knife in the window, and then return to me.' So the lady did, and returned to Carradora, who said : ' Witches come by night to suck the blood of thy child, and it must be prevented.'

" Then the witch took *corbezzole*, and thorns, and put them in red bags and bound them to the door-posts and windows, and then took the entrails of a very small pig (*un maialino*), and said :—

> " ' Questi sono gl'interiori
> D'un piccolo maiale,
> Che servono per le strege
> Discacciar, e gl'interiori
> Di si bella bambina
> Sono giovani quanto lei cara,
> Ed e proprio ad atta
> Per amare. E le corne
> Alle strege bisogna fare,
> Che qui dentro non possino più entrare.'

" Then Carradora took the child and made a skein of thread (*ne fecè un gomitolo*) and threw it in the air, and so it was cured."

The story was imperfectly told, because it was mentioned in connection with it, that thorns in the form of a cross were either laid in the window or should be put in a window to keep witches from entering.

Carna or *Cardæa* was a very ancient Roman minor goddess. " Some writers," says PRELLER, " describe her as a goddess who strengthened the heart and entrails. Others call her *Cardea*, a goddess of the door-hinges, and class her with *Forculus* and *Limentius*." Of her he relates the following, which has certainly an extra-ordinary resemblance to what I have related :—

" There was by the Tiber an ancient grove of Helernus, to which the *Pontifices* brought offerings. Hence came the nymph who was really called Cranæ, but who, by means of Janus, became Carna, or goddess of all hinges of doors (doors ?) and entrances or exits. As a nymph she was chaste as Diana, and by speedy flight avoided the glance of every man. But she could not escape the double sight of Janus who won her love and gave her for reward the *jus cardinis*, or sway over all hinges, and the white thorn (*spina alba*) in order to keep evil from all doors, and especially to exclude the witches who come in the night to suck the blood of children.

" Proca was the daughter of a Latin prince. When the child was only five days old the witches began to suck its blood. The nurse came and saw the marks of the witches' claws on the baby's cheeks—the child was pale as a faded leaf. So they went to Carna—or Cardea—who first touched the door-posts and threshold thrice with arbutus (Italian, *corbezzole*), and sprinkled the entrance with water, and took the entrails of a sucking-pig in her hand. Then she said :—

> "'Ye night-birds (witches) spare the bowels of the babe
> The tender creature is for dainty boys;
> Heart for heart !
> Bowels for bowels !
> Soul for soul !'

"Then she laid the entrails in the open air, and no one dared to look at them." (This, I am sure, means that they went away without looking back at them.) "After that no witch could enter, and the child soon recovered."

This is essentially the same story with the one previously narrated. But quite independently of it, I was informed long before that the *white thorn* laid in a window kept witches from entering, and that the entrails of a pig were a most potent means of exorcising them. That the Latin Cardea should have become Carradora is natural enough.

Carnea-Cardea seems to have been interested in pigs. It is remarkable that the dish of pork and beans (which, as Sir THOMAS BROWNE remarks, the Jews and Pythagoreans contrived to spoil between them) was sacred to her ; it was eaten in her honour on the 1st of June. This fact alone would convince any native of Boston that she must have been the most genial, humane, and æsthetic spirit in existence—*cui pulte fabacia et larido sacrificatur* [1]—and I am not sure that, if a copy of this work should ever find its way to the Hub, the modern Athenians will not erect a church or temple to her, unless indeed they have one already, for there are few things which they do not know, and nothing which they have not tried in the way of religion. In any case it is a remarkable historical fact that pork and beans—probably baked—was an Athenian dish, associated with the deepest mythological mysteries.

VIRA

Of this spirit I have the following account and story :—

"Vira is a fairy who, from a fairy (*fate*) in her life, became a spirit who by day and night is always in the forests. And when she sees any handsome young man busy in cutting wood, or making charcoal, if he pleases her she appears to him in the form of a very beautiful girl—*da farne a bagliare*—such as to dazzle him —and then he finds his work all done to his hand, or else she shows him a treasure.

"One day she found a handsome youth who was in great sorrow because he was so poor. He began to cut wood, yet wept while so doing because he could bring nothing home to his mother. Then Vira appeared to him and said :—

---

[1] MACROBIUS, i., 12, 33

" ' Buon giovane non ti disperare,
A far fortuna ti voglio mandare,
Vi e un piccolo paiese vicina à Benevento
E la vi e la figlia del re
Che aspetta il mago delle sette teste,
Che vada a mangiarla l'aspetta,
A sedere al balcone ma pero basta
Che uno vada dal re con le teste del mago,
Che sia stato capace d'ammazzarlo.'

(" ' Good youth be not in despair !
There's a small place near Benevento
Where dwells a king who has a daughter fair,
Who waits for the seven-headed ogre
Who will devour her, but her father there
Hopes that some one ere long may slay him,
And bring the ogre's heads unto him.')

" ' And he who will do this may wed the princess. Now this ogre has been slain by the Signore Slaniani, who will now carry the heads to the king and claim the hand of his daughter, but that is reserved for thee and not for him. For when the heads were put on a waggon to be carried to the king I took from them their seven tongues, and thou shalt carry these tongues to the king and say that thou didst slay the ogre and that thou dost wish for his daughter. Then the king will say that it was another who gained the victory, the proof being that he has the heads. To which thou wilt reply, " Who should be the conqueror—the one who has the heads or the tongues ? " And it will be admitted that the victor would have secured the tongues although he might have neglected the heads, but that it would be most unlikely that he would have cut out and thrown away the tongues.'

"And thus did Vira ;
The youth was clad in splendid attire,
He too was very beautiful,
Boldly he went to the king,
Boldly he claimed to have slain,
Single-handed, the ogre,
And asked for the beautiful princess
As a reward for his valour.
' It may not be ' said the king ;
' He who slew the monster
Has brought with him its heads,
No better proof can be found.'
' A better proof is the tongues,'
Answered the youth, undaunted,
' And I can show all the seven.'

" But the Signore Slaniani maintained that these were not the tongues of the ogre, because no one could have taken them from the heads, which had never been out of his sight. Then the king said :—

" ' Well, then bring here the heads !
If they all have their tongues
The princess shall be your wife,
And this youth must be cast into prison,

But, if the tongues are gone,
Gone with them are your chances,
You'll be a prisoner then,
And the youth shall have the maiden.'

"But as he had no witnesses Signore Slaniani depended on the heads, and what was his amazement to find when they were brought that the tongues were gone.

"Therefore it came to pass
That the poor youth who was favoured
By the help of the fairy
Carried away the reward.
So it often goes in this world—
He who does the hard work
Often misses his pay,
When some one more favoured by fortune
Steps in and secures the prize.
Higher beings than man
Play with us all like toys.
The youth was as nothing in this;
All that he won he owed
To the loving spirit Vira."

This is, as regards the incident of the dragon's or *maga's* heads and tongues, a very common fairy tale. We have the last echo of it in Quentin Durward, where the hero appears with the head of William de la Mark, the Wild Boar of Ardennes. But it is very peculiar that in this version the whole principle of the story is reversed. In the others it is the true slayer of the dragon who gets the tongues, and the impostor who has the heads but in this story.

"The page slew the boar,
The king had the gloire."

This indicates an extremely archaic form of the tale. Among rude races it is the crafty man who is most admired. The Algonkin Indians call their great god *Glooskap* or *Glūsgabe*, which means "the Liar," as Dr. J. G. Brinton declares, because they thought it the most distinguishing attribute of wisdom to be able to deceive. Highly civilised people are ashamed to boldly admire such a mean trick as that which was played by the *protégé* of Vira. It cannot have escaped the reader that, taking these tales and myths as a whole, they indicate a really primæval antiquity. Their morality is antique and they are all based on the idea that human beings or fairies who are a kind of human beings (a belief which Prætorius and many more defended only two hundred years ago), became spirits or deities. This is the very oldest form of supernaturalism, or animism. And in accordance with it is this naïf admiration of deceit.

But what is most interesting in this tale is the name VIRA, that of the heroine who is described distinctly as a fairy "who is always in the forests." In ancient times the *Vira* was strictly a sylvan spirit, and is thus mentioned by PRELLER (*Rom. Myth.*, p. 89) : "But the women of ancient times whom we call *scias* (wise women or witches) . . . were also called in early times *Viræ* or *Vires*, for this form also occurs, and they were indeed chiefly known as *Baumnymphen* (*tree*-nymphs) the word *virere* and *viridis* being clearly connected with this name." But the name being very old Italian, seems to be peculiarly appropriate to a very old story of the Toscana Romagna. "The race of wood women," says PRELLER, " is generally indicated by the Greek names of *Nymphs* and *Dryads*, while in the very earliest Italian antiquity, and in hoary popular tradition, they are called *Viræ*, *Vires*, *Virgines* and *Viragines.*" In the story which we have given, Vira acts more like a witch than a fairy.

Taking the name Vira into consideration, with other characteristics, it is therefore possible that we have here perhaps the most ancient form of the legend.

BERGOIA

Bergoia is a spirit *sempre perfido*, always treacherous, who was in her lifetime a very mischievous witch. Yet when young she was really good, and she was in a great and wealthy family by whom she was loved like a daughter. And there was a young girl, a daughter of the family, who also loved her very dearly. But little by little, no one knew how or why it was, Bergoia began to change her nature and became as evil as she had before been amiable.

" Now the change was so great that the young lady was certain that some strange cause lay behind it, and being a very shrewd girl she resolved to watch Bergoia closely, and find out what it meant. And one evening when Bergoia bade her go to bed early, she did so, but kept awake to watch. And when midnight came, she heard the voice of a man without, singing :—

<blockquote>
" ' O Bergoia ! o bella Bergoia !
Vieni mi aprire,
Che da questa finestra,
Non posso salire,
Bada i tuoi padroni non sveglia,
Perche con te una affare
Abbiamo da combinare ;
Se questa affare combineramo,
La tua signorina stregheremo,
</blockquote>

Se la tua signorina
Non mi farai stregare,
Una strega di te faro diventare.'

("'O Bergoia! fair Bergoia!
Come open unto me!
For thou knowest through the window
I cannot come to thee.
Beware, lest the master wakes,
For we have work to do ;
There is witch-work which calls us, Bergoia !
Witch-work for me and you ;
We must bewitch the maiden
And win her from her home.;
Unless the spell pass on her,
A witch thou must become !')

" Then the young lady, terrified at what she had so nearly escaped, ran screaming to her parents, and told them what she heard. Then he who had called, and who stood without, in a rage changed himself into a black dog,[1] and disappeared in a terrible flash of lightning with Bergoia, who was never seen on earth as a true woman again.

" After her death, Bergoia became a spirit of thunder and lightning, and was seen darting in the fire— *si converte molte volte in saietta.* She, however, often took human form, and would go to a house and ask for food and shelter ; if she obtained it she would content herself with making thunder and lightning roar and flash, and if her hosts showed fear then there would come hail to devastate their crops. But woe to those who utterly refused her shelter, for then there would come a flash (*saietta*) which would destroy or burn the house, or set fire to the trees.

" So men lose thousands on thousands
Of money by crops destroyed,
For the flash is a ray of fire,
And the bolt like a splint of iron,
And he who is struck by it dies,
As he may by the deadly odour
Which lightning spreads around.
Such is the work of Bergoia.

"Sometimes it comes to pass that *Bergoia* fancies a youth, and passes the night with him. He is bewitched and makes love, but never sees her, for she comes and goes in darkness, and suddenly departs in a flash of lightning which kills her paramour.

" And so she is ever doing evil to all,
Evil to those who have never done her wrong."

The Tusci, as OTTFRIED MÜLLER observes, had in their mythology an extraordinary number of spirits of thunder and lightning, furies and infernal witches,

---

[1] " Any voodoo is supposed to change himself into a black dog, black wolf, black cat, owl or bat at night. The way to stop the metamorphosis is to find either the human or the animal skin and salt it. These black animals spit fire at you if you have their human skin ; but you must not fear, but hold it fast until you have salted it well."—MARY A. OWEN.

and, as I have observed, there are a great many in the Romagnolo mythology.[1]
The Etruscan, like the Turanian everywhere—and the Mexican so far as we know
it—seems to have been a religion or cult which was, especially in a certain stage,
one of blood and of the grotesque horrors which always appeal to primitive man. In
such religions thunder and storms, death, bloody sacrifices and evil spirits take
precedence of more refined conceptions. The god is always a human sorcerer who
continues to haunt mankind and exercise the same functions which he practised
while living. No one can fail to recognise very distinct traces of this in these
Romagnolo traditions.

This account speaks of " the deadly odour which lightning spreads around."
The Hungarian gypsies say that it has a smell like garlic.

It may be observed that these Tuscan legends deal, not indirectly, but very
evidently and closely, with their original myths. Many of the names of Etrusco-
Italian deities are preserved in them almost unchanged. Now in no part of the
Roman empire was the worship of Ceres so zealously maintained as in the Tuscan
land ; hence the idea of a wandering goddess, going about in disguise, soliciting
shelter and food, and cruelly punishing those who treat her unkindly, appears more
than once in these traditions. And it cannot be denied that by considering them
as a whole, comparing one incident with another, or all the special characteristics
of the legends, no one can fail to see that all agree marvellously with what we
know of Etrurian or Old Latin origins, and manifest little admixture from other
sources.

This being true, it is curious that there was an Etruscan minor goddess
named *Begoe* who appears to have communicated to mortals the whole theory and
system of thunder, or an *ars fulguritorum*, which was preserved with other
writings, after the time of Augustus, in the temple of the Palatine Apollo.
Fulguritus really means *id quod est fulmine ictum*—that which is thunderstruck.
Begoe was at least one who was concerned with thunder, storms, and the spoiling
of harvests. But here—as in all such cases—I only make a mere suggestion, to be
corrected or set aside by those who are better qualified to decide.

Bergoia in this Tuscan myth kills animals and men at a flash or in an instant.

---

[1] The Tuscans (*Tusker*) who devoted much attention to investigating thunder and lightning . .
recognised three kinds—that which gave counsel or advice, that which confirmed events and indicated how
something which had happened would turn out, and the third which came unexpectedly and predicted according
to circumstances. It would weary the reader should I relate more of this greatly spun-out lightning-lore.
For further details he may consult : SENECA, *Naturæ Quest.*, ii., 32, &c. ; PLINY, *Hist. Nat.*, ii., 53 ;
VALERIAN, *De fulminum significationobus in Grævii Thesaur.*, v., p. 600 ; MÜLLER, *Die Etrusker ;* CREUZER,
Symbolik, 3rd ed., vol. iii., p. 650 ; NORK, *Real Worterbuch*, vol. i., p. 160 ; DÖLLINGER *Heidenthum*,
p. 461 ; FRIEDRICH, *Symbolik der Natur.*

BEGOE (THE FIGURES FROM GORI MUS. ETRUS.)

"Begoe," as we are told (*History of Etruria*, by Mrs. Hamilton Gray) "slew an ox simply by whispering in its ear the fearful *name* of the Highest." This I think refers to lightning. "The highest and most irresistible of all the powers dwells in the divine and mysterious *name*—"the supreme name," with which Hea alone is acquainted. Before this name everything bows in heaven and in earth and in Hades, and it alone can conquer the Maskin (evil spirits), and stop their ravages. "Awe her (Ninkigal) with the names of the great gods" (Fox Talbot, cited in Lenormant, *Magie Chaldaienne*). Thus *nomen est numen*, according to Varro, to which we may here appropriately add *et numen est lumen*—the divinity being lightning.

BUGHIN

Of this spirit I have the following account :—

"*Bughin* is a spirit who does both good and evil. About harvest time he causes the *carbonchiato* [1] in the grain, or makes it become black, whence the bread made from it is also dark, having such a vile smell and taste that it cannot be eaten, which is a sad loss for the poor peasants—*e così i poveri contadini se avessero la disgrazia*. And when they have suffered much from this, say for three or four years, then they take two or three ears of wheat or of the grain (*spighe di grano*). These the peasant must husk or shell (*sfarlo*), clean, and put them on the hearth where it is very hot, and throw the refuse out-of-doors, and when putting the grain on the hearth say :— .

> "'Metto questo grano carbonchiato
> Perche lo spirito di Bughin mi ha rovinato,
> A lui mi voglio raccomandare,
> E lo voglio tanto pregare,
> Che aquesta male voglia riparare ;
> Se questa grazia mi vuol fare,
> Questo grano in mezzo della stanza
> Mi deve fare saltare !'

> ("'As these rusted grains I see,
> I fear Bughin hath ruined me !
> Therefore unto him I pray,
> That this harm may pass away ;
> May this corn now be a sign
> That all is well for me and mine,
> May it, if I escape a doom,
> Jump to the middle of the room !')

"Should the heated grains burst and jump well, it is a sign that the rust or mildew will not attack the grain. But the peasant must be on the look-out to secure two grains of wheat of the very first which ripen before the smut, or *carbonchiato*, manifests itself."

The Romans had a god or rural deity who presided over the rust in wheat.

[1] *Carbonchio*, a disease in grain by which it appears black and scorched. The smut or mildew. *Carbonchioso*, affected with the smut, burnt or scorched (BARETTI'S *Italian Dictionary*).

His name was *Robigo*, and there is much about him in the lore of the Latin harvest gods, of whom I would say incidentally that they seem to have been the prototypes of the same "Corn gods" in Germany, or sprung from the same source. The Latins had indeed quite a minor mythology of these. Seia, or Segetia, guarded the seed while in the ground. She was also called Fructiseia and Semonia. Segesta attended to it when sprouting. The Deus Nodotus aided the development of the joints—*dicitur deus qui ad nodos perducit res satas* (ARNOBIUS, iv. 7 ; ap. PRELLER). Volutina formed the husk, Patelena opened the ear (*vide* Patelana). With these were twelve male gods who presided over all the separate processes of sowing and harvesting, besides the Deus Spinensis who was invoked to keep the crop free from thorns and weeds. In Bolognese, *Robigo* would easily and naturally be changed to *Bughin—big*, the root, becoming *bug* or *bugh* by many analogies. *In* is a common termination for proper names.

GANZIO

"Festa para Conso : Consus tibi cætera dicet;
Ipso festa die dum sua sacra canes."

OVID, *Fastorum Lib.* iii

The *contadino* when in difficulty on any subject has always his choice between appealing to a Christian saint or an ancient heathen god : "One good if the other fails." So if his horse be ill, he may begin with a prayer to Saint Antony of whom I was told that :—

" He is a saint who protects all animals, especially horses. And when one has a horse in bad condition he goes to Saint Antonio and says :—

" ' Saint Antonio mio benigno !
Di pregarvi non son digno ;
Ma voglio voi pregare,
Che il mio cavallo mi volete liberare
Da tutte le malattie;
Sano et svelte me le farete stare ! '

(" ' Most benign Saint Antony !
Though unworthy I may be,
Yet to thee I pray, of course,
And beg that thou wilt free my horse
From all evils in him found,
Make the creature safe and sound ! ' ")

But should Saint Antony turn a deaf ear to this humble petition, the suppliant appeals to a much older, and therefore probably more experienced deity, that is *Ganzio*, who is "of the horse, horsey," as he dwells in stables, and who, though not devoid of trick or vice, is always willing to give his aid as an experienced " vet." when politely requested. Of him I have the following account :—

" *Ganzio* is the spirit who is over horses. Now it is not with evil intent but for fun that it often happens when a coachman goes into the stables Ganzio makes the horses misbehave, and throws impediments in the way, especially if the master be waiting without, and very impatient, begins to scold.

"However, if the master do not become too angry, or treat the coachman badly, Ganzio contents himself with making the horse rear and curvet a little (*fa fare qualche capriciola*). But if the master is unreasonably angry, then the horse will take the wrong road if it be possible, or get into a dangerous place, or leap or bolt, but still without hurting his rider.

" Now if it be thought that Ganzio is playing these tricks the rider should say :—

> " 'Ganzio, Ganzio, benedetto tu siei !
> Buono quante bello. Son cattivo, ai
> Bene ragione trattero bene i servitori,
> Giacche tu me ai data
> Una lezione, ma ti vengo a pregare,
> Ganzio non me piu spaventare
> Che mi ai fatto una gran paura
> Ma e vero la valuta,
> Ganzio viene in casa mia,
> Vieni a tenermi compagnia
> Ma non farmi spaventare,
> Nei burroni non mi gettare.'

> ("' Ganzio, Ganzio, heed my song !
> Thou art right and I am wrong,
> I will treat the servants better,
> And will mind thee to the letter ;
> For the present I implore,
> That thou frighten me no more !
> Also that thou'lt ever be
> In my house, as company ;
> And may I ne'er again be seen
> So near the edge of a ravine !'")

I must remark that my informant did not very well recall this incantation, and " pieced it up," so to speak, as well as she could. But who was this Ganzio originally? *Consus* was a very old Roman minor deity, who was closely connected with animals, and especially with horses and races. " The Greeks," says PRELLER, " declared that on account of the chariot-races at his festival, and his altar buried in the earth that he was the same as their Poseidon Hippios." It is to be remarked that he was regarded as being very kind and considerate to animals, therefore on his festival all horses and mules were allowed to rest, and were crowned with flowers and otherwise well treated. Consus would naturally become Conso or Consio in Italian, which in Tuscan is *Chonsio*, the *ch* in Romagnola often changing to a *g*, as, for instance, *lonbrigoli* for *lombrici* (earthworms), and *piga* for *pica* (wood-pecker or magpie), old Umbrian *pei qu*. This etymology may or may not "hold water," I only suggest it as the only one which occurs to me. But, according to it, Consus would almost inevitably become Consio and Ganzio.

I forgot to mention that Ganzio may be invoked for any matter relative to a horse.

ALPENA

"Der Name der Göttin Alpan erklärt sich durch Vergleichung stammverwandter Namen von ähnlichen Gottheiten bei den Indern und Germanen." "Diese schafft und bringt nach der Darstellung des Spiegelbildes durch die Luft dahin schwebend den Schmuck der Pflanzenwelt."—CORSSEN, *Über die Sprache der Etrusker*.

Alpena, as I was told, is a beautiful female spirit who always flies in the air. She is very charming, and in addition to her name is entitled *La Bellaria*. She is a *la dea dei fiori*—the goddess of flowers. The name recalls the Etruscan ALPAN, who was also an aerial goddess, or rather peri, who appears on a mirror from Vulci now in the Vatican (*vide Mus. Etrusc. Vaticana*, i., vol. xxiii., and Gerhard, *Etrus. Spiegel*, v., 28 f. t., cccxxxi. f. 2141) as holding leaves or flowers. Every detail as given to me agrees curiously with what is said of Alpan, by Corssen (*Über die Sprache der Etrusker*, vol. i., p. 255). "Alpan," he says, "creates the ornamental part of the world of plants, and brings it, sweeping through the air, in the train of Adonis, the goddess of spring." The name *Alpena*, with the description of her attributes, were given to me, not as the result of inquiry, but as information, volunteered by a peasant woman.

As Alpena or Alpan is, like Albina, one of the *Lichtgöttinin*, or goddesses of light, it is probable, from the similarity of name, that they are the same. From Alpan the Etruscans developed another goddess, *Alpanu*, or *Alpnu*, who appears to have been an inferior form of Venus (*vide* CORSSEN, *Über die Sprache der Etrusker* —a work of no value as to philology, but full of curious materials).

It is remarkable that in modern Tuscan tradition there are several spirits of light and air called Bellaria, corresponding to the Etrusco-Roman group of Eos and the nymphs of the dawn. Though Eos had few temples ("*rarissima templa per orbem*," OVID, *Met.*, xiii., 588), the Etruscans made great account of her, and her son Memnon (Memrun) often occurs on vases (*vide Die Weltkörper in ihrer mythisch symbolischen Bedeutung*, von J. B. Friedrich, 1864).   All of the Etruscan

ALPAN   (*Alpena or Albina*)
(From Corssen.   The ornament from a vase.)

winged spirits bearing flowers, and connected with rainbows, clouds, air, and light, were in fact *Bellarie*, and a part of the *Lasæ*, who carry bottles probably of perfume—though it may have been something more substantial—wherewith to welcome the soul of the life-weary mortal entering heaven. As is beautifully set forth in my own French romance of *Le Lutin du Chateau*, which was refused by Hachette because of its worldly-minded gaiety and freedom from blue-nosed straight-lacedness.

CHAPTER VII

TITUNO

"Tituno is the spirit of thunder—*forgore*—and he is known in all the Romagnie." So asserts Naudo Papetti. Another authority (Peppino) gives the name as Tit'uno "*lo spirito del folgore*," adding that he regrets that he cannot communicate much on the subject, but that when the season of the silk-worms shall have passed he will go forth among the *contadini*, and gather up what unearthly lore he can. Meanwhile he has noted down as to Tit'uno the following :—

"This spirit did marvellous things in the ancient time when Jupiter [1] was wont to let loose his thunder-bolts over great plains, destroying everything. Then the people invoked this spirit, saying :—

"'Spirito infernale ti scongiuro
In nome di Dio e del santo Isodorio.'

"Then they took salt and holy water and sprinkled the house or the place where they were. Then the thunder departed and did not return to repeat the mischief, the invocation being a protection. And I have found a *contadino* who repeats it, but he says there was a time when every one in the Romagna did so."

It cannot have failed to strike the reader, as I have indeed observed it more than once in this book, that there are many spirits of thunder and lightning, which was also the case with the Etruscans of olden time.

[1] This was written by a youth who had received some education, hence the association with *Giove* or Jove. Here the latter is *deus ex machina*.

ALBINA

" Obstinet dicebant antiqui quod nunc ostendit, ut in veteribus carminibus: sed iam se cælo cedens Aurora obstinet suum patrem."—FESTUS, p. 197

It will come to pass, and that at no very distant day, when—although there will be no lack of people who will understand this book perhaps better than I do— there will not be a soul living who can *feel* it. For a copy may be kept in some library, even unto the time when there will be no more wild woods, or wilder- nesses, either rural or human ; when every tree and rock will be recorded, and every man and woman be well educated—and all the better for them—probably into something far more sensible than sentimentalism or superstition, but the ancient spirit in which the past was lived will be irrecoverably lost. I have no fear that the *outlines*, or drawing, of my humble pictures will perish, but I know that the colours will inevitably fade, and yet it is the colour which most impresses me as I now write. A few days ago a dealer in bric-a-brac here in Florence showed me a picture which he said was by Beato Angelico. It was not by that master, for it was very correctly and beautifully drawn ; what was remarkable in it was that it was utterly faded, all was dead grey-white, figures as well as ground being quite uniform. But the artist had outlined, or stamped every detail with tracer or wheel, so that the original conception of form still remained, and I—knowing the time and school to which it belonged—could conjecture what it must once have been. So I beg the reader to endeavour to re-colour or revive these outlines. After all, that is a poor portrait which only conveys an idea of the great *skill* of the artist ; at least half of its effect should consist in giving us some vivid idea of what the original must have been, as man or woman, and a very badly executed sketch often does that, better than a very artistic work, as cheap popular caricatures of public characters abundantly prove.

These thoughts occurred while disentangling the meaning of a rude fragment which was half-recited and half-sung to me, and then written down as roughly as it had been repeated, yet in which there is a certain mysterious beauty, as of a dayspring obscured by clouds. It is of a spirit of the dawn who is supposed very appropriately to herald a bright day, or promise hope to unfortunate lovers.

" Albina is a fairy who appears when morning dawns—*quando spunta l'alba*—to lovers who love in vain. She herself once, when in life, loved and was beloved, but she was in the power of an aunt who was a sorceress, and who opposed her love, and said to her : ' Leave this lover of thine, or evil shall befall thee. Firstly, thou shalt be a fairy, and when I die thou wilt take my witchcraft and never more have peace nor happiness.'

"Albina replied : 'Though all the world should perish, I will wed my love, and if I must become witch or fairy, then I will use all my power to benefit lovers.'

"'I will do evil to women who betray their lovers.' So Albina kept her word. If a youth in love prays to her at early dawn he will be sure to gain her favour.

"When a youth loves and meets with no return he must rise before daybreak, and, kneeling in an open field, say :—

> "'Alba, alba, che tu spunti
> Fa spuntar per me l'aurora !
> Che l'Albina venga fuori !
> Una grazia mi deve fare
> A lei mi vengo a raccomandare,
> Dalla mia amante sono disccaciato,
> Sa anche l'Albina per amore,
> Quante mia passate sa che l'amore,
> E tanto forte che si preferisce,
> Preferisce piu tosto la morte,
> Che da un amante abandonati.' "

Albina is, by name, allied to Alba the dawn, or is plainly enough Aurora herself. Further questioning I leave to the learned. But what is worth remarking is that in this wild, imperfect sketch we have the fragment of some ancient and possibly far more perfect poem, utterly beyond the creative power of a mere illiterate *contadina*. Albina dreads the becoming a fairy, spirit, or witch. It may be observed that in all this lore there is something mysterious and terrible, to gentle natures, connected with the transfiguring of mortality into *folletti*. Albina fears it, but rather than relinquish her faith to her lover, and even though she lose him, she will not yield one whit, and declares that if unearthly power be forced upon her, she will exert it in behalf of unfortunate lovers. Which is realised.

All of this is not clearly and artistically developed in the incantation, but it was apparent enough in the glances and expression of the *strega*, who simply had a rough diamond which she could not polish. To better understand this let the reader suppose a Hampshire peasant singing such a song.

There was an old Roman, now Tuscan, town called *Albinia*.

VERBIO

The strange manner in which dim recollections of ancient myths are handed down in names, and how they are worked over and varied by the people, is illustrated by the following story from the Romagnola :—

"*Verbio* was a beautiful youth, as good as he was beautiful, and he loved with all his heart a maid who seemed to return his love.

" But she soon was tempted,
Tempted by another
Youth of greater beauty,
Which was like enchantment ;
Yet he was a stranger,
And he had no story,
For this handsome stranger,
Verbio was slighted.

" Then Verbio fell ill in despair, and seemed to be dying, and the girl learning this repented, and in grief said to her new lover : ' I have done wrong, and I now see that Verbio loved me truly as thou dost not and no one can.' Then her lover gazed at her and she saw he was not a man but a devil. And he said :—

" ' See what thou hast done,
See how thou art wicked,
Leaving one who loved thee
With all soul sincerely !
Yet for me you left him,
Yes, for me, a devil ;
Now you both are lost,
For thou'st truly promisèd
To be mine for ever,
As thou holdest Verbio.
But if you will sign
With your blood a contract
To be mine, I'll grant ye
Many, many years
Of happiness together.'

" Now Verbio did not believe in the power of devils, and was only too glad to get his love again, and so signed the contract, as she did also. And they lived happily indeed for many years ; but years must end, and so it came to pass that when the time of the contract expired both died at once. And all at once there was an awful storm over all the land, the heavens grew dark by day, and horrible fires flashed out of the darkness, and amid the storm was heard a voice which sang :—

" ' Women, learn to love
One true love, and truly ;
When you're truly loved
Be warned by my example !
Now I pay the fee
For my fatal falsehood.'

" And since that time the two have gone about as spirits knowing no rest."

Virbius was the attendant—" *genius* or *indiges* of the forests of Diana, or the oldest king and priest—*rex Nemorensis*—who founded her worship." He was, says PRELLER, a male demon, worshipped with Diana. He was compared with and in fact was, " the Greek Hippolytus who, after he had been trampled to death by the wild horses of Poseidon, was revived and carried away by Diana."

Diana is known popularly to-day as the Queen of the Witches, but rather as Hecate, in a dark and terrible sense. And if Verbio be the modern form of Virbius it is evident how he has become a spirit of the night, knowing no rest. I suspect that in an older version of this story Verbio dies and is revived.

Pico de Mirandola, attacking the moral character of Diana, declares that "she was very liberal with that virginity which she feigned to adore, possibly to stimulate those who hated luxury. Thus, as the moon, Endymion lay with her, as did Hippolytus and Virbio." And Tertullian (*De falsa Religione*, lib. i., cap. 17), who naturally wanted to destroy the good fame and name of every lady in every mythology not Christian, holds forth in much the same manner, asking why she should take such pains to save Virbius from being killed by the horses—" *qui erat turbatis distractus equis* "—*unless*—— " What, I ask," cries the holy man, inspired, " does all this nasty horse-business mean ? (*quid equorum tam pertinax abominatio*) —unless it be a *conscientia stupri, et amorem minime virginalem ?*—a con- sciousness of—ahem !—and a love of anything but a virginal sort ? " Exactly. And so, ever since then Diana, as the ever-wandering moon, and Virbio—the man in the moon—have gone wandering over the face of the heavens " as spirits finding no rest."

I suspect that there is much more to be found out about this Romagnolo Verbio, and that what I have given is like many other accounts—only a mere fragment of some much completer story. The idea of signing a compact and assigning the soul is a very late Christian invention, though Horst finds traces of it a thousand years ago.

DUSIO

" Augustine (testimonio famoso) dice al quindicesimo libro della Citta di Dio, che i Silvani ed i Fauni (volgarmente detti Incubi), di molte volte sono stati maligni verso le, donne, e che le hanno desiderate, e finalmente son giacuti con loro, e che alcuni demonj, chiamati da Franzesi *Dusi* del continuo vanno cercando-tal disonestà, e mettonla ad effetto."—*La Strega di Pico della Mirandola.*

In what may be called the Irregular Minor Mythology of Anglo-Saxony, or Saxonyankeedom, and in which Jingo and the Dickens are prominent deities, there is one power known as the *Deuce*. I have always inclined to think that this word is only the Latin *Deus*, but philologists deduce it from a French goblin, one *Dus*, who is described as early as the fifth century as *Dusius*. *Deus* means God, while *Dus*, according to DU CANGE, is found in almost all the Slavonic, Celtic, and Teutonic tongues of Europe, always as a kind of devilkin, a seducer of virgins and a being of familiar, easy, make-yourself-at-home habits. It is true, however, that the word for God has been elsewhere made to do diabolical service. In English gypsy it is *Dùvel,* from the same Aryan root as Deus. Some years ago an English lady teaching religion to some gypsy children, asked them how the Creator was called? Whereupon a small traveller, thinking the name was wanted in Romany, cried out " *Dùvel."* Soon after there appeared in the newspapers an Appalling instance of Ignorance and Depravity, showing that the lower orders actually believed that the world and all things were made by the devil—*à la* MOLOCH or MALLOCH. For they do indeed sound very much alike (*i.e.,* Duvel and Devil), and when we consider the extraordinary preponderance of power awarded to the devil in Catholic Christianity, it is a marvel that these names were not interchanged long ago.

Isidore of Seville (*in Gloss*) speaks of Dusii as *demones.* Another ancient authority declares that there are actually women so devoid of decency or so worldly-minded as to solicit the embraces of those demons, *quos Galli Dusios nuncupant, qua assidue hanc peragunt immunditiam*—"whom the French call Dusii because they so constantly persevere in such impurity." PAPIAS writes: " *Dusios nominant quas Romani faunos ficarias vocant* " (" They call those Dusii whom the Romans call Faunos ficarios "). THOMAS of CANTERBURY speaks of them as forest or sylvan gods in Prussia, and that the " gentiles " there dare not cut the woods consecrated to them. And a Codex of the eighth century, cited by DU CANGE, speaks of *aliqui rustici homines,* "some rustics who believe in witches, *dusiolas* and *acquaticas* or *genisons."*

But the word seems to exist in most Northern languages. ZEUSS gives *Dusmus, diabolus,* for Dusius. DIEFENBACH (*Origines*) finds a Prussian Dussia or Dussas, "perhaps *dwæse, geist,* a spirit." And VILLEMARQUÉ, gives as British or Breton, *Dus, Duz,* plural, *Duzed,* an incubus. *Dus* appears also in Old Friesic as Dûs, and in Middle High German as *Daus.* I conjecture that there was an Etruscan or Sabine *Dus*—the parent or origin of the domestic goblin, also of the fauns. There occurs very often on vases the fox-tailed, phallic, laughing god with a flat face and snubbed nose—always as wanton and indecent.

None of the authors whom I have cited mention any Italian equivalent for the word. I was therefore pleased at finding on inquiry that not only was the name at once recognised, but that the description of the goblin corresponded in every detail to that which appears in all the earlier writers. This is the more interesting because *Dus,* at present, in all the rest of Europe is little heard of, and may perhaps be put down as one of the gods gone to sleep. This is what was told me :—

" *Dusio* is a mischievous little *folletto*, or goblin.   He teases girls, sometimes he acts as a nightmare, very often he inspires lascivious dreams and has connection with women.   Sometimes as a little imp not more than three inches high he perches on their pillows.   He is not bad, but mischievous.   He haunts houses and fireplaces."

Afterwards the following was first narrated and then written out for me :—

" Dusio is a *folletto*—goblin or spirit—who sits on girls' shoulders.   In a district of La Romagna there was a girl at service in a gentleman's family.   In this palace the aunt of the proprietor had died.   The family consisted only of two brothers, a young son, and a girl.   After the aunt died, . . . the father also passed away.   And after these deaths there was no peace in the house for strange noises.

" At first the girl was afraid, but she soon became accustomed to the sounds.   Steps were heard all the time going up and down stairs, doors banging.   Then Virginia—such was her name—beheld at times a form as of a lady dressed in black enter and sweep by.   And then came the *Dusio*, who played her all kinds of wanton tricks, *e faceva l'amore*.   Now Virginia did not like this, for she had a lover who wrote frequently to her, and she had carefully hidden these letters for fear lest *i padroni* or her masters and mistresses should find them.   One night Dusio entered, and began his pranks.   First he teased her in every way—*faceva tutti i dispetti*—and pulled all the bed-covering, sheets and all, from Virginia.   Then he went and brought out some of her letters, and lighting them at the candle burned them all up in the *scaldino*, or brasier.

" The next day she went to walk with an old woman who was to her as a mother, to whom she told all the tricks which Dusio played, and how he was teasing the very life out of her.   Then the old woman said : ' Should he try to do that again say to him :—

" ' Dusio—*diosio*—vattene via !
Vattene in pace che Dio ti benedica !

" ' And then he will go away and trouble you no more.'
" But Virginia was so forgetful, or so much excited, that instead of repeating these words she said :—

" ' Dusio, Dusio, cosa fai ? '

" That s, ' Dusio, Dusio, what are you doing ? '   And he, bursting into a loud laugh, said : ' Taking care lest your master and mistress find your letters.' "

I have omitted from this story some family details and their name and the place where it occurred.   I was assured with great earnestness that it all really took place as I have given it.   What is remarkable in it, beyond the fact that Dusio corresponds exactly to the wanton sprite *Dusius* of the old writers, is the word *diosio* in the incantation.   My informant could not explain it.   I think I have met with it before, but cannot remember where.   I conjecture, haphazardly, that it is equivalent to " Thou who mayest be, or art, a god "—*i.e., dio sia !*

Prætorius has, in his *Blockes Berges Berichtung* (1669), something to say about Dusius, and of course in his fashion it is something quaint and strange. " It hath been observed," he states, " yea, and experienced and made known by many credible men, that the Sylvani or Little Forest men and *Inni*, which are otherwise commonly known as Incubos and Squatters (*Auflröcker*) are madly lewd for women.   And there are others of the same kind whom the French call *Dusii* who are fully their equals in such impurity, so that it is verily a sin and a shame, and Giraldus, Livy, and Isidore l. 1, testify to it.   But they have all been wrecked on the word Dusius.   For it should be *Drusius*, and mean forest-devil, whom the Latins in the same sense call *Silvanus.*   So that which Saint Augustine saith, that our ancestors of old time called these spirits and devils *Druten* is most probable, since the word agrees well with that of *Druids* who lived in wood and forests."

Which may or may not be.   *Dus* is distinctly marked in all its early forms, although the intercalation of *r* is extremely common, even to children.

Pliny tells us that hand-mills were invented at Volsinii, and that some of them turned of their own accord (Pliny, xxxvi. 29), "from which," says Dennis, "it would appear probable that 'that shrewd and knavish sprite called Robin Goodfellow' was of Etruscan origin—a fact worthy the attention of all Etrusco-Celtic theorists."   The reader will find in several chapters of this my book much to confirm this conjecture.

REMLE

The following account as to this spirit came from a family living near Forli :—

"*Remle* is the spirit of the mills, and when a peasant who has offended him in any manner takes his corn to be ground, then the miller finds that something is out of order and that the wheel will not turn, because Remle has meddled with the works (*va in mezzo alla macina*), and hinders the grinding of the grain.
"Then the miller must say :—

> "'Remle, Remle, a ti mi raccomando,
> Che siei tanto buono e grande,
> Ti prego la macina lasciami andare,
> Perche a da fare, e il contadino ti mandero,
> A far ti ringraziare ! '"

> ("'Remle, Remle, on thee I wait,
> For thou art so good and great,
> I pray thee let the mill-wheel go,
> For there's work to do, and the peasant shall know
> How much to thee he doth truly owe ! '")

I can find no name like that of *Remle* connected with any early Tuscan or Latin divinity.   In Italian *Remolare* means to retard, or to hinder, and as Remle retards or hinders the working of the mill, it is most probable that this is the origin of the word.   *Mola,* a mill-stone, *permolare,* to grind, *moláto* (Ital.) ground, seem all to be closely associated with it.   In Romagnolo the word *Remle* is the same as the Italian *crusca,* or bran.   Yet I doubt whether this be the original name or indicative of its real meaning. It is worth noting that it seems very natural to suppose that there is a goblin dwelling in the mysterious chiaro-oscuro of a mill—

> " Made misty by the floating meal."

JANO, MEANA, MONTULGA, AND TALENA

> " Now, by two-headed Janus !
> Nature hath formed strange fellows in her time."

" Quod quidem apud Thuscos Italiæ populos accidisse, historia traditur, neque ego hæc loquor quasi poëticum fabulam."—*Psellus de Daemonibus.*

As my limits forbid much further printing, I include in one section four spirits who came flying in late after the rest. The first of these is *Jano*, who is thus described :—

" JANO is a spirit with two heads, one of a Christian (*i.e.*, human), and one of an animal, and yet he hath a good heart, especially that of the animal,[1] and whoever desires a favour from them should invoke (*deve pregarle*) both, and to do this he must take two cards of a *tarocco* pack, generally the wheel of fortune and the *diavolo indiavolato*, and put them on the iron (frame) of the bed, and say :—

> " ' Diavolo che sei capo
> Di tutti i diavoli !
> La testa ti voglio stiacciare
> Fino che o spirito di Jano
> Per me non vai a pregare ! ' "

> (" ' Thou devil who art chief
> Of all the fiends !
> I will crush thy head
> Until the spirit of Jano
> Thou callest for me ! ' ' ")

Jano is here plainly enough Janus, who was of yore a god of chance and fortune, and who has descended legitimately and naturally, as surveying the past and future, to association with cards. I have seen an early Romanesque or Lombard statue of this god in which one of the heads was of an animal and the other human (*vide Gypsy Sorcery*, p. 208, in which, however, *both* heads are erroneously given as animal).

I believe that there were few gods with whom there were so many occult, strange, and forbidden mysteries connected, as with Janus, and there are marked

---

[1] There is manifest confusion here.

traces of this in the modern tradition. As having two heads, or being all-seeing, he became the symbol of Prudence—the *Prudentia* of *Gothic* sculpture, which is also the mystic Baphomet, or two-headed figure girt with a serpent, of the Knights Templars. There is one of these on the door of the Baptistery here, in Florence. The Baphomet signified secrecy and "illumination"—or, properly, freethought, nature-worship, or agnosticism to the *adepti*. Janus was *the god of the door*, *i.e.*, the entrance or admission to the mysteries. By him the chief devil (or evil) is conquered, and fortune or fate mastered. The incantation to Jano is therefore of great interest and value as possibly indicating a very curious tradition handed down from the old initiation. He is the *weird*, *i.e.*, prophetic spirit.

MEANA —Of this spirit I have the following written :—

"Meana is a spirit who is amiably inclined to people, and especially to lovers. When we desire a favour of her we should say :—

> " ' Per l'imagine di Meana !
> E per la sua bella persona
> Uno che la guardi bisogna
> Che l'adori sulla sua tomba
> Preghero fin che il suo spirito non vedro,
> Se vederlo io protro il suo spirito
> Sempre preghero che nessun spirito maligno
> Mi possa molestare
> E Satanas le converra
> Sempre lasciarmi stare
> Lo spirito di Meana sempre preghero
> E saro certo che mai non periro ! ' "

As this is to me intranslatable nonsense, I have not attempted to give a version of it. MEANA, according to Eduard Gerhard (*Gesammelte Alcademische Abhandlungen*, 1866), the Etruscan name of a winged goddess of fate. He connects it with *mens*, *Menerva* (Minerva) and Mnemosyne. Her pictures as given indicate an aerial, *lasa-like* spirit, resembling Bellaria, or such as in popular tradition is connected with benevolence and love.

Since writing the foregoing there has fallen into my possession, " for the second time in life," a copy of the *Miracles of the Living and of the Dead*, by Henry Kornmann, Frankfort, 1614. I have not now space wherein to print all that I have learned regarding *Meana ;* suffice it to say that as a love-goddess, specially devoted to *brides*, she is identical with *Mena*, thus described by Kornmann in language which I really *must* be excused from translating :—

" *Quæstiuncula. Cur novis nuptis Mena appareat?*

" Latet ibi mysterium magnum serpentis antiqui. Id quod et Romanis ignotum non fuit. Quia nova nupta super ingentem fascinum, id est membrum Priapi sedere jubebatur, qui erat in loco altiori, quem indicat Lucanus inquiens. Torvus stat, id est, stratum, pendulum, et erectum. In quod ascendebatur gradibus ebore ornatis, hoc autem fiebat propterea, ut illarum pudicitiam prior Deus delibasse videretur, docet ex Varrone Aurel. Augustinus lib. 6, Civit Dei, c. 9, et Lactantius, lib. 1.

According to that strange book, the *Delineatio Impotentiæ Conjugalis* of John G. Simon, 1682, the serpent, if not conciliated and buried under the threshold, prevented conception. *Vide* also *De Natura Hermaphroditorum*, of Caspar Bauhinus, 1614, containing interesting chapters on satyrs, fauns, &c. The tale of the Æolian virgin and her serpent-love belongs to this series.

Last of all there was sent to me a very long paper stating that MENA or MERNA is a spirit who appears to brides in the Romagna Toscana in the form of a serpent. But only to those who know the proper invocation. Should the serpent appear *perpendicularly*, at full length (*i.e.*, Phallic), this means a long life, and happy ; if twisted up, it presages many sorrows, &c. ; but if Mena comes as a woman, it forbodes unhappiness and discord. The incantation is as follows in such a case :—

> " Ti scongiuro, o Serpente !
> Merna ! Merna ! Merna !
> Del malaugurio, e che
> Tu mi faccia tornare
> In pace col mio marito !
> Se no come mi indichera
> La fata Merna, io ti confinero
> Nel piu profondo abisso
> Che possa esistere
> Soprà la terra. Merna ! Merna ! "

Then if Mena appears as a serpent all is well ; but if not, the bride must sit for three nights under a juniper-tree by a running stream, and cast into it three juniper berries, make a fire of three twigs of birch (*beto*), throw the ashes into the brook, and repeat :—

> " Fata Merna, ti 'nvoco !
> Per la tranquillita
> Dell' anima mia, e per quello
> Di mio caro marito ! "

Then the spirit will appear in the form of a fish, and bid the bride take of the mud of the stream, mingle it with salt and oil, warm it, if possible, against the husband's body, make it into a box (or take a box) and put the mud into it shaped like fish, carry it into the church where the wedding took place.

Then Mena appears and tells the bride in long detail to be three nights in the church, and to burn the box and fish with *cypress* wood, and cause the husband to swallow the ashes in soup. Then all will be well.

MONTULGA —Of this spirit I am told :—

"Montulga is a very beautiful spirit, called *Montulga della Bellaria*. Unto him who believes in her all his affairs will prosper. He who would invoke her should go into a pine-tree grove and say :—

" ' Qui si resposa,
Al odore dei pini
L'odore piu bello,
Piu bello che ci sia,
E qui inginnochio
. . . di un pino io mi metto
A pregare la regina—
La regina delle stelle—
O sia regina della luna
E del sole la prottetrice—
Prottetrice dell' amore
Lo regina dell' aria pura
Che di par bene
Agli infelici
Sempre si chura (cura).' "

I believe that *Montulga* may be the Etruscan *Munthuch*. A *Bellaria* in modern Tuscan tradition is an aerial spirit of grace, and flowers, of which family are Albina, or Alpena, and these are the companions or counterparts of Venus. Of Munthuch I learn from Corssen that the name had also the older form, *Munthu-chā*. "She belongs to the world of plants in spring. In one mirror she dances with a satyr," all of which associates her with fields and forests, "piny grove and shady fountain." If Muntucha be the name, the *l* and *g* come naturally into *Muntulga* in Bolognese.

MUNTHUCHA, OR MONTULGA

TALENA —This is written Salena, I *think*, in the letter in which this spirit is given, but I am altogether uncertain as to the initial. She is thus described :—

"Talena is a female spirit which causes terror in the night. She is clad in white." [1]

---

[1] The manuscript being here illegible it was mislaid, hence a portion is wanting.

BELLARIA

If this name be Talena there is nothing in the description which connects it with that of Talena, or Thalna, of the Etruscans, of whom Gerhard says, "Thalna, and Thalne, and perhaps also *Talena* . . . is on the Etruscan mirrors a goddess," of whom I may briefly say (to condense the mass of authorities whom he cites) has been believed to be a form of Venus, Juno, and Diana, *none* of whom is a nightmare. If it be *Salena* there is no deity known to me with whom she corresponds.

The woman who sent me the information relative to these four spirits, adds in a postscript : " This is all which I have been able to learn from several people." I believe that the information was chiefly, if not all, derived from Volterra, but to what degree I could not verify.

PICO

Of this spirit I am very uncertain, and regarding him I know nothing. I find him entered among notes taken and neglected as " un piccolo spirito colla beretta," a goblin with a cap, probably a form of the Red Caps or House Goblins. He is, almost certainly, the ancient Picus, or red-headed wood-pecker spirit.

Still later, while this work was being printed, I collected, or received in letters, accounts of, or tales relating to, a number of spirits, which, if fully translated, would have made perhaps sixty more pages, for which there is, of course, no space. These were briefly and in part as follows :—

Nurbia e la Pietra di Salute (cf. *Nurbia*, the spirit of disease, who is invoked while preparing the stone of health, or a pebble used to cure rheumatism, &c.).

Lamia, or the serpent-witch. A story and a long poem, now lost, I fear.

La Strega Zumia.

Il prete Stregone Arrimini (" The wizard-priest Arrimini ").

La fata Julda. A tale. Including an account of the three spirits *Trillo, Jullo,* and *Burillo.*

The Witch-spirits Gerda and *Meta.* With a tale.

The Baker Tozzi and his Daughter Fiorlinda. A tale.

La Penna Maligna. An indescribably revolting ceremony with incantation. From Volterra.

La Corda, or the Incantation of the Vintage (Roman Catholic).

To these I may add many poems or ballads all referring to witchcraft, and all, with one exception, as yet unpublished. These would fill about one hundred and fifty pages.

CHAPTER VIII

FLORIA

"Dictes moy, en quel pays,
Est Flora la belle Romaine."

FRANÇOIS VILLON

HIS very curious tale was one of my latest discoveries :—

"This spirit, Floria, was once a fair girl who loved a youth who loved her as well. But Floria had a female friend, and they trusted in and told to one another everything. And Floria did not know that her friend was a witch, or that she loved her own lover and hid it all from her. But it was true, and the witch was very jealous and envious and evil. And so one day when they were walking alone in the country the witch slew Floria, and put on her garments. Then in the evening she came to the lover.

"'Alla sera, 'la sera,
Se presente al giovane
Col nome di Floria,
Essendo una strega.'

(" ' In the evening, the evening,
She came unto the youth,
With the name (form) of Floria,
As a witch she had the power.')

" So the youth married her, and she had a beautiful boy. But one night as the mother held it there came the spirit Floria, who took the child and put it under the bed, and said to the husband —

" ' Guarda che quella non é Floria !
Floria son'io, io sempre,
Quella che tu hai sposato,
E l'amica che m'uccise
Per sposarti, ma guarda
Che a mezza notte ti scappa,
Perche non e che una strega.

(" ' Seest thou that is not Floria—
I am Floria, I ever ;
She there whom thou hast married
Is the evil friend who slew me
That she might marry you ; but watch
Lest she slip away at midnight,
For she is a sorceress truly.')

" And further that if he would slay the witch, she would ever protect him and the babe, and come every night to visit him.

" Then the youth seized the witch by the hair and bound her to the bed, and she howled and blasphemed horribly (from midnight) till three o'clock. Then her witch-power left her, and she became as other women, and said to her husband :—

" ' Look at the baby,
Look in his bed,
There thou wilt find
Crosses and garlands.
It is a year now
He has been enchanted.'

" Then (the husband) gave her a blow with a hammer and slew her, so that she died. And from this time he always loved the spirit of Floria."

In this tale, which was collected and sent to me by Peppino, it is properly Floria who gives the blow with the hammer, and it is evident that Floria is the real mother of the child, and that the witch came after the marriage in the wife's form. Floria—Flora—was certainly equivalent with Horta, who in Etruscan times was one with Nortia—Fortuna—who drove the nails of Fate. I forget now whether it is in the work of Inghirami or that of Eduard Gerhard that she is twice depicted as holding a hammer. Padre Secchi follows Müller (*Etrusker*, iii. 3, 7) in declaring that Horta, an Etruscan goddess, equivalent to Salus, gave name to Orte, and that she is distinct from Nortia, or Fortuna, the great goddess of Volsinii. "A distinction between her and Fortuna is indicated by Tacitus" (*vide* Dennis, *Cities of Etruria*, vol. i., p. 140 in note). But these very objections prove that Nortia of the hammer was regarded as one with Horta by many. And this legend of Peppino agrees curiously with it. Dennis suggests that Horta was a goddess of gardens, therefore a synonyme with Flora. Pomona was also a form of Flora, and in her legend, by a strange change, it is not the witch who takes a female form, but Vertumnus who appears to her as an old woman. Confused as all this seems, I believe this legend to be ancient or classic. But it is very significant indeed that on Etruscan vases the hammer specially occurs as the implement of death in the hands of the equivalent of Nemesis, as in this tale. It is, in fact, the invariable symbol of death, and is in the hands of Charun and all the demons. Lanzi gives a beautiful female spirit holding it.

The crosses and garlands alluded to, refer to the "*guirlanda delle strege*," or Witches' Ladder, elsewhere described.

RA

I am indebted to Mrs. Hayllar for the information that there is a spirit named *Ra,* who is much talked of in Volterra. I had not far to go for knowledge as to this *folletto,* for the first native of the town, a young shoemaker, who was questioned on the subject, at once narrated the following :—

"Ra is a spirit who protects children. When they are in danger the parents apply to him, and *li incanta*, charm him with these words :—

"'Dormi, dormi bambino mio !
Dormi il sonno degli angioli,
Quando tu ti sveglierai,
La felicita riaquisterai.'

("'Sleep, sleep, my little one !
Sleep the sleep of angels,
When thou shalt awaken
Thou shalt be happy again.')

"Then the child will awake free from pain or trouble, secured from all danger, especially from that of falling into the *balze* (precipices, subterranean pits or cavities) of San Giosto in Volterra.

"This spirit Ra was known in Volterra in the year 1001, for just in that year he protected a little child which had been enchanted to him, which fell from a height of several yards in the *balze*, but upon a pile of broom-plant (*ginestra*). Then the peasants came running to save him, but he kept crying, ' Ra! Ra! ' and when they had let him down a ladder, he would not climb it. And while they stood above there came a strange signore, who said : ' Ye cannot save him ; I only can do it by supernatural power. I am the spirit *Ra*, and now ye shall see how I will effect it.'

" Saying this, he stamped thrice on the ground, when there rose a great mass of broom-plants growing, by means of which, as from branch to branch of a tree, they descended and brought up the child."

I am indebted to Professor Senator Comparetti for the suggestion that Ra may be *Rhea Sylvia*. The Etruscans made all their deities male and female. Rhea Cybele, the wife and sister of Cronos, and mother of Jupiter, was specially the patroness of ravines, cliffs, and rocks (*Die Götter und Heroen. von Stoll*). And it is as at home in ravines that Ra appears. Rhea was also a nursing goddess, or protector of children. The change of sex is of no consequence, for, as we have seen, Cupra and Siera have changed theirs, and this was even commoner of yore. In the story Ra raises a poor child from an abyss by means of the broom-plant, and it is a curious coincidence that Deus exaltat humiles (God exalteth the lowly) was always in the Middle Ages the motto accompanying the *ginestra*, both being worn by Louis the Pious of France in 1234 (Helyot. *Description of knightly and monkish orders*. German version, 1756).

BOVO

" Come conosci tu Buovo? Mi sapresti dare notizia alcuna di esso ?"—*I Reali di Francia.*

It is an extraordinary fact that one may ask a hundred peasants or other humble folk in Tuscany for mythical folk-lore and not find a trace thereof, and then meet with one who would seem to be the chronicler, or keeper of a museum of such curiosities. This is just the same among American Red Indians, and it was explained to me in Florence, as it had been in America, by the fact that in certain families only are such records preserved. Thus, while my very intelligent friend, Signora la Marchesa di T., could not by the most masterly and adroit cross-questioning elicit from her maid, who was of Volterra, the least indication of any knowledge of such things as sorcery or spirits, I, on the contrary, got from the young shoemaker of that ancient *ville* much that was marvellous, and, thereamong, the following relative to the spirit Bovo :—

" Volterra was not the first name of our city, for that was Antona, the second Voltona, and the third Volterra. In the time when it was called Antona there lived a prince called Bovo di Antona, who was held by the people to be a *stregone*, or wizard; they also said he was immensely rich, because he had made a golden chariot with four horses of gold, and when in his last illness he reclined (*si fece adagiare*) in it, and there died after long suffering. And when dead, his spirit appeared and ordered that they should set in motion the grand carriage bearing his body, and going forth from Volterra unto a mountain called Chatini (Catini), which is in sight of the city, there bury him. This was done, and the people believe that the chariot and the body of the king still exist. For there have been many excavations in which they have found relics of ancient days recording the epoch of this Bovo di Antona, and in recent times they found, *le sue carte*, his records with pictures representing his age (*raffiguranti i medesimi tempi*), but they have not found as yet the great chariot.

"After this burial the spirit of Bovo returned at night to his palace, which he adorned with all possible magnificence, and illuminated brilliantly.[1] And all the multitude seeing this illumination and festival could not imagine what it meant, knowing that the prince Bovo was alone. But one evening certain bold spirits among them, moved by curiosity, knocked at the gate, but there was no reply. After midnight they heard merry laughter, and then they knocked again, when the gate opened by magic, but in an instant all was dark, and the people entering found all things as they had been in the time of the late king's life.

"Then they knew not what had become of all that splendour which they had seen from the outside, and concluded it must be done by the spirit of Bovo. So it was decided that the boldest four among them should remain there the following night, which they did. And at midnight all the carpets and tapestries began to wave and move, and all the furniture changed into objects of great value. Then they decided to invoke the spirit of Bovo, which being done, he appeared, wrapped in a great white cloak, and when asked what he required" (*i.e.*, what made him restless and haunt the palace), " replied :—

"'Never having been loved by woman in all my life, I wish that this palace shall be inhabited by a beautiful girl, to whom I will appear as a beautiful youth. Should my subjects not succeed in finding such a *bella donna*, then I shall be confined in this palace, disturbing the peace of the citizens. But if it should be done, in recompense I will appear to him who brought it to pass. At midnight he may invoke the spirit of Bovo and I will ever aid to do him good.'"

This is evidently only the beginning of a legend. Buovo of Antona as a hero of popular romance is well known. There are poems on him, and Reiner has written a monograph on the subject, showing that he was one of the champions of Christendom, and, in fact, our old friend Bevis of Southampton. But I suspect that in this particular case a local *folletto* with a similar name has borrowed the fame of the mediæval hero. For, having read the popular romance of *Buovo di Antona*, which forms the fourth part, or 142 pages, of the *Reali di Francia* (Florence, 1890), I find that there is not in it *a single point* of resemblance to the hero of this story, and that, far from having lived unloved, the champion wooed and wedded the beautiful Drusiana, who died of grief for him forty days after his death. The only Antona recognised in the chronicle is very evidently the seaport of Southampton in England, founded by Bovetto and named after his queen, *Librantona*.

---

[1] The sequel indicates that this was only done temporarily, by magic illusion or glamour.

ATTILIO

Attilio, Atiglio, Ottilio or Tilio—for I cannot quite determine his name—is a *buon folletto*—a merry devil, very much the same as *Dusio*, or a jolly Brownie in English folk-lore. But he is an awful tease, especially of servant-girls, to whom, however, he makes love and with whom he behaves quite like Dusio, sharing their couch, and in grateful return doing all the housework for them, and making them no end of presents. And it must be reluctantly admitted that despite his immoral character Attilio is very popular with them.

GUISEPPE PITRÉ, who certainly cannot be accused of credulity remarks (*Bib.*, vol. xviii., p. 163), that if we listen to what people of the lower class relate, in all honesty, we must remain uncertain whether these men and women are a prey to continual visions, or whether we ourselves are dreaming with our eyes wide open. For my own part, I firmly believe that in very credulous communities there are people, especially girls, who honestly believe that they see, and sometimes hear and touch, supernatural beings. There are powers latent in us of which we have no comprehension whatever, and one of these is that of creating sensations, that is of reproducing or forming from Memory any sensations, be they of touch or taste, which we have once experienced.

Unless this be true, I absolutely cannot explain many things which I met with among the believers in all these marvels. The *strege*, with all their tricks, believe in their own art, and carry fetishes. And that there are girls who have Attilios and Dusios, and people who catch glances of Faflon in the vineyards at sunset and in the wine cellar at midnight, cannot be denied. So all life is for them a fine-land fairyland, or a witch and devil dream, according to their disposition or freedom from dyspepsia.

The following is the history and mystery of ATTILIO, as it was narrated to me on the 1st of January, 1891, by a Maddalena from Rocca Casciano :—

"Attilio is a good goblin, but he does everything he can think of to worry servant-girls. There was once a very pretty one, but she had harsh and exacting *padroni* " (superiors—master or mistress). "Well, it happened that every day for three days, when the poor girl had cooked the dinner, and gone to spread the table, she found on returning that all the food had been overturned and scattered about. The maid wept bitterly, but she did not know what to do. *Was she scolded?*—indeed she was, till she was almost mad.

"But when the dinner was ruined on the third day in the same manner, the master and mistress were *tutti arrabiati*. Then they said that they were tired of going out to the *trattoria* to dinner, and that she must do the best she could *a rifare* to dress up the remains. So she went into the kitchen, sorrowfully enough, and felt more sorrowful still when she looked over the wreck, and saw how little could be made of it. When all at once she heard the sweetest voice close by her sing these words :—

" ' Dimmi a me Attilio,
  Se ami Attilio,
  Perche se mi ami,
  Il pranzo sara gia pronto.'

" And as she stood amazed and speechless, lo there stood before her the most beautiful young fellow she had ever seen in all her life. He was dressed in old style with long stockings, and velvet tunic, with long curling golden locks and a little velvet cap with a white feather, and the maid felt as if she could fall down and worship him, he was so elegant and stylish." And what he sang was in English :—

" ' Say you love Attilio,
  For his love is steady,
  And if you will love me
  Dinner shall soon be ready.'

" To which the girl, quite enraptured, could only answer, ' Si—si—yes, indeed ! ' Then Attilio sang :—

" ' Attilio son io,
  Ed io' bisogna d'amare
  E tu sei quella,
  Chi mi ai ispirato
  Tanto amore.'

(" ' I am Attilio,
  My heart for love doth call ;
  And thou art the beauty
  Who inspired it all.')

" You may suppose that the girl was pleased. And he sang on :—

" ' Si ti amo
  E ti amo tanto ;
  Siei tu mi ami
  Sono Attilio.
  E sono un spirto folletto ! '

(" ' If thou wilt love me
  I'll come at thy call ;
  All because I love thee,
  For I am Attilio,
  The merriest sprite of all.')

" When lo ! at a touch the dinner was all right again, and when the girl served it the *padroni* said they had never enjoyed such a nice meal. And every day Attilio did most of the work and was always with her, and she could see him though he was invisible to every one else."

It is remarkable that while in all the Oriental and German or French mediæval tales it is a knight or favoured man who wins the love of a spirit, the Italian rather give the fairy lovers to girls. This is a very curious point in folk-lore.

The Dusio and Faun, and every one of the *prototypes* of Robin Goodfellow and Puck, and the House-Brownie are represented as frolicking sprites, always misleading girls. In the North, under chaster influences, these wanton sprites soon sobered down into very moral beings, not going beyond boyish mischief. But in Italy nothing has changed, and so they still remain the same rogues among the girls which they were even while satyrs hopped about in the woods, and lemures prowled near tombs and witches took out men's hearts—and people were all so happy!

Attilio is certainly here a *lar familiaris*, a spirit of the fireplace, a sprite who ever since the days of Tarquin and Tanquil has seduced the servant-maid in Tuscan families, even as he seduced Ocris, "she who waited on the table" of yore He is in the kitchen and he cooks the dinner, and is altogether of the fireplace Of his existence I have but a single authority or witness. He corresponds altogether to the French *Lutin*.

LA BELLA MARTA

(*La Madre del Giorno, or Mother of the Day*)

" Nam et Romulus post mortem Quirinus factus est, et Leda Nemesis, et Circe Marica, et Ino, postquam se precipitavit in Mare, Lucothea, Mater que Matuta."—LACTANTIUS, *Div. Institut. de falsa Religione*, lib. i., cap. 21

By far the most prominent character in the popular mythology of Tuscany, or of that which is not Catholic, is *La bella Marta*, also called *Madre del Giorno*, or the Mother of the Day. I was at first misled by the name into believing that it was Saint Martha confused, as are Saints Antony and Simeon, with old heathen deities. But I soon found that she had nothing in common with the Martha of the Bible, nor the one of Roman Catholic hagiology whose image conquering the Tarascon I copied in the cloister at Arles in 1846. I have, indeed, very little doubt that this beautiful Martha is a transformation of the ancient *Mater Matuta*, in which I am guided not so much by the resemblance of *name* as by the fact that she has as *Beinahme*, or attribute, that of *del giorno*, " of the day."

" There was," writes MÜLLER, "in the haven Pyrgoi, the great and richly endowed temple of a goddess who was generally called by the Greeks Leukothea. . . . It was doubtless the honoured *Mater Matuta*, worshipped since the time of Servius in Rome in the Volscican land and also in Etruria. The Greek and Roman antiquaries classed the two as one. However, in Rome this Mater Matuta was regarded much more as a goddess of the morning than as of the sea, for her name clearly means *the Mother of the Day*, and when the Greeks translated it to Leukothea, or white goddess, they may have thought more of early morning light than on the white foam of the sea. The mother of the light of day could readily be regarded as the deity which led man to daylight ; for which reason, as it would appear, STRABO called her Eileithyia. According to this the goddess of Pyrgoi was one of the dawn, and of mankind."

The Bella Marta of Tuscany dwells in forests or fields, and, though a spirit of the day, is worshipped by night. This, however, is to be explained by the fact that all "spirits" are connected with the old religion, now called witchcraft, and that its rites are conducted in secrecy and obscurity. Martha is favourable to lovers and conjugal love. The following incantation, which tells its own story, indicates clearly as can be the fact that the sylvan gods are still literally worshipped like saints, and are not merely evoked like goblins. A wife or girl who is jealous of her lover goes by night to the most beautiful garden to which she has access, and kneeling pronounces—

THE PRAYER TO LA BELLA MARTA

"Bella Marta! Bella Marta! Bella Marta!
Tu sei bella come una stella,
Io ti vengo a rimirare,
E da te mi vengo ad inginnochiare
Per poter ti meglio pregare.
La mezza notte e ora suonata,
E da te sono inginnochiata,
In mezzo ad un bel giardino,
Che tu Marta Bella ne sei regina,
Io ti porto un fazzoletto
In una punta troverai,
I capelli del mio amor
E tu bella Marta fannecio
Che vuoi, purche il mio bene
Tu faccia tribolare,
E mio marito tu lo faccia diventare,
E che altra donna non possa mai amare :
Se questa grazia mi farai,
Tutte le sere una candela
Accesa tu l'avrai,
Questa grazia certo tu mi ai fatto,
Bella Marta ti ringrazio ;

In English :—

"Beautiful Martha! Beautiful Martha! Beautiful Martha
Thou art beautiful as a star.
I come to behold you once more,
Once more to kneel before you,
That I may adore you better.
Midnight has struck,
I am kneeling before you ;
Kneeling in a fair garden,
Where thou, beautiful Martha, art queen.
I bring thee a handkerchief ;

In a corner thou wilt find
The hairs of my beloved,
And thou, oh Martha, cause
What thou wilt that my trouble may pass to my good,
Cause him to marry me,
May he never love other women ;
Grant me this grace,
And thou shalt have
Every evening a lighted candle.
This thou wilt surely grant me,
Beautiful Martha, I thank thee ! "

In the next incantation *La bella Marta* is distinctly invoked from hell. I do not think that she is at all popularly regarded as infernal or evil, but that this was done to distinctly distinguish her from the *saints*—a matter which is strictly observed among the sorcerers. And as the priests have always taught the people that *all* spirits not sanctioned by the Church are devils, it indicates great constancy to the customs of their ancestors that the peasants continue to adore them even as infernal.

THE INVOCATION TO LA BELLA MARTA BY NIGHT

" For this you should go into a wood or forest at midnight and look at a star, and say :—

" ' Buona notte o Donna Marta,
Non chiamo la Marta di casa del Paradiso,
Ma chiamo quella di casa dell' inferno.
Prenditi dei panni belli
Alla presenza de . . .
Prima mi era tanto amico,
Ora mi e tanto nemico,
Amici e nemici,
Tutti gli sembrino brutta gente,
Fuor che io la sua stella rilucente,
A stella stella da levante oscie,
Da lui portante :
Cinque dita per lui io batto al muro.
Cinque anime io scongiuro,
Cinque preti, cinque frati,
Cinque anime dannate,
All anima, alla vita
Del tal. . . .
In vita ne anderete,
In pensiero la porterete,
Per la barba e capelli lo piglierete,
Col pensiero da me la strascinerete ;
Se questo mi farete,
Tre segni mi darete,

Porta picchiare,
Cane abbiare,
Unno fistiare ;
Se questo mi farai,
Tre segni mi darai ! ' "

Or in English :—

" Good evening, O Lady Martha ;
I do not call thee Martha called of heaven,
I call upon the Martha named of hell.
Take these fine cloths
In the presence of . . . (here the name is given).
Once he was so much my friend,
Now he is so much my foe :
May enemies and friends
All seem the same to him
Save me, his shining star.

I beat five fingers for him on the wall,
Five souls do I conjure,
Five priests, five friars,
Five damned souls,
Into the soul, into the life
Of . . .
May they pass into the life !
Bear this into his thoughts,
Drag him by beard and hair,
Drag him by remembrances of me !
If you will do this for me,
Three signs you will give me—
A knocking at the door,
A dog barking,
A man whistling.
Should'st thou favourable be,
These three signs thou'lt grant to me ! "

This is considered as a very serious, terrible, and powerful incantation or imprecation. The looking steadily at a star connects Martha apparently with Mater Matuta or Leucothea, the goddess of light, and Marta of the Day, for this star I suppose is Venus or the Morning Star. There is a portion of this incantation which occurs in others. This is the invoking several *fives* of priests and devils to enter into the soul and life of the one banned. This, both as regards a category of numbers and calling on the spirits to enter into the life and soul and body of some one, corresponds precisely to what is found in Chaldæan spells.

A Paracelsian, or almost any writer of the sixteenth century, would have recognised in this regarding the star an invocation of the astral spirit, especially as it is mysteriously connected with ordering spirits to *possess* a certain person. I do not doubt that there are in it strange relics of ancient beliefs; one thing is certain, it is regarded as very powerful by the witches, who recite it with deep feeling. And it is remarkable how passionately this witch spirit manifests itself when seriously relating spells or even while writing them down.

Bella Marta appears in one narrative as one of the benevolent witches of Benevento, and also as a dryad.

BELLA MARTA AND THE YOUNG CONTADINO

"Once there was in Benevento a great tree—*o sia una quercia*—probably an oak, in which there was a cavity. The peasants passing by it often saw a very beautiful woman, who disappeared they knew not where.

"But there was one young man who, moved by curiosity, said: 'I will come here early, and I will follow the lady, and find out where she dwells.' So he went to the wood, and quietly waited till she appeared, and then went after her till she came to the great oak and entered it as if it were a door.

"And then he also stepped in after, and lo, he found himself in a great and splendid palace! One might have walked three days in it from room to room without entering a new one—*camminando tre giorni, non si sarebbe mai finito di girare*—and all of marvellous beauty.

> "And so the peasant stood amazed,
> As on the wondrous scene he gazed,
> When entering the oak-tree there,
> He found a palace wondrous fair:
> He knew not where to turn his feet,
> To forward go or back retreat——

"When all at once a small white hand was laid on his shoulder, and a soft sweet voice was heard saying, 'Welcome!' And turning, he saw the beautiful lady of the forest whom he had followed, and she said: 'Be not afraid, I welcome thee, and will make thee happy, for thou art a good youth. And I am the Bella Marta. Go thou and play, and always win, and when thou wilt have anything, pronounce this spell:—

> "'Bella Marta! bella Marta! bella Marta!
> Sei più bella d'una santa
> Al albero tuo vengo a pregare,
> Se una grazia mi vuoi fare,
> Se questa grazia mi farai,
> La mia padrona tu sarai,
> Qualunque casa mi chiederai,
> Bella Marta tu l'avrai.'

> "'Lovely Martha, this I vow,
> Fairer than any saint art thou.
> Here I stand before thy tree,
> Grant, I pray, a grace to me,

And thou my patron ever shalt be,
And if there's aught beneath the sun
Which I can do, it shall be done
For thee, thou ever lovely one.'

" *Qalunque.cosa mi chiederai—bella Marta tu l'avrai.* So, whenever you see a great oak in the forest, and repeat to it this incantation, you will do well."

Here Marta is unquestionably a dryad, and the *contadino* is RHŒCUS. Rhœcus was a great player—it was because he was absorbed in a game of draughts that he beat the bee who told the nymph who blinded the boy who cut down the tree which fell on the youth who had such a passion for gambling.

This may be all guess-work and pot-shot hunting or point-blank firing, but here in Tuscany the spirit of the olden time is still alive, and I am writing in sight of olive-trees and crumbling towers of the Middle Ages, and these stories of Rhœcus and the fair Martha, and the mystic oak, seem, I will not say more credible, but more connected and intelligible than they would in the North.

In the year 1846, in Florence, an English gentleman who had passed most of his life in Italy, consulted me gravely and seriously as to what numbers of several which he had chosen would win in a lottery. This spirit of play and chance and of inspiration connected with it enters deeply here into all Italian life, as it did of yore. Therefore I am not astonished that it was the first thought of the beautiful nymph. She knew her man.

It is worth noting that in Sicily the Mother of Light is invoked when salt is spilt (PITRÉ, *Bib.*, vol. iv., p. 144)—

" Matri di lu lumi, cugghitivillu vui."

La bella Marta is invoked when three girls, always stark-naked, consult the *taróco*, or cards, to know whether a lover is true or who shall be married. This is, indeed, connected with the two incantations already given. According to PITRÉ, Saint Martha is one of those who are sometimes consulted in sorcery. Thus Archbishop TORRES (*Ricordi di Confessori*, &c. ; PITRÉ, *Bib.*, vol. iv., p. 148) excommunicates " those who utter prayers which are not approved, or even disapproved of by the Holy Church, to bring about lascivious and dishonest love, and such are the prayers falsely attributed to Saint Daniel, Saint *Marta*, Saint Helena, and the like." The Mater Matuta, or Mother of the Dawn—that is, Venus—may very well have been the patroness of lovers and the *Donna del Giorno*, but it is difficult to connect the Martha of the Bible or the Provencal conqueror of the Tarascon with any such aiding and abetting of amours (to say nothing of card-playing or divination) as we find in this Queen of Beauty and Fortune-telling.

As regards the *three* girls meeting to divine who shall be married, I think it is DION CASSIUS who remarks as regards divination by means of ashes, "Vel cum aliquem tres personas cogitare jubet, quibuscum matrimonii inire optet, tum tres ducunt sulcos in cinere" ("When three meet to find out whom they are to marry, they draw three lines in the ashes"). This confirms in the main the antiquity of the rite. The reader will find more as regards this in the chapter on Divination by Ashes.

It may be observed that in the last incantation Bella Marta is addressed as being "fairer than *any* saint." Here the Romagnola *stregeria*, or witchcraft, which is utterly heathen and always jealous of Roman Catholic influence, shows itself.

The festivals of the Mater Matuta, which were widely spread in Italy, were called *Matralia* or Martralia, may give some clue to the modern name of Marta. But I repeat here that I at first attached no significance to the resemblance of the word Martha or Marta to *Mater*, though there is absolutely no reason why it may not have been derived from the latter, just as "pattering," or talking slang has been conjectured to have come from *pater* in the *paternoster*. But I have since found that M. L. F. Alfred Maury, in *Les Fées du Moyen Age*, had the same idea as to a perfectly analogous conception. He writes :—

"Les epithetes données sans cesse aux fées, sont celles de bonnes, bonnes dames, bonnes et franches pucelles. Ces qualifications ne sont évidemment que la traduction du titre de *bonæ* donné aux parques, plutôt sans doute par anti phrase que par reconnaissance, et de *puellæ* attribué aussi bien aux nymphes qu'aux fata. Le nom de *Matte* donné à une fée célèbre d'Eauze, pour laquelle on avait reproduit la fable du Minotaure, semble venir du mort *mater* abrégé."

On this name Fraser (*The Etruscans*) has the following :—

"Max Müller also speculates (*Science of Languages*, vol. ii., p. 152) on the derivation of *mane* and *matutæ*. He says : ' From this it would appear that in Latin the root *man*, which in the other Aryan languages is best known in the sense of thinking, was at a very early time put aside, like the Sanskrit *budh*, to express the revived consciousness of the whole of Nature at the approach of the light of the morning, unless there was another totally distinct root peculiar to Latin expression of that idea.'"

Was this root possibly *mat?* It is worth observing that Tertullian observes that the Etruscan Venus was called *Murtia* (*vide* Dennis, *Cities of Et.*, vol. i., p. 58). And as Bella Marta is called the most beautiful of the spirits, is associated with cards, and is identified with the morning star, it seems probable that she is a form of Aphrodite or Venus.

DIANA AND HERODIAS

(The Queens of the Witches in Italy)

" Horsù dimmi, o buona Strega, che vuoi dire che non andavi a questi balli e giuochi di Diana o di Herodiade, ovvero sì come le chiamate, a quelli de la Donna ? "—*La Strega di Pico della Mirandola.*

" Hecate trium potestatum numen est. Ipsa est enim Luna, Diana Proserpina."—SERVIUS.

It is remarkable that while witchcraft was regarded in later times among Northern races as a creation of Satan, it never lost in Italy a classic character. In this country the witch is only a sorceress, and she is often a beneficent fairy. Her ruler is not the devil, but DIANA, with whom, as I shall show, there is associated HERODIAS. The latter, as presiding at the dances of the witches, was naturally connected with the Herodias of the New Testament, but there was an older Herodias, a counterpart of Lilith, the first wife of Adam, by whom she became the mother of all the minor devils or goblins.

It is evident that in this capacity Herodias was confused with Diana. The latter had been as Hecate the ruler of all the witches, while Lilith-Herodias was the same among the Jews. There is a passage in Odericus Vitalis (born in England in 1075—*Hist. Eccl.* v. 556) which illustrates this, that Diana was parent or protectress of goblins. It is as follows :—

" Deinde Taurinus fanum Dianæ intravit. Zabulon que coram populo visibilem adstare coegit, quo viso ethnica plebs valde timuit. Nam manifeste apparuit eis æthiops niger et fuligo, barbam habens prolixam et scintillas igneas ex ore mittens. . . . Dæmon adhuc in eadem urbe degit et in variis frequenter formis apparens, neminem laedit. Hanc vulgus Gobelinum appellat."

("Then Taurinus entered the temple of Diana and compelled Zabulon to appear visibly before the people, who, being seen, was greatly dreaded by the heathen folk. For he plainly showed himself as a black, grimy Ethiopian, having a full beard and emitting sparks of fire from his mouth. The demon went forth often in the same town, appearing in many forms, yet injured no one. The common people called him *Goblin*, and declare that by the merits of Saint Taurinus he was withheld from doing harm.")

Here we have the Goblin as the familiar spirit of the temple of Diana, the witch-mother, just as the Jews declared that goblins were the children of Lilith-Herodias. How it was that the Shemitic myth came to unite with the Graeco-Roman is a matter for investigation. That it existed is proved by the testimony of several old writers.

In the *Dæmonomagie* of HORST (1818), a writer who was far beyond his time, I find the following :—

" In the indictments of witches it is generally stated that ——, the party accused, acted with " (worshipped) " Diana and Herodias. It is very remarkable that we find this among the declarations of public Church council—that of Ancyra in the middle of the fifth century—just as in later witch-trials. It was asserted that certain women imagined that they flew by night through the air with *Diana* and *Herodias*. But as this was spoken of at the Council of Ancyra as a well-known thing, the belief must be much older, and I do not doubt that there exist much earlier historical records of this, which are unknown to me."

PAULUS GRILLANDUS, in his *Treatise on Witches* (1547), a great authority in its time, speaks several times to the same effect, that witches—*putant Dianam et Herodiam esse veras deas*—" think that Diana and Herodias are true goddesses, so deeply are they involved in the error of the pagans." And he deduces all the evil of their ways from this false and heathenish beginning—*ex qua omnes alii errores et illusiones successive dependent cum credant illas Dianam et Herodiadem esse veras deas*. In which he very inconsistently ignores the fact that he has elsewhere declared Satan to be sole master of the entire sisterhood.

JEROME CARDANUS (*De Subtilitate,* l. 19), in describing an altogether diabolical evocation by a sorcerer of his time (*Quoties veneficus ille rem non divinam sed diabolicam facturus esset*) says no word of the devil whatever, but represents Hecate, or Diana, as the leading spirit (*Execratur illis precibus, Hecate dictante, primum adorandam,* &c.). That Diana-Hecate was Queen of the witches in classic times is known from many authors ; also that she was invoked in all *chthonic*, dark, or nocturnal sorcery. She was compared, as the goddess of the moon, to a cat which chases the star-mice. Herein she was like Bast of Bubastis, the cat-goddess of Egypt ; and Freya, of the North, whose car is drawn by cats, is clearly a Norse Diana. What is remarkable, and to my purpose, is that while witches in Italy are supposed to do harm like Canidia of yore, they do it simply as *sorceresses*. The Catholic Church imposed on the popular belief in witchcraft much that was foreign to it, in Christian diabolism, and yet it is most remarkable that even to-day Diana, and not Satan, is the leader and ruler of Italian witches.

And there are many points in this popular belief which are much more ancient than Christianity. Thus in Venice, as in Florence, witchcraft is not at all a result of a compact with the devil, but a peculiar endowment, which may be transferred, even by a trick, to an innocent person. I will illustrate this with a story which I heard told in good faith in 1886 as having happened in Florence, and which has already appeared in my book on *Gypsy Sorcery :*—

"There was a girl here in the city who became a witch against her will. And how ? She was ill in a hospital, and by her in a bed was *una vecchia ammalata gravamente, e non poteva morire*—an old woman seriously ill, yet who could not die. And the old woman groaned and cried continually, ' *Oimé! muoio!*

A chi lasciò? Non diceva che' ('Alas, I die! To whom shall I leave——') But she did not say *what.* Then the poor girl, thinking, of course, she meant property, said : '*Lasciate à me—son tanto povera!*' ('Leave it to me—I am so poor'). At once the old woman died, and *la povera giovana se è trovato in eredita della streghoneria* (the poor girl found she had inherited witchcraft).

"Now the girl went home to where she lived with her mother and brother. And having become a witch, she began to go out often by night ; which the mother observing, said to her son : '*Qualche volta tu troverai tua sorella colla pancia grassa*' ('Some day you will find your sister with child'). 'Don't think such a thing, mamma,' he replied. 'However, I will find out where it is she goes.'

"So he watched, and one night he saw his sister go out of the door *sullo punto della mezza-notte* (just at midnight). Then he caught her by the hair and twisted it round his arm. She began to scream terribly, when—*ecco !*—there came running a great number of cats (*e cominciarono à miolare, e fare un gran chiasso*) they began to mew and make a great row, and for an hour the sister struggled to escape, but in vain, for her hair was fast, and screamed, while the cats screeched, till it struck one, when the cats vanished, and the *sorella* was insensible. But from that time she had no witchcraft in her and became a *buona donna,* or a good girl—*come era prima*—as she had been before."

There is nothing of a compact with Satan in this—it is a witch of Diana, bound to the spell of the moon, one of the cats of the night. In the Venetian stories a witch loses all her power if she is wounded and spills a drop of blood, or even if detected. It is true enough that the monks imported and *forced* into popular Italian superstition strong infusions of the devil. Yet with all this, in the main, the real Italian witch has nothing to do with Satan or a Christian hell, and remains as of yore a daughter of Diana. There is something almost reviving or refreshing in the thought that there is one place in the world—and that in papal Italy itself—where the poison of diabolism did not utterly prevail.

There are in the treatise on the Magic Walnut Tree of Benevento, by P. Pipernus (Naples, 1647), several passages in reference to Diana as Queen of the Witches, one of which is curious as it seems in a manner to identify Lamia with Lilith and Diana. It is to the effect that the witches who of yore seduced youths to their death, were the same with Lamia—*a Lilith hebraeo,* whence the Empusæ, Marmoliciæ or Lares and Lemures, appearing on one foot in various figures dedicated to Diana—in variis figuris Dianæ dedicatis. But Elias Schedius (see *Dis Germanis,* Amsterdam, 1648), has with great industry brought together from many sources, Hebrew and others, strong proof that Diana was identical with Lilith, the two being identified in the Roman Lucina :—

> " Tu Lucina volentibus
> Juno dicta puerperis
> Dicta lumine Luna."
>
> (*Catullus Epigr.,* 35)

Luna meaning here, Diana.

Another singular remark is to the effect that there were as communities of witches in ancient times the Eriphiæ, from Eriphia, the Michaleiæ, from Michala, Hecateiæ, Medeæ Circeæ, Thessalæ, in Sicilia Cyclopas Lestrygonas and Herodiades—"communiori vocabulo in aliquibus regionibus nuncupantur ex Idumæa *Herodiade* prope Jordani flumen habitante, choreis, ludisque venereis effuse fruente, quæ multos et multas ad suum convictum trahebat, Dianæ ludorum memorans." In another passage Pipernus conjectures that there was a Herodias earlier than the one who was the cause of the death of Saint John.

In the Slavonian spells and charms, which are generally very ancient, and of Oriental origin, Lilith appears the same as Herodias. She has twelve daughters who are the twelve kinds of fever. This arrangement of diseases, or evil spirits, into categories of sevens, twelves, &c., is found in the Chaldæan magic as given by Lenormant. All things duly considered, I agree with Pipernus that there was a Herodias long before the lady of the New Testament who danced Herod off his head and the head off Saint John.

In regard to which transaction I marvel that I have never yet seen it treated by any writer from a modern society-Christian practical point of view. Suppose a lady, an intelligent, accomplished widow, who had a good thing of it as wife of the governor-general of—say Cathay. The governor dies and his brother succeeds to the appointment, and marries the widow (a thing actually commanded in the Old Testament, and a common custom in the later time), or it may be the fraternal divorced wife. Uprises a clergyman of a new sect, with eccentric new views, who has tremendous influence among the people, and informs the governor that his marriage is illegal. And then fancy the feelings of Herodias! On one hand, divorce—perhaps death or poverty—with a charming daughter just coming out ; on the other, a prophet of the wildest description. And it was considered to be such a remarkably natural, trifling, and commonplace thing in those days to put anybody to death who was in your way, if you had the power to do it—just as CALVIN did with SERVETUS when the latter got in *his* way, or as some millions of heretics were disposed of—some for their money—by Mother Church. And so Herodias did what I believe a very great majority of worldly-minded High or Low Church Christian matrons and mammas would do to-day under the same circumstances—if they *could*—and put Saint John out of the way.

What I most wonder at in this story is, who *was* this Herodias—what was her blood, what were her "havings," or belongings? There is nothing whatever, after all, in this story of commonplace revenge to account for her being taken up and made to occupy the position of joint-queen with Diana of an immensely widely-spread confederacy of sorcerers and witches. Above all, how came it that her daughter, presumably a Roman or Jewish young lady, who had been respectably brought up, danced a gypsy can-can *pas seul* before Herod and his court? The mediæval writers have it that she "tombelede," or tumbled, *i.e.*, threw flip-flaps, and " made the wheel" (as POCAHONTAS used to do for the common soldiers in Virginia—as I have read), but then they knew nothing about it. Or was she perhaps really one of those Syrian-Hindoo-with-a-touch-of-Persian dancers — actually *gypsies*—who in those days strayed about to every corner of the Roman empire?

There were mixed marriages in those days, even as there are now, and there lives at present in England a lady with a very great title, who was once a dancing Hungarian gypsy. One of these *ballerine* might have wedded Herod's brother. Assuredly the dance which Miss Herodias executed was not the holy *Chagag* which David danced before the Lord (2 Sam. vi.), the sight of which had, however, such an effect on the king's daughter Michal. And yet even the holy *Chagag* was considered a vulgar performance—Princess MICHAL called it shameless—from which we may infer what kind of a wasp or busy-bee performance the after-supper tipsy-chorean bayadere *posing* of Mademoiselle Erodiade must have been! No, it was *not* the *Chagag* which Rabbi DAVID KIMICHI says was danced to the singing of the forty-seventh Psalm, but a very different kind of a gag indeed, and in faster time.

But admitting that there was—'tis a mere conjecture, my cousin—a strain of Syrian-gipsy—witch and devil-blood in these Herodiades—I can well understand how the whole sisterhood of fortune-tellers and sorceresses took up the story, and made the most of it—how one of their kind had bewitched a tetrarch, and played Lola Montez queen in a kind of Hamlet drama.

The dance was in ancient days something so wild and passionate, so bewildering and maddening, that we of the present day can form no conception of its real nature. I can remember when TAGLIONI, and ELLSLER, and CARLOTTA GRISI, and CERITO turned the heads of the world, as no dancer has ever done since. Before them *others* had maddened the multitude still more, so it went back in compound ratio till we come to the witch-times. Now, whether witches and wizards ever practised sorcery or not—whatever that was—one thing is certain, that bands of male and female sinners believing themselves to be inspired by the devil—and I doubt not being very much inclined to raise him in a general way—went forth by moonlight, armed with sundry brooms, divers pitchforks, certain goats, *et cætera*, and did drink, dissipate, and dance all night.

Dance! I should think so! PRÆTORIUS says: "But the dances of the sorcerers make people *mad* and *raging*, so that the women lose the fruit of their bodies." Now it *may* be natural for certain females everywhere in every country to dance naked and mad—even among those in the first court circles—but I must declare that the traditions of antiquity all point to a certain Syrian-Indo-Persian origin for all this. MOSES MAIMOND tells us that when the sun rose the daughters of the ancient Persians danced naked, singing to music. DELANCRE, writing of witches, observed that witches did the same as Persian girls at sacrifices in this respect. Now to this day the dancing women of India and Persia are of common stock and origin. Tradition says that a certain king of India once sent ten thousand dancers and musicians as a present to the king of Persia, and that they all turned out to be irreclaimable vagabonds. And all of these dancers in all times formed a close corporation. It was only professionals who danced. So that, taking everything into consideration, I think it possible, if not probable, that Herodias, mother and daughter, belonged to the very ancient if not honourable company of witches and gypsies, and that their name, while coinciding with that of Herod, had been attached in earlier times to a form of Lilith. And it is not impossible that the chance coincidence of this name of Herodias with that of the earlier witch-queen, had as much to do with raising the Idumean damsel to celebrity among the witches as her share in the decapitation of Saint John. For, justly considered, this latter gives us no reason at all why she should have been preferred to such position, while her bearing such a name would account for it all.

There are many people in Italy, and I have met such, who, while knowing nothing about Diana as a Roman goddess, are quite familiar with her as Queen of the Witches. One day I had brought to me as an invaluable secret of witch-lore something which had been treasured up by the sisterhood for a long time. What was my astonishment to find that it was an old chemical trick, which, discovered by some disciple of Paracelsus or Scheele, became common in books of " natural magic " in the last century, and was familiar to me in my tenth year in the *Boy's Own Book*. This is simply a composition of nitrate of silver and mercury, or silver and mercury in aqua-fortis, which, when put into a flask, causes an incrustation like foliage, whence it is called the Tree of Diana. That name was enough for my innocent witches who, not doubting that it was a deep work of dark magic, had treasured it up accordingly, perhaps for generations, and gave it to me with the superscription : *Albero di Diana—la Mga (magia) delle Streghe* (The Tree of Diana, the magic mistress of the Witches).

On one occasion I was given as a great find in the way of sorcery and witchcraft, some poetry which I soon found consisted of about one hundred and fifty lines from Ariosto. Truly it was full of supernatural diabolical description, but it was not exactly what I wanted. At which my friend who had written it out was very much astonished, declaring that as it was all about supernatural things she thought it must be all right. And—" Dove diavolo avete pigliato tutto questo coglionerie ? " I asked in the words of Cardinal d'Este—" Where didst thou rake out this trash ? "   " *Ma Signore*, I got it from an old woman who had kept it for a long time as *streghoneria*," *i.e.*, magic.

As regards Diana, it may be observed that in the Roman times she was specially worshipped by fugitive slaves, " perhaps because they hid themselves in the forests." Thus it may be that the witches and wizards as outcasts inherited a certain predilection for her. As goddess of secrecy and of sorcery she would also be the patroness of those who shunned the day and intercourse with mankind. Witches, outlaws, broken men, runaway slaves, minions of the moon, and all the Children of the Night were under her protection, and it is pleasant to think that in ages when there was such enormous oppression of the unfortunate, that the victims had, if not a God, at least a goddess to whom they could pray.

OFFERINGS TO SPIRITS

As the same spirits of rock and river, fountain, cavern, and forest, are believed in and invoked as in the earliest Tuscan time, so the same offerings continue to be made to them as of yore. And when asking for information on the subject, I promptly received several explanations or illustrations of what the auditors understood by votive gifts. It must be understood that these differ entirely in spirit and in form from anything which is given to saints.

" Yes. For instance, if a *contadino* passes by a grove or a rock where *folletti* or fairies or spirits live, he will there put into the ground money or pins to please them, and say :—

> " ' Questo lo sotterro
> Per far piacere
> Agli spiriti (o alle strege)
> Che ne potrebbero
> Avere bisogna,
> E così a me
> Pure mi contra,
> Cambierrano
> Colla buona fortuna ! '

> (" ' These things I bury,
> That I may gratify
> Spirits or witches !
> That they may never
> Such things be wanting !
> Or go against me,
> Changing my fortune
> From good unto evil ! ')

" Or it may be that he passes by a fountain or a stream, when he will throw his gift into it and repeat the same words, adapted to it."

But I was further informed on the subject in these words :—

" Offerings to spirits or *folletti ? Si.* When a spirit comes by night into a house and causes much annoyance as a nightmare, sitting on people's breasts, and stifling them, when, if they show fear, the *folletto* will tear all the covering from them, pull them out of bed, and depart with a roar of laughter.

" To prevent this, make him an offering. What he likes best is three sunflowers, laid outside on the window-sill. Then say :—

> " ' Metto questi tre girasoli
> Alla finestra, perche lo spirito
> Non mi venga tormentare,
> Dove si trova il sole a girare,
> Se in casa mia vuol venire,
> Almeno non mi faccia ingrullire,
> La notte in pace mi faccia dormire ! '

> (" ' In the window sunflowers three
> I put ; and may the spirit be
> Here no longer to torment me,
> And with that I will content me,
> If so long as the sun goes round
> He may ne'er in my house be found ;
> Let at least his troubling cease,
> So that I may sleep in peace ! ')

" And when this is done and said, the spirit will cease from troubling—*non potra più darle noia*—and the weary will be at rest."

The next illustration is very curious :—

" Sometimes goblins and witches meet in groves or gardens, and should any one care to know who or what they are, let him watch from a window at midnight. And he will see forms assembling under the trees, with one who is *capo*, or their head, who gives orders. If they appear in human forms they are spirits who pass freely as they will, and therefore remain as they are. But if they are witches and wizards, they come in the shapes of goats, kids, moles, or other animals, because when they leave their homes they also leave their human forms asleep in their beds, even to their shirts, and so must assume the appearance of or become animals.

" Now, these witches do much harm by pulling up plants and breaking boughs to make beds for their love-making, and so the *contadini*, or the owners of the gardens or groves, spread hay or leaves or herbs as an offering, and say while so doing :—

> " ' Questa erba fresca per terra
> Voglio spandere perche le strege
> Vengono a riposare coll'amante.'

> (" ' I lay this grass upon the ground,
> So that if witches here are found
> They may comfortably rest,
> Each with him whom she likes best.')

" And this is the power which they have, that if they assume the form of goats, they can take people who are not witches, be they gentle or simple, in their sleep, away to their witch-meetings, and so they choose the most beautiful youths and girls to make love with. Now, among the wizards and witches are even princes and princesses, who, to conceal their debauchery and dishonour, take the goat form and carry away partners for the dance, bearing them on their backs ; and so they fly many miles in a few minutes, and go with them to distant cities or other places, where they feast, drink, dance, and make love. But when dawn approaches they carry these partners home again, and when they awake they think they have had pleasant dreams. But indeed their diversion was more real than they suppose.

" But if they look about they will always find in their room some money, be it copper or silver, for this witch-money must always be paid. And when they find it, or any pins or needles, they ought to cast them all into a running river or current, for thus they will be freed (revenged on *potrebbe essere vendetta*) from witchcraft."

The object of laying sunflowers on the window-sill, according to ancient symbolism, is to detect or find out the offender ; that is to signify to him that he is found out or known. Thus, in accordance with this, ALBERTUS MAGNUS informs us that if any man has been robbed, if he will sleep with sunflowers under his pillow, he will dream who was the thief. For it is an emblem of the sun which shines on—that is, who sees and searches out—all things. And as an image of the day it frightens away spirits of darkness.

The third illustration, while it apparently flies wide of the mark, is extremely valuable in really explaining one reason at least why coins and pins are thrown into fountains. And it is of very great importance as casting quite a new light on the cause of the transformation of witches into animals. For in all the many works which I have read on witchcraft I do not remember to have seen it explained why witches assume the shapes of animals. According to this probably ancient theory, their bodies—as BAPTISTA PORTA and many more believed—remain asleep while the soul goes forth, or else the witch-ride is only dreamed. According to my Romagnola authority, the witch-soul, for want of a better shape, enters into some animal.

And yet further. In the works of PRÆTORIUS and others I have met with mention of people who had often gone on goats to the Sabbat and returned, yet who had never been wizards or witches. There is a story in several books of a man who said he was wicked enough to have done so several times in his youth, but who had discontinued the practice. I confess that this puzzled me much, and often till I heard this explanation of it. Those who took the goat-ride were not wizards, but the mere dupes or victims of the *stregoni*. Still, they had enjoyed the frolic, and were willing to have such dreams again. What the basis for it all was I do not know, but incline to think that persons, while under the influence of opiates or narcotics, were taken to wild-dances, then dosed again and taken home, as happened to the shoemaker described by Shakespeare.

CHAPTER IX

Il Spirito del Scaldino

URING the reign of Charles the Second it was often said in England that the women of Holland became pregnant simply from their habit of carrying and keeping under their petticoats a small receptacle, or hand-stove, in which burning charcoals were placed. These hand-stoves, made of wood and tin, may still be seen among market - women in Philadelphia. The result of such pregnancy was a small elf or goblin, that is, a strange little creature of flesh and blood.

In Italy women carry a *scaldino*, a receptacle exactly in the form of a basket, but made of glazed earthenware. It is filled with ashes and charcoal, and is so common that there are as many of them in Italy as there are inhabitants—at least, in the north. And as they are very often put under the garments next to the body, it is not remarkable that the idea that the very agreeable warmth would be impregnating should have occurred. It was known in earliest times, and Spenser has told us in the "Faerie Queene" how a beautiful lady, falling asleep, was exposed to the rays of the sun, which, entering her person, caused her to bear a child.

The Tuscan, more poetical or more classically-minded than the Dutchman, believes that the hand-stove makes the *donna incinta*, or *enceinte*, but with a *folletto* or pretty airy fairy, the rule of whose life is "light come, light go," since it is but a short time in the womb, and escapes, or is born unnoted at night, vanishing unnoted, like air.

When a girl or woman suspects that she has thus been made a *madre*, or mother, should she desire to see her offspring she repeats the following lines :—

> " Folletto !   Folletto !   Folletto !
> Che vole per l'aria,
> Piu lesto che del vento,
> Tu fai per non farti vedere
> Da 'alcuno, ma io
> Che desidero di vederti
> Sono una persona
> Che tanto ti amo ;
> Sono la tua vera madre,
> Per cio mi raccomando
> Che tu ti faccia vedere
> Al me per una volta ! "

> ("Spirit !   Spirit !   Spirit !
> Airy fairy light,
> Fleeter than the wind,
> Thou keepest from my sight,
> And from all ; but now
> Come unto my spell,
> Truly I am one
> Of all who loves thee well,
> Thy mother, too, I am,
> And that I may see
> What my child is like,
> Come, I pray, to me !")

So he cometh in a dream, or it may be in reality—who knows? Who knows anything of it all, or in what life they live who believe in these things ? Something must be seen or imagined, else how can these people maintain these fancies from age to age, from father to child, ever on. Or is all life a dream?

And yet how they *can* do it appears intelligible on reflection. When a man is not entirely absorbed by the life of cities, in factories, counting-houses, or "society," and when he is at home "in woodlands wild where the sweet birdes singe," then nature, or his instinct for companionship, makes him feel as if there were souls in trees, a spirit dwelling in the hearth, under the threshold, even in the *scaldino* of glowing coals. The *polypantheistic* stage, when man was passing from the phase of making gods of every object, to that of feeling *one* spirit *in* all, must have been coeval with a somewhat greater development of social life, yet when out-of-doors, rural or wild life or nature still exerted a deep influence. In such a life we gladly surround ourselves with strange companions, and believe that nature, which is so wonderful and apparently inspired with life and thought as a whole, also exists in separate beings. Men do not reason this out in these words, but Red Indians or Tuscan peasants feel it and act in its spirit.

While this spirit of nature still existed, SHAKESPEARE wrote under its inspiration, and artists painted, and all art came from it. And since it died out, what we *call* poetry and art are imitations of what they really did who lived in it.

What is most curious as regards this having a child begotten by fire in such a familiar domestic manner is that the very oldest story of the kind in existence is Etruscan. The tale is told by DIONYS, OVID, and PLUTARCH, and runs thus:—

"Tarquinius and his wife, the wise Tanaquil, were seated at their meal, while Ocris, the captive daughter of the king of Corniculum, waited on them. As she went to the fire to throw into it the usual offering to the *Lar familiaris* there came out of the flames a *fascinum* (phallus). Alarmed at this she told it to Tanaquil, who bade her dress herself in bridal array and sit on the hearth. She did so, and conceived from the heat, and bore a son, Servius Tullius. And it was said that when he once slept his hair appeared to be like flames."

This is effectively in another form the story of the child begotten by the Scaldino. The reader will observe that Dusio, Cupra, Attilio or the *lar familiaris* who is the spirit of the fireplace, in these Tuscan tales, always seduces a *maid-servant*. And this suggests a remark which the reader would do well to bear in mind. It is that, taking them all together, one with another—modern popular Tuscan tales, spells, incantations, and observances or descriptions of spirits—and comparing them with what is given by Latin writers, we find the ancient continually confirming the extreme antiquity of the modern. Be it a tract here, a small observance there, now an herb in an incantation, and anon a couplet in a charm, they continually interlace, cross, touch, and coincide. I find these unobserved small identities continually manifesting themselves, and they form a chain of intrinsic evidence which is as valuable to a truly critical scholar as any historical or directly traditional confirmation. That fire was a creature, or a living existence (as is still recognised by the Church of England) was believed in by all religions of all ages, as is illustrated by Schedius and Friedrich with a vast array of authorities. That it should as a spirit be capable of begetting spiritual children was a natural sequence. I think therefore that, all things duly considered, we have in the belief in the Scaldino a probably well-established continuation of the old Etruscan tale of the goblin of the fire and the fair queen's daughter, fallen to a servant-maid.

It is worth remarking that in the Tomba Golini at Orvieto, as in Pompeii, a fascinum, or phallus, was depicted over the oven or fireplace, probably to signify the spirit of the fireside.

ARTEMISIA

I was astonished to find that the name Artemisia is known only as that of a *strega*—here a vampire—who sucks the blood of the dead in their graves. This indicates some connection with Diana as a witch of the evil kind. The name was promptly recognised, but I could learn nothing more regarding her. PRELLER identifies Diana Artemis with Hecate. As to which as with all others, I leave it to the more learned to investigate, examine, prove or disprove to their heart's content, I only professing to record, as in every case, what was told me.

RED CAP

" Lord Foulis sat within his tower,
    And beside him old Red Cap sly ;
' Now tell me thou sprite who art mickle of might,
    The death that I shall die.' "
                    Minstrelsy of the Border

" Here is an ancient description of the dress of the fairies : ' They wear a red conical cap ; a mantle of green cloth inlaid with wild flowers ; green pantaloons, buttoned with bobs of silk, and silver shoon. They carry quivers of arrow-slough, and bows made of the ribs of a man buried where " three lairds " lands meet ; their arrows are made of bog-reed tipped with white flints and dipped in the dew of hemlock ; they ride on steeds whose hoofs would not " dash the dew from the cup of a harebell." ' "—*Anonymous*

There are in the Romagna Tuscana a class of goblins or fairies who are almost identical with the Irish Leprachaun who possesses treasures which are yielded only under compulsion. I could not learn that the Italian elf has any other name than *Il Folletto colla Beretta*—the imp with the cap. He was described as follows :—

" When mysterious noises and knocks or a rummaging sound are heard in your rooms by night, and you are sure it is made by unearthly visitors, prepare for them by putting a lighted lamp in the room, and covering it over with an earthen pot, but very carefully so that not a gleam can be seen.

" Then when you hear a noise in the room, uncover the light as quickly as possible, and if goblins are there catch the cap from one if you can and say :—

> " ' La beretta ti ho portato via !
> Ma non ti ho portato via,
> Ma la pace che più non ti daro
> Se non mi dice prima
> Dov'e nascosto il tesoro.'

Which is in Romagnola :—

> " ' A t'o porte via la bretta,
> Ma an tó porte via la bretta ;
> A to porte via la pes,
> Che piu an te daro in fé
> Che tun ma vre det en dove
> Le piate e tesor ! '

> (" ' I have taken thy cap away,
> And yet 'tis not a cap I say,
> But thy peace which I'll not give
> Unto thee while thou dost live,
> Till thou tellst me, as thou'rt bid,
> Where a treasure now lies hid.')

" Then the spirit, to redeem his cap, will tell where a treasure is concealed."

This is classic enough. " They knew in Italy," says PRELLER (*Römische Mythologie*, p. 488), " a class of spirits who knew where treasures were hidden, and who guarded them. They were called *Incubones*, and wore caps (the symbols of their hidden secret natures). If any one can steal these caps he can compel them to tell where these treasures are hidden " (PETRONIUS, s. 38 ; see GRIMM, *Deutsche Mythologie*, 479).

This elf with the red cap and a scanty shirt is common in Roman mural paintings and on Etruscan vases. He spread all over the world, unto Germany and the Scandinavian countries, even the Algonkin Indians of America got him from the Norsemen. But it is very probable that the Etruscans or their neighbours had him first of all. Which, however, I leave for more learned men to determine. It is, however, certain that the Red Indians and Romagnolo peasants are the only people at the present day who really believe in him as existing.

It is not improbable that the goblin with the red cap is derived from the red-headed wood-pecker Picus, who was in the earliest times believed in Italy to be a sprite who guarded treasures, and sometimes, under compulsion, showed where they were hidden, as is shown in another chapter. All of which—as with everything else in this work—I submit as material only, the real value of which others must determine.

Preller assumes, quite as a matter of course, that the red-caps and other

RED-CAP ON A ROMAN LAMP

minor deities, or house-goblins of a frolicsome brownie character, belong rather to Teutonic and Celtic mythologies than to the Italian. Herein he quite forgets that though the world has through Grimm's fables or early personal influences learned to associate these sprites with the North, yet that in reality written and authentic history shows them as familiar to early Latins centuries long before German or Celtic beliefs were, so to speak, ever heard of. According to David MacRitchie, the origin of all "wee folk" is to be sought in antecedent dwarf races, driven out by larger and more vigorous people—a process which probably went on all over the world. This would not interfere with the creation of other personifications of manikins, such as the very obvious one which occurs to most children of treating the thumb and fingers as a kind of fairies, or believing that frogs and birds assumed dwarf human forms. As regards Red-cap, as I have already said, testimony seems to indicate that he is of Etruscan origin, and is a personification of the red-headed wood-pecker; that is, a small form of Picus or Picumnus.[1]

[1] "The negroes and half-breeds in Missouri consider the red-headed wood-pecker a great sorcerer, who can appear either as a bird or as a red man with a mantle or cloak on his arm. He is supposed to be very grateful and very vengeful. He made the bat by putting a rat and a bird together. He sometimes bores holes in the heads of his enemies while they sleep and puts in maggots which keep them for ever restless or crazy."—Note by MARY A. OWEN

The Italian house-goblins, like those of the North, are given to imitating sounds. One of the sixteenth-century writers tells us that the day before a party of merchants arrive at a country house the people dwelling therein often hear the Elves imitating the sound of scales rattling as if making weight, the ring of money, and all the circumstance of buying and selling. And it is very remarkable that, as one may see by the *Etruscan Museum* of Gori, the red-cap goblins of ancient Italy are sometimes represented with weights and scales and behaving like merchants. But in all countries they are given to holding fairs, as Christina Rossetti's "Goblin Market" bears witness. He who finds himself in such fairs may buy diamonds and pearls by the pound for a penny, but he must escape ere they close, or he will come to woes. And ere a visitor arrives his voice may be heard, and the night before a rain or a storm the little people make sounds as of a shower or the blowing of winds when all is still.

> " What ripples and rapples so fast and near ?
> Is it the rain on the roof I hear?
> It is not rain, it is not hail,
> But the Elves and Witches who dance in a gale.
> First in a patter and then in a prance,
> That is the way the Elfin dance."

A writer in the *Philadelphia News* sums up the different names by which the wee folk are known. These are "fairies, elves, elfe-folks, fays, urchins, ouphes, ell-maids, ell-women, dwarfs, trolls, norns, nisses, kobolds, duende, brownies, necks, stromkarls, fates, little wights, undines, nixes, salamanders, goblins, hobgoblins, poukes, banshees, kelpies, pixies, moss people, good people, good neighbours, men of peace, wild women, white ladies, peris, djinns, genii, and gnomes."

Making allowance for mere synonyme, all of these are to be found in early Italian lore, and they still exist in the mountains. But in reality they may be found all the world over, be it in Eastern lands or in America.

OF SORCERY IN ANCIENT ART

(The Interlace, or Twining Serpents, Vines, and Knots, as believed in in Tuscany.)

> " Twist ye, twine ye, even so,
> Mingle threads of joy and woe."
>
> GUY MANNERING

" Pingue duos angues : pueri, locus est sacer."—PERSIUS (sat. i. 113)

There is a passage in Heine's preface to his Germany which must appeal to every collector of folk-lore.   In speaking of the traditions and tales of the humbler rural folk he says :—

"I have here given more than one of these which I myself heard by hearths in huts, narrated by some vagabond beggar or old and blind grandmother, but the strange, uncanny reflection which the flickering fire of twigs cast on the face of the narrator, and the beating of the hearts of the hearers who listened in happy silence I could not render, and these rustic, well-nigh barbaric stories when deprived of that lose their wondrous and secret charm."

Heine had been, as we may gather from his life, perhaps half a dozen times in such scenes, and heard, it may be, about as many tales of the Grimm kind.   I wonder what he would have written had he been for years almost constantly among gypsies and witches, especially the latter, and seen and felt to perfection the survival of the strange wild classic *strega*, whose soul is still inspired with early Latin or Etruscan sorcery, and from whose inner life was ever and anon flashing out something far more uncanny and unearthly than all the flames of twigs which he had ever seen.   Many a time have I been awed at these living dreams, these forgotten visions of yore, incarnate in strange women, who spoke of an old, old faith, long in its grave, once held by a race whose very language is now as unknown, as their origin.   And I avow that this has ever moved me as a sincere lover of antiquity as a real romance, without equal in this our age of prose.

She was seated by the table on which was one of those simple, beautiful long brass lamps with three lights, such as have come down unchanged since the Roman time ; in her hands she held a *scaldino*, which was all the fire for warmth known to her ; in the window grew herbs of deeply mystical meaning, not for show but for sorcery, when I by chance asked her if people found many objects of antiquity where she dwelt.   And reflecting an instant as usual—which always inspired a marvellously antique-wild expression which suggested classic art—she said :—

"*Molti.*   Strangers come to us and dig up vases, black and yellow, which our ancestors made long ago. There at Cesena, for example.   Cesena, is in the Romagna.   Sometimes the *contadini*, excavating the ground for a building, find medals as well as antique vases, thousands of years old.

"And these were all made for witches according to their belief, and all these things are of magic and witchcraft, for in those times all the land was full of witches.   And the reason why they are found in secret places and old ruins and the like is this: When the priests came in, they would not let the witches be buried in the *campo santi*, because they said the witches and wizards were *scomunicati*—excommunicated.

"So they arranged it to bury one another, and when one witch died the others interred her secretly in her own cellar or house [1] with her vases and witch-medals, and all the things which she used in her art.   And before dying she taught all her secrets to the others.   And this is why it is we never find them buried in

---

[1] As the Etruscan tombs were often exact copies of the homes of the departed, this idea would be very naturally formed by the peasantry.

Christian burying grounds, and why we do find vases and very ancient medals in their graves, for these things are all of their own ancient belief, or for witchcraft, and so they could not be placed in the *campo santi.*

"For in the old times witchcraft had a religion, and it was called *la religione della stregoneria*—the religion of sorcery—and what you see on the old vases are the names and portraits of witches and wizards of the olden time. And on them are the pictures of Tigna and Faflon and all other witches or magicians who became spirits." [1]

I have read of a man who had " foregone to be a Christian reality, and per-verted himself into a Pagan idealist." This was in a novel, but my friends were *real* Pagan survivals, and though the spirit fire had burned low, so that it smoul-dered in the ashes, and only now and then sent out a jet of flame, still it was marvellous to me—yea, *awful*—that through the ages such a glimmering had come down of a heathen faith outworn, and that women now live who speak of the Etruscan Jupiter and Bacchus as of deities whom a few still adore, and whose pic-tures are to be seen on ancient vases ! Though degraded to the humblest condition and fast fleeting, *Stregoneria* is still a belief, and not mere fragments of folk-lore or of ancient superstitions. Yes, the ceremonies and incantations, charms and amu-lets which I have so often seen practised or prepared, till they were to me as familiar things—all, as I have elsewhere shown, were of the same hoar antiquity.

Heine could not give the flicker of the fire nor the beating of hearts ; what I would fain convey is the classically stern, almost terrible beauty which appears in the face of an old Italian witch when it is illuminated by an earnest thought, and the same beauty in the thoughts themselves. The reason why there seems to be so much light in an Italian smile, such intensity in the passion, even of peasants, allied to a certain indescribable picturesqueness, is because all their habits of thought and traditions have been derived for thou-sands of years from stages of society in which *Art* and Faith in their most com-prehensive sense influenced every act of life. And though the Art no longer exists, the impulses which it created still live in blood and brains, and are trans-mitted by heredity—even as the water of a stream continues to leap and sparkle long after it has passed some mighty cataract. That was Art which inspired Etruscan vases, and jewellery, and mirrors ; not less artistic was the feeling which created deities, goblins, *spiriti folletti*, and elves, with their lays and legends, and mystical cognate sorcery. Faith without art is an egg not yet hatched ; art with-out faith is an empty egg-shell worth nothing—unless it be for some wizard, like Zola, to make a boat of to ride to the devil withal. These descendants of the old

[1] The nakedness, the dancing and wild revelry depicted on the Etrusco-Greek vases, with their satyrs, goblins, and winged *lases* and mysterious emblems or hieroglyphs, would all very naturally suggest to the *contadini* magic and sorcery. Does not all this Greek beauty and joyousness seem even to us like a dream of fairyland—a Paradise ?

Italians who have kept in simple faith their old superstitions, have also kept with them, unconsciously, the *art* which giveth life—and life is light and fire and feeling.

This speaking of old Etruscan art made me think of serpents, and I asked if the peasants in *le Romagne* had any beliefs regarding them.

> " Yes. They sometimes paint a serpent on the wall to keep away the evil eye or witch evils, and to bring good luck. But the head must be down and interlaced, and the tail uppermost." [1]
>
> " And do interlaced serpents mean good fortune? "
>
> " Ah, that is a well-known thing, and not as to serpents alone, but all kinds of interweaving and braiding and interlacing cords, or whatever can attract the eyes of the witches. When a family is afraid of witchery they should undertake some kind of *lavori intrecciati*—braided work—for witches cannot enter a house where there is anything of the kind hung up, as for instance, patterns of two or three serpents twining together, *o altri ricami*, or other kinds of embroidery, but always of intertwining patterns. So in making shirts or drawers or any garments for men or women—*camice, mutande o vestiti*—one should always in sewing try to cross the cotton (thread) as shoemakers do when they stitch shoes, and make a cross-stitch, because shoes are most susceptible to witchcraft (*perche le scarpe sono quelle più facile a prendere le stregonerie*). And when the witches see such interlacings they can do nothing, because they cannot count either the threads nor the stitches (*ne il filo ne i punti*). And if we have on or about us anything of the kind they cannot enter because it bewilders or dazzles their sight (*le fa a bagliare la vista*), and they are incapable of mischief. And to do this well (*tenere il sistema*) you should take cotton, or silk, or linen thread, and make a braid of six, seven, or eight columns, as many as you will—the more the better—and always carry it in your pocket, and this will protect you from witches. You can get such braids very beautifully made of silk of all colours in some shops ; and they keep them for charms against the evil eye."

I took great pains to have this carefully recorded, for it is intimately connected with an interesting subject which possibly enters into the *raison d'etre* or real inspiration of all the most characteristic decorative art of all Europe, especially during the Middle Ages. In my work on *Gypsy Sorcery* the following passage occurs (page 98) :—

> " There is a very curious belief or principle attached to the use of songs in conjuring witches or in averting their own sorcery. It is that the witch is obliged, willy-nilly, to listen to the end what is in metre—an idea founded on the attraction of melody, which is much stronger among savages and children than with civilised adults. Nearly allied to this is the belief that if the witch sees interlaced, or bewildering and confused patterns, she *must* follow them out, and by means of this her thoughts are diverted or scattered. Hence the serpentine inscriptions of the Celts and Norsemen, and their intertwining bands which were firmly believed to bring good luck, or avert evil influence. A traveller in Persia states that the patterns of the carpets of that country are made as bewildering as possible 'to avert the evil eye.' And it is with this purpose that, in Italian as in all other witchcraft, so many spells and charms depend on interwoven braided cords (*vide* the Spell of the Holy Stone).
>
> " The basis for this belief is the fascination or interest which many persons, especially children, feel to trace out patterns, to thread the mazes of labyrinths, or to analyse and distangle knots and 'cats' cradles.' Did space permit, nor inclination fail, I could point out some curious proofs that the old belief in the power of long and curling hair to fascinate, was derived not only from its beauty, but also because of the magic of its curves and entanglements."

---

[1] Probably the caduceus of Mercury, which often appears on vases as simply two serpents with interlaced heads.

I have made serious and extensive study of interlaced patterns, beginning with Westwood's *Palæographia Picta* in which the claims of the Irish to be the originators of such art are upheld, down to the latest works on design. I have studied them with intense interest in the museums of Ireland, Norway, Sweden, and Denmark, England, and Scotland, and copied literally thousands of them. And I was deeply convinced from the beginning that in all these Celtic intertwinings of infinite Irish lizards, and eternal Scandinavian serpents, down to Gothic ribbon and Florentine cord and vine braidings, there ran a mystic meaning, expressing as it were in an occult writing, deep and strange secrets of sorcery. What gave me the suggestion is worth mentioning. There is a book of which TROLLOPE declared that he believed he was the only person in Europe who had ever read it. I had, however, perused it thrice in as many versions before I was sixteen years of age, which I mention to show what an impression it made on me, for such reading at such an age sinks deep into the soul. This was *The Unheard-of Curiosities*, by GAFFAREL, in which he sets forth naïvely, yet strikingly, a grand Paracelsian idea that the stars in heaven in their relative aspects and courses form the points of Hebrew or geomantic letters, and that the lines on the bark of all trees, and the marks on sea-shells and fishes, the curve of the waters as they wind in the brook or bound upwards in the ocean-wave, the flight of the bird and the flickering bend of a flame ; or all forms, inspired by the spirit of Nature, or the *Archæus*, form eternally varied hieroglyphics of a vast writing, to which we may get the key by inspiration and study. The poetry of this idea entered into my soul, and I cherished it for a long time, the more so as I read much in Wordsworth and Shelley. It was in my first year at college, where I took daily long and lonely walks in wild woods, and seated by grey rocks and silent waters, tried to trace by the aid of poetry some of this Divine caligraphy. About the same time I began to study Gothic art, and to copy illuminations, and, as may be supposed, the spirit of Gaffarelius guided me here to many deep and strange conclusions. And from it I have since drawn many more which have apparently no connection with it. That some tradition and association, some extremely deeply-seated feeling and serious sense of meaning must have attached itself to this immensity, this universality of a system of *design* which endured for a thousand years, and was found in every work of art, every letter, every article of Northern jewellery, stands to reason. In an age when symbolism and magic permeated everything it would have been a miracle indeed if Art were meaningless. And what the Interlace meant everywhere has been, as I think, clearly set forth by the Italian *strega* in the preceding pages.

Identical with this law, or instinct, by which the evil eye must perforce trace out patterns is that which compels the witch to count, *con gré mal gré*, all the grains of rice or sesame or corn which she may encounter. So in the *Arabian Nights* the ghoul Amina *must* eat her rice grain by grain with a bodkin. In South Carolina, rice strewed in the form of a cross about a bed prevents a witch from getting at her victim, for she must remove it, grain and grain, ere she can reach him, nor must she shirk the task. And as I have elsewhere shown the *erba Rosolaccio*, or Rice of the Goddess of the Four Winds, is esteemed as a protective, because the witches cannot count its rice-like leaves, and so they get bewildered in them. This belief was carried to the extent of regarding corrugated and rugged surfaces of any kind as protecting from evil. Hence the stalagmite, or salagrana stone, is very popular against *malocchio*, which means *all* inimical sorcery.

I conjecture—for it is not as yet a matter of *proof*—that the Celtic peoples from the earliest times, in the East, during the migration of races, *e.g.*, through Hungary, and in Great Britain and Gaul, had the interlace and constantly used it. The Britons, generally, made gaily-painted baskets—*bascaudæ*—which were sent to Rome. This suggests interlaces. The Irish monks and artisans developed these basket-patterns, manifestly using, as a more pliable *suggestive*, ribbons, ropes, or cords, as I have often done myself to make designs. I do not think it necessary to adopt the rather unpleasant idea set forth in a great book on needlework that the entrails of animals were thus used for models. A month's work of intelligent designing is worth all the theory in the world, and I no more believe that "insides" were employed to suggest motives than I do that earth-worms were taken for the same purpose, as was indeed once suggested to me by a certain wood-carver, who could see no beauty in anything save *baroque* patterns.

I have been told, or I have read, that the theory of the basket-pattern is now "exploded" as also that of the Irish claim to have developed or invented the interlace; in fact, I find that everything nowadays is "exploded" almost before the powder has been put into it. Thus a certain blue-stocking lady, speaking to me of agnosticism, declared languidly that she had gone through with it all, and that it was a vanished quantity. I begged her to define it for me. "Let me hear your definition first?" asked the *blasée-bleue*. But I was not to be caught thus, and the learned dame, with an ill grace, explained that an agnostic was "a kind of infidel-sceptic,—but all that sort of thing is quite out of fashion now, you know." So I have been told, on the best authority, that somebody—I forget who—has exploded the Altaic-Tartar Accadian theory—a theory which, however, the firm and gentle Sayce and the fiery Oppert still maintain. And I am also told by other men that Fetishism is exploded, or utterly blown up, though I have before me, specially manufactured for my own use, as undeniable specimens of fetishes of many kinds as could emanate from the brains of Italian witches and American Voodoos. So they go on, building up every man his little cardboard system and blowing down those of others— "and one live nigger would walk over the whole of them," as I heard it tersely expressed at the termination of the Folk-lore Congress of 1891.

But to return to the interlace, or the magic power of intertwining knots, for there is more of it in the lore of the *strege*. The mulberry-tree, being of great importance in Italy, has, of course, its peculiar superstitions, and curious among them is the following :—

> "When a peasant prunes the mulberry-trees which are for silkworms, he must trim them so that the boughs *restino intrecciati*—may remain interlaced—in which case the silkworms will be protected against any *malocchio*, or evil influence from any witch.
>
> "But care must also be taken that, however fine (*belli*) the silkworms may be, no one shall say so, because calling them 'fine' during the three trials (*malattie*) which they pass through before spinning their silk would cause their death.
>
> "Be therefore attentive that if any one entering the house should say, '*Belli quei bacchi*' ('Those are fine silkworms'), to throw at that person a handful of leaves, because the person, being vexed, will throw the leaves at the silkworms, and the evil charm, if they have taken it, will be removed."

In Italy, as in the East, there is great dread of unpremeditated praise, be it of animals or children, because those who fascinate or bewitch always use it. The convolvulus, which includes the honeysuckle and morning-glory, and indeed all that twineth as a vine or "bine," is also a protection against witches, owing to its twisted tendrils.

> "Those who fear enchantment or the evil eye should have the *convolvolo* in their gardens or in a pot in the window, because it is of all others the flower which witches cannot endure. And they cannot enter a house where it is, because it bears tendrils (*nerbolini*) like a mass of little serpents intertwined (*come tante piccole serpia rotolate*) and all entangled, for which reason it keeps them out. This plant flowers by night, and its beautiful flowers in a bouquet and its tendrils bewilder the sight (*fa affogliare la vista*) of sorceresses, and keeps them afar."

All of which, if the reader be "a thinking character," may give him something to think over when he sees a Gothic interlace, or serpentine ornaments, or love-knots, or fish-nets, or Hegel's sentences !

Lenormant, in his *Magie Chaldaienne*, speaks of the very ancient weaving of magic knots—that is, plaiting interlaces, as old Assyrian, of which he says that the efficacy was so firmly believed in, even up to the Middle Ages, and gives in illustration the following against a disease or pain in the head :—

"Knot on the right and arrange flat in regular bands—on the left a woman's diadem ;
divide it twice in seven little bands ;
gird the head of the invalid with it ;
gird the forehead of the invalid with it ;
gird the seat of life with it ;
gird his hands and his feet ;
seat him on his bed ;
pour on him enchanted waters.
Let the disease of his head be carried away into the heavens like a violent wind ;
may the earth swallow it up like passing waters !"

From which we can see that plaiting the hair in interlaces was a charm for a headache. Taking it altogether, this application of interlacing cords to the temple or other parts of the body is quite identical with modern usage.

This subject of the interlace as a guard against evil magic, or an amulet, is nearly allied to the idea of holes and corrugations in stones—*vide* the Sala-grana—to magic rhymes and bewildering music, and mingled colours, and all that attracts and confuses the mind. All produce one effect.

I am indebted to Miss Mary Owen, of Missouri, for the following (learned from a black sorceress), which is nearly connected with the interlace :—

"When a man is visited in sleep by witches who ride or torment him, you should fasten in the chimney a coarse linen cloth or a sieve ; tie at the head of the bed a pair of wool cords or a branch of fern leaves, in which the seeds are almost ripe ; sprinkle a cup of mustard seed on the door-sill. The witch must count the interstices of the cloth or sieve, the seeds of the fern or the teeth of the cords, and must pick up every mustard seed, counting as she does so, ere she is free to torment the sleepers by knotting their feathers, riding on their breasts, or whispering to them awful dreams."

The black Takroori, or sorcerers of Africa, draw their magic and lore largely from Arabic-cabalistic sorcerers, as I know, having examined their books when in Egypt, and all this is known to the Arabs. It is very curious that Prætorius speaks of a man who, in jest, used curry-combs or wool-cords to defend himself from a nightmare witch. Here, I think, in these cases we probably have tradition or transmission.

THE GODDESS OF THE FOUR WINDS—L'ERBA ROSOLACCIO

"Come from the four winds, O breath, and breathe upon these slain, that they may live" (*Ezekiel* xxxvii. 9)

Among all primitive or superstitious people, the medicinal or other virtues of herbs are attributed to some deeply mysterious cause of a supernatural nature. In the Romagna, just as among the Red Indians of America, this faith is carried so far that certain plants are regarded as being in some strange way fairies or spirits in themselves. He who bears one of these about him—always in a red bag, as in old Etrusco-Roman times—carries a small guardian angel, or, if he plants it in a pot, he will be like the ancient Egyptians of whom Juvenal said they had gods growing in their gardens—in allusion to their reverence for onions or garlic.

One of these plants which is an object of culture not only in a literal, but also in a religious and æsthetic sense, is the *Rosolaccio* which has also the curious double-meaning name of the rice (*riso*), also laughter, or the smile, of the Goddess of the Four Winds. I had the following account given to me with a specimen of the herb :—

" " *Rosolaccio* is a plant the leaves of which, drawn up like a many-fingered little hand, look like grains of rice, whence it is called the rice (or the smile) of the Goddess of the Four Winds. It is also called the plant of good luck because it brings great good fortune. A sprig of it may be kept growing in a small pot, or, if this be impossible, in a red bag. If the former, it must always be in the window, if in a bag, the latter should be hung up behind the window, and this done, no witches can enter, for there are so many grains (or grain-like leaves), or eyes, that the witches cannot count them and therefore cannot pass by. For they are so closed together that counting is impossible. And should it happen that in any family a child or grown person is bewitched, then we take this plant, either growing or else in the bag, and go to the sufferer who must be fasting, even from water, early in the morning, and say :—

> " ' Dea, o dea dei quattri venti,
> Non ci e altra bella al par di te
> Un' erba miracolosa l'hai fatta nascere,
> Perche la stregoneria passi . . . ! '

> (" ' Goddess, O goddess of the four winds !
> There is no one equal to thee in beauty,
> Thou hast made a miraculous plant to grow,
> That the bewitchment may pass from . . .')

Then let the sign of the cross be made three times with the herb, and this must be done for three mornings.

" ' But who was the Goddess of the Four Winds ? '

" Well, I have heard that her mother was a beautiful girl who was of great rank, perhaps a princess ; however she loved a poor young man, and her parents would not hear of such a match.

" How it came to pass, who knows ? but the young man dwelt near her, and they found a subterranean passage which led to her room—some say she had it dug, for she was of fairy kind—but it came to a trap-door in her room, and under her bed.

" And the end was that she was with child, and remained many months in her room, lest the world should know it. And she prepared a fine cradle *all made of roses*. And her mother, who was a fairy, kept her secret, and aided her, and when the time came for the princess to give birth to the child, the mother made a fire of laurel, so that in its crackling the cries of the babe should not be heard.

" And when this happened, and while the mother burned the laurel, she said :—

> " ' Figlia mia, amata, amata,
>   A batta di lauro tu sei nata,
>   E di rose conbugigata,
>   Figlia mia, amata, amata,
>   Una fata di te pure ho fatta.'

> (" ' Darling daughter in the morn,
>   To the sound of laurel thou wert born ;
>   Wrapped in roses thou shalt be,
>   Daughter, daughter, dear to me,
>   A fairy I have made of thee.')

" And this child was the Goddess of the Four Winds. *E questa fu la fata detta la dea dei quattro venti.*"

This marvellous and mysterious story can hardly fail to suggest much to every folk-lorist. First of all the infant goddess of the wind is rocked in a cradle of *roses.* FRIEDRICH (*Symbolik d. Natur*) observes that in the Greek myth, the Wind, Æolos, has in his home six sons and six daughters—*wohl die älteste Andeutung einer Windrose*—"the first indication of the wind-rose or anemone." The real *rosalaccio* (rose-lace) is the red poppy or corn-flower, but the name *rose* refers to the colour. We have in it, however, a connection of roses with the wind, and of the dew-drop, "rocked by the wind in the cradle of a rose." The anemone or wind-flower sprung from the blood of Adonis, that is, in the flower he lives again as a spirit of the wind. Adonis, the spirit of spring, is the same with Favonius, "the Greek zephyr, the sweet and fructifying south wind who comes with the swallow and the spring." It can hardly be denied that all this seems to be indicated in this strange Tuscan tale.

The burning of laurel twigs so that they shall make a noise is of ripe antiquity. " There was a special divination or foretelling the future by burning laurel leaves, and it was regarded as a good sign if they crackled and made a loud noise " (TIBULLUS, *Eleg.*, ii. 6, 81). Hence came a common proverb, *Clamosior lauro ardente*—" Noisier than burning laurel." Or, as we are told by the author of the *Trinum Magicum* (A.D. 1611), " Et lauri quoque ramis divinatio sumebatur, and there was also divination by a branch of laurel, which if it made a loud sound was a good sign, and the contrary if it burned out quietly."

But the chief aim of this story is to show how it was that the babe was made to pass from a mere mortal into a fairy or goddess, as Ceres attempted to do with the infant Triptolemus. She also employed a fire, but I do not know that it was of laurel boughs. But the laurel, as FRIEDRICH declares, was not only consecrated to prophecy or magic, and, as an evergreen, to immortality, but it was peculiarly a symbol of a new life—*neues Leben im Tode.* " Among the Romans the corpse in a funeral was sprinkled with water from laurel boughs ; and in the early times of Christianity the dead were laid on laurel leaves to signify that those who died in Christ had not ceased to live. And the baptism, or the new life in CHRIST, was also symbolised by laurel" (WINCKELMANN, *Versuch einer Allegorie, besonders für die Kunst*, iii. c. ; also HARTUNG, *die Relig. der Römer*, part i., p. 46). WINCKEL-MANN also mentions that on a rare medal, Lucilla, the wife of the Emperor Lucius Verus, is represented as holding a branch of laurel, near her kneels a woman drawing water, and there stands by her a half-naked child awaiting baptism. This has a special application to the Tuscan tale, with this difference—that in one case there is a baptism by fire, and in the other by water. In both the babe is to be prepared for a new life by means of the mystic laurel.

There is some obscurity in this myth, but it may be remarked that the zephyr, the dew-drop, and the rose, were mystically combined in ancient fable, and that they reappear in the birth of the Goddess of the Four Winds. Again, peasants usually retain, or relate, only fairy stories, whereas this is not a *tale* at all in the real sense of the word, but an explanation of the origin of a spirit who is, we may say, worshipped in a plant.

In another Romagnolo legend the Wind appears as male and female. It is as follows :—

"The Wind is a magician (*mago*) and Corina (Romagnolo, *Curena*) is his sister.

"A youth had a sweetheart and believed she had been false to him while she was innocent. But the youth in his sorrow fled far, far away so that he might see her no more.

"Then she went to a wise old woman, who consulted the cards (that is 'divined' in any way), to know if she would ever find her lover again, and the old woman bade her go to the Wind, and to his sister Curena." (Here there is a manifest hiatus.) "And they departed with her ; the morning had just dawned when they came to a city, they put her down before the window of her love, and she sang :—

"'Love, thou hast been false to me,
While I was ever true to thee,
Thou for me didst leave thy home,
Now unto thee I have come,
In two hours' time I travelled here,
Yet 'twas the journey of a year.
The wild wind bore me like a cloud,
And Curena whistled loud,
They have put me on thy track,
Thou from me wilt ne'er turn back ;
Now our sufferings are o'er,
Thou shalt leave me nevermore.'

"So they were united, and lived happily ever after."

It is *possible* that in this *Curena* we have the Teutonic "Wind's bride," who is ever hunting, and who blows a horn which is indicated in *cor* or *curen*. Corinth, Corinna, and Curena seem to be certainly allied to *Coronis*, the wind : raven, typical of the north-west wind, or *Skiron*.

As regards the *rosalaccio* it is evident that the names and associations of the herb which I have described are confused and intermingled with those of the poppy or red corn-flower, which is the true rosalaccio, and the red anemone or wind-flower. And there are those in Ireland who maintain that the so-called wild wind-flower, which is white, and has a triple leaf, is the real shamrock. Out of all which those who have better material wherewith to work than I, may make what they can. There are some also who assert that the *red* sorrel is the true shamrock because the blood of the Saviour dropped upon it, even as the blood of Adonis dropped on the anemone.

Of which confusion there is a great deal in all legends of a people in which old tradition has long since run into decay and new growth, and I beg the reader to pardon me if I cannot clear it up.

MADONNA DEL FUOCO

" Sic in igne praeter alia elementa, sacra omnia insistebant, quod is, credo, proximus cœlo sit, quod in specie ignis Deus Mosen primum allocutus."—ELIAS SCHEDIUS, *De Dis Germanis*, 1648

It was formerly a custom at Forli in the Romagna Toscana to give annually a grand procession, the occasion of which was the showing an image of the Virgin seated on a dragon surrounded by flames. This extremely heathen ceremony is now discontinued, so far as Forli is concerned, but it is still kept up in the neighbouring small town of Civitella.

I have looked over a rather large Latin work, profusely illustrated, published about two hundred years ago, which is entirely devoted to describing this Madonna of Fire and Dragons, from which I gather that once upon a time the festival must have been very magnificent. It is remarkable that the witches and wizards, either guided by a sagacious intuition or ancient tradition, regard this Madonna as one of their own heathen deities who has been unjustly filched from them, and placed in the Christian pantheon. On which subject one of the sister-hood expressed herself not without a certain amount of righteous or pious indignation, to the effect that the Lady of the Fire was a great spirit before the other Madonna was ever heard of ; her words being, in part, as follows :—

" She was a spirit (*i.e.*, heathen) who indeed worked many miracles, and so the priests took her and called her *la donna miracolosa del fuoco*.

"But in truth the priests knew that this Madonna del Fuoco did many miracles, and revived those who had fallen dead, before they had ever done anything. (The sense here is that she did all this before she was claimed or known as Christian.)

"The first that was known of her was that she appeared as a beautiful lady in a certain garden, and so all the neighbourhood began to talk of her and said it was Our Lady, or the Madonna.

"In Civitella there was an ancient and rich family. And in their fields there was a very small boy who kept sheep and was dumb. One morning the lady came to him, and this child who was mute began to speak and said : ' Lady, I could never speak before, dumb I was from my birth. Thou art a miraculous virgin. Tell me what I must do to express my thanks.'

"And she replied : ' Go to the great family and tell them they must go to Rome for a certain large stone and send it to me, and that by doing this their race will never end, but if they neglect it their troubles will never cease.'

"This he did, but was treated as a lunatic. Yet while they did this there appeared before them great flashes of fire—*gran fiaccole del fuoco*—and they knew it was the Lady of Fire. So they sent for the stone, and as soon as the lady had it she ascended it and remained there as an image. So they bore it to a church and placed it there—*e le misero nome, la Madonna del Fuoco, la Madonna Miraculosa*—and called it the Lady of Fire and the Miraculous Madonna.

"And this family left it by will that the festival with miraculous fire should be continually kept up. And all peasants when they have any illness or bad crops, or any trouble, attend this ceremony."

Ottfried Müller and Preller observe from good authority that the Etruscans paid very great attention to thunder and lightning, and that all their principal gods and goddesses were believed to wield, during certain months, the terrible power. Traces of this continually reappear in the legends of Le Romagne, as the reader may find in several places in this work, such as the tale of the Spirito del Giuoco. I think that this, taken in connection with the witch belief that this Madonna del Fuoco is really one of their own spirits, indicates a pre-Christian origin for the Madonna del Fuoco. It may be, indeed, that she is Vesta, the Roman goddess of fire, converted and Christianised. The miraculous stone refers possibly to the flint from which fire is struck.

LA CAVALLETTA

" Thou holdest the Cicada by the wings."—ARCHILOCHUS

La Cavalletta is defined as " a locust or grasshopper," but as I understand, it is neither, but what is known in America as the *Katydid*, a cicada which indeed resembles the Oriental locust in its general shape, but is somewhat larger, and is of a clear green colour, its wings being quite like leaves. Its cry is like that of the locust, but much louder. It appears to play an important part among the superstitions of the Romanga.[1]

[1] " That animal which the French call sauterelle, we a grasshopper, is named Ακρις by the Greeks, by the Latines locusta, and by ourselves a locust. Again, between a cicada and that we call a grasshopper the

I was first induced to notice it by hearing a woman sing a song, *alla conta-dinesca*, about it, in *Romagnola*, which I wrote down, and then received the following account in Italian :—

" The *Cavalletta* is an insect of a green colour with long legs.   It is a sign of good luck—*e tanto di buon augurio*.   When it comes into a room one should at once close the windows to prevent its escaping, and if there should happen to be sleeping children in bed, so much the better.   Then one should tie a thread to the leg of the *Cavalletta* and the other end to the bed, and say or sing :—

  " 'O Cavalletta che tanto bello sei !
   E da per tutto la buona fortuna porti,
   E quando va via tu la lasci,
   Percio sei venuto in casa mia
   Per portarmi la buona fortuna,
   E neppure non riportarmela via,
   La buon' fortuna lascia in casa mia ;
   E specialmente ai figli miei,
   Che eri tu pure in vita una donzella
   Bella e buona e piena di talento,
   E cosi ti prego se tu vuoi far' venire
   I figli miei di gran talento,
   E se cosi farai ne sarai sempre benedetta ;
   E ben vero che ora tu hai
   La forma di una bestia, ma una bestia tu non sei
   Sei uno spirito della buona fortuna.'

  (" 'Oh, Katydid, so fine and fair,
   Who bringst good fortune everywhere !
   Leave good luck in this my home
   Since into the house you've come.
   Bring it unto me I pray,
   And do not take the least away ;
   Bring it to me and every one,
   Most of all unto my son ;
   In life you were a lady, full
   Of talent, good and beautiful,
   Let me pray, as this is true,
   You'll give my children talents too,
   And where you fly from East to West,
   May you in turn be truly blest !
   Since though an insect form you wear,
   You are a spirit good and fair ! ')

---

differences are very many, as may be observed in themselves, or their descriptions in Matthiolus Aldrovandus and Muffetus. . . . Our word is borrowed from the Saxon Graest-hopp, which our ancestors, who never beheld the cicada, used for that insect which we yet call a grasshopper " (*Pseudoxia Epidemica* (*Vulgar Errors*), by Sir THOMAS BROWN, London, 1672).

"Then when the child shall be of an age to understand this, he should be taught to sing, when he sees a Katydid :—

> " ' Io son giovane e vero,
>   Ma lo tengo un gran talento,
>   Un gran uomo io saro,
>   Ma la cavalletta posso ringraziare,
>   Per che nella culla il gran talento
>   Mi e venuto a porta mia,
>   Portato la buona fortuna per la cavalletta.'

> (" ' I am but little, as you see,
>   And yet I may a genius be,
>   And if when grown I should be great,
>   And make a name in Church or State,
>   I'll not forget that one fine day,
>   As I in cradle sleeping lay,
>   How all my wit, as mother bid,
>   Was brought me by the Katydid.')

" But when the Cavalletta has been tied one hour to the cradle of the child, it must be freed, and the window opened, and it should be allowed to depart—not driven away—but suffered to leave at its own free will."

It is altogether impossible to separate the ancient folk-lore of the locust, grass-hopper, and cricket, or cicada. FRIEDRICH remarks that in the magical practices of the ancients the grasshopper was supposed to possess such powers of divination that it was called μαντις, or the soothsayer. It often occurs on monuments as an amulet against evil. One which represents a Cupid holding a butterfly, while a grasshopper is close by on an ear of corn, seems to me to set forth the spirit of the song which I have cited.

But the cavalletta is properly in legend the same as the *cicada* which was regarded as the emblem, and almost as the genius, of song and poetry, or the highest forms of intellect. The Greeks and old Italians loved this insect more than the nightingale, they associated it strangely with a higher genius and stronger powers of magic and prophecy. It was to them the herald of spring, a song of rivulets and fountains sparkling in the shade, a calling to green fields, a voice of the flowers.

Thus ANACREON sings :—

> " We praise thee auspicious Cicada, enthroned like a king
>   On the tree's summit, thou cheer'st us with exquisite song,
>   Living on dew-drops, and all men bestow on thee honour
>   As the sweet prophet of summer—the Muses all love thee,
>   So does Apollo the golden who gave thee thy song."

Ulysses holding a cicada to Cerberus, as it occurs in gems, signifies the power of evil or horror, captivated by genius or song. The old story was that these insects were once men and women, who, having heard the Muses sing, were so enchanted or enraptured that they could think of nothing else—yes, they forgot all earthly things, including eating and drinking, and so starved to death in pure æsthetic absence of mind. So the Muses turned them into the beautiful cicadæ, which, when they have sung themselves out in summer shades, return to the Muses. Therefore the Athenian ladies wore golden cicadæ in their hair as a sign of culture and refinement, also to indicate their patriotic attachment to their small country or city, because it is said that the insect never quits the place where it is born.

The whole spirit of the ancient belief in the cicada, or grasshopper, as a prophetic spirit, and the genius of song, is perfectly reflected in this Romagnolo ballad, which is in reality a rough but very fine diamond. For it is beautiful to see how the refined old classic feeling that the cicada is the spirit of genius and poetry has survived among these humble peasants, and how as a *mantis* it is believed to be capable of bestowing genius on the little *bambino*. It is absolutely the same idea or inspiration, but in a far sweeter and nobler form, which made the Greek maiden wear a golden cicada in her hair, that induces the Italian mother to tie a cavalletta by the leg to her baby's cradle, and sing to it the incantation or prayer to give it talents or genius, or make of it a poet.

There is something very antique in all this, as well as original and beautiful, so that, taking all others into consideration, I have very little doubt that this ceremony, as well as its song, may have come to us from the early spring-time of Latin, Greek, or Etruscan song. Ancient !—why there is nothing of the kind here given which is not, as the Germans say, stone-old, among the mountains of La Romagna Toscana. Every idea there which has a form, took it in neolithic or certainly bronze times. This of the cavalletta can at least be proved to be almost prehistoric.

The original Romagnolo which was sung like all contadino songs to a monotonous air, which, like the words, gave the impression that it was being improvised, was as follows :—

> " E spirit la cavaletta,
> Le un spirit et bona fortona,
> E sla ven in ca' vostra
> Nola fe mai scape.
>
> Sla ven in ca' vostra
> Piutost lighela a una gamba

E po lighela a e let de vostra bordel
E quella lav portera fortona
Ai vostre fial.

Lav portara fortona
Ai vostre fial e lai portra
La fortona pur et gran talent,
E la vi librara pur dal regiment.

En fen caiari pze an pense mai,
A quant chi andara a fer i solde
Ma quan chi e grend e chi belle aloe
Per vo o sara un gran dalor.

Per cio pensei sempre per temp,
Arcorder ed la Cavalletta,
Per che se le a pregari i vostre fiol,
Da feri solde ai librari a punti ste sicur."

It may be observed that this was described to me as *Lo Spirito la Cavalletta*—
the Spirit Cavalletta. That is to say the insect is recognised as a spirit which was
once human, just as it is set forth in the Latin or Greek legend. The ancient
myth declares that the cicadæ were once very much refined maidens, who were
turned to insects by the Muses. The modern incantation says that the katydid
was in life—

> " a lady full
> Of talent good and beautiful."

Of those who attribute all of these identities in tradition to *chance* coincidences
and " development under like causes," one can only say, as did the old orthodox
Christian of the doctrine of atoms, and fortuitous combinations, that it put upon
the back of Chance more than it would bear.

CHAPTER X

CUPRA

" Ex eo tempore . . . illum sic concubisse secum, ut viri cum fœminis solent, nec percipiente viro, cum simul in lecto essent,"—BODINUS, lib. 2, capit. 7

F this spirit all that I know is given in the following strange story :—

" Cupra is a *folletto*, or spirit, who when *se prende a sinpatia una donna*, he takes a liking to a woman, and inspires her with it, follows her about all the time even by day.

" There was once in a town in La Romagna a girl of extraordinary beauty, who was moreover strangely fortunate in all things—*quello che desiderava e quello che le appariva*. Now it came to pass that waking in the night she found that she had by her a very beautiful youth, and this happened often, till at last she told her mother of it.

" Her mother bade her carefully close the door, and not to go to bed till morning. And he came all the same ; but the mother, who was secretly watching, saw no one. Then she strewed leaves all about, thinking that when this mysterious lover passed over them there would be a rustling. And he came and made a great noise with the leaves and laughed loudly, but not a leaf stirred. Then the mother, being angry, said to her daughter : ' Go to bed, and I will lie by thy side ; but I do not believe that there is any one here save us.'

" Then Cupra laughed aloud and sang :—

" ' Si—sono a letto,
 Con tua figlia,
 E incinta
 D'un bel bambino :
 Son' un spirito folletto
 Che la tua figlia voglio amar,
 E molti figli voglio creiar,
 Molti figli io l'avro,
 E tua figlia
 Sempre amero.'

(" ' Yes—I am lying
 Here by thy daughter ;
 She has by me, too, unborn,
 A beautiful boy.
 I am a spirit
 Who loves her—you'll see
 She will bear many
 More children to me,
 And your fair daughter
 Long loved shall be ! ')

" Now after this nobody would marry her ; yet she was happy and contented, for she had all she desired, being long and well loved by her *amante*."

There is in this a little, as it were, of Cupid and Psyche, which beautiful myth doubtless grew out of some rude and simple old story of a girl and a spirit lover. I have no doubt that the tale as here given is a mere fragment. As among the Red Indians, we find loose pieces of stories, sometimes fitted into one another.

It cannot fail to strike the reader that there is a very loose moral tone—a gay and festive sensuousness evident in these tales. These *folletti* are all, when not terrible, very much like the Fauns and Sylvans, spirits of yore, from whom they are, beyond all doubt, legitimately descended. In fact the spirit of Dyonisia, the worship of Bacchus and Venus, and of Pan—of Dryads and Oreads, and a multitude of hard-drinking, free-loving, rakish divinities, all of whom, from great Jove himself down to the Satyrs, set the example of embracing every pretty woman who came in their way, could hardly be wanting among people who still actually invoke these deities by their old names. And this is—*inter alia*—a strong confirmation of the heathen antiquity of all this Tuscan lore.

I deem this thing well worth dwelling on, that while in the folk-lore and fairy-tales of the rest of Europe there is but little account of fairies, brownies, elves, and sylvan goblins seducing maidens and abusing wives, it is in the Romagna at the present day their chief mission or amusement. A ringing melody of forest glee does not come more surely from the *Waldhorn* of a hunter when sounded by some skilful woodcraftsman than a tale which is "naughty, but nice," to youthful sinners, comes when conversation turns on these mysterious beings. I could have made a very distinguished acquaintance indeed—namely, that of the Lord Chancellor—had I published in a book all the Merrie Tales of the kind which I have, or could have, heard of such "shoking" culpabilities—which seem to be almost the only kind of abilities now manifested by these "geniuses." In all which they are true as steel to the traditions of their ancestors, the *dii minores*, the minor or sylvan gods, of whom Pico della Mirandola—whose tomb is not far off from here—informs us that "Saint Augustin declares in the fifteenth book of the City of God, that 'the *Silvani* and *Fauni* have many times sinned with women, who, however, greatly desired it, the end thereof being that they lay with them. And that certain demons, called by the French Dusii, went about continually seeking such carnal iniquity, and—*mettendola ad effetto*—putting it into effect.'"

All of these, as I have shown in chapters on them—Fauns, Silvani, and Dusii —still live in the Romagnola. There the *contadina* maiden half fears and half hopes in the forest shades, as twilight falls, to meet with a handsome, roguish, leering, laughing lover; there, it may be, among reedy rocks, will rise from the whitening water of the headlong stream some irresistible Elf. *Ma—che volete?* Girls will be girls!

This Cupra tale is much like one in BODINUS, where, however, the devil him- self is the lover, and a girl of twelve his *bonne fortune*. They may both have come from a common source.

According to PRELLER (*Römische Mythologie*), there was on the coast of Picenum a goddess named *Cupra*, who is supposed to be a Juno, of Etruscan origin. Her temple was renewed by Hadrian. "But the name is probably to be explained by the Sabine word *cyprus* (good), whence the Vicus Cyprius in Rome and a *Mars Cyprius* in Umbria." I do not feel authorised to suggest any con- nection between these names and that of the Cupra in the story. Nor do I insist on any *positive* identity of *any* of my discoveries with ancient ones. There may have been, for aught I know, mistakes or misunderstandings as regards any or all these names. I have simply written down what I gathered, and I dare say there will be correctors enough in due time to verify or disprove it all.

All of the old Etrusco-Roman deities were in pairs, male and female, hence possibly the modern confusion as to certain names. They also "crossed" one another. "Thalna, or Cupra," says George Dennis (*The Cities and Cemeteries of Etruria*, 1878), "was the Etruscan Hera or Juno, and her principal shrines seem to have been at Veii, Falerii, and Perusia. Like her counterpart among the Greeks and Romans, she appears to have been worshipped under other forms, according to her various attributes, as Feronia, Uni, Eilithya-Lucothea." The incident of the leaves connects Cupra with classic lore. Gerard (*Gottheit : der Etrusker*, p. 40) thinks Thalna is descriptive of Cupra as a goddess of births and light. We learn the name of Cupra from Strabo, v., p. 241. Of which Noel des Vergers says in *L'Etrurie et les Etrusques*, Paris, 1862, that :—

"Junon, que Strabo appelle Cupra, bien que nous ne trouvious pas ce nom sur les monuments cerami-ques ou les miroirs, avait comme Jupiter un temple dans l'arx ou la citadelle des villes Etrusques."

Walnut Witches

" In Benevento a nut-tree stands,
And thither by night from many lands,
Over the waters and on the wind,
Come witches flying of every kind,
On goats, and boars, and bears, and cats,
Some upon broomsticks, some like bats,
Howling, hurtling, hurrying, all
Come to the tree at the master's call."

Dom Piccini, *Ottava della Notte*

" Sott'acqua e sotta viento,
Sott' 'e nuce 'e Veneviento."
Neapolitan Saying

It is probable that one of the earliest supernatural conceptions formed by man was that of the *T'abu*, or *Taboo*. It was that if the witch, or shaman, or conjuror wished to guard, or keep, or protect a certain property from depredators, he by magic power or spells caused the person trespassing to suffer. If a sorcerer or a chief had a valuable weapon or ornament, spells were pronounced over it to protect it, and if it were stolen some mysterious disease soon after attacked the thief. By a little judicious poisoning here and there of suspected offenders, the *taboo* of course soon came to be firmly believed in and dreaded. Naturally enough it was extended to trees bearing valuable fruit, fields and their crops, wives and cattle. Then in time everything belonging to priests and chiefs was *tabooed*. In the Pacific islands at the present day where the natives have not been civilised, it often happens that a man who has eaten fruit, or even touched an article belonging to a chief, though he did not know at the time that it was prohibited, will soon die of mere fear. The laws of *taboo* in Fiji and many other places were so numerous and intricate that if written out they would make a work quite as extensive and difficult to master as Blackstone's Commentary. Little by little it entered into every relation of life. Wherever the power of the priest came—and it went everywhere—there was the terrible *taboo*. It sat by every fireside—it was with man when he awoke in the night; there were kinds of food which must not be eaten, certain positions which must not be assumed, thoughts which must not be entertained. There were words which must never be spoken, names of the dead which must never be uttered; and as people were named from things, therefore language was continually changing. Over all and under all and through all was the *taboo*, or will of the priest.

In CATLIN'S great work on the North American Indians there is the portrait of a Chippeway emaciated to a living skeleton. There was, about fifty years since, in his country, in a remote place, a vast mass of virgin copper, which was regarded with superstitious reverence. The sorcerers of the tribe had decreed that any Indian who should guide a white man to this great nugget would surely be accursed and die. One man, tempted by gifts, and in an hour of temporary free-thought, broke the ban and led a white trader to the mysterious *manitou*. Then came the reaction. He believed himself to be accursed, and so pined away. A traveller in Fiji has recorded that a native having once by mere accident touched something which belonged to a chief, and learned that it was *taboo*, died in a few days from terror.

An accurate and impartial history of the development of *taboo*, or prohibition, would be the history of religion and of the human race. As regards church property it became known as *sacrilege*—the conversion of sacred things to secular uses. The *exempla* of the preachers of the Middle Ages show us the doctrine of *taboo* carried to the extremes of absurdity. RABELAIS ridiculed these extrava-gances, but the shafts of his wit fell back blunted, even as the arrows of the scoffer missed the mark when shot at a leaf taken from the Holy Decretals. But *taboo* is yet strong everywhere. I can remember that once when I was a very small boy I unwittingly—this was in a New England village—injured a pamphlet or book which had been lent by the local clergyman. "Don't you know," exclaimed a lady who was reproving me, "that that book belongs to Dr. L—— ? " And I was aghast, for I felt that the crime was far greater than if the injured property had belonged to one of the laity.

Making every allowance for the natural limitations and necessities of Evolu-tion, *taboo* was productive of some good but also of great evil. At present, its old mission being worked out among enlightened people, the bad is predominant. Under the influences of the Church it was so freely, so recklessly, and so unscru-pulously applied that millions of lives were crushed by it or made needlessly miserable. It enforced celibacy; it compelled injudicious charity, which enlarged the area of poverty instead of relieving it; it made idleness, coloured by superstition, holy ; it exalted in every way the worthless idle shaman, or sorcerer, above the productive citizen ; it laid great curses and eternal damnation on trifling offences, on no offences, and on the exercise of natural human rights and privileges. And it still contrives to do so to an extent which few realise. For the prohibition or punishment, or causing suffering in any form whatever, when it is applied to anything which is not in itself wrong, is *taboo*. But what *is* wrong? That which injures others. And what are injuries? Firstly, those which the law defines as to person and property, directly or indirectly, in law or equity. Secondly, those which are conventional and spring out of our artificial social conditions. These are mostly of the feelings, or sentimental—regarding which it becomes us to exercise the strictest discipline over ourselves, and to make the *utmost* allowance for others.

It is as regards these conventional and sentimental wrongs in social relations, and in really *artificial* matters, that *taboo*, be it religious or secular, makes its tyranny most keenly felt. Not to wander too widely from the subject, I can only say that a vast amount of all social injustice does not spring, as is generally assumed, or supposed, from unavoidable current causes, but from mere custom and use derived from tradition. He who will look carefully, honestly, and above all boldly, into this, will be astonished to learn how powerful still is the old shaman of the very earliest stage of barbarism. The demon of the Threshold—he who lay in wait at the very entrance of the first hut of humanity—is still lurking by thine though thou seest him not.

It would be interesting to know how many objects which were regarded as accursed and bedevilled owed their evil repute in the beginning to *taboo*. During the Middle Ages, and indeed from earlier times, the walnut-tree was regarded as being dear to demons and specially chosen by witches as a place of meeting. Among the Romans it typified darkness or evil, hence it was believed that if it stood near an oak they mutually injured one another, because the latter was sacred to Jove, the god of lightning, the principle of light (NORK, *Realwörterbuch*, vol. iii., p. 387. FRIEDRICH). In the earliest mythologies the nut was an erotic symbol. On the bridal night the married pair among the Jews praise God for planting the nut-tree in the Garden of Eden ; and among the Romans it was a custom *spargere nuces* to scatter nuts on such occasions. " But as sensual passion is allied to sin, it is plain that the walnut-tree is also a demoniac symbol. The Rabbis declared that the devil chose it for a favourite resting-place, and advised people never to sleep under it, because every twig thereof has nine leaves, and on every leaf dwells a devil " (FRIEDRICH, *Symbolik*, p. 315).

BUNSEN (*Rom.* iii., 3, 210), tells us that there once stood in the *Piazza della*

Chiesa del Populo a great walnut-tree whose leaves were so infested by devils that Pope PASCHAL the Second cursed it, had it cut down, and a church built where it had stood—an act quite becoming a shaman or voodoo in every respect. *Maledicta sis o nuce !* " Be thou d——d, oh walnut-tree, root and branch, nuts and bark, und to hell vit you ! "

All of this rubbish of eroticism, diablerie and darkness, doubtlessly gathered about the tree from many sources, but the beginning of it all was that some early sorcerer, to save his walnuts, informed his neighbours that the tree was *tabooed*, and that devils sat on it to torment those who should rob it. I have heard of a German preacher of the mob who explained the origin of evil by the fact that, " Eve did rop a *Baumgart* " (or orchard), and I know a perfectly authentic case of theology in the nursery, in which a small girl, being asked why God forbade Adam and Eve to eat the apples, replied that He wanted them for pies, but was corrected by another, who told her, " No—that He wanted to keep them for his *winter apples* "—that kind being usually prohibited to children. However, in any case it was the first *taboo* on record ; and because simple Adam and Eve had been created of a heedless curious human nature, and not wise enough to resist Satan, the incarnate spirit of genius and evil, their descendants have been damned eternally to hell by hundreds of millions. Which cheerful myth in *no* respect invalidates the many great truths which abound in the Bible, as PAINE and INGERSOLL argue—nay, it contains a *great* truth : that idle curiosity and childish disobedience are a great source of evil. The Jews regarded unflinching, unconditional obedience, with no allowance for human weakness, as the law of laws. It was well for them as they were, but it was going too far to make it all in all. It had held Egypt together in good condition for thousands of years, and MOSES, who was a great student of laws, applied it. But it is not applicable to England. or America, or indeed to any republic, or semi-republic, to-day. Freethought now has its rights, and is a law like others.

But to return to our trysting-tree—the walnut. As all the witches of Germany were accustomed to assemble on the Blocksberg, so those of all Italy had their rendezvous or sabbat, or, in Italian, *treguenda*, at a great walnut-tree in Benevento.

This terrible tree is mentioned by many writers on witchcraft, and allusions to it are very common in Italian literature, but I never met with anything in detail till I found a pamphlet—*De Nuce Maga Beneventana*—which is by PETER PIPERNUS, and forms a supplement to his work *De Effectibus Magicis*, of which I have elsewhere written. In which, as it never rains but it pours, I met with such an excess of information that I had some trouble in condensing it, the work being composed on the picturesque, but not lucid principle, followed by

PRÆTORIUS, of writing down anything whatever about everything which comes into one's head, on slips of paper, which are then thrown into a basket without numbers, and set up by the printer as they occur. So, after eight pages of skimble-skamble, including a short essay on the sins of keeping bad company and of telling indecent stories, or *comicas fabulas de stupris virginum*, we see a gleam of coming day in a chapter on Nuts in general, with the comforting assurance that, as a tree, the walnut is endowed by Nature with both good and bad qualities—of which chapter we may note that if the walnut really does possess the extraordinary number of medical and other virtues ascribed to it by PIPERNUS, it is no wonder that it was supposed to be in the highest degree supernatural— albeit not a word is said in it of catsup or pickles. Could the men of old have foreseen the sauces of to-day, and the part which walnuts would play in them all, Heaven only knows what witchcraft they would have ascribed to them!

Finally we come to the fact that from the testimony and traditions recorded in the manuscripts of an old witch-trial, and from information gathered by many holy Inquisitors, that it was believed in the fraternity of sorcerers that not only from the times of the Lombards, but even from those of the ancient Samnites, there had ever been at Benevento an immense walnut-tree which was in leaf all the year (the same tale was told of old Druidical and German oaks), the nuts of which were of a pyramidal form, "*qua tragularibus lineis emittebat.*" These nuts sold for a high price, people believing that they protected against accidents, earthquakes, and cured epilepsy, also that they were sure to produce male off- spring, *retentis intra matricem nucleis.* And they were also valuable amulets against witchcraft, though used by witches in much deviltry. I think that we have here a hint of the curious triangular nuts which come from the East, and of which such numbers are sold in Florence, made into rosaries. These are also carried singly as magical amulets. There is a variety of them found in China which exactly resembles the head of a buffalo, horns and all. I have specimens of both kinds.

Next we have the topography of the region where the tree grew—for PIPERNUS approaches the enemy very gradually—and finally of the field in which this King of Darkness stands, as our author puts it very neatly, "more like a *Nox* than a *Nux.*" Which pun of darkness casts, however, not a little light on the tenebrific nature of this tree, and its noxious nature, with the suggestion that it was the mere resemblance of name which drew to it an associa- tion with the powers of the underworld. PIPERNUS gives us a long array of causes why the nut-tree was dreaded by Christians, and loved by witches, the only sensible one of which is that it was of yore, because of its dense shade, sacred to Proserpine, Night, and the Infernal Gods.

Well, as it happened that the good people of Benevento had a great walnut-tree where they worshipped serpents, or "divinity in the likeness of a beast, which is vulgarly called a viper," and what was also horrible, held horse-races in which the riders caught at bunches of sumach suspended in the tree—after the fashion of the profane and ungodly game of flying horses and hand-organ which we have seen at irreligious, worldly-minded, country fairs. There was in Benevento a great saint, Barbatus, to whom these goings-on of the heathen with their great moral show of snakes and races, and the rest of the circus, were a terrible annoyance—for then, as now, two of a trade did never yet agree. Competition was not, with him, the soul of business. The ruler of that region was ROMUALDUS, who was a heathen. And BARBATUS tried to convert him, but he did not convert worth a button. In vain did BARBATUS flourish and coruscate his miracles—*et miraculis coruscans*—round the head of this impenitent mule—I could almost fancy that Rom must have been a gypsy. His only reply was to the effect that "that cock won't fight." For I must mention that it is also recorded that he kept race-horses and game-cocks—and that there is in bad Latin mournful evidence of the truth of it all.

By and by there were rumours of war in the land. Constantinople—I mean CONSTANTIUS—the emperor, was coming *innumera multitudine suorum collecta*, with a vast army to wipe out Benevento. Romualdus was a hard fighting man, but as Saint CHRYSOSTOM said, "There is no use in a goat's trying to buck against a bull." He was reduced to extremes, and it was finally found that CONSTANTINE, like a true and gentle Christian, had decreed that on a certain day he would take the city and put every human being in it, *utriusque sexus*, to death.

Arrepta occasione—BARBATUS saw his opportunity and improved it. He held a grand public meeting, in which he attributed all these troubles to that nasty Viper, and their heathenish horse-races, and wicked walnuts. I dare say, too, that they had wine with their walnuts—but of this the history says nothing. And he ended by telling them that if they would raise their eyes above vipers and walnuts, and the turf, up to heaven, they would all be saved. Whereupon Romualdus said if that would save the town, he, for one, would raise *his*—and, to cut the tale short, CÆSAR CONSTANTINE and his army, *Beneventum non penetrabit*—"did *not* take Beneventum."

And then BARBATUS had a beautiful time. He cut down the walnut-tree, killed the snakes, stopped the horse-races, confiscated all the "poultry" of the cock-fights, threw the gaffs into the river ("they used slasher-gaffs in all pits in those days," *Alectromachia*, vol. i.), and what with baptizing, confessing, and burying, got to be as rich as a Jew.

It is not difficult to see how this miracle was worked. When you are in correspondence with your CONSTANTINE, it is easy to arrange that he should not penetrate to your Beneventum. A chief who, like ROMUALDUS, might be obliged to fight to the death by force of public opinion when it was only a question of war, could nicely compromise on a miracle. The entire history of the progress of Christianity in Sweden, Norway, and Denmark, is a chronicle of heathenism extinguished by brute force, or marriages, or by this same old trick of BARBATUS.

The nut-tree was cut down, but the king never dies. It is true, adds PIPERNUS, that there is now in the same place another tall and great walnut-tree, in the hollow of which three men might hide—and near this are sometimes found bones and bits of flesh, the signs of witches' banquets—probably chosen to take the place of the ancient one. As appeared by the testimony of one VIOLANTA, who being interrogated—probably with a rack and red-hot pincers in the Christian manner of 1519 (that being the date)—said that she had been at such a tree. There they worshipped Diana (not the devil—he was only adored in Germany) or Herodias, the goddess of dancing, who, however, as before said, appears in Rabbinical writings as Lilith, who was the Hebrew Diana, or mother of all the witches, and held high revel and "had a good time."

It may be observed that PIPERNUS declared that women became pregnant simply by means of the nuts from this tree. There is no mention of male assistance in this matter. Very recently, as a write, I inquired in Florence if there was any account current of magical properties in walnuts, and was promptly told the following tale, regarding which I had made no suggestions and given no hints whatever. It was written out for me, not by any means in choice Italian.

"The country of *Benevento* is in the Romagna, and that is the real *posto delle streghe*, or witch meeting-place. One evening a gentleman went to walk with his daughter whom he adored. And as they passed under a walnut-tree, and there were so many fine nuts, she desired to eat of them. But hardly had she eaten one when she felt herself ill, *allo stomaco*, and went at once home, and to bed. And all her family were in despair, because they loved her tenderly.

"Nor was it long before they saw her body increasing in size, and thought she was *incinta*, or with child, and began to treat her harshly, till at the end of nine months she gave birth to a little lamb ; it was very beautiful, and her parents knew not what to think of this phenomenon. And they questioned her closely as to whether she had ever had a lover, but she swore this had never been the case, and knew nothing beyond this—that she felt ill after having eaten the walnut.

"Then the father took his daughter to the tree, and she ate another nut ; when all at once the tree vanished, and there appeared an old witch, who touched the lamb, when it became a handsome young man, and the witch said, ' This is the lover whom you would not permit your daughter to marry. I by my sorcery made him enter and leave her (*sortire dalle sue viscere*), and so shall she be compelled to wed him.' "

On hearing this mystical tale I remarked, "Then the lover became father to himself?" "*Sicuro*—certainly," was the reply. Here I might tell the story of the nun who became possessed, or as some say, *enceinte,* by swallowing a *diavoletto,* or little devil, in a lettuce leaf, she having taken her salad without first praying, and so on, such tales, suggested by meditations on immaculate conception not being rare. But what is to the purpose is to show that the idea of the walnuts of the tree of Benevento producing such results is ancient and widely spread. The story seems to be a witch parody of the birth of Christ.

The witches of Benevento do not seem to have been by any means a bad lot. In this story they appear as succouring—in a strange way to be sure—a pair of unfortunate lovers, which is certainly the ideal of human benevolence to most young ladies. And in Spain, Ireland, and elsewhere, the fairies have taken from them the credit of a tale which is very much to their credit, and which was attributed to them lang syne. This is the story of the Hunchback who lost his hump. Among the two or three hundred jolly little comediettas in which good-natured, honest *dummklug* STENTORELLO is the hero, and which are played at present all the time in Florence, there is one called The Witches of Benevento, which is founded on the legend, and I find it in PIPERNUS. Perhaps your memory may be a little rusty— *nulladiméno*—anyhow, I will tell it, with interpolations.

" There was a man named Lambertus Alutarius, who was a hunch-back, gay and cheerful, popular with everybody. One night, returning home by the light of the moon, he passed near the great Walnut-Tree of Benevento. There he saw a great assembly of people, men and women, in fine array, dancing and singing, jolly as sand-boys—but their song was strange and somewhat monotonous, for it was merely :—

" *' Ben venga il Giovedi e Venerdi.'*

(" 'Welcome Thursday and Friday !')

" Thinking they were a party of reapers—*putans esse messores*—by way of helping them on, Lambert, catching the tune, sang in rhythm :—

" ' E lo Sabato, e la Domenica.'

(" 'And Saturday—Sunday too.')

" Which was so well done that the dancers all burst out laughing, and feeling respect for such an admirable poet, pulled him out, made him dance and feast with them. And then a merry devil " (PIPERNUS calls him a *diabolus,* but he must have been a jolly one) "jumped up behind, and with one tremendous jerk, which was like drawing a tooth, causing great but momentary pain—*intenso sed momentaneo dolore*—took away his hump. At which Lambert screamed out, *O* JESU, *Virgo* MARIA ! when the whole *spuk,* or enchantment, vanished— lights, plate, dishes, all the splendour and glory of the festival had gone. Still Lambert had not exactly the feeling of one who treads alone some banquet hall deserted—for the hump had gone too with all the witches, and he found himself a magnificently tall, straight figure ;—when witches *do* do a thing, they ' does it hand- some,' as a certain ' unfortunate nobleman ' was in the habit of saying.

" He went home and knocked in the early dawn, while it was three-quarters dark, and la signora Lambert looking out bade him begone. *Quis est iste temerarius ?*—' Who is that chèeky vagabond ?' was her indignant cry. *Lambertus tuus*—"Thy Lambert!' he replied. 'The voice indeed is Lambert's,' she answered, 'but you're not the man.' And then *alta voce proclamans*—raising a row—she called in all the neighbours and relations, who, after duly examining him and listening with awe and delight to his tale of the adventure by the great Walnut-Tree, passed him on as all right. But the change in his personal appearance must have been very great, for our author states that 'the next day when he walked the streets of Altavilla even his best creditors did not recognise him.' To which he adds in an airy, impudent manner, 'Such cases are very common with us,' and many writers record them *quos brevitate omittimus*—which I omit for want of room.' "

I should like to have seen some of those "numerous cases."

It is—as I have before remarked—very remarkable that in Italy there are two very distinct and contradictory currents of Witch-lore. One is the true old Latin-Etruscan legend, in which the witch is merely a sorceress or enchantress, generally benevolent and kind. She is really a *fata*, like the French *fée*, who is always a lady, loving children and helping poor men. There is in this witch-craft nothing to speak of, of selling souls to the devil, and all the loathsome abominations of living only for evil. There are good witches and bad, the old Canidia of Horace still exists, but though she lames donkeys and blasts vines, she does not make a specialty of getting people to hell. The Italians seem to have believed that men could do that abundantly well for themselves, without help.

The other current is of the diabolical sort, and it is due almost entirely to the Church and the priests. This is the kind which caused the witch-mania, with its tortures and burnings. It is very curious that despite all the efforts of Saint Barbato, and an army of theologians after him, the old genial classic associations still survive, and the witches of Benevento are still believed to be a beautiful, gay and festive society, whose queen is Diana—with very little of Hecate-Hexe in her. In proof of this I am supplied with another legend by the same authority as that from whom I obtained the tale of the lamb.

" There was at Benevento a poor family whose members gained their living by going about the country and getting fruit, which they sold. One day the youngest son was roaming, trying to see what he could find, when he beheld a Walnut-tree—but one so beautiful *che era una cosa di non credere*—'twas hardly credible what nuts were on it !

" Truly he thought he had a good thing of it, but as he gathered the nuts they opened, and from every one came a beautiful little lady who at once grew to life-size. They were gay and merry, and so fair— *parevano occhi di sole*—they seemed like eyes of the sun. Sweet music sounded from the leaves, they made him dance ; 'twas a fine festa !

" But he did not for all that forget why he had come there, and that the family at home wanted bread. But the ladies, who were fairies (*fate*), knew this, and when the dancing was over they gave him some of the nuts. And they said : 'When you shall be at home open two of these, keep a third for the king's daughter, and take this little basket- (*pagnerina*) full to the king. And tell the queen's daughter not to open her walnut till she shall have gone to bed.'

" And when he had returned and opened his nut there poured from it such a stream of gold that he found himself richer than the king. So he built himself a castle of extraordinary splendour, all of precious stones. And opening the second nut there came from it such a magnificent suit of clothes that when he put it on he was the handsomest man in the world.

"So he went to the king and was well received. But when he asked for the hand of the princess, the monarch replied that he was very sorry, but he had promised his daughter to another prince. For this other the princess had no love at all, but she was enamoured *à prima vista* with the youth.

"So she accepted the nut, and went to bed, but oh wonder! what should come out of it but the young man who had asked her in marriage! Now as she could not help herself, and, moreover, had no special desire to be helped, she made the best of it, and suffered him not only to remain, but to return, which he did, zealously, full many a time ; with the natural result that in the course of events the princess found herself *incinta*, or with child, and declared that 'something must be done.'

"And this was arranged. She went to her father and said that she would never marry the prince to whom he had betrothed her, and that there should be a grand assembly of youths, and they should agree that, let her choose whom she would, they would support her choice. So it was done, and there were feasts, balls, and at last a great assembly of young men.

"Among these appeared her own lover—*quel giovane delle noce*—'that young man of the walnuts.' And he was dressed like a poor peasant, and sat at the table among the humblest who were there. Then the princess went from one to the other of those who wished to marry her. And she found some fault in every one, till she came to her own lover, and said : ' That is the one whom I choose,' and threw her handkerchief at him—which was the sign that she would marry him.

"Then all who were present were enraged that she should have selected such a *pezzente*, or beggar, nor was the king himself well pleased. At last it was arranged that there should be a combat, and that if the young man could hold his own in it he might marry the princess.

"Now he was strong and brave, yet this was a great trial. But the Ladies of the Walnut Tree helped their friend, so that all fell before him. Never a sword or lance touched him in the fray, he bore a charmed life, and the opposing knights went down before him like sheep before a wolf.

"*Fu il vicitore.* He was the victor. And he wedded the daughter of the king ; and after a few months she gave birth to a *bel bambino*—a beautiful babe who was called, in gratitude to the fairy ladies, The Nut of Benevento. And so they were happy and contented."

I have done scant justice to this poem—for a poem it was, as I heard it sung with feeling and expression, and yet there was in it neither metre to speak of nor rhyme to mention, only such as the beautiful Italian language supplies to all who can sing. It does not seem to be known to all that all Italian fairy tales are really poems, and often sung by the *contadine*—as were all the American Red Indian traditions. The witches of the Walnut-Tree appear in this tale as fairies, but 'tis all one—they are the same charming souls as those who remove Lamberto's hump, and make the young man his own father. I cannot deny that they certainly do manifest a decided disposition to play the most eccentric erotic tricks, and confirm what William Grant Stewart says of the Scotch fairies, that "their appetites are as keen and voluptuous as their inclinations are corrupt and wicked "—wicked here meaning what I once heard another Scotchman define as "vara leecherous." It will be observed that the walnut which produces a child is effectively given in another guise in this tale, and that this, coupled with the assertion of PIPERNUS, induces me to believe that in substance these two tales are extremely ancient. They are also valuable in proof of the fact that, in spite of the incessant efforts of the monks to carry out the declaration made in *Psalm* xcvi. 5, that "all the gods of the Gentiles are devils," there were exceptions in which the beautiful and benevolent spirits of the ancient time survived the Hebrew-Catholic calumnies. It is worth noting that the last half of this tale corresponds exactly with an incident narrated in an Icelandic saga.

But to return to our Walnut-tree. Janet Ross tells us in her *Land of Manfred* that Monsignor SCHINOSI gave her the following from a MS. history of Benevento by Nicastro :—

> "In the time of Romuald the Longobards worshipped golden vipers, and the Duke himself, though he had promised to Bishop Barbatus that he would embrace Christianity, had an altar in his palace on which stood a winged two-headed golden dragon, with two sphinxes in jasper on either side, and various idols from the temple of Isis. This angered the bishop, who, helped by the Duchess Theodorada, his disciple, went with an axe and broke the dragon and idols to pieces. Of the fragments of the winged monster he made a chalice for his church. He then cut down the tree."

It may be all as true as the other tale, but this account of gold vipers, dragons, and Egyptian idols has a bric-à-brac shop-look which seems to have come—if a look can come—from the rococoanut of some later writer. But it may be all right. *Non nobis tantæ componere lites.*

WITCHES AND WITCHCRAFT

> "Oc eru ther hiner mestu flaugd konur, ther kanna Galldra oc fiolkyngi, so ecki standist noytt vid them."
>
> ("And there are many evil women who know incantations and magic, so that no one can harm them.")—
> ULF UGGASON'S *Saga*.

"It seems to me strange," I remarked one day, "that no *men* seem to practise witchcraft!"

"Oh, but there are, though," remarked my Head-Collectress. "Why, there is a *priest* here in Florence who is a *streghone.*"

"Santo! Now, if you had told me there was a thief in the police I should not have been astonished. But he can't be a real wizard."

"*Ma sì.* GESUALDA there knows him. And you can see him yourself if you want to."

I thought on the whole I did not want to. For I knew that, in the first place, I should be introduced as a *stregone Inglese,* and then something came into my head about one CATO, who marvelled that one agur could look another in the face. Not that I had any fear of mutual smiling or winking—the confessional gives a command of countenance beyond words. But I was seized with great admiration of a priest who could be honest enough to call himself by his right name, and asked how he came to practise our noble profession.

"Ah!" cried the witch, with a smile, "he couldn't help himself. He *had* to become one. He was called in to confess a witch who was dying, and did not know with whom he had to deal. So she got her confession, and then said she had something to leave him. Would he have it? Oh, wouldn't he! *Si, sicuro*. 'Then,' she cried, 'I leave you my witchcraft!' And before he could say a word she was dead and off, and he found himself a wizard."

Some time after I had written the foregoing sentence I received from another source the following additional authentic information regarding this goblin priest, of whose real existence I have not the least doubt :—

"This priest was called in to convert an old woman, who, saying that she had something, continually repeated : ' I have no relations—to whom shall I leave it ? to whom shall I leave it ? I cannot leave this world till that is left.' Then the priest said : ' Leave it to me !' Then the old woman at once gave him a small key to a certain box or casket, and died. When the priest opened the casket he found in it a mouse. And so the spirit of witchcraft came on him.

"And when it comes, if the witch touches any person, he or she will be bewitched, and waste away or die. But this priest, being a good man, would not touch or embrace people at such times, but, going into the country, touched trees, or grain, or maize, and whatever he touched dried up. So he did as little harm as was possible ; but for all this he could not help being a wizard."

This story is extremely interesting from the mention of the mouse. This was the soul of the witch. Prætorius, in his *Anthropodemus Plutonicus*, tells a marvellous story of a witch whose soul came out of her mouth as a red mouse, which idea Goethe uses in Faust. As my informant was herself in the sisterhood of sorcery, I have no doubt that she made out as strong a case as was possible to prove that all the power and sanctity of the Church and of Christianity could not avail to remove the awful might of *stregoneria*. But she *believed* what she narrated to me, and it is interesting to know that in the city of Florence in the month of January, 1891, there were people who believe in a prehistoric Shamanism which is stronger and mightier than that of the Church. Ages have lapped over ages, the Etruscan and Sabine-Latin and Roman and Christian cults have succeeded one to the other, but through it all the witch and wizard, humble and unnoted, have held their own.

But, in fact, as I became familiar with the real, deeply seated belief in a religion of witchcraft in Tuscany, I found that there is no such great anomaly after all in a priest's being a wizard, for witchcraft is a business, like any other. Or it may come upon you like love, or a cold, or a profession, and you must bear it till you can give it or your practice to somebody else. What is pleasant to reflect on is that there is no *devil* in it. If you lose it you at once become good, and you cannot die till you get rid of it. It is not considered by any means a Christianly, pious possession, but in some strange way the *strega* works clear of Theology. True, there are witches good and bad, but all whom I ever met belonged entirely to the *buone*. It was their rivals and enemies who were *maladette streghe, et cetera*, but the latter I never met. We were all good.

What seems incredible and utterly contradictory to all this is the fact that during the Middle Ages witchcraft, supposed to be based on a compact with the devil, raged in Italy—witness the rubbish written by PICUS DE MIRANDOLA, GRILLANDUS, PETER PIPERNUS, and scores more. And it is absolutely true that before this Hell carnival, and after it, and deep, deep under it, there was alive all the time among the *people* the old ante-Etrusco-Roman sorcery, and with it another witchcraft which had nothing to do with hell or devils, or original sin or anything Hebrew-Persian-Christian—and it lived, unheeding learned men and priests and their piety.

The witch-mania died, and the Church is dying fast, and yet here, in Tuscany, the witchcraft without a devil or a god—the Shamanism of oldest times with a little later Etruscan-Roman colouring, still survives—as indeed everything in this book indicates. The knowledge inspires a very strange reflection as to what the *real* nature of the Northern Italian can be like. For such a capacity for survival indicates character. The conservatism of the old Roman was his peculiar trait. It was not a blind adherence like that of the Egyptian to an established order of things, for it was based on common sense. This is strongly manifested in the works of CATO and of VARRO on agriculture. They strictly observed all the old rites ; nay, they even taught spells, much like the incantations of the witches. But under it all there was a spirit of independence. CATO says (*De Agricultura*, c. 3, 5): " Rem divinam, nisi Conpitalibus in conpito aut in foco ne facit—haruspicem, augurem, hariolum, Chaldæum ne quem consulisse velit, segetem ne defrudet, nam id infelix est."

Italy has never wanted in her darkest hours—as in the days of CRESCENTIUS, or in those of the Borgias—for CÆSAR BORGIA aimed at a united Italy ; and MACHIAVELLI was a true patriot—a few enlightened minds. So it seems to me that even in this peasant witchcraft which held its own despite the Church, there is a kind of conservatism which will not yield to the Church, that is to a form of supernaturalism which is too powerful. It is blind, humble, and ignorant, but it has a kind of vitality and of independence which indicates great power.

It is not so very absurd, in the face of hypnotism and the known influences of the imagination (whatever that may be), for ignorant peasants to believe in a *limited* amount of spells and magic. CATO did as much, and he was as sensible a man as ever lived. What is wonderful in it is that this limited amount of superstition has held its own against the stupendous, subtle influence of a far greater superstition. It may be as Marcellus says, *Venenum veneno vincitur*.

When I have been asked by people of average ordinary minds " In what do gypsies believe?" it often occurred to me that the proper answer would be " In just what you do—that is, in nothing at all." For the mere indifferent, unthinking admission of the truths of a religion, or the existence of a God, does not constitute *faith*, and there are very few persons, let us say in London, who, if a new kind of religion should become fashionable, would not fall in to it with very little thought as to its real nature. But a question in science, be it of chemistry, political economy, public health, navigation, or morals, cannot be thus easily acquiesced in, for it demands *active* intelligence. A priest settles a disputed point in theology very easily by his *ipse dixit*, but a lawyer cannot clear his client by merely expressing his conviction of his innocence. He must work hard to prove his point.

But however lukewarm an indifferent Christian may be, there is always that to be drawn from his general course of life which shows the faith in which he was born, and so as regards Tuscan or other witches and wizards, while they make no profession of any doctrines, one can deduce from their traditions and spells several curious and very original points, which were doubtless at one time taught or believed in with great zeal. They are as follows :—

The reader will have observed from several passages or anecdotes in this work that witchcraft as it now exists in Italy is utterly unlike the same as it was or is represented to be in Northern Europe. Sometimes the latter as it was taught by priests, with its principle of selling the soul to the devil, and as a thing entirely vile and diabolical, appears. But this is all Christian. The real *stregoneria* of Italy, and especially of Tuscany, is *in se* absolutely heathen. It has nothing to do with pacts with Satan, or hell, or heaven. When the devil, or devils, are mentioned in it, they are under false colours, for they are simply spirits, perhaps evil, but not beings solely intent on destroying souls. According to Roman Catholic, and I may truly add early Protestant, doctrines there are incredible swarms of devils (far outnumbering the good spirits), who are all the time occupied in tempting and damning mankind, in most cases succeeding with great ease.

The Italian *stregoneria* is like an endowment. It may be voluntarily assumed by keeping company with witches, studying their lore, and taking part in their enchantments. But this may be done either in a good or evil spirit, and in neither case is the soul to be damned for it in a Christian sense. The witches evidently are not so far advanced in humanity and the religion of illimitable Divine mercy and love as to conceive that a soul can be sent to hell eternally for a forgotten *Ave Maria*, as is beautifully illustrated by a number of well-authenticated Catholic tales. The gift of witchcraft is not indeed for every one. Many long for it, but in fact very few attain it in its upper or higher grades. But one who gets it must keep it till some other person will take it—in which case the witch is, as it were, absolved and washed clean of all her sins. Nay, she can cunningly induce an unsuspicious person to take the power, by pretending to leave her a legacy—the precious legacy being her *stregeria*. For as she cannot die while she is a witch, and very often desires to do so, either to go to heaven or otherwise occupy herself, it sometimes requires all her ingenuity to work off the commodity. As I have mentioned, there is now a priest in Florence who was thus taken in by a dying witch, who after getting absolution from him, ungratefully swindled him by offering a legacy which he accepted and which turned him into a wizard. And now he runs about town, alternately confessing and conjuring—giving the sacraments I suppose " in either form," like an eclectic doctor who treats his patients either allopathically or homeopathically, just as they prefer.

Italian witchcraft may be lost, in Venice, by the witch's spilling even one drop of blood while she is exercising her supernatural power, or even by being caught at it. In a Florentine story, told in another place, a girl is *un*-witched by being violently detained from going to the sabbat. All of this indicates a radically different kind of witch from the one described by Sprenger Bodinus, Wierus, and a thousand other writers.

But what is most remarkable of all is the belief that very great wizards and witches when they die become great spirits, who sweep over the country in clouds or vapours or storms, or wander on earth disguised as mortals. This is precisely the doctrine of North American Red Indians, among whom one hears continually of Glooskaps, Manobozhos, and Hiawathas, once human sorcerers, but never a word of any Great Spirit, except at treaties with the Government and interviews with missionaries, such a being having been quite unknown to them till they heard of him from the whites. In the shamanistic stage, man is always Euhemeristic, and makes his departed friends or great men into spirits.

It is also believed in the Romagna that those who are specially of the *strega* faith die, but reappear again in human forms. This is a rather obscure esoteric doctrine, known in the witch families but not much talked about. A child is born, when, after due family consultation, some very old and wise *strega* detects in it a long-departed grandfather by his smile, features, or expression. So the world-old Shamanism of the Grand Lama of Thibet is maintained—that strange and mysterious centre of the world's earliest " religion."

Dr. O. W. HOLMES has shrewdly observed that when a child is born, some person old enough to have triangulated the descent, can recognise very often the grandparent or great-uncle in the descendant. In the witch families, who cling together and intermarry, these triangulations lead to more frequent discoveries of palingenesis than in others. In one of the strange stories in this book relating to Benevento, a father is born again as his own child, and then marries his second mother. But the spirit of the departed wizard has at times certainly some choice in the matter, and he occasionally elects to be born again as a nobleman or prince. Hence the now and then startling phenomenon of a count or marquis with an unusual amount of intelligence, for which nobody can account, not even on the ground of a clever and handsome German tutor, or a season in London or Paris. There are always some wise men in Italy who are true and honest patriots, and according to the doctrines of *stregeria* we owe them all to the very ancient and learned if not quite respectable college of wizards, to which, however, if this doctrine be true, the country owes its salvation. At any rate the idea is original, and it might be adopted to advantage in some other countries where the statesmen are certainly no conjurors.

Since writing the above I obtained the following information regarding the transmigration of souls, and the reappearance of ancestors in their descendants. And a precious time I had to disentangle or make sense of it—which may serve as a hint to those who come after the pioneer in such a wilderness, who has made the path straight for them, not to sneer at him for " inaccuracy." Truly my informant was not wanting in faith or zeal, but she was far inferior to a Passamaquoddy Indian who has been trained in tradition in the art of understanding one's self.

" Sometimes in his life a man may say, 'After my death I may be born again a wizard, (for) I would like to live again !' But it is not necessary even to declare this, because if he has said such a thing, even unthinkingly to witches—*senza neppure pensarvi ai stregoni*—they hear and observe it. So it will come to pass that he may be born again even from the children of the children of his children, and so be his own great-great grandson, or great-grandson, or grandson.

" And when such a one is born he or she is known as wizard or witch, for such an one will have fierce eyes (*con occhi burberi*), very lowering or evil, very thick hair, and such are the most malignant of all. And such a one was born in a part of the Romagna called Castrocaro. This was a girl who grew up with a wicked mind, and a hard heart, or rather no heart at all, so that as a woman she had none for her own children. And she said one day that she would be born again as a witch to be revenged on those whom she hated, which meant everybody, for she loved nobody.

" And so it came to pass many years after, the wife of her nephew gave birth to a daughter with lowering bad eyes, and heavy black hair, the very picture of a witch. And in a dream the mother heard :—

" 'This thy child
Is not thy child,
But an evil witch
Who will be full wild !

And befal what may befal,
She will do much ill to all ! '

" And so it turned out that she was re-born a girl in form, but really a spirit of evil and revenge ; for before long everybody in Castrocaro was ill and the children bewitched. The poor mother was obliged to become a witch, and obey her terrible daughter, and do all the wicked deeds which she commanded, and dared confess it to no one.

"The father of this terrible being at last understood the whole, and acted thus : He arranged a grand festivity and ball in a great open public place. And he assembled there on one side all who had been the victims of the witch, while on the other were many priests with holy water. At eleven o'clock they had supper, and at *twelve* the witches wished to escape. But the priests held them fast, and obliged the daughter to cure, or *unbewitch*, all her victims. And they bound her with ropes and sang : —

" ' Tutto il male che tu ai fatta,
Tu lo possa riparare,
E in cielo tu tu non possa andare,
Ne in forma di gatto e di nessuno animale,
Tu possa tornare
Requia sean tinpace. Amen ! '

(" ' Every sin beneath the sun
Due to thee must be undone !
Happiness thou ne'er shalt know,
Unto heaven thou canst not go,
As a cat no more thou'lt glide,
Or in such form on earth abide,
Neither shalt thou vex or slay men,
Requiescat in pace. Amen ! ')

" And then the witch-spirit, making a terrible sound as of rattling chains, and spreading fire, disappeared and was never seen again."

In this we may trace the process by which the witch or sorcerer, by being *re-born*, becomes more powerful, and passes to the higher stage of a spirit. This is extremely interesting, because it gives a clearer understanding of the method by which the man or woman who is feared is developed to a god. It is quite the same in Brahminism, or Buddhism, or Tibetan Shamanism. New incarnations in human form give greater power. This story is the more remarkable because the narrator was perfectly convinced of its truth.

In connection with this tale, the narrator observed that there are witches very good as well as very bad, and an aristocracy far above the vulgar or common kind. She, in fact, impressed it on me that there are the same distinctions in the world of sorcery as in this of ours.

" The belief that men could become gods," writes Mrs. Hamilton Gray (*Hist. of Etruria*), " is very old Etruscan. In the Acherontic Books of Tages, translated by Labeo, there were certain rites through which the souls of men could become gods, entitled " Dii-Animales," because they had been human souls. These were first Penates and Lares, before they could become superior divinities." Which agrees accurately with the modern belief as here set forth.

What is very peculiar is that these devotees believe in *two* distinct sets or systems of supernatural beings—one of the saints, angels, and the " hierarchy celestial " of the Scriptures, and the other of " the spirits," which latter, when examined, turns out to be the old Etruscan mythology, with such Shamanic additions as have been made to it by the deaths of distinguished wizards. As illustrating both this and the belief in the power of a promise or vow once made to the spirits, I give a curious story, which is the more curious because the woman from whom I obtained it absolutely believed in its truth. Its proper place would perhaps have been among the Spirits, as it was given me to illustrate the manner in which spirits, or *folletti*, came into existence ; but it has a closer relation to what is discussed in this chapter.

ZANCHI

" Zanchi was a man who was generally loved and esteemed, and who was devoted to his family. He had first one wife, who died, and then another, who did not live long, and by each of these he had a son. His heart was, however, passionately set on having a daughter. Then he married again, and had two more sons by this third wife, at which he was *tutto disperato*, or almost desperate, to think that he could not have so small a favour granted, which would have been such a great one to him. Now, of his children all died save two. And he continued to pray for a daughter, and appealed not only to all the saints, but also to the ancient spirits of the land, declaring that if he could only have his desire he would gladly die —that is, provided he could revisit earth and see the child.

" Now this vow did not pass unnoticed ; for though the saints heeded it not the spirits did, and not long after he had a daughter, whom he loved dearly ; but when the little girl was eight months old, the vow was called for, and the father left this world for another. Now his widow was a tender-hearted and devout woman, loving the sons of her husband as much as her own daughter. And every night she prayed before an image for her son and husband who had passed away.

" And one night she saw a form bending over the sleeping daughter, and as it looked up she saw that it was the spirit of her husband. And so he came night after night. In time the widow died ; but Zanchi, from his vow, became a spirit, and continued to visit his children, especially the daughter."

Here we see that a man, by a prayer to the heathen spirits of old, becomes one of them. There is no indication that he is punished—he simply is transferred entirely into another region.

It may be observed from all the incantations in this book, that even the worst of the mischief-making by Italian witches is based on individual ill-feeling. In German or English witchcraft the sorceress acts from " pure cussedness," on general principles, not sparing friend or foe, and doing anything which would please the devil. The *Stregone* or the *strega*, acts from jealousy, envy, or personal hatred. Or he or she injures a person because of being paid to do it to please a third person. The *folletti*, or spirits, do mischief, but it is because the peasants never bless them, or, worse still, speak disrespectfully of them. It is said quite exceptionally of *Spulviero* that, when alive as a wizard, he was so evilly-disposed that he injured every one indifferently. This would have only been his duty, according to the pictures of his class as drawn by the old ecclesiastical witch-doctors. In Italy revenge is almost as deeply cherished as it is in the frontier lands of America—hence we find a great deal of it in witchcraft ; but this is mere human nature.

The following sketch of witchcraft is very curious, as giving in fullest form the counter-charm against sorcery. It was partly recited, partly sung or murmured :—

"In the Tuscan Romagna are always many witches, and twice a week they meet in council.

" Witches great and small,
Meet to consider
What they must be doing
On Friday and Tuesday.
On Friday and Tuesday
Then they hold meeting
In other forms, changed
To dogs, cats, or mules,
Of goats there are many,
And go forth to follow
The tasks which are set them.

" Now it happened two years ago (1889) that a poor woman had a very beautiful baby, two months old. And one morning, after having attended to it, she went forth to work out of the house, when, turning round, she saw a strange cat leap out of her door. And feeling that it was a witch who had injured her child, grasping the cat in a great rage, she tore from it a handful of fur.

" Entering the house,
She sought in the chamber—
Sought for her infant—
On the bed, under,
But nowhere could find it,
When in the fireplace
She heard a strange wailing ;
And in the fireplace,
On coals hot-glowing,
'Mid the wood flaming,
She saw the baby,
As in a glory,
Quietly seated,
Harmed in nothing.

" So she took her child up, and being sure that this was witchcraft, she made a charm.

> " For she put the cat's hair
> In a red scarlet bag,
> With the juniper berries,
> Frankincense and cummin,
> Salt, crumbs of bread,
> Many iron filings,
> Horse-scrapings in powder,
> With a witch-medal,
> Three black-headed pins,
> Three red, and three yellow,
> Three cards from a pack—
> From a pack which is Roman—
> The seven of spades,
> Which causes confusion ;
> The seven of clubs,
> Which makes tears and sorrow ;
> And the queen of spades,
> Ordained for the witches.[1]

" Then all this is put under a heavy weight—let it be as heavy as possible—and then say :—

> " ' All of this I do
> For the accursed witch,
> That she may not live,
> Nor eat, nor drink (in peace) !
> And I put not this bag
> Under the weight,
> But the body and soul
> Of that witch accursed,
> That she may not live or stand
> Until she gives health
> Again to my child ! '

" Then the witch will come again to the door every day in the form of a cat, wailing and imploring peace.   And so this one came ; and then the woman took a skein (*gomitolo*, a bottom) of thread, and threw it three times in the air.   Then the child recovered its health and the mother burned the cat's hair ; and so there was an end to the bewitchment." [2]

It seems as if, by the putting the child in the fire, where it sat unharmed, there is a reminscence of Ceres, who did the same with the infant Triptolemus, to make it immortal.   Perhaps the witch did it to make a witch of it.   There is no explanation of the reason, and it seems altogether misplaced and mysterious, unless this be the cause of it.   If we take it altogether, this story is as strange —one may say as classical—as any of Roman times.

[1] In the original—" Che si battezza per la strega " : that is, baptised or consecrated for the witch.
[2] I am obliged to omit the original text for want of space.

Witches of a certain class have their homes in wild and strange places. Thus I have been told that—

" When one passes by a cavern where witches dwell—*o sian folletti, o siano le fate*—or it may be goblins or fairies—one makes the sign of *la castagna*, and repeats :—

> " ' O strega maladetta !
>   Che da me tu possa stare
>   Sempre distante ! ' "

> (" ' Oh witch accursed !
>   Mayst thou ever be
>   Far away from me ! ' ")

Information on this subject was often given to me in such a mad, eccentric manner with wild sounds that it is really difficult to convey it by writing. The following was half-sung, half-recited ; but the " *si, si*," or " yes, yes," was always sung, and sometimes with a strange laugh :—

" Witches make boats with the feathers of birds. And in a minute they fly—

> " In a minute they fly
>   Over land and rivers ;
>   But you must beware, *si, si !*
> How you make children's beds with feathers.
>   And if one has children, *si, si !*
> With the feathers of beds they will do them great harm.
>   And you'll find within them, *si, si !*
> Crowns made with feathers in the form of a capon.
>   And look out for that, *si, si !*
>   *Dal farci dormir i bambi*
>   *Se non veli volete fare stregar.*
>   If you want the children to sleep,
>   And not have them bewitched,
> You must keep them away from feathers.
>   And now it is finished, *si, si !*
>   Tell your story, my friend, *si, si !*
>   For mine has come to an end, *si, si !* "

In this wild song, which was not improvised but repeated as if it were well known, and a part of some longer narrative (my informant was very particular as to my putting *si, si* in the right places), the allusion to boats made of feathers is classical. " Feathers," says FRIEDRICH, " are a symbol of flight and inspiration. So the Muses were represented as having feathers on their heads to express poetic flight and rapture." " They had won them from the Sirens." The allusion to the capons is explained in the chapter on the Spell of the Black Hen.

But there was in all this mad witch-song a something mocking, and, as it were, unexplained.   Perhaps the final recommendation to keep children from *feathers*—that is, from poetry and inspiration—unless we would have them become witches or lunatics, explains it all.   But the reader cannot fail to observe that in many of the incantations which I have given there is an inexplicably wild *mysterious* spirit, which seems derived from unknown sources, and which differs entirely from those of other countries.   There is hardly a trace of it in the gypsy incantations of WLISLOCKI, or in those of the English Book of Fate.

As there are witches good and bad, so they give presents which may bring good or evil fortune ; but these must be accepted with great suspicion, or a man may find himself *indiavolato*, or bedevilled, ere he knows it.   If one has unwittingly accepted from some old woman dried chestnuts, or nuts, or almonds, and then suspects she is a witch, they should not be eaten, or he may find himself bewitched.

" In such a case, let him wait till Tuesday or Friday, and then take green broom-plant (*ginestra*), exactly at noon or midnight.   Then make the broom into a cross, and put it on the fire, and on it the gifts of the suspected witch, and say :—

> " ' Se sei una strega !
> Strega, strega, strega !
> Tu sia maladetta,
> E sia per il camin
> Maladetta, tu possa saltare
> Come queste nuoce—
> (O qualunque altra cosa sia)
> Brucciata tu possa restare ! '

> (" ' If thou art a witch !
> Witch, witch, witch !
> Cursed shalt thou be !
> And if, like these nuts,
> I can see thee jump,
> Jump up through the chimney,
> And burn away from me !')

" But the witches are crafty.   One of their tricks is to let fall an enchanted ring.   And if any person picks this up, and puts it on a finger, he will begin to waste away like a burning candle.   Then he, finding this, must make a great fire of broom (*ginestra*), and *barracocolo di ginestra* and put the ring close by the fire and say :—

> " ' Se questo anello e strègato
> Su per il cammino possa saltare,
> Incompagnia della granata
> Che io ho appogiato,
> Appogiato al focolare ! '

(" ' If this ring should be bewitched,
May it up the chimney fly
With the broom which I for peace
Have leaned against the mantlepiece ! ')

"Then if the ring be bewitched it will fly up the chimney, but be prompt at that instant to make the *castagna* with both hands, else it will fall back and the man be as bewitched as ever."

There is yet another incantation when one has received any gift of eatables from an old woman. Take a broom and put it by the fire, and throw some of the suspected food into the flame and say :—

" ' Se la robba
Che tu o vecchia indegnata
Mi ha data,
Lei e' stregata,
Nel tempo stesso che la butto,
Nel fuoco o vecchia indegnata :
Tre colpi possa fare,
Uno sopra il cammino,
Che tu possa accetare,
Uno dalla finestra,
Che quella sempre arda e la tempesta,
Ed uno della porta
Che in casa mia entrare
Più non possa !
Strega, strega, strega !
Vile e nera, brutta strega ! ' "

(" ' If these things which here I see,
By thee, vile witch, bewitched be,
In the fire the things I throw,
And as sign to let thee know :
Three blows I strike, to let thee see—
One on the chimney, straight at thee,
One on the window at thy form—
And may it stir thee like a storm—
And one at last upon the door,
That thou mayst never enter more !
Witch, witch, accursed witch,
Vile and dark and black as pitch ! ' ")

It may be here observed that witches of the wicked kind work their worst spells by means of giving food, and that this forms a much more prominent feature in Italian sorcery than in any other. Thus they make people into animals or compel them to believe themselves changed into persons of another sex. For this they were famed of old as Fulgosus (lib. 8, cap. 2) relates : "There are in Italy certain women, who by certain kinds of food, act on human minds so that they believe themselves to be what they are not." These ideas were probably produced firstly by *suggestion* or hypnotism, and secondly by administering certain poisons, such as stramonium which causes strange delusions. Fulgosus, indeed, suggests that these are delusions, and that probably the turning men into pigs by Circe, and the Egyptian girl who believed herself to be a mare and was cured by Hilarion, were all cakes baked from the same meal. In which the reader will no doubt agree with him.

The street-boys and canaille, who are as cruel in Italy as in other countries, have a very easy method for ascertaining whether an old woman is a witch. Should you see one in the street, you must follow her, making the sign of the *castagna*, and cry out many times aloud at her, "Witch, witch, witch! *Fico !*' (a-fig, meaning the sign of the *castagna*). And if she turns round and answers : "Zident !" (Romagnola, in Italian, *Accidente !*) "Bad luck to you !" you may be sure she is a witch. But she must reply with this word, and not with any other.

The witch is not so much identified in Italy with the broom as a steed, as in Northern Europe. She generally rides a goat. But she is kept away or exorcised with a broom, which is of very old Latin origin. The broom was anciently a symbol of purification—hence a magic protection against evil spirits who love dirt. Thus VARRO relates that when a child was born, the threshold was touched with a broom, a hatchet, and a pestle, to keep away spirits, which is quite like the Romagnola custom of laying a broom across the door to prevent the entrance of witches. In fact, in every one of the instances which I have collected the only allusion to the broom as regards witches is as a thing which they utterly dread. What Silvanus (regarded as a mischief-making spirit) chiefly dreaded was the broom, the hatchet, and the pestle, or the three principal symbols of culture, cleanliness, and fertility.

Since writing the foregoing I have learned the following, which proves that the whole of the ancient rite as described by VARRO is still observed.

" When a babe is born, to free it from witches one should take a hatchet, a pestle, and a broom, and all these are to be put in a cross on the threshold of the door, and the one who does this must say :---

" ' Tutto questo l'ho incrociato
Perche voialtre strege maladette,
Il soglio della mia (casa)
Non potete traversare ! ' "

(" ' With these things a cross I make,
Cursed witches, for your sake,
That ye may no further come,
To trouble me in this my home ! ' ")

The *pestle*, for some reason, is regarded as being very effective in magic.

Witches in Italy as in the Danubian provinces love to dance and rock and fly in wild mazes, chasing one another on the summits of waving branches, and when these move much in but little wind you may be sure that they or the fairies are there.

> " On the tops of waving trees,
> When they're bending in the breeze,
> That is where the witches dance,
> How they caper, and they prance !
> Up and down to a piper's tune,
> Frisking in the light of the moon ! "

Hail and Cloud Men

" Hast thou entered into the treasures of the Snow ? or hast thou seen the treasures of the Hail ? "— Job. xxxviii. 22.

" Fleeting clouds—sailors of the air ! "—Schiller

I think it is Washington Irving who describes a man who wished that he were superstitious because he fancied that such a person must live in a kind of fairy-land. Walter Scott, too, was always wanting to believe what his strong Scotch common sense, fortified by education, rejected. And if the faith of the Middle Ages had not taught men that every supernatural conception whatever not included in the teachings of the Church was hellish, and fairies and elves, devils, men might certainly in the old days of belief have been much happier, and surrounded themselves with ever-varying, many-wreathing, golden-starred canopies, recognising a spirit-artist's hand in the dew, decking with liquid pearl the bladed grass, seeing eyes of light in rain-drops, and hearing love-whispers in the breeze. It is worth considering that though Chaucer wrote that in his time—

> " Now can no man see non elvés mo,"

Yet that the instant the curse, or ban, of the Church was removed from poetry by the Reformation, Fairy-land revived and flourished in the works of Shakespeare, and indeed in those of hundreds if not thousands of other writers. In truth, although its *first* causes were dying out, it received such a great development that its real power was greater than ever, like a strawberry-vine, which, dying in one place, sends out its tendrils to another, and from being barren at first, becomes in a few removes fertile, bearing abundant ivory blossoms and coral golden-spotted fruit. Which indeed holds well, because the strawberry is *par eminence* the fairy-fruit—Jerome Bosch in a picture gives it the power of changing men into strange beings. This has been little considered. The Elf, who had been a literal and yet very limited, or almost commonplace being to the peasant, became apotheosised to the refined and cultivated minds of the golden age of English literature into an Ariel. And in sober truth, there is no such exquisite worship of Elfland as is to be found in the works of SHAKESPEARE, HERRICK, DRAYTON, and in innumerable ballads and legends which this fairy Renaissance called to life. Bishop CORBET was quite wrong when he said that the fairies

> "Were of the old profession,"

or Catholic. They were all devils damned under the Church, and only became delightful little deities to the Protestants.

This view may be new to many of my readers, but it is worth seriously considering how *very* valuable a highly cultivated sense of art, or an instinct for the beautiful, preserves men from evil and revolting influences. The peasantry in Italy to this day do not quite identify witches with the horrible hags of Germany and England, who meet simply to worship the devil. Their chief is not the dirty vulgar Devil but beautiful lady-like Diana. Herein we have the result of a certain refinement of art which even the monks could never quite extinguish.

Not only is it true that a man who believes—like a Red Indian—that every tree and stone has its indwelling spirit, is always in a kind of fairy-land, but what is also worth envying, he is never *alone*. When he sits in woodland wild 'neath green or russet tree, he knows the presence of the Elves, or sees by many a sign where they have passed. Every relic of the olden time, arrow-heads, pottery, and hollow flints, have been touched by fairy hands, much more those older relics of an older time, rocks, rivers, and forests.

There is to the truly refined or cultivated mind an infinite field for this feeling, if its possessor is very familiar with such lore, for with it we too can live in Fairyland, and—

> " By a spell to us unknown,
> We can never be alone."

I do not think that SHAKESPEARE or HERRICK really "believed " in the existence of fairies, but I am very sure that no peasant of the tenth century ever peopled the forests and fields with more beautiful fairies and associations than they did. And, after all, *who knows* how much life and mystery and fairydom and spirithood *really* lies hidden in nature—what elements and senses and laws underlying laws not as yet known to us? Sleep on, and dream—it is not yet time for man to be quite aroused from his rest—you may lie a little longer!

Read, master, and inwardly digest, oh reader, all this folk-lore of the olden time. It will do you no harm though your mind were as full of fairy fancies as ever that of Don Quixote's was of the dreams of chivalry. For while the childlike charm or poetry is none the less, the historical value and the lessons which it teaches are of very great value. You will have read this book to little purpose if it has not induced you to reflect on the fact that by studying the stupendous errors of the past we learn how much of them still remain, and how few of us *realise* it.

There is, however, a distinct charm in knowledge of what man has really believed, whether it be true or false. I love to look at the knurls or knots in trees, and remember that they are caused by the heads of witches buried near them, and forcing themselves again to life ; or to peer through a flint with a hole in it to help my sight, and perhaps see Elves. Or watch the clouds like ships—" sailors of the air "—and think of the "treasures of hail " stored in them !

And this recalls one of the strangest and most daintily beautiful conceptions of the olden time—that there is afar in Cloudland a mysterious city called Magonia, where the hail is manufactured, and whence it is carried in ships which look to us like " clouds sailing along in golden sunset green."

The monks who bedevilled, belittled, and dirtied everything, added to this fancy that these ships were loaded and manned by witches and devils in order to destroy crops, and that for return cargo they were freighted with the fruit thus injured or destroyed. On which subject the tenth-century Archbishop AGOBARD of Lyons delivered himself as follows [1] :—

"Most people are so stupid and unintelligent that they believe and declare that there is a land called Magonia, from which come ships sailing through the air, which receive on board all the fruit which is destroyed by hail and storms. And that the sorcerers who cause the storms are in connection with the ship-people, and are paid by them."

The same bishop relates that he himself once saved the lives of four human beings, three men and a woman, whom the populace wished to stone to death because they believed that they were people from Magonia, who had fallen from a cloud-vessel, having been " shipwrecked " during a thunder-storm. It is to be

[1] *Des Deutschen Mittelalters Volksglauben und Heroensagen*, von F. L. F. von DOBENECK. Preface by JEAN PAUL RICHTER, Berlin, 1815. This Bishop Agobard was a noble-minded man, a miracle for his age, quite free from vulgar superstition, and determinedly opposed to that kind of Christianity which believes that there are a million of devils tempting man where one angel comes to his aid, and that the devil is far superior to God in power, since he gains more souls than are saved. For such views the bishop was greatly persecuted by the Orthodox believers, and died in misery (*vide* HORST, *Dæmonomagia*).

deeply regretted that the bishop did not give us some account of this quartette—
how they looked, and what language they spoke. I fancy myself that they would
have proved to be gypsies !

"Like ships far off and out at sea !" Reader, is there not a charm in this
conception ; and will you not *sometimes* recall it when you sit at evening and look
at the rosy, golden sunset—it may be at the trysting-tree—and see the cloudlets
steering in the fiery sea, and wish that you two could take passage therein for the
beautiful, far-away, forgotten city—for Magonia, whose walls are of aerial
amethyst, and citadels of vapoury emerald ?

> "All over doth this outer earth
>   An inner earth enfold,
> And sounds may reach us of its mirth,
>   Over its pales of gold ;
> There spirits live, unwedded all
>   From the shapes and lives they wore,
> Though oft their printless footsteps fall
>   By the hearths they loved before.
> We mark them not, nor hear the sound
>   They make in threading all around,
> Their bidding sweet and voiceless prayer
>   Float without echo through the air ;
> Yet often in unworldly places,
>   Soft Sorrow's silent vales,
> We mark them with uncovered faces
>   Outside their golden pales ;
> Yet dim as they must ever be,
>   Like ships far off and out at sea,
> With the sun upon their sails."

Floating away, away, and ever on : gleaming in glory on the heavenly plane—
blending in darkness, glittering in rain, or in hail-diamonds seeking earth again,
mingling and changing like all things for ever ! *Thou* hast been there many a time
and oft in very truth, and there thou wilt be many time, thou Child of the Mist,
or ever Eternity shall end !

Sic vita. But I learn from PRÆTORIUS, in his *Anthropodemus Plutonicus*,
that these *Graupenmenschen*, or Hail-men of Magonia, are rare elfin-artists, and that
now and then they fashion their ware in strange forms, and even enter into their
work themselves, or else by magic might cause small fairies to appear in it, in order
to mystically forebode strange things.

"Very memorable is that which happened in the year of Christ 1395, when there fell, like a rain of
pebbles, wonderful hailstones on which were human faces, both male and female. The former had beards like
those of men. The female bore long hair and veils, which were seen by a very credible man, who also had
them in his hands, as CRANZIUS declares in *Wandal*, lib. 9, c. 3.

"And in Cremona, in the year 1240, in the cloister of Saint Gabriel, there fell a hailstone on which could be seen, as if most carefully engraved, the form of a cross, with the face of the Lord Christ, and the letters JESUS NAZARENUS. And one of the drops of water from it wetting the eyes of a blind man caused him to see. As appears by the writer VINSICH, *Histor.* lib. 30, c. 138, and from him MAJOLUS, p. 15. d. tom. ; also NAUCLERUS, *Gener.* 41."

Which well-authenticated fact should of itself show that the inhabitants of Magonia were good Christians—"and wider."

"M. HEINRICH GOBALD in *Breviar. Histor.*, p. 473, declares that in 1650, on the 18th of June, as announced from Presburg, there was a terrible hailstorm, such as no one had ever beheld. The stones were of very varied forms, and some of them were like Turk's heads."

From which soon came wars, famines, revelations and revolutions, adulterers and harlots struck dead, and from this it was deduced that—

"A Child of Midnight will ere long reign, and his rule will be hard as iron and full of grief ; when pestilence, hunger, and war will take the upper hand. Yet first will he govern Moscow with much peace, and become a mighty monarch."

Which is followed by forty pages of grim and wild prophesying as to what will take place in the year 1666, as foreboded by the hailstones.

I, and it may be you also, oh reader, have seen a great and a small hailstone stuck together, so as to much resemble a Turk's head with a turban ; but truly it never occurred to us that there was a volume of political presage therein. We did not even think of the Child of Midnight which, by the way, is a fine term, and might serve for the title of a novel or poem. Yet when you see the cloud-ships far sailing in the sky, you may perchance recall the mysterious city of Magonia, and when hit by a hailstone regard it as done in sport by the fairy artisans of that famed town.

What appears from several authorities is that what seem to us to be "fleeting clouds—sailors of the air," are in reality mysterious barks, or very often spirits, hastening across the sky, the ships and sailors of "cloud-land gorgeous land" bent on errands far away ; of which there is a very strange story told by Meteranus (*Niederland Histor.*, b. 28). Firstly be it remembered that as the Norse heroes of Valhalla meet every day to rehearse their ancient duels, and fight and be killed, and then revived, so the mysterious dwellers in the land of air return to earth on the anniversary of some great battle of the olden time, just as in America the battles of Bunker Hill, Concord, Saratoga, and others, even as late as that of Gettysburg, are celebrated by spectral armies, who fight by night the conflict o'er again. So it came to pass that in the land of Angoulême in France, in December, 1608, many small clouds came drifting o'er the sky, looking like the pebbles on the strand moved by the rising tide. Then, one by one and two by two, they began to fall, softly and gently as snowflakes, to earth—" One by one and two by two, they to a mighty squadron grew "—and as they touched ground they suddenly became warriors. " All," as Meteranus declares, " were very tall, straight, handsome men, having blue weapons, flags, and everything else cerulean or sky-blue—and of them all were 12,900. And they divided into two armies, and fought from five o'clock in the afternoon till nine, when they all vanished."

But it is mostly in the silent desert or in lonely mountains, in hidden places far beyond the plain, that we see these beings who are *corpore aërea, tempore eterna* (airy of form, yet with eternal soul), who go fleeting over the sky on mystic errands bent. Sometimes they pause, however, for a time, either of their own free-will or at a sorcerer's spell, and build up, at a thought, cloud-capt towers and gorgeous palaces, rosy and golden in the setting sun, pillared domes, pearly citadels, and rows on rows of battlements, repeated like giant stairs until high lost in the air. To those who are " gifted," these appear to be actually humanly built ; and no wonder, for they are only made to seem like clouds to delude mankind. For Magonia truly is—

> " A great strange city, lovelier in its lights
>   Than all the golden greenness of the hills,
>   And in its shadows glorious far beyond
>   The purple dropping skirts of thunder-cloud,
>   A city of all colours and fair shapes,
>   And gleams of falling water day and night . . .
>   Lit up with rainbow fountains in the day,
>   Lit up with rain of coloured stars by night . .
>   And out beyond and sleeping in the light
>   The islands and the azure of the sea,
>   And upwards, through a labyrinth of spires
>   And turrets, and steep alabaster walls,
>   The city rises—all its jewelled fronts
>   Shining to seaward . . .
>   Until at last through miles of shadowy air
>   The blue and violet mountains shut the sky." [1]

I had written the foregoing in the city of Florence in May, 1891, when I was conversing one day with a woman who came into the house just as a storm was raging without. And she said : " I was going to the post-office, and as I went some one said to me, 'Truly thou art a witch, for the hailstones leap up from beneath thy feet.'"

----

[1] *The Disciples*, by Harriet E. H. King

Then we all laughed, and I asked if witches made hail ; and this was the answer, which I wrote down, word for word, in Italian :—

" People say that when the weather becomes bad (*quando il tempo si guasta*), and thunder and lightning begin, that it is a storm caused by wind, and that the dark clouds are water, and the wind bears along those clouds which shed water. But really it is a very different thing. For up in the sky there are cities made by the witches and wizards who were once driven out of paradise or who left this world, and they have made for themselves another world in heaven.

" But even in heaven they keep those evil feelings (*tengono sempre i suoi rancori*) which they ever had, and so they choose the worst weather, so that they may do much mischief to men. And then they enter a vessel (*barca*) and load it with hail ; and all the clouds which we see are not clouds of air, but boats. Then their leader takes a hailstone and throws it at a witch, and so they all pelt one another and sing :—

> " ' Tiro queste granate,
> Ma non tiro le granate,
> Le tiro perche si devono
> Convertire tutte in grandine
> E voglio sperare
> Che tutta la campagna
> A male voglia andare
> E cosi tutti di fame
> In terra dovranno andare ! ' "

This spell was sung also in Romagnola, and it means :—

> " I throw these grains of hail,
> But not merely these grains,
> I throw them that they may convert
> All (the rain) to hail ;
> And I wish, I hope,
> That all the country
> May suffer from it,
> And all the people therein
> May go their graves from hunger ! "

Of this Hail-land in heaven I received another history, which is different in a few details, but which, I think, is not less interesting :—

" People when they see clouds in air say it is *air* (vapour) and a sign of rain, but there is more in them than they suppose. For there is in the sky another world made by wizards and witches who, when they died, were not admitted to heaven, and so they made a world for themselves, which has a sea (lake) in it. And when the weather is dark, and clouds fly before the storm, those clouds are boats full of hail, and in them are wizards and witches, who throw the hail at one another, and so it falls to earth and does great harm. When this happens one should invoke the spirit of thunder (Tituno or Tignia).

" The light, small clouds which pass along in sunlight in fine weather are small boats in which are girls and children whom the witches have taken and keep as prisoners. But sometimes when it is pleasant they send them out sailing in the air."

I have, indeed, a third account in MS. devoted to these captives, but after six readings I have been obliged to give it up as unintelligible. It is only additional testimony. There is something to the effect that the witches have mirrors with which they flash out signals to the boats to return, or with which they make lightning.

Witches on earth sometimes pay visits to this Magonia, or Cloud City land, but they run a risk of being caught or killed in the storms of their own raising. Thus Friedrich Panzer tells us in his Bavarian Tales, that during the first half of the last century there was such a tremendous tempest, with hail, in Forchheim in Upper Franconia, that the people feared lest the whole town should be destroyed. Then the Franciscan brothers met in their cloister garden, when, just as the first blessing was pronounced, lo ! a beautiful woman, stark-naked, was thrown headlong from a passing thunderstorm on the grass in their midst ; and the holy brothers, greatly amazed at this, doubtless to them, utterly novel sight, drew near, when they recognised in her who had indeed dropped in on them so suddenly, the wife of the town miller, a woman long suspected of witchcraft. Whereupon one of the monks threw a garment over her, and she was brought into the cloister—" By means of which," says the account (somewhat obscurely), "they averted from her the death by fire." Which means, I suppose, that she made so favourable an impression on the Franciscans that they protected their *proie inattendue* (vide *Le Moyen de Parvenir*) from being roasted.

The conduct of these sorcerers and witches, unfit for heaven and averse to earth, building for themselves starry palaces and rose-red citadels with all the glory Dream to genius yields, reminds me of what Professor Shairp remarks of Shelley, and that very markedly indeed :—

"" The real world-existence as it is to other minds he recoiled from—shrank from the dull, gross earth which we see around us—nor less from the unseen world of Righteous Law and Will which we apprehend. The solid earth he did not care for. Heaven—a *moral* heaven—there was that in him which he would not tolerate. So, as Mr. Hutton has said, his mind made for itself a dwelling-place midway between heaven and earth, equally remote from both—some interstellar region, some clear, cold place

' Pinnacled dim in the interse inane,'

which he peopled with ideal shapes and abstractions wonderful or weird, beautiful or fantastic, all woven out of his own dreaming phantasy.''

Once in a while one of these dwellers in the violet Nifelheim, or Magonia, escapes and comes down to earth, and is born as a Shelley or a Keats—I think that Mr. J. A. Symonds is really one of them—or a Swinburne, or Ruskin, or Heine, or Carlyle, or Victor Hugo, or anybody else who is magnificently illogical, splendidly rhapsodical, sublimely egoistical (or subjective)—men whose thoughts are streamed and dashed with startling hues, and who think showers of stars, and who, when they do teach us something new—

> " Shoot out a scarlet light which seems as if
> The torch of some explorer shone in them,
> Revealing mysteries of caverns deep
> Which had been hidden from the birth of Time."

So from old days these hardened stories live as if trenched in ice, like mammoths in Siberia, to the world unknown till some discoverer reveals them, and then there is marvelling here and there that such things could have been so long frozen up. So into time old time returns again, and the ancient medals, thus disinterred, are all the more beautiful for their rust. And it went deeply to my heart that after I had read the story of Magonia, and thought it was a tale utterly dead on earth and embalmed in a chronicle, to find a sorceress in whose faith it *lives*. It was as if an Egyptian mummy, revived, had suddenly spoken to me, and told me a tale of Thebes, or declared that Cloud-Cuckoo land was a reality which he had known when he beheld—

> " Against an orange sky a purple cloud,
> A cloud that did not change nor melt nor move,
> And still there were faint shadows in the cloud ;
> A mystery of towers and walls and hills,
> And the shadow of a great dome in the midst,
> All purple."

How deeply (or one may say how terribly) impressed the Italian peasantry are by the belief that hail is caused by devils and witches appears from the following from a London newspaper of September, 1891. It is curious as involving the ancient Roman belief in the sacred power of bells as devil-drivers which was in later times turned to such good account by the priests :—

" The schoolmaster is still but very moderately abroad in Italy, as the priest of Montalto in that country has too good reason to know. When a storm comes on there it is the practice to ring frantically one of the church bells, which is supposed to have good effect on the temper of the clerk of the weather. This was duly done by the sexton one day last week, and indeed it is lucky for him that he does not hold office in our climate, or he would scarce have left the belfry this summer. However, the priest has the misfortune to be far too much ahead of his flock, and stopped the ringing, telling the people to come into church. As soon as the bell ceased the hail began, and no sooner had the priest reached the altar than a peasant named Marca bitterly upbraided him for causing the hail by stopping the bell. Producing a billhook, he attacked the priest, who parried one·blow, but presently received a fearful gash, a woman, said to be Marca's mother, meanwhile calling out, ' Give it him ! ' Marca then fled, and has not yet been caught. A little more spent by the Italian Government on spelling-books and a little less on ironclads might possibly prevent such unpleasant contingencies."

Truly Marca was much more of a heathen than a Christian. The spirit of old Rome was great in him—he would not yield to feeble modern faith.

Stories of Witches and Goblins

Story-telling in the Tuscan Romagna is an institution with observances. The peasants in winter meet together, "perhaps ten, there may be twenty or thirty, around a fire, and first of all recite with due solemnity a *rosario*, or five paternosters with the *aves* and other prayers, and then begin to *raccontare*, or relate tales of fairies, witches and *folletti*." This very ancient custom is still very generally observed. First of all some old man gives a story, which is commented on, eliciting from the hearers their own reminiscences, then another is suggested, and so the folk-lore is kept alive. In the year 1808 there was published in Bulgnese, or Bolognese—which is, with trifling difference, the same dialect as that which these peasants speak—a translation of Neapolitan fairy tales, which appears to be in the main taken from the Pentamerone of Gian Battista Basile, but which is very much varied to suit new surroundings. Hence the same stories, now known all over Italy, have penetrated to the Romagna. But they have, in the Bolognese region, many of which no traces are to be found in the usual range of Italian legends, and very often even the latter have here either taken of later years, or derived from very ancient sources, elements and characteristics which are quite peculiar, and often bewildering ; all of which the folk-lorists of the future will doubtless duly consider and sift even to powder.

The following are a few of the tales which I have heard. I could have given many more—several do indeed occur in other portions of this work—but I have been too much occupied with other subjects, nor indeed would space or the publisher permit further addition.

The Witches and the Boat

" There were two witches, mother and daughter, who lived by the sea-side, and the younger was a beauti-ful girl, who had a lover, and they were soon to be married. But it began to be reported that the women were given to sorcery and had wild ways, and some one told the young man of it, and that he should not take such a wife. So he resolved to see for himself by going to their house, but intending to remain till midnight, when, he knew, if they were witches they could not remain longer at home. And he went and made love, and sat till it was after eleven, and when they bade him go home he replied, ' Let me sit a little longer,' and so again, till they were out of patience.

" Then seeing that he would not go, they cast him by their witchcraft into a deep sleep, and with a small tube sucked all his blood from his veins, and made it into a blood pudding or sausage (*migliaccino*), which they carried with them. And this gave them the power to' be invisible till they should return.

" But there was another man on the look-out for them that night, and that was the brother of the youth whom they had put to sleep, for he had long suspected them, and it was he who had warned his brother. Now he had a boat, and as he observed for some time every morning that it had been untied and used by some one in the night, he concluded it was done by these witches. So he hid himself on board carefully, and waited and watched well.

"At midnight the two witches came. They wished to go to Jerusalem to get *garofani* (clove gilly flowers, or the clove plant, much used in magic). And when they got into the boat the mother said :—

"' Boat, boat, go for two !'

"But the boat did not move. Then the mother said to the daughter, " Perhaps you are with child— that would make three." But the daughter denied it. Then the mother cried again :—

"' Boat, boat, go for two !'

"Still it did not move, so the mother cried again :—

"' Vai per due, vai per tre,
Per quattro, per cuanto tu vuoi !'

("' Go for two or three or still
For four, as many as you will !')

"Then the boat shot away like an arrow, like lightning, like thought, and they soon came to Jerusalem, where they gathered their flowers, and, re-entering the boat, returned. Then the boatman was well satisfied that the women were witches, and went home to tell his brother, whom he found nearly dead and almost out of his mind. So he went to the witches and threatened them, till they gave the youth the *migliaccino*. And when he had eaten it, all his blood and life returned, and he was well as before. But the witches flew away as he arose, over the house-tops, and over the hill, and unless they have stopped they are flying still.

BERNONI tells this story in his narratives of Venetian witches, but less perfectly, since he makes no mention of a lover or of the witches sucking and restoring his blood. In the classical tales of APULEIUS and others, sucking the blood was the chief occupation of the *striga*, for which reason I think that this may be the earliest version of the tale. In the Venetian story the boat goes to Alexandria and the boatman while there obtains fresh dates and leaves, which he exhibits on returning as a proof of his adventure. The obtaining the mystic clove flowers gives a far better reason for the voyage. HAWTHORNE has written a story in which a boat full of witches, in the form of cats, make such a trip to obtain *rosemary*, also a witch-herb.

LA VENDETTA DI PIPPO

"There was a man named PIPPO, and he had not been long married to a young and beautiful wife when he was obliged to go on a long journey. And it so chanced that this journey was by accident prolonged, nor did his letters reach home, so that his wife, who was young and very simple, believing all the gossip and mischievous hints of everybody, soon thought that her husband had run away. Now there was a priest in the village who was *bastanza furbo*—not a little of a knave—and to him she bitterly complained that her husband had abandoned her, leaving her *incinta*, or with child.

" At this the priest looked very grave, and said that it was very wicked in her husband to act as he had done ; yes, that it was a mortal sin for which both she and PIPPO would be damned, even to the lowest depth of hell, because she would give birth to a child which had only been begun, and not finished, for that it would probably be born without a head or limbs, and she would be very lucky if only a hand and foot, or the eyes were wanting. And that all women who bear such monsters would be certainly condemned to the worst.

" Now the wife, being only a simple *contadina*, was very devout, and went frequently to confession, and, believing every word which the priest said, was terribly frightened, and asked him what could be done in this case ? Then he replied that there was a way to remedy it, which he should most unwillingly employ, yet still to save her soul, and for the child's sake, he would try it. And this was that she should pass the night with him, when by his miraculous power as a priest, and by his prayers, he would so effect it that the infant would be perfected—and so she could be freed from sin. But he made her swear an oath not to tell a word of all this to any human being, and especially not to PIPPO, else all would fail. So she assented, and the priest had his will.

" Now no one knew it, but PIPPO was a *streghone*, or wizard, and casting his mind forth to know how all was going on at home, learned all this fine affair which had passed. Then returning, instead of going to his house, he put on the form of a beautiful nun, and went to the priest's. The priest had two young sisters, famous for their extraordinary beauty, and PIPPO was very kindly received by them as well as by the brother. And when he begged for a night's lodging, the two young girls bade him sleep with them, which he did, of course seducing them thoroughly.

" The next morning, being alone with the priest, he first ogled him, and as the other caught eagerly at the chance of sinning with a nun, he plainly asked him if they should not go into the cellar, *per fare l'amore*. At which the priest was enraptured ;' but when they were alone together PIPPO assumed his natural form, which was a terrible one, and said : ' I am PIPPO, whose wife thou didst wrong with thy lies. Evil hast thou done to me, but I have done worse to thy sisters, and worst of all to thee, for now thou art accursed before God, thou false priest ! ' And the *prete* could do nothing and say nothing. And there came before him all the time many spirits who mocked him, and he had to leave holy orders. And this was the revenge of PIPPO."

I should have omitted this very Bocaccian tale had it not been that it illustrates very strikingly the antipathy of the believers in witchcraft and the spirits of old for the priests. A merely loose, licentious story makes no such deep moral or immoral impression on the Southern European mind as it does on the Northern, but the distinctly placing wizard against priest, or old sorcery against Christianity, is, if the reader will reflect, a very singular incident. It is in this that the point lies for a *strega*, and it is most remarkable as showing that such antagonism between Shamanism and the Church should still exist, as it has undoubtedly existed through the ages. I may add that among the tales received after this work had gone to press is one entitled *The priest Arrimini*, in which a priest becomes a wizard, manifesting, like this narrative, a marked heathen or anti-Christian spirit.

PISPI

" In a district of La Romagna, there was a man named PISPI, who was a great robber ; yes, one who carried away vast treasures and yet was never detected. He would go to a *café* and meet gentlemen whom he had plundered immensely, and on departing he would say, ' Signori, I am PISPI, the famous robber,' but nobody could catch him or lay hands on him, and when they met him they did not recognise him at any time, for he changed his face and form continually, until at last it was generally believed that he was a devil.

" But he really was a wizard. And at last he lay dying, but could not die. And he groaned, and implored those present to take his power, but none would accept it because he was believed to be a devil, At last some one put two brooms under his bed, and so he died. But his spirit had no peace, for he had left a treasure. Now PISPI was really a good spirit, because he robbed very rich people and gave a great deal to the poor. Then he sought about for some poor and deserving man, and finally found one in a prisoner who was condemned to the galleys for life, and he said to him, ' I will by my conjuring deliver thee from thy sufferings and set thee free. Then go into the woods in such a place, and there stands an oak-tree called *Istia*, buried one yard's depth you will find a treasure, it is in a boot and in an earthen pot. And when thou art rich and free do not forget the poor ! ' And so PISPI had peace, and the poor prisoner became rich and happy."

It would not have been worth while to give this vulgar and rather flat tale, had it not been for the name of its hero. PISPI is a typical thief, and in Holland the mandrake, which is there supposed to grow from the droppings of a thief's brain, &c., on the gallows, is called *Pisdifje*, or little brain-thief. He who has this *pisdifje* can enter all houses, open all doors, and rob freely, without being detected. This root was called by many names, such as mandrake, mandragora, alraun, gallows, mannikin and earth-mannikin in Germany, and was regarded as a demon and received offerings or a kind of worship. There is of course no rational philological connection between the names of Pispi and Pisdifje, but the connection of associations between these names and the thief who could never be detected, and the root-demon who enables a thief to avoid detection, is very curious indeed. It may be remarked in this connection that the *Vocabulario delle Lingue Furbesche*—or Vocabulary of Thieves' Tongues—indicates much intercourse in common between the thieves of Northern Italy and those of Germany.

THE WITCH CAT

It has been well said that one half the world does not know how the other half lives, and while collecting these instances of strange superstitions, I am tempted to think that almost one half does not at all understand how the others think, feel, or what is the moral atmosphere which they breathe. We *know* that there is no truth in anything supernatural, but these others who appear to be so ignorant and indifferent live in a different life, and see and hear—or believe they see and hear—ghosts and marvels and all strange things. Witness the following, which the woman who told it to me certainly believed she had witnessed :—

" When I was a small child I went frequently to the house of a woman who had a *bambina*—a girl baby —and we often made a noise when playing together, but woe to us whenever we did so, playing with the cat, for the child's mother said that cats are all wizards and witches.   As I indeed learned only too soon how true it was.

" There lived near us another woman who had also a little girl ; this child was very impertinent.   One day while we three were playing together and making a tumult, my friend gave this other one a cuff.   So she ran howling to her mother, and the woman said to the mother of my friend, ' I will be revenged for this ; ' and, *per troppo fu vero*, it was only too true.   For after a few days my little friend fell ill and no one knew what was the matter, nor could any doctor explain the malady.

" Then her mother began to think that the woman who had threatened vengeance was a witch.   And she was sure of it when she observed that a cat came by night into her house, and that it, instead of lying down always remained standing ! So she watched, and when at midnight the cat came again, she took it and bound it to the child's bed and beat it with all her might, saying, ' Cure my child or I will kill you ! '

" Then the cat spoke with a human voice, and said, ' I can endure no more.   Let me go and your child shall be well.'   But at that instant there was heard a horrible roar and clanking of chains as if many demons were about, and the mother instead of letting the cat free went and called the priest that he might give his blessing.   And the mother clipped the hair from the cat, and in the morning when the church-bell rang the cat became nothing more nor less—*non divento altro*—than the woman who had vowed revenge.   And so she could no longer be a witch ; and all the neighbours seeing her naked, and without a hair left, knew what she was, and so she practised witchcraft no more."

This is interesting because it shows plainly the belief derived from pre-Christian times, that the witch once detected, or stripped—in this case literally—of her disguise, can no longer be a witch.   Here it is not a question of a soul sold to the devil, but only of power held on a very precarious condition.

Apropos of this subject, I have the following in a letter by Miss Mary A. Owen :—

The negroes in Missouri say some cats are real cats and some are devils, you never can tell " which is which," so for safety it is well to whip them all soundly.   The voodoo does not whip her own cat, but she excepts none other. A strange black cat that runs in at one of your doors and out at another, puts " a trick " on somebody in the house.   A grown-up black cat which comes and cannot be driven away voodoos the whole house in spite of blows.

THE DWARFS

" Von wilden Getwergen
Han ich gehoeret sagen,
Sie sin in Holn Bergen."
Das Nibelungenlied

One day I inquired if there were any Elves, or little dwarfs, in La Romagna ; and I was at once informed that there were, in these words :—

" *Dei nani !* Dwarfs ! There are many. They dwell in lonely places, far away in the ᴜ ᴊuntians, deep in them, in caves or among old ruins, and rocks. Sometimes a *contadino* sees one or more ; he may behold them far away, going home very early between night and day, hurrying before the sun rises to get into their homes. They live like other people, they are good and bad like other people, but they are *folletti*, really. I will tell you an old, a very old, story about them :—

" Once there was a girl who had been betrayed by her lover and abandoned for another, and so she, in a wild fit, determined to go in search of him.

> " Over the high blue mountain,
> Over the rolling rivers,
> Through the wet grass,
> Along the hard highway,
> Into noisy cities, in churches,
> Where there were people or none,
> *Si mise in cammino*
> *D'andare in cerca di lui,*
> She set herself on the journey
> To go in search of him.

" And when she had travelled many days and longed for a little rest, she came to a small house far away among the rocks and knocked at the door. There came out a little dwarf, who asked her what she wanted. And she answered :—

> " ' Good friend, a little lodging,
> I beg it in charity,
> For my feet are weak and weary ;
> I am seeking, seeking my lover,
> Whom I wish to kill for his falsehood,
> Yet I hope I shall not find him,
> Because I love him still.'

" Then she entered and supped and went to bed. And at midnight there came leaping and laughing and frolicking into the room swarms of little dwarfs or goblins—*tutti uomini piccioli*—who shouted for joy at seeing her. And they pulled her hair and danced on her, and tweaked her ears and nose, and she, in a rage, pushed and beat them and gathered them up and threw them as she could against the wall, but they did not mind it in the least, but climbed in crowds like bees on her bed till dawn came, when they disappeared, when she fell asleep.

" And waking she rose and went her way, when from a hill came out another dwarf, who said :—

> " ' Stop and talk with me ;
> I can truly tell thee
> Where to find thy lover,
> And if thou would'st find him
> Come to me at midnight,
> And I'll truly tell thee
> Where to find thy lover ! '

" Then the girl replied :—

> " ' *Dammi la tua mano,*
> *Pegno de la parola !* '

> (" ' Give me, then, thy hand ;
> Pledge that truth thou speakest. ')

" But the dwarf answered :—

> " ' I cannot give my hand,
> As 'tis given by mortals,
> For I am a spirit,
> And spirits were the goblins
> Who this night did tease thee,
> Still thou didst well please them
> For thou didst show spirit.'

" Then at midnight the girl went to the dwarf, and he gave her a feather, and she was turned into a swallow, and he said :—

> " ' Fly upon the wind
> As the wind directs thee ;
> Follow, follow, follow,
> And thou'lt find thy lover
> And when thou hast found him
> Then thou wilt have travelled
> Two months' distance, but I
> By my incantation
> Truly shall have made thee
> Fly it in a minute.
> When thou seest thy lover
> Touch him with this feather,
> Then he'll love thee only,
> Nor think upon the other.'

" Then he will wed thee after three days, but during the time thou must come every day at noon to my grotto and say :—

> " ' Grotto, grotto, grotto !
> By the incantation
> To call on all good spirits,
> Enchant, I pray, my lover,
> So that he may never
> Love another woman !
> So that three days over,
> He may be my husband !'

" And when the three days had passed she touched him with the feather, and resumed her own form, and by his side—

> " E si incominciaro
> A baciare,
> E altre donne
> Non potiede più amare

> La sua prima amante
> Le tocco sposare.
> Tutto e finito
> Non voglio piu narrare."

> " Then the pair began
> Kissing as before;
> And to other women
> He made love no more,
> But married her ; the story
> Now is fairly o'er."

The swallow as the bird of spring brings luck ; hence in Tuscany swallows' feathers tied with a red string form an amulet. This story is only a variation from one in Grimm's *Kinder und Haus Mährchen,* but it may be observed that there is in the Tuscan tale more of chiaro-oscuro and incantation. In fact I cannot imagine one of this country without the latter. The magic song enters into everything of the kind. This was probably the case in ancient times in Germany, but as stories become fairy tales for children alone, it naturally disappears, and the narrative alone is then the subject of interest. These Romagnolo stories are all in that state when the narrator—as I have often tested—will tell or sing them just as requested. This is the case among all primitive people in the magic epoch, and I might with truth, had I pleased, have given any story in rude metre as well as prose. Sometimes the rhymes and attempt at metre are unmistakable, and in such cases I have given them in a form as near to the original as I could make it. But in the original, two or even three lines are often run into one and the voice modulated to suit the variation.

THE APPLE-TREE

Had I found the following story in any country save the Romagna Tuscana, I might have passed it by as possibly modern. But in this region the peasantry have learned so very little that is new, that novelty in their legends and customs is very exceptional. This is the tale, which I have somewhat abridged :—

" Once there was a beautiful lady who married a wealthy and handsome lord. And the great desire of his heart was to have an heir, but as his wife bore no children he became almost mad with disappointment and rage, threatening her with the worst ill-usage and torture unless she became a mother. And she spent all her time in prayer and all her money on the poor, but in vain. Then her husband hated her altogether, and took a maid-servant in her place. And finding her one day giving a piece of bread to some poor person, he had her hands cut off, so that she could no more give alms. And she lived among the lowest servants in great distress.

" One day there came to the castle a friar, who begged for something in charity of her ; and she replied that she had nothing to give, and that if she had aught she could not give it, being without hands.   And so he learned how she had been treated, for she said :—

> " ' Because I have not bore a child
> My husband is with anger wild,
> For giving alms, the truth I say,
> He had my hands both cut away ;
> Heaven help me, and help the poor !
> For I can give them nothing more ! '

" Then the friar looked a long time at her in silence, considering her extreme misery and goodness, and said :—

> " ' Lady, in the garden go,
> Where an apple-tree doth grow,
> Fairer one did never see ;
> Lady fair, embrace that tree,
> And as you embrace it, say
> These words as closely as you may :

> " ' " Pano o mio bel pomo !
> A te con grande amore,
> Ti voglio abbraciare,
> Che mio marito
> In letto con se questa notte,
> Mi possa portare,
> E cosi possa ingravidare
> E che il mio marito
> Mi possa amare ! " '

> (" ' " Apple-tree, fair apple-tree !
> With my love I come to thee.
> I would be to-night in bed
> With my husband as when wed :
> May I so become a mother.
> Grant this favour ; and another
> Still I earnestly implore—
> May he love me as before ! " ')

" ' And this done, take from the tree two apples and eat them.   And go to your husband and he will love you and take you to his bed, and you will in time bear two beautiful babes.'

" And so it came to pass, and the husband bitterly regretted his cruelty and the loss of her hands.   And she bore the two children ; but the girl who had been a servant and his mistress persuaded him that his wife had been unfaithful, and that they were not his.   Then he took a donkey, on it were two panniers, and he put a babe into each and sat her in the middle, and bade her ride away.

" So she rode on in utter grief and sorrow, hardly able with her stumps of arms to manage the children or to drive.   But at last she came to a well and stooped to drink.   And lo ! as soon as she did this her hands grew again, for it was the fountain which renews youth and life.   Then her heart grew light, for she felt that fortune had not left her.   And indeed all went well, for she came to a castle where no one was to be seen. And she entered and found food on the tables, and wine and all she required everywhere, and when she and the children had eaten, at the next meal there was food again. Now this castle belonged to fairies, who, seeing her there, pitied her and cared for her in this manner.

"And considering her case they sent a Dream to her husband. And the Dream came to him by night and told him all the truth, how his wife had been true to him, and how evilly he had done. Then he rode forth and sought far for the castle till he found it. And he took her and the children home. And as they came near the gate they saw before it a statue which had never been there. Now the wicked servant had said, ' May I be turned to stone if this be not true which I have said of thy wife.' And the words were remembered by the fairies (spirits), for they hear all things. And the statue was the figure of the girl turned to stone. But the husband and the wife lived together happily ever after."

The story is the widely spread one of patient Griselda and Genevieve de Brabant, and was perhaps in truth that of many a suffering wife in early times. But the conception from the apple-tree suggests the story of Juno, who conceived Mars without the help of Jupiter from the touch of a flower (OVID, *Fasti*, v. 253). The fountain of youth in this story also recalls the golden apples of the Hesperides, and especially those guarded by the Scandinavian Iduna, which kept the gods young. There is a mass of myths in all countries connecting the apple-tree with generation and birth. So in this story, as in all which come from this country, there are throughout sketches and touches which are possibly copied from more ancient pictures. It is worth observing, that even in this story the incantation must be spoken to the tree before it exerts its fertilising power.

IL SPIRITO DEL GIUOCO

This is a curious and evidently very ancient tale, probably modernised :—

"He is an evil spirit now—as one may say, a devil—but he was once long ago, before any tree which is now growing had begun to sprout, a handsome and rich young lord : yes, he had as many olive-trees as I ever ate olives, and more vines than I ever drank glasses of wine ; but he wanted more, and so he gambled. Now some men spend all their patrimony in a jolly way, but he wasted his, quarrelling, cursing, and blaspheming. And at last, when nothing was left of all he had but some barren fields, and he was mad for money to play with, he looked at the wretched farm which remained and said :—

> " ' This, too, I would sell,
> Yes, and to the devil,
> And give him my soul to boot
> When my life comes to an end :
> Yes ; he might kill me with lightning.
> And a roaring crash of thunder
> Bursting up from the earth,
> If, when I went, I could burn
> All the crops of grain,
> Vines, mulberries, figs,
> And the olives—blast them !

Which I see all around and afar !
Once they were mine ; see the grain
Shining like gold in the sun ;
Gold I had—gold I lost !
Gold is our only life ;
What if the devil could give me
Power to win at play !
And then when I won
To hear the thunder roar,
With a flash of lightning,
As the card turned !
Burning the crops,
Homes and all,
Of those who once stripped me.
Aye ; and when dead—
E quando saro morto !—
I would haunt the gambling room,
And if some fellow won
Make him hear thunder
And see lightning to fright him
(Of course burning his crops).
But if some poor devil—like me—
Would pray to me for aid
When he has lost at play,
Then I would gladly give him
The devil's own luck at cards,
And—burn up the crops of his enemies,
To whom he had sold his lands ! '

" When the young man returned home he found *un bel signore*—a fine gentleman—waiting to see him. And the stranger said, very politely :—

" ' You wish to sell, I think,
That little estate of yours,
And I am willing to buy :
You are a bold, brave fellow—
Galante di prim'ordine.
I like to please such men,
For I know when the time shall come
For them to enter my service,
They make the best of servants.
Well, I agree to your terms,
All your demand you shall have :
Luck at cards for life—
Thunder and lightning included—
You shall have your riches again:
Le richezze torneranno.'

" So it came to pass, and for a long time he won. And it was observed that when he played high at he last card there always was heard a clap of thunder, and a great storm raged somewhere, near or far. Years passed, but one day, when his time had come, there was a tremendous burst of fire which lighted the room—and lo ! the gambler appeared all at once like a glowing coal from head to foot, and a voice exclaimed :—

> " ' That which was asked for
> Was granted to fulness ;
> This is thy last day,
> This is thy final hour ;
> Thou didst ask for the lightning—
> Thou hast had it ;
> Thou hast it now—
> Now live in its fire ! '

" *E così sprafondo nella terra*—and so he sank into the ground. And they remembered what he had said, and many regretted him, and when they were in trouble and needed his help they called on him. And they said :—

> " ' Spirit of thunder and lightning !
> Spirit of help ! Help us !
> For of thee we have great need !
> As thou wert as are we,
> Aid us, aid us in our play !
> Make us win much money,
> Else ruin is before us ;
> Thou wilt not abandon us !
> We hope that thou wilt come
> And play in our company."

There is apparent in this tale something of a modern spirit of composition, as if it had been subjected to liberties. But though the form may have been changed, there is reason to believe that under the mosses and flowers is an ancient rock. As no one can listen long to an Algonkin Indian story without coming to *meteoulin*, or sorcery, so all these Romagnolo tales turn on the transformation of a man to a spirit, and are therefore myths, and extremely interesting as indicating the process by which myths were first made. Gambling is so deeply seated in the Italian, as it was in the old Latin, nature—every man, woman, and child in the entire population buys, on an average, at least ten lottery tickets every year—that a spirit of play would naturally be one of the first placed in a popular pantheon. Therefore it is probable that from an early time there has been a legend of some Don Juan or Don Giovanni di Tenorio, whose main vice was not women but play. It may be remarked, indeed, that in a great proportion of Italian tales gambling, and not drinking or lust, is supposed to be the chief cause of moral destruction.

PATÁNA

" *Patalena* protected the growing or shooting corn.   In Germany such a deity was called the *Roggenmutter*, whence the saying to children :

> " ' Leave the flowers standing !
> Go not into the corn !
> There the Roggenmutter
> Stands from night to morn ;
> Now adown she's ducking,
> Now all up she's looking,
> She will catch the children all,
> Who look for flowers, great or small.' "
>
> FRIEDRICH, *Symbolik*

The following story is very curious in several respects :—

" Patána was a beautiful girl, but she had a stepmother who was a witch, and malicious too, so that she kept Patána shut up in a tower, into which no one was allowed to go.   The old woman went every day into the city to sell milk.   One day she passed by the king's palace.   Now the king had a son whom he loved so much that there was nothing else in the world for which he cared.

" The young prince was at the palace window, and held in his hand some pebbles.   The old woman came and sat down opposite, putting her pitchers of milk on the ground.   And the young prince, out of heedless mischief, threw a pebble and broke a pitcher.   The old woman, being angry, cried to the youth :—

> " ' Tu sei il figlio del re
> E crederesti di esser piu potente di me,
> Ed io ti faro vedere, ai !
> Che saro piu potente assai.'

> " ' Though the king's son thou mayst be,
> And think thou hast more power than me,
> I can show thee, and I will,
> That I have more power still ;
> Thou shalt have no joy in life
> Till fair Patána is thy wife,
> And that will never come to pass,
> For thou shalt never have the lass.'

" Then the prince had no more rest nor happiness by day or night.   And at last he went out into the world to seek for Patána, travelling far, till one day he met a poor old man who begged something to eat for he was starving.   The prince gave him something, and said, ' Thou art not so wretched as I am, for I can have no rest till I shall have found the beautiful Patána, and I know not where she is.'

" The old man replied, ' That I can tell thee—

> " ' Go along the road
> Till thou seest a tower
> Rising in a forest ;

> There Patána dwells
> With her stepmother,
> But be sure to go
> When the witch is absent,
> And be sure to give
> Food to everything
> Which is in the tower,
> Even the smallest pot
> By a magic spell
> Will tell the old witch all,
> Unless it has been fed ;
> Take this pebble too,
> It will give thee power
> To speak with the witch's voice,
> And then cry aloud :
> " Beautiful Patána,
> Fairer than a sun ray,
> Let thy tresses down
> And then draw me up ! " '

" So he did, and was drawn up into the tower, where Patána received him with joy. Then they made a great pot full of *pappa* (bread crumbs boiled), and he fed, as he thought, all the furniture and utensils, all except one earthenware pot, which he forgot. And this was the chief spy, and it betrayed him.

" Then Patána took a comb, a knife, and a fork, and said, ' Let us be free ! ' and the door of the tower opened, and they fled. But before long beautiful Patána, looking behind, saw her mother-in-law flying after them, for the pot which had not been fed had told her all, and the way which they had gone. Then beautiful Patána stuck the fork in the earth, and it became a church and she was the sacristan. And the witch, not recognising her, asked her if she had seen the king's son go by with a girl. And the sacristan replied :—

> " ' This is not a time
> To answer idle questions,
> Twice the bell has rung
> For mass, come in and hear it ! '

" Then the witch went away in a rage, and they proceeded. But before long they saw her flying after them again. Then the beautiful Patána threw down the comb and it became a garden and she the gardener. When the witch came up she put the same question as before, and Patána answered :—

> " ' If you wish to chase them,
> You'll have need of horses ;
> I have two to sell you,
> Fine ones at a bargain,
> Pray come in and see them ! '

" Then the witch in a rage went home to the tower, and the pot told her that the garden was only a comb and that the gardener was the beautiful Patána. So she set out again, and they soon saw her flying after them. Then beautiful Patána threw down the knife, and she became a *vasca* (basin of a fountain or reservoir), and the prince a fish swimming in it. But this time ere she made the change she said :—

> " ' Here I take this knife
> And plant it in the ground,
> That I may become
> Now a sparkling fountain,
> And my love a fish ;
> May he swim so well
> That the witch now coming
> May never, never catch him ! '

" And the witch coming up tried and tried to catch the fish, but in vain.　So at last in a rage she cried :—

> " ' Mayst thou leave Patána,
> Leave her in the castle,
> If to thy home returning
> Once thy mother kiss thee
> Thou'lt forget Patána ! '

" So she departed.　And when they came to the castle the young prince left Patána there for a while to go and see his parents, being determined, however, that his mother should not kiss him.　And she, being overjoyed to see him, tried to do so, but he avoided it.　Then every preparation was made for his marriage, and he, being weary, fell asleep, and then his mother kissed him.　When he awoke he saw all things got ready for a wedding, but he could not remember anything about the bride.

" So time passed, and he was about to marry another lady.　When beautiful Patána heard this she went to the palace and said to the cook, ' I am the lady of the castle, and I wish to make a present for the wedding dinner, and that it shall be two fishes.'　Then she had the oven made ready, and bade the wood go into it, and it went in of itself, and then bade it burn, and then went into the fire and came out, and there were two such fine fish as no one had ever beheld.　And when they were carried to the table everybody was amazed at them, and the cook being called, when asked where they were caught, replied they had not been caught but made by the lady of the castle as a gift.

" Then the bride, who was herself something of a witch, said, " Oh, that is nothing ; I can do that.'　But the wood did not obey her, and when she entered the oven it blazed up and she was burned to death.

" And as this was done the two fishes on the table began to converse one with the other, as follows :—

> " ' Dost thou remember
> How the king's son
> Entered the tower ? '

> " ' Well I remember
> How he fled away
> With beautiful Patána.'

> " ' Dost thou remember
> How she preserved him
> From the wild sorceress ? '

> " ' Well I remember
> The church and the garden,
> The fish and the fountain.'

> " ' Dost thou remember
> His mother's kiss,
> How he forgot Patána ? '

> " ' Well I remember
> All the strange story,
> But now he remembers.'

"Then the prince, who heard this, remembered all. So he married the beautiful Patána, she who is now the Queen of the Fairies."

This is perhaps the commonest of all Italian fairy tales, and in some form it is known all over Europe. I have given it here because the name of the heroine, *Patána*, is interesting as connected with some of the incidents of the story. *Patána* was a Roman goddess who appears with greatly varied names, sometimes as a derivation from Ceres or a Cerean deity, and sometimes as Ceres herself. Thus there was Patelena, who opened the husk of grain, Patellana and Patella, who induced the grain to come forth, or presided over it when it came to light. She was the goddess of the sprouting grain or of *growth* (*Vide* Bughin, p. 160).

"Thus," says PRELLER (*R. Myth.*, p. 592), "she was the goddess of the harvest, the blonde Ceres of the Greeks, and, in fact, as the goddess of crops seems to have been chiefly known under this name in ancient Italy. At least the Inguvinic tablets mention a goddess Padella, and the Oscan votive tablet a PATANA, which are most probably identical with Patella, as is the deity Panda. It even seems that this name was the common one for such a goddess instead of the Roman-Latin Ceres."

I had asked my authority if she knew the name of any spirit who caused crops, trees, or the like, to grow. She at once suggested *Patána*, who in a tale made a garden, a church, and a fountain spring out of the earth. These are of some little value taken in connection with the name. VARRO [*De vita pop. Ro. cited in* PRELLER] mentions that this Panda, or Pandana, " whom AELIUS thought was Ceres, had a sanctuary where bread was given to those who took refuge in it." In the Italian tale bread boiled in water is given to all the articles of furniture and utensils to eat, even as the spirits of the dead are pacified by food ; here the furniture may mean the refugees, who receive pap or boiled bread.

As *Patána* has been confused with Ceres, and made into her minor, or daughter, so it is possible that the heroine of the story has changed place with the stepmother. In this case we have a very curious parallel to Ceres pursuing Persephone, or Proserpina. In the one, as in the other, a mother— mother-in-law—pursues the fugitives, Ceres puts Triptolemus on the fire to make him immortal (which occurs in a Romagnola witch-tale), in this story *Patána* herself enters the fire. In Rome Ceres was regarded as a foe to marriage, "*Alii dicunt Cererem propter raptum filire nuptias execratam* (SERV. V. A. iii., 139). And it is evident that in our legend she opposes the match for no apparent reason. Ceres in the Latin legend is mocked by a boy, the son of Metanira, and punishes him by changing him to a lizard, the witch mother of *Patána* is angered by the young prince and inflicts a penalty.

It is perfectly true that with some ingenuity parallels like these may be established between almost any fairy tale and some ancient myth. But where we have a leading *name* in common with corresponding incidents, we may almost assume an identity of origin. If we found the story of Whittington and his cat among South American Indians we might suppose it had originated there. But if the hero was called Whittington, or even Vidindono—as it probably would be—we might very well assume transmission. Till within a very few years the apparent coincidence system as a proof of origin was extravagantly overdone, and has since been succeeded by an opposite one, which has in turn been carried to as absurd extremes. The best test for the value of these Romagnolo traditions, as remains of antiquity, is to carefully study them *as a whole*, and compare them as a whole with what we know of Etrusco-Latin myth and legend. There may be error in *any* one minor detail, however strong the identity may appear to be, but there can be none as regards the æsthetic or historic spirit and character of a great number of *incidents* taken together.

It may be added in reference to the tell-tale pot which was not fed, that the forgotten or neglected fairy who revenges herself for the slight is of very ancient origin. We find her first in Discord, who was enraged at not being invited to the marriage of Tethys and Pelius (LUCIAN, *Dialog. Marin.*, v. ; cf. HYGNI, *fol.* 92, COLUTHUS, *De raptu Helen*, v. 60). This incident reappears in the Middle Ages in the fairy who was not invited to be present at the birth of Oberon, and therefore condemned him to remain a dwarf. This is not necessarily derived from tradition, but it may have its value, as indeed all incidents may in folk-lore—a fact which is much too frequently and rudely set aside by a large class of the critics who peel away the onion till there is nothing left, forgetting that to have any result or profit one must stop after removing the rough outside leaves. There is a spirit in tradition as well as the letter.

Schedius in an enumeration of minor Roman deities includes "Patellana seu Patula."

Il Moro

"There was in the Romagne a rich lady who was unkindly treated by her husband because she had no children. And he often said to her that unless she gave birth to a son or daughter, and that soon, he would leave her and take another. So the poor signora went every day to the church to pray to God that He would be so gracious as to give her a child; but it was not granted to her, therefore after a time she went no more to church and ceased to give alms.

"One day she stood quite disconsolate at the window, because she loved her husband and met with no return, when, from a window opposite, a dark signore (*Signore Moro*—a Moor or Negro, as in German) called to her, and she, raising her head, asked him what he would have?

"The Moor, who was a wizard, or magician (*uno streghone, o sia uno magliatore, o maliardo*), replied, 'Look me steadily in the eyes, and then all will go well with thee. And this night when thy husband shall embrace thee think steadily of me, and thus thou wilt be *incinta*, or with child.'

"This came to pass, and the poor lady was very happy to regain the love of her husband, and at the same time become a mother. But joy flies like the clouds, and so did hers, for when her child was born it was dark as the Moor, yes, and looked altogether like the Moor himself. Then the husband abandoned both wife and child, saying that the infant was none of his. And the lady reproved the Moor, saying that he had betrayed her.

"But the Moor replied, 'Grieve not, O good lady, for I can still make peace between thee and thy husband. To-morrow a charity sermon will be preached, and when the friar shall give thee benediction, put the child on the ground and let it go whither it will.' So the lady did. Now her husband never went to any church, but, hearing that there was to be a famous preacher this day, he was present. And when the lady put the little babe on the ground, what was her utter amazement to see it rise and run on its little feet, and go to its father, and embrace him with its little hands, and say, in distinct words : '*Babbo, perdona mamma, è innocente*'—'Papa, pardon mamma, she is innocent; and thou seest it is a miracle of God that I have come to thee.' And from that time the babe never uttered a word till he had come to the age when children usually talk.

"Then the father, being moved by the miracle, was reconciled with his wife, and they returned home together and lived happily."

This will suggest much which is familiar to the reader, such as Othello, Tamora, and Aaron, the beautiful sorceress and her negro in the *Arabian Nights*, and chiefly the mysterious story of the French queen and the black page. What is chiefly remarkable in it is that sorcery is made superior to religion, for all is effected by the Moor, though in the end the miracle is wrought in a church, and is, so to speak, given to God.

The incident of a babe's speaking is found in the folk-lore of every land ; but it is remarkable that the earliest instance of it in Europe is that of the Etruscan infant Tages, who was ploughed out—possibly in the place whence I derived this tale.

The Witch Lea

"This witch was a wealthy lady, very self-willed and licentious, who often changed her lovers. So she would keep one for a time, and when she was tired of him she would lead him into a room in which there was a trap-door in the floor, through which he would fall into a deep pit, and into a subterranean dungeon, where he miserably perished. And so she had many victims, and the more she sacrificed the better pleased she was, for she was a wicked sorceress, insatiable in lust and murder.

"But it went not thus with one of her lovers, who knew her nature. And when she asked him to pass the secret gate, he replied :—

> " 'Thou, vilest of women,
>   Thinkest because thou art rich and powerful
>   That all must bow before thee?
>   Rich and powerful, and beyond that
>   A harlot and coquette,
>   Vile thou art. To hide thy dishonour,
>   Thou sendest many to God—
>   Makest thy lovers die.

" 'But so thou wilt not do with me, for I too am of the wizards, a son of a witch, and more powerful than thou art. And at once thou shalt have proof of it.

> " 'Three times I call thee,
>   Lea, Lea, O Lea !
>   Thou art cursed from the very heart,
>   By my mother and by me,
>   For thou didst kill my brother ;
>   For that I come to condemn thee ;
>   A serpent thou shalt become,
>   Every night as a serpent
>   Thou shalt suck the blood of corpses—
>   The corpses of thy dead lovers ;
>   But first of all thou shalt go
>   Unto the body of my brother,
>   Thou shalt put life into him,
>   Breathe into him, revive him.
>   Henceforth all men shall know thee
>   As an accursed witch !'

"And so it came to pass that after three days the dead brother was revived, but the beautiful Lea was always a serpent witch."

It would seem as if there were an echo in this tale of the Libitina, the goddess of lust itself, as well as of death. "Ab lubendo libido, lubidinosus, ac Venus Libentina et Libitina" (VARRO, l. i, vi. 47 ; apud PRELLER, p. 387.) She was also the generally recognised goddess of corpses and of the dead. PRELLER quotes several instances to illustrate the fact that death and luxuriant life — *schwellendes Leben*—were thus intimately connected in one myth, in a single person, and that the Sabine Feronia was paralleled with the Greek Persephone, and Flora. There are also the affinities between Venus and Proserpine.

The story has a great resemblance to one of Odin, which has been set forth in a German poem by Herz. It also recalls—

> " The proud and stately queen
> By whose command, De Buridan
> Was thrown at midnight in the Seine."

That is to say, the well-known legend of the Tour de Nesle. But I believe that this is a very old Italian tale, and possibly archaic, because the connection between lust and death is so strongly and strangely marked in it. That Lea is given the form of a serpent in order to revive the dead cannot fail to strike every one who is familiar with classic serpent-lore.

It is far too bold a conjecture that the word Lia or Lea is derived from Libitina; but it is certain that the characteristics of the two are the same. Libitina was also known among the Romans as Lubia, and as a goddess of lust (PRELLER, 581), "*cui nomen ab libidine*" (AUGUST. iv. 8), and the name may have been still more abbreviated. The step from Libia, or Livia, to Lia, would be in peasant dialect almost inevitable. We must always remember the fact in such cases that the tale is from the same country as the ancient characters.

WIZARD SAINTS

It was the most natural thing in the world that there should be certain blendings, compromises, and points of affinity between the Stregeria—witchcraft, or " old religion," founded on the Etruscan or Roman mythology and rites—and the Roman Catholic : both were based on magic, both used fetishes, amulets, incantations, and had recourse to spirits. In some cases these Christian spirits or saints corresponded with, and were actually derived from, the same source as the heathen. The sorcerers among the Tuscan peasantry were not slow to perceive this. How deeply rooted the old religion really is, occasionally, even to-day, may be inferred from the story told in *Faflon*, of the peasant who, whatever happened, never neglected to bless the *folletti*—meaning the rural deities. As for the families in which *stregheria*, or a knowledge of charms, old traditions and songs is preserved, they do not among themselves pretend to be even Christian. That is to say, they maintain outward observances, and bring the children up as Catholics, and " keep in " with the priest, but as the children grow older, if any aptitude is observed in 'them for sorcery, some old grandmother or aunt takes them in hand, and initiates them into the ancient faith. That is to say it was so, for now all this is passing away rapidly.

Certain saints are regarded as being *folletti*. A *folletto* is a generic term for almost any kind of spirit not Christian. Fairies, goblins, spectres, nymphs, are all called by this name. There is a *Manuale di Spiriti Folletti* published at Asti (1864), which includes devils, vampires, undines, and *comets* under this word.[1]

The chief of the goblin-saints is Saint Antonio, Antony, or Anthony. This character was remarkably familiar with strange spirits of all kinds. The priests represented that he was beset and tempted by devils ; but the sorcerers knew that all their dear and beautiful gods, or *folletti* — their Faflon-Bacchus and Bella Marta of the Morning — were called devils, and so had their own ideas on the subject. They did not object to being tempted by these "devils" when they came as beings of enchanting beauty, to fill their wine-cellars and give them no end of good luck in gambling and naughty love. Even the priests made it very prominent that Antony *commanded* all kinds of devils and *folletti*—ergo he was a conjuror and *streghone* and "in the business," like themselves. "Saints Antonio and Simeone cannot be saints," said a *strega* to me, "because we always perform incantations to them in a cellar by night." This of course is always done to heathen spirits, and never to saints. But what is very conclusive is this : It is decidedly a matter of witchcraft, and most un-Christian, to say the Lord's prayer either backwards, or "double"—that is, to repeat every sentence twice. This—the *pater-noster a doppio*—will call any heathen spirit in double quick time ; and it is peculiarly addressed to Saint Antony, and bears his name.

Thus when one has lost anything—*quando si perde qualche cosa*—you say a double paternoster to San Antonio, thus :—

> " Pater noster—Pater noster !
> Qui es in coelis—Qui es in coelis !" &c., &c.

"Ma dire il paternoster cosi e della stregheria, e non della vera religione Cattolica " (" But to say the paternoster thus, is of witchcraft, and not the real Catholic religion "). So said one who had received a liberal education in the art.

Quite as heathen does this saint appear in the following ceremony, every detail of which is taken from ancient sorcery : When a girl wishes to win or reclaim a lover, or, indeed, if anybody wants anything at all, he—or generally

---

[1] According to PITRÈ (*Usie Custome*, &c., vol. iv., p. 69) the *folletto* in Southern Italy is only one kind of spirit—*non se ne può ammettere più d'uno*. This is a *buon diavoletto*, and the exact counterpart of *Dusio*, or Puck, a trifling airy Robin Goodfellow, or fairy of the Shakespeare and Drayton type,

she—puts two flower-pots, containing *l'érba San Antonio*, one on either side of an open window at midnight, with a pot of *rue* in the centre. These must be bound with a red-scarlet ribbon, made in three knots, and pierced or dotted with pins, as a tassel (*fatto con tre nodi e puntati con tre spilli per fiocchio*), and turning to the window, say :—

> "Sant' Antonio, mio benigno,
> Di pregarvi non son digno,
> Se questa grazia mi farete,
> Tre fiammi di fuoco per me facete ;
> Una sopra la mia testa,
> Che per me arde e tempesta,
> Una canto al mio cuore,
> Che mi levi da questo dolore,
> Una vicino alla mia porta
> Che di questa grazia non se ne sorta ;
> Se questa grazia mi avete fatto,
> Fate mi sentir tre voci !
>> Porta bussare
>> Uomo fistiare,
> E cane abbiare !

English :—

> (" My benign Saint Antony !
> I am not worthy to pray to thee,
> This grace I modestly require ;
> Pray light for me three flames of fire,
> And of these the first in turn
> On my head may storm and burn,
> One I pray within my heart,
> That all pain from me depart,
> And the third beside my door,
> That it may never leave me more.
> If this grace be granted me,
> Let three sounds be heard by me :
>> A knock at a door,
>> A whistle, before,
> Or the bark of a dog—I ask no more.)

"When this prayer shall have been uttered, wait attentively at the window, and if a knock at a door be heard, or a man whistling, or a dog barking, then the request—*grazia*—will be granted ; one alone of these sounds will suffice to make it known. But should a dark (*nero*) horse or mule pass, or a hearse, bearing a corpse, then the prayer is refused.

"But if a *white* horse goes by, the favour will be conceded—*ma con molto tempo*—after some time shall have passed."

It may always be borne in mind that though this be addressed to a mediæval saint, there is every probability, and, judging by every analogy and association, a certainty, that San Antonio is some Roman or Etruscan spirit in Christian disguise. For all the details of the ceremony are old heathen, as is the divination by sounds.

Saint Antony protects his friends from many troubles, but specially from witchcraft. Therefore they say to him in Romagnola :—

> " Sant' Antogne, Sant' Antogne
> Sopre came, liberez dai sase !
> Liberez dai asase !
> E dal streghi chliùvengu,
> In camia a stregem
> I mi burdel chi 'e tent bel !
> Sant' Antogne e santa pia,
> Tui lontan el Streghi da camia,
> So ven el streghi in camia
> Ai buttar dre la graneda,
> Chi vega via ! "

In Italian :—

> " Santo Anto super (sopra) il cammino
> Liberate ci dagli assassini !
> Liberate ci dagli assassini !
> E dalle Strege che non vengano
> In casa mia a stregare
> I miei bambini che sono tanti belli,
> Santo mio, Santo pio !
> Tenetemi lontano le streghe.
> Di casa mio !
> Se viene le strege in casa mia,
> Buttatele dietro la granata
> Che vadino via ! "

> (" Saint Antony on the chimney-piece
> Let our fears of murderers cease !
> Free us from all evil which is
> Round us—specially from witches
> Who come in our minds bewilderin'
> To enchant my pretty children :
> Saint Antonio—I pray—
> Keep such creatures far away !
> If you'll throw the broom behind 'em,
> I at least will never mind 'em ! ")

This is not very beautiful poetry, but it is as good as the original, which is not in either form " written in choice Italian." The reader may judge from them what trouble I have sometimes had to disentangle an incantation from the bristling dialect in which it was surrounded.

In allusion to Saint Antony on the chimney-piece I was informed that he is specially the *folletto*, or spirit, of the fireplace. Which makes him quite the same as the Russian Domovoy, and gives him—which is worth noting—a distinct place as a Lar or *spiritus domesticus, lar familiaris.*

Santo Eliseo is unquestionably at first sight Elisha. He has a bald head, and appears as the destroyer of bad boys. But—scratch a Russian and you find a Tartar—when we look into this interesting Christian he appears to be sadly heathen, even Jovial, for there is a distinct trace of Jupiter in him. When a young lady finds that her lover is going astray, she, after the fashion followed in the blackest witchcraft, takes some of the hair of her lover, goes into a cellar at midnight and curses, blasphemes, and conjures after the following good old Tuscan style :—

> " Santo Elisæo dalla testa pelata,
> Una grazia mi vorrete fare,
> I ragazzi da un leone
> Li avete fatti mangiare,
> Spero di me vi non vorrete dimenticare
> Stanotte a mezza notte,
> Dentro alla cantina,
> Vi verro a portare
> I peli del amor mio
> Perche una paruccha
> Ve ne potrete fare,
> E nel posto dei peli
> Del amor mio
> Tutti diavoli e strege
> Li farete diventare,
> Che non possa vivere,
> Non possa stare,
> Che non abbia più pace,
> Ne a bere ne a mangiare,
> Fino che l'amor mio
> Alle porte di casa mia,
> Non fanno ritornare ;
> Non le diano pace,
> E con altre donne
> Non la facciano parlare ! "

In English :—

> " Saint Elisæo, bald-headed one !
> For a special favour I pray ;
> 'Tis said that boys once by a lion
> Were eaten for you one day ;

Therefore I trust from your memory
I shall ·not pass away.
Here in this cellar at midnight
Ever devoted and true,
I have brought some hair from my lover,
To make a wig for you :
And for all the hairs
Which I have taken away,
May just as many devils
About him ever play,
May he not live,
Or stand or think,
Or know any peace,
Or eat or drink
Until he shall come
Again to my door,
With true love returning
As once before,
Nor with other women
Make love any more ! "

Truly a curious invocation, and a nice occupation for a Christian saint! But who was this Elisæo, or Elisæus? There was of yore a certain Jupiter Elicœus, or Aelisæus, not unconnected with lions, who was well known in this same Tuscan land ; but I leave all this to others. Elisha of the Bible was a wonderful worker of miracles, and this may have established him as a magician among the Tuscans.

Saint Elia is Saint Elias. He appears in the following prescription and invocation :—

" To cure an affliction of the eyes, take three roots bound with a red ribbon, three leaves of trefoil and then say :—

" ' Stacco queste trefoglie per Santo Elia,
Che il mal d'occhio mi mandi via.'

(" 'I take these three leaves by Saint Elias,
That he may banish the pain from my eyes.')

" Then take three peppercorns and a bit of cinnamon, three cloves, and a large handful of salt, and put all to boil in a new earthenware pot, and let it boil for a quarter of an hour. During this time put your face over it so that the eyes may be steamed, and keep making *la castagna* (the sign of the thumb between the fingers) into the pot and say :—

" ' Per —— che maladetto sia !
(Then spit thrice behind you)
Per Santo Elia, Santo Elia, Santo Elia !
Che il male degli occhi mi mandi via ! '

" And this must be done for three days."

Another sorcerer-saint is Simeon. As he is sometimes called Simeone Mago, there cannot be the least doubt that he is quite confused with Simon the Magician ; in fact, I ascertained as much from a witch who was much above the average of the common people as regarded education. For when people are not encouraged to study the Bible, such little mistakes are of unavoidable occurrence. But before I conclude this chapter I shall show that there is a complete confusion in Italy between old sorcery and Christianity, and that the priests, far from opposing it, in a way actually encourage and aid it, on the principle that you can always sell more goods where there is a rival in competition. The following was taken down word by word from a witch :—

" IL VECCHIO SIMEONE SANTO

"This saint is a *folletto*—*i.e.*, a heathen spirit. There are many of these spirits who in witchcraft are called saints. And this is not all. For as you invoke Simeon, so you may call other spirits *faccendo la Novena*—repeating the Novena." (This is a Roman Catholic incantation, a copy of which was purchased for me in a cross and rosary shop.) "You simply substitute the name of a *folletto* for Simeon—any spirit you want.

"But for Simon himself, when you go to bed you must repeat his *Novena* three nights in succession at midnight.

"But you must be fearless (*bisogna essere di coraggio*), for he will come in many forms or figures, dressed like a priest in white, or like a friar with a long beard. But do not be afraid however he may change his form. Then he will ask, ' Cosa volete che mi avete scommodato ? ' ('What do you want, that you trouble me thus ? ') Then answer promptly whatever it may be that you require —three numbers in the lottery, or where a hidden treasure is concealed, or how you may get the love of a certain woman : *qualunque fortuna si desidera*—what-ever fortune you desire.

"But be very careful in repeating the *Novena* not to err in a single syllable, and to repeat it with a fearless mind (*colla mente molto ferma*), and so you will get from him what you want.

"But if you are not [fearless] and prompt to answer, he will give you a *stiaffo forte* (a sound slap or cuff), so that the five fingers will remain marked on your face—yes, and sometimes they never disappear."

The *Novena* itself is as follows :—

" O gloriossissimo S. Vecchio Simeone che meritaste ed aveste la bella sorte di ricevere e portare nella vostre fortunate braccie il Divin Pargoletto Gesù—E le annunziaste e profetiziaste e le vostre Profezie furono sante verità—Oh Santo concedetomi la grazia che vi addomando. *Amen.*"

This is the inscription under a coloured print in which Saint Simon is represented as clad in a grey skirt to the ground, a scarlet gown to the knee, a yellow sash and girdle, and a kind of high mitred cap—quite such as was worn by magi and sorcerers and Egyptian priests of yore—whence it came in the second or third century with a mass of other Oriental properties and wardrobes to the Roman Catholic manager of the Grand Opera of Saint Peter.

This is the account of the spell as given by one who was a believer in this heathen Tuscan magic. In it we have, plainly and clearly, an old heathen spirit or the magician Simon, who changed his forms like Proteus. It is very curious to contrast this with the following Roman Catholic method of working the oracle, as given in the *Libretto di Stregonerie*, a halfpenny popular, half-pious work.

" IL BUON VECCHIO SIMEONE

" Procure an image or statuette in plaster of this great saint, who presided at the circumcision of our Lord Jesus Christ, with the old Saint Joseph and the Virgin Mary, both being the very much beloved progenitors of the Lord God the Redeemer.

" It makes no difference if the image of the saint be of plaster or a picture, if we repeat the marvellous Oration (*Novena*) dedicated to him, and if according to the instructions in it we recite the customary prayer.

" And it is certain that after the *Novena*, the good old man will appear in some form, and give to the one praying his request ; but what he principally bestows is lucky numbers in the lottery.

" There is no occasion to fear, for the saint generally appears in a dream while you sleep, and his form is so good and benevolent that there is no danger of awaking trembling and terrified.

" The whole difficulty is to know how to decipher the exact meaning of the words and signs which the saint will give. Many people miss their meaning, according to what many have experienced, so difficult is it to decipher and unravel the problems or ' figurations.' " [1]

There, reader, you have the two—take your choice. One is the downright grim old heathen classic Proteus Simon, who requires the courage of an old Norse hero to face him, or one of the kind who—

" Ransacked the tombs of heroes old,
And falchions wrenched from corpses' hold,"

while the other is all rose-water—*sucré*—and light pink ribbons. But you should have seen the sorceress who prescribed the allopathic spell ! She *looked*

[1] It is a fact worth noting that in all religions of all ages the inspiring spirit of oracles, like Martin Van Buren, the American President, seems to suffer from a decided inability to give a plain straightforward answer to a plain question. The prophecies of the Old Testament, like those of the Pythoness, or Merlin, or Thomas Nixon, or Mother Bunch, or True Thomas, or Nostradamus, are all frightfully muddled. I believe that no theologian has ever accounted for this divine inability to speak directly or to the point.

her part. One day I said to her that I wanted a photograph of a certain other old woman professor of the art, but she must look animated like a witch. " Oh, you want her to look like THIS ! " cried my oracle. And she put on for an instant the witch-look—and, as Byron says of Gulleyaz, it was like a short glimpse of hell. She actually seemed to be another person. Then I realised what the Pythia of yore must have looked like when inspired—or the old Etruscan sorceress described in *The Last Days of Pompeii*—who was possibly an ancestress of my friend. A photograph of *that !* Why, it would be like the likeness of a devil with the hydrophobia.

One day I gave a young woman an amulet—a stone in the form of a mouse— for luck. Her first question was, "Will it enable me to win in the lottery?" " For that," I replied, "you must put it under your pillow, and pray to San Simeone." " *Si—si*," she eagerly cried, " I know the *Novena*." When I met her some time after she declared that the mouse (which she was wearing in a little red bag hung from her neck, but hidden), had promptly brought her a prize in the lottery, and much other unexpected good luck.

What we have here are two forms of sorcery—one the old Roman-Etruscan, and the other its modification under Roman Catholic influence. I suspect that the first was in the beginning purely Etruscan, but modified to agree with Simon Magus. I have other forms of diabolical or heathen spells which are unquestionably *ante* or anti-Christian, and which agree with it so much as to prove a common origin. I will now proceed to " further instances."

It is not remarkable that there should be saints half heathen in a country where the established Christian religion itself makes extraordinary and frequent compromises with common sorcery and black witchcraft. In old times those souls of men who had slain many victims were invoked above all others, the belief being that they carried into the other world the audacious power which they had won by blood. This foul and atrocious worship of dead criminals is to-day in full action in Sicily with the cordial sanction of the priesthood, as the reader may learn in detail from a chapter in the *Biblioteca delle Tradizioni popolari Siciliane*, edited by GIUSEPPE PITRÉ, vol. xvii., Palermo, 1889. In it we are told that when murderers and other atrocious criminals have been beheaded, if they do but confess and receive absolution before death, they are believed to become a specially favoured kind of saints, who, if invoked when any one is in danger of being robbed and slain, come down from heaven and aid the victim. And this is carried so far that there is actually a *chiesa delle anime de corpi decollati* (a " church of the souls of beheaded bodies ") in Palermo, with many pictures of the holy miracles wrought by the sainted murderers. M. PITRÉ has devoted twenty-five pages to this subject, showing the extent of this vilest form of superstition and witchcraft, the zeal of its worshippers, and the degree to which it is encouraged by the priests. There is a work entitled *Saint Francis of Assissi, Sacred Discourses*, delivered by the Rev. FORTUNATO MONDELLO, Palermo, 1874, in which such worship is commended and exalted with much sham-second-hand fervour, in that wretched fervid style of writing, which reminds one of third-rate plaster statues of saints in Jesuit churches of the last century, which the sculptor attempts to make holy-sentimental but has only succeeded in rendering spasmodically silly. There is, according to him, something exquisitely tender and beautiful in giving "to these pilgrims of eternity when about to rise to heaven, the refreshment of that sublime word, "Sons of penitence—fly—fly to glory!" "So religion ennobles and sanctifies their death when they take the cross of the Redeemer," &c., and so forth, as usual, when the stream of such holy commonplaces is once turned on.

What this really *is*, is devil-worship. These saints have been the very scum of Sicilian brigandance, outrage, robbery, and wickedness—incarnate fiends ; and now, because they went through a mere form of words and were sprinkled and oiled, they are adored like God, are prayed to, and their relations are proud of them. In all this there does not appear a word as to their unfortunate victims. No ; because these latter went straight to hell, having mostly died "in sin," without confession.

"It is believed about Naples or in Sicily, that a man will be safe not to go to hell if he will take some flour, roll it up in a paper, carry it to a priest who lays it on the altar near the cup and renders it potent with the words of the consecration " (*Ibid.*, p. 142). This practice was condemned in 1638, but there are many similar ceremonies still practised with the aid of priests. Thus in Florence if a woman wishes to be with child, she goes to a priest and gets from him an enchanted apple, after which she repairs to Saint Anna, *la San 'Na* who was Lucina of Roman times, and repeats a prayer or spell. And all this is not sorcery! Oh dear no—that is *quite* a different thing! Thana was in fact the Etruscan Lucina, or goddess of birth, and Anna may be derived from this. She was identical with Losna.

Saint Lawrence, or San Lorenzo, is another old heathen in disguise. He was grilled on a gridiron. His day is the 10th of August, when innumerable children visit his church and turn three times round before the altar, or go round it thrice for good luck, reciting *orazioni*, incantations, and prayers. "E ciascuna volta far mostra d'uscise di Chiesa."

This turning or going round for *luck* is a remnant of the old worship of

Fortune, and of the turning of her wheel. To this day in Sicily the turning a knife or spinning a chair is an invocation of *Fortune* according to Pitré.

To recur to Simon, one can hardly fail to inquire of him as the Christian Saint of the Circumcision, since he performed the deed and Christ submitted to it), giving us thereby a divine example, and since the circumcision is glorified in every church, and in thousands of pictures, as in this Novena), why do not all Catholics submit to it? Surely the Pope, cardinals, and priesthood should conform to that which they glorify, and set the example of. " Or if so, why not?" " Matter of breviary, quoth Friar John."

Simeone as the Saint of Dreams has taken the place of Somnus. It may be that Somnus, who became Somno, may have been called *Somnone* and so coalesced with Simeone. This is mere conjecture, but by a guess hypothesis begins, and then in time a place as theory wins. The difference between Santo Simeone and Santo Somnone is not tremendous—and Simeone is the Saint of Dreams.

While these sheets were going through the press, I received several curious documents which I regret that I cannot give in detail. The first is a legend of a spirit or sorcerer, who was on earth a priest named *Arrimini*, who hid in the magic walnut-tree (probably of Benevento), and acquired magic power by means of a cat-witch's blood. The second is a strange and interesting tale of the rivalry of two witches named *Meta* and *Goda*, in which the latter comes to grief by endeavouring to bewitch the king's son. Both of these tales are from the Tuscan Romagna, that of Arrimini comes from Premilcuore, and is written by Peppino, who has been several times referred to in this book. I may here lay stress on the fact that these witch or sorcery legends have a marked character of their own, being all harsher, cruder, and more uncanny than the usual Italian fairy tales, in which latter there are, however, many traces of the former. I mention this, because in marked contrast to them I have received with the others the tale of *Il Fornaio*, or of the baker *Tozzi* and his daughter the fair *Fiorlinda*, which is made up of the usual nursery-tale elements, or the cruel stepmother, the benevolent fairy, the ugly envious daughter of the stepmother, and the young prince. The real witch tales are told among witches and grown people, and have a far grimmer, darker, and more occult tone than the latter. Thus in the story of *Arrimini* it is not the *narrative* by any means which forms its strength, but the description of the magic means and materials obtained, which would be of no interest to any one save to adult " professionals."

DVSIO

PART SECOND

PART SECOND

INCANTATION, DIVINATION, CHARMS AND CURES, MEDICINE, AMULETS

CHAPTER I

LA STALLA DI MAIALE
—DREAMING IN A
PIGSTY AND SWINE
LORE

E are told in the *Heimskringla*, an early history of Norway, that when Ragnhild, the wife of King Halfdan the Swarthy, was with child she dreamed marvellous dreams. Once she seemed to be standing in a garden trying to take a thorn out of her chemise, but the thorn grew in her hand until it was like a long spindle. One end of it took root in the earth, while the other shot up into a great tree, so high that her eye could scarcely reach the top of it. The lower part of the trunk was red as blood, further up it was green and fair, while the branches were white as snow. They were of very unequal size, and it seemed to her that they spread out over the whole kingdom of Norway.

King Halfdan hearing this wished to dream also, to further explain the mystery. He consulted a magician, who told him that the sure way to have truly prophetic dreams was to sleep in a pigsty. The king did so, and dreamed that his hair grew to be very long and beautiful. It fell in bright locks about his head and shoulders, but they were of unequal length and colour ; and one lock was longer, brighter, and more beautiful than the others. This was interpreted to mean that a mighty race of kings should spring from him, though they would be unequal in fame. The largest lock was in after days, according to Snorro Sturleson, supposed to indicate Olof the Saint. As for the queen she bore a son, Harold, who became famous for his long locks whence he was called Harold Harfagr, or, Harold the Fair-haired.

The belief that prophetic dreams can be secured by sleeping in a pig-pen is widely spread. The Roumanians and so-called Saxons, and probably all the Slavonian and gypsy inhabitants of Hungary, are familiar with it. Therefore I was not astonished when on asking my fortune-teller from the Tuscan Romagna whether people ever slept in a *stalla di maiale*, or pig-pen, she at once replied that *per avere un vero sogno*—to have a true dream—it was the most approved method known, and proceeded to explain how it should be done, in these words :—

" To learn the future in a dream one must sleep in a pigsty, and above all be sure that the pen is occupied by a *maiala incinta o gravida*—a sow with young. And he must sleep *alla boccone*, that is on his face, and crouched up, or else flat on his back, but not on his side. And before going to sleep he must say :—

> " ' Mi addormento
> Per fare un buon sogno,
> Sant' Antonio che siete
> Sopra i maiale,
> Fate mi la grazia
> Che possa fare
> Un buon sogno,
> Secondo il mio desidirio ! '

> (" ' I sleep that I may
> Have a propitious dream.
> Saint Antonio who art
> Placed over the pigs ;
> Grant me the grace,
> That I may have a good dream,
> Such as I desire ! ')

" And doing this he will surely see in a dream that which will set forth or explain what he wishes to know."

"In Germany," says De Gubernatis, "common people often go to sleep on Christmas Day in the pigsty, hoping to dream there ; and this dream is the presage of good luck. The new sun is born in the sty of the winter hog."

It is worth observing that as everything which was connected with generation or begetting, such as life, love, revival, birth, fruitfulness, and coupling of the sexes, was associated with light and reviving springtime, therefore the pig, though it was as a wild boar a symbol of death and darkness, yet because it is enormously prolific "and one of the most libidinous of animals, was sacred to Venus, and for this reason, according to the Pythagoreans, lustful men are transformed into hogs" (*De Gubernatis*, vol. ii., p. 6). In fact the *pudendum fem.* itself, as a symbol of

THE ATTITUDE FOR DREAMING

fruitfulness, was known as a pig, and has for this reason always been worn as a charm for luck. The cowrie shell, from its resemblance to the same organ was also called a pig, and is extensively used at the present day in the East as a charm against the evil eye. In Varro (*De re Rustica*, ii. 4) we read :—

" Nuptiarum initio, antiqui reges ac sublimes viri in Hetruria in conjunctione nuptiali nova nupta, et novus maritus primum porcum immolant ; prisci quoque Latini et etiam Græci in Italia fecisse videntur, nam et nostræ mulieres, maxime nutrices *naturam*, qua fœminæ sunt, in virginibus appellant *porcum*, et Græce *choiron*, significantes esse dignum insigni nuptiarum."

As sleeping in a pigsty gives true dreams, so the pig seems of old in many lands to have been closely allied to truth, for Romans, Scandinavians, and Germans all swore by it (*Livius*, i., 24 ; *Mome, Geschichte des Heidenthums*, i., p. 259 ; *Claudius Paradinus Symbola heroica* (Antwerp, 1583), p. 8. Also in the *Hervor Saga*, King Heidreck swears by a boar, the symbol sacred to Frey. The pig was so generally used in sacrifices, and was so closely connected with mysteries and holy rites, that a German, Casselius, published a work on the subject—*De Sacrificiis porcinis in cultu deorum veterum*, Bremen, 1769. For much erudition on the subject of swine in ancient mythology and legend the reader may consult *Die Symbolik und Mythologie der Natur*, von J. B. Friedrich. Wurzburg, 1859. It is not generally known that the reason which the Turks give for not eating pork is that all living things were converted to Mahometanism except the pig, who remained a heathen. And in the Netherlands the peasants have a proverb of " the pig under the barrel," which refers to the Jews refraining from " the unclean beast," and tell a story accounting for it :—

" When Christ once went to Flanders the Jews ridiculed His teaching, and to test His wisdom they hid one of their number under a barrel, and asked Him what was there ; and He answered, " A pig." So they laughed Him to scorn. But lo ! when they lifted the barrel, there was their friend changed into a hog. And he ran forth and mingled with the other swine, and because the Jews could not pick him out, to this day they have eaten no pork for fear of devouring him or his descendants."

There is another old and curious Norse story of dreaming in a pig-pen. When Earl Haakon was fleeing (A.D. 995), from his subjects, who had risen in rebellion, he went with a single thrall, a slave named Kark, who had been his playmate from his boyhood, to his mistress Thora of Rimul. And she hid the two in a deep ditch under her pigsty. This was covered over with boards and earth, and the pigs were over it.

" Then came Olaf Tryggvesson, of the race of Harold the Fair-haired, to Rimul to seek and slay Haakon. And calling his men together he mounted a great stone close to the pigsty and declared in a loud voice that he would give a great reward to any one who would find the earl and slay him.

" The earl heard this, and saw that the thrall Kark was listening eagerly.

" ' Why art thou now so pale,' asked the earl, ' and now again as black as earth ? Is it that thou wilt betray me ? '

" ' No,' replied Kark.

" ' We were both born in the same night,' said the earl, ' and our deaths will not be far apart.'

" They sat in silence. At last Kark slept, but he tossed and talked in his sleep. The earl waked him, and asked what he had dreamed.

" ' I dreamed,' answered Kark, ' that we were both on board a ship, and that I stood at the helm.'

" ' That must mean that thou rulest over thy own life as well as mine. Be faithful to me and I will reward thee when better times come.'

" Once more the thrall fell asleep, and had a nightmare. The earl woke him again, and asked him his dream.

" ' I thought I was at Hlode,' said Kark, ' and Olaf Tryggvesson put a golden ring about my neck.'

" ' The meaning of that,' said the earl, ' is that Olaf will put a red ring about thy neck if thou goest to seek him. Therefore beware of him, and be true to me.'

" But when the earl fell asleep Kark slew his master with his knife, thrusting it into his throat. Soon after he came to Olaf with Haakon's head, and claimed the reward promised. But Olaf verified the murdered man's prophecy. He put, not a ring of gold, but one of blood round Kark's neck, for he beheaded him.

" For though Haakon Jarlo Earl Haco had been his bitterest foe, and done him great evil all his life long, he little liked it that so great a man should be treacherously slain by a slave whom he had ever treated kindly. And as the saga ends :—

" Oc er Olafr kiendi thetta var hofut Hakonar Jarlo, tha reddist han thrælnum, oc bad han uppfesta, oc sagdi hann hofa skild maklig laun, fyri sin Drottin svik. Sveik hann Hakon Jarl, svikia mann hann mik, ef han ma. Enn sua skal leida drottins svikun."

English :—

" And when Olaf knew that it was the head of Earl Haakon he was enraged at the thrall, and ordered him to be hanged, and said, ' He shall have evil boot for betraying his master. For if he deceived Earl Haakon so would he betray me if he could—and so shall all treason to a master be rewarded.' "

As we are influenced by surroundings, it is natural that certain places should have been chosen to dream in. "We have read," says Pico de Mirandola in his *Witch*, "that the physicians of Calabria and Taurus were wont to sleep in the sepulchre of Podalirius, and others in that of Esculapius." A pig-pen is, however, several degrees removed from a temple, or even a tomb. As the former seems to be distinctly Northern, it may have come into the Romagna from the Lombards. It may be observed that it is only in the Italian traditions that the minutiæ of the ceremony are given. The presence of the sow with pig is significant. It was by a prediction referring to such a sow that Odin caused himself to be suspected by King Heidreck in the Hervor Saga.

But not long after I had written the foregoing remarks, I came across a certain passage in the *Symbolik* of Creuzer (whom, by the way, I knew in Heidelberg in 1847), which seems to cast much light on this connection of the pig-pen with the temple.[1]

"Unto Demeter or Ceres pregnant sows were specially offered in sacrifice, as Cornutus, the Stoic, who lived sixty-eight years after Christ, informs us, as does Arnobius (*Disput. adversus Gentes*, edit. Elmenhorst, p. 135), adding that it was because of the great fertility of this animal." Therefore it came to pass that pigs were kept in the cellars of the temple of Ceres and Proserpine, as Creuzer relates : "In honour of these goddesses the Bõotians put little pigs into subterranean chapels, which the next year were seen in the meadows of Dodona. Pausanias and Clemens Alexandrinus speaks of the same thing as observed in other places." [2] Ceres was pre-eminently a goddess of fertility, therefore of good luck and all genial influences ; hence little gold and silver pigs were offered to her, and also worn by Roman ladies, partly to insure pregnancy, and partly for luck—a custom

[1] *L. Annæus Cornutus de natura deorum*, 211, pub. by Fr. Osann, 1844
[2] *Pausanii De. Græciæ*, lib. ix., c. 8

which was revived as a fashion a few years ago in Paris, and a very funny one it was when adopted by unmarried virgins. Of which gold and silver pig-norance some note has been taken in a French novel, entitled *Le Cochon d'Or.*

It is remarkable that the Italian superstition requires that there must be in the pig-pen a sow with young. According to Aristophanes, the sacrifice of the sow must be made when any one was initiated into the mysteries. For information on this subject consult also *Bayerische Sagen und Bräuche, Beitrag zur Deutschen Mythologie, von Friedrich Panzer. München,* 1848.

From what is here cited it appears that of old people slept in certain temples of the gods to have true dreams, and that these temples were used partially as pig-pens. And this much seems to be certain, that Ceres was greatly consulted by means of dreams, and that this dreaming was specially in her temples in which pigs were kept.

The Spell of the Ivy and the Statue

" Cur hederâ cincta est ? hedera est gratissima Baccho,
Hoc quoque, curita sit, dicere nulla mora est.
Nysiades Nymphæ puerum quærente noverâ
Hanc frondem cunis apposuêre novis."

Ovid, *Fasti.* iii

The first of the medical magical cures of Marcellus of Bordeaux is as follows :—

"Herba in capite statuæ cujus libet nasci solet, ea decrescente luna, sublata capitique circumligata dolorem tollit."

("If grass growing on the head of any statue be plucked in the waning of the moon and taken away, be bound about the head, it removes pain.")

The sixth is much the same :—

"Herba vel hedera in capite statuæ cujus libet nasci solet, ea si in panno rufo ligata capiti vel temporibus alligetur, mirum remedium hemicraniæ vel heterocraniæ prestabit."

("If grass or ivy grows on the head of any statue and it be gathered and tied in a red cloth to the head or temples, it will be a marvellous remedy for headache or neuralgia.")

I inquired for a long time in Florence before I found the following cure for a headache. It was not only repeated to me, but also written :—

"When you take grass from the head of a statue to cure a headache you must say :—

> " ' Non prendo l'erba,
> Ma prendo la magia
> Che il mal di capo mi vada via,
> E chi mi ha dato la malia
> Il diavolo la porta via.'

" And then you must make *le corne* (the sign of the horns or *jettatura*) behind you."

That is to say, cast it in the old Roman fashion over your right shoulder. In English this is :—

> " I do not take the grass or ivy,
> But I take the magic power,
> That the headache may leave me,
> And may the devil carry away
> The one who gave it to me ! "

Now it may be observed that whenever any of these magical prescriptions are wanting, as regards an incantation, they are always imperfect.

MARCELLUS, as the imperial court physician, probably did not obtain his prescriptions very accurately from the people. I am quite sure that this Italian incantation is far older than the third century. It is in the same form as many others ; but what is most conclusive, it assumes, as a matter of course, that even a headache must be the result of evil magic. This is the very oldest form of sorcery.

I have no doubt that Ivy was the original plant used in this cure. In early religious symbolism, as wreathing the head of Bacchus, it meant *life* itself, and that very deeply and significantly. Therefore, when it was found growing of itself on a statue, it was of course supposed to be very effective. The early Christians borrowed much from the Dionysiacs—among other things, the Ivy. They laid it in coffins as a symbol of new life in Christ.[1]

I have said that ivy on the head of a statue was especially typical of health and life in Roman symbolism. It also signified on any head—as a garland, a fillet, or wreath—poetry, inspiration, or active genius. As appears from the following from Ovid :—

---

[1] " Hedera quoque vel laurus et hujusmodi : quæ semper servant vivorem in sarcophago corpori subster-nantur ad significandum, quod qui moriantur in Christo, vivere non desinant, nam licet mundo moriantur secundum corpus, tamen secundum animam vivunt et reviviscunt in Deo."—DURANDUS, *Ration. Div. Offic.*, lib. vii., c. 35

" Siquis habes nostris similes in imagine vultus,
Deme meis hederas Bacchica serta comis,
Ista decent lætos felicia signa poetas,
Temporibus non est apta corona meis."

Tristium, lib. i., cl. 6

Of which crowning with ivy or roses, and many other customs, it can be truly said that we know very little as regards all the feeling, sentiment, and associations which attached to them in the days of yore.

It is remarkable that, according to the very ancient and widely-spread tradition, any plant which grows off, away from, or above the earth, is believed to have magic or healing virtues, or to be spirit-haunted. The mistletoe, from its aerial nature, became almost the centre of Druid observance, and moss has many mysteries. The house-leek—in German *Hauswurz* or *Donnerkraut*—is believed to guard a house from lightning (Grimm, *D. M.*, 2 ed. B. 1, s. 445)—the mountain-ash being also dedicated to Thor, or thunder. But remember that whenever you see grass or herbage, ivy or flowers, on old walls or ruins grey, there the owls wone, and elves and fairies delight to dwell or dance, or pass the time, as has been so well approved by much observation that to deny it were enough to deny all testimony of tradition. So rest ye firm in the faith that wherever—

" High on the towers
Grow beautiful flowers,
Wall-flowers, ivy and grass ;
There in the light
Of a moonshine night
You can see the fairies pass."

THE SPELL OF THE HARE

" Flevit lepus parvulus
Clamans altis vocibus,
Quid feci hominibus:
Ut me sequuntur canibus?"

German Latin Song, Twelfth Century

" First catch your hare . . ."

Attributed, wrongly, to Mrs. Glasse

There is among the spells of MARCELLUS one (84, GRIMM) to relieve the *coli dolor*—inflammation of the colon, possibly here the colic—which is very curious :—

" Lepori vivo talum abstrahes, pilos ejus de sub ventre tolles atque ipsum vivum dimittes. De illis pilis vel lana filum validum facies, et ex eo talum leporis conligabis corpusque laborantis præcinges : miro remedio subvenies. Efficacius tamen erit remedium, ita ut incredibile sit, si casu os ipsum, id est talum leporis in stercore lupi inveneris, quod ita custodire debes, ne aut terram tangat aut a muliere contingatur, sed nec filum illud de lana leporis debet mulier ulla contingere. Hoc autem remedium cum uni profuerit ad alios translatum cum volueris, et quotiens volueris proderit. Filum quoque, quod ex lana vel pilis, quos de ventre leporis tulis, solus purus et nitidus facies, quod si ita ventri laborantis subligaveris plurimum proderit, ut sublata lana leporem vivum dimittas et dicas ei, dum dimittis eum :—

> " ' Fuge, fuge lepuscule !
> Et tecum aufer dolorem ! ' "

("Take from a live hare the ankle-bone (or heel-bone), remove the hair from his belly, and let him go alive From that hair, or fur, make a thread, and with it bind the bone to the body of the sufferer, and you will see a wonderful cure. But the remedy will be more efficacious—yea, incredible—should you by chance find that bone in the dung of a wolf. In which case so guard it that it shall not touch the earth nor be touched by a woman, nor should any woman touch the thread made of the hare's wool. But the remedy may be transferred from one to another patient as often as you will. But carefully wash the thread, every time, for more avail. And when you shall have shorn it away, let the hare run away alive and say :—

> " ' Run, run little hare
> And carry the colic with you ! ' ")

The following prescription is given word for word as it was told me in Florence :—

" Take or catch a hare without doing it the least harm and say :—

> " ' Lepre vi prendo,
> Ti porto a casa mia,
> Che tu mi porti
> La buona fortuna,
> Fa porti via la male di . . .'

> (" ' Hare, I take you,
> I bear you to my home,
> That you may bring me
> A good fortune ;
> Bear away the illness of . . .")
> [Here the name of the patient is mentioned.]

" And when the hare is carried home you must cut, or shave, away its fur in the form of a cross. And this done, hold the hare towards the invalid with a third person, and put it on the neck of the one who suffers. Then let the hare run away, making the sign of the chestnut (or *la fica*), saying :—

> " ' Vai ! e la malora
> E il male tu possa portarlo con te ;
> E lasciarci noi
> Tutti in liberta,
> Colla buona salute !

(" ' Go ! and mayst thou bear
All the trouble and ill with thee !
And leave us free
With good health.')

"Then spit behind you thrice, *and look not behind you*, and go not out from the house for three-quarters of an hour."

I have no doubt that the incantation on catching the hare is as old as the rest, but was unknown to Marcellus. The cutting the fur away in the form of a cross is evidently modern. The spitting thrice and the sign of the *castagna* are old Roman, and formed a part of all such ceremonies. It will be seen that all of the Roman prescription is given in the Italian version, the concluding incantations being almost identical. I suspect that Marcellus really abridged most of his accounts. They may have been at first hurriedly noted down, and transcribed a long time after from the notes. GRIMM, in fact, points out, with much sagacity, that they bear evidences of copying. It is, indeed, not in the nature of things that such a troublesome task as catching and shaving a hare, and extracting the *talus*, &c., should have been " worked off," or dismissed, so abruptly as Marcellus describes it.

There is not a negro in North America, and I suppose very few white men, who have not heard that the fore-foot of a rabbit (the hare being there unknown), is a charm for luck. The fore-foot brings fortune, the hind-foot prevents evil from overtaking the bearer. This world-old, widely-spread belief owes its origin to a faith in the *talus*, or ankle-bone. I possess specimens of these amulets, or fetishes, which were obtained from Voodoo sorcerers by Miss Mary Owen, of Saint Joseph, Missouri.

All mediæval magic, as well as Roman, abounds in allusions to the effect that while engaged in incantation the operator must not look behind him. And if a traveller be followed by an evil spirit or fiend, the latter will have no power over him until he " turns around his head."

The injunction not to look behind one involves some very curious and very ancient lore. In Tuscany if one gathers ashes or other objects for magic, he or she in departing must not look round. So in Theocritus (Idyl 91), on gathering ashes such retrospection is forbidden. Also Virgil (Eclogue 8) writes :—

" Fers cineris Amarylli foras, rivoque fluenti
Transque caput jace ne respexeris."

HILDEBRAND (*Theurgia*, p. 297) tells a marvellous tale, how a young man of noble birth was tormented by demons. His guardian angel promised him that if he would pray to God, not drink with the devils, and not once look behind him, *bey Verlust seines Lebens*—on his life, and could hold out till cock-crow, he would be all right. Which so happened. PRÆTORIUS, who gives several pages to the subject "Why witches when riding on their brooms must not look behind them lest they fall off"—which it seems is a condition of broom and goat-riding (*Blocksberg*, p. 414)—very shrewdly conjectures that Satan got the idea from Lot's wife. This not turning round is probably connected with the unbroken attention or unintermitted thought which enters largely into all execution of spells. When the witch's attention is distracted by intricate patterns, grains, or by songs, her evil power for the time is suspended.

The Spell of the Spider

"L'araignée est un signe de bonheur et annonce particulierement de l'argent pour la personne sur laquelle est trouvè."

As is very natural, the spider appears in Folk-lore as both bad and good, lucky and unlucky. From its ugliness and poison it is an emblem of enmity and hatred. "The Tarantula causes by its bite a species of madness, which, according to popular superstition, can only be cured by dancing." For this cure there is a physical explanation. Violent exercise often works off ill humours in the blood. A typhoid fever may be averted by hard labour. In Western America a man bitten by a rattlesnake must drink all the whiskey he can swallow, and run or walk till he drops with fatigue. Thus the Tarantella is a well-known dance, which popular superstition assigns to witches. It is the awakening dance at their Treguenda, or Sabbat.

There is a legend which states that this Tarantella dance originated as follows: A priest bearing the sacrament passed by a party of dancers who did not salute it. So he caused them to dance on and more madly than ever (*Naturgeschichte zur Dämpfung des Aberglaubens* (Hamburg, 1793), p. 102). But while there are many legends of evil spirits appearing as spiders, on the other hand the extraordinary instinct, or ingenuity displayed by the insect in making its web, and its habit of always being in one place at home, and its foresight as regards the weather, have made it a generally recognised symbol for industry, cleverness, domestic steady habits, and prophecy. Therefore it brings good luck, and is a type of thrift and wealth. If a spider creeps over you and you do it no harm "there is money coming." Again, its wonderful perseverance in re-spinning its web, or in getting to a predetermined place, has pointed many a moral and adorned many a tale from the days of the Bruce to these our own times.

Of course it found a place in magical medicine. MARCELLUS (cap. 14, p. 104) gives the following :—

"Araneam quæ sursum versus subit et taxit prendes, et nomen ejus dices cui medendum erit, et adjicies : *Sic cito subeat uva ejus*—quem nomino, quomodo aranea haec sursum repit et texit, tum ipsam araneam in chartam virginem lino ligabis et collo laborantis suspendes die Jovis, sed dum prendes araneam vel phylacterium, alligas ter in terram spues."

Which is to the effect that when you see a spider weaving upwards, you name your invalid, and take the spider, and put it in a bag of virgin linen, and hang it round the neck of the patient, but while taking and bagging your spider, spit thrice on the ground.[1]

All of which is nearly the same in Tuscany, but with it there must be pronounced the following incantation :—

> " Ragno, o mio bel ragno ;
> Benedetto che tu sia !
> La tela che tu fai,
> Lascia la in casa mia,
> La tela che tu fai,
> Falla con buona fortuna,
> E con malissima fortuna,
> E che la fortuna resti in casa mia,
> Quando la tela l'hai fatta,
> Vattene o ragno mio !
> Ma non di casa mia,
> Vattene dalla tela,
> Che tu mi hai fatto,
> Mi hai fatto con buona fortuna ;
> E io la prendero
> In un sacchetto di lana rosso la mettero.
> E dentro un marengo d'oro vi uniro,
> E cosi sempre più buona fortuna io l'avro,
> E questo sacchetino
> Come un oracolo la terro,
> E la terro dentro al seno,
> E mai più lo lasciero ! "

> (" Spider, O my pretty spider,
> Blessed be thou !
> The web which thou weavest,
> Leave it in my house !

---

[1] The spiders that come to your house (so says the negro), indicate the number of your friends. If you kill a spider you will certainly lose a friend. At the same time, certain kinds of spiders cooked in the food are supposed to cause death. "A spider in the dumpling" is a name for secret poisoning. Spider-webs are found on the bodies of feeble babies. —Note by MARY A. OWEN

The web which thou makest
Make it lucky (with good fortune),
Or with the worst fortune.
And may the luck abide in my ouse,
When thy web is spun
Leap out, O my spider !
But not from my house.
Go from thy web,
Which thou hast woven for me,
Which thou hast made with good luck,
And I will take it,
I will put it in a bag of red woollen !
And there with a golden spangle,
Thus I shall ever have good luck,
And this bag
I will always keep as an oracle,
I will keep it within my bosom,
And I will never leave it !")

This incantation speaks of putting the *web* and not the spider in a bag of red woollen. But MARCELLUS in other cases orders the red woollen bag. As for the spitting thrice on the ground, it is a common formula at the end of many Tuscan incantations. I may say that it and the sign of the *fica*, also of the *jettatura*, go *ad libitum* with all of them.

There is no proof, but there is always a possibility, that all these modern incantations may be translations from the Latin, while it is almost certain that the Latin were in turn taken from the Etruscan, or Oscan, or some early tongue. If so, future researches into the earliest languages of Italy may verify the assertion.

As regards the web of the spider, there is a pretty German fancy that when the Virgin Mary ascended to heaven, her veil, falling off, was carried about and torn to pieces by the winds. Therefore the silvery spider-webs which are seen in summer floating in the air are called *Mariengarn*, or Mary's yarn, or that which is spun.

It is worth noting that in SCOTT's novel of *Waverley*, Meg Merrilies while braiding differently coloured threads in a charm—which custom still exists in Italy —sings :—

" Twist ye, twine ye even so,
Mingle threads of joy and woe !"

And that this is almost exactly the same with a passage in the Tuscan incantation to the spider :—

" La tela che tu fai
Fa la con buona fortuna
E con malissima fortuna ! "

The spider is, according to several learned authorities, often carried in Germany in a walnut-shell as an amulet, and then, after several years, it turns to a gem. The explanation of this is that, as the yolk of a very hard-boiled egg, if kept for several years, becomes almost like a stone, so the mass of substance from which a spider spins her web hardens to a semi-transparent ball. Here I may remark that wherever we find any such superstitious custom followed without an incantation, we may be sure that it is imperfect, for in early times nothing was " locked," or made sure, without its charm. In Tuscany this spider spell exists in its ancient form, and I here give it literally *in nuce*—in a nut-shell :—

"Do you want a charm to bring good fortune or much money ? This is the way to make it—the more you believe in it the better your luck will be : Take a great spider. *Si mette in una nuoce*—you put it into a walnut-shell ; and, if you can get it, let this be a walnut-shell of *three* pieces—*una nuoce a tre canti*—and put with the spider, *comigno*—cummin—frankincense, and salt, and a little bit of a red (woollen) garment, and a bit of iron magnet. Then close the shell, glue it up, and say :—

" ' Non porta nuoce,
Ma porto la fortuna,
Che non mi abbandone mai ! ' "

(" ' I do not bear the nut,
But I carry the good luck,
That it never may leave me ! ' ")

This is an extremely curious and ancient formula of declaring that whatever one does is not to stop at a certain point. By means of it almost any action is turned into magic. Thus to find and pick up *anything*, at once converts it into a fetish, or insures that all will go well with it if we say when taking it : " I do not pick up " —naming the object—" I pick up good luck, which may never abandon me ! " It is an incantation of universal application, enabling one to secure a wish out of every chance occurrence.

The spider is also used in divination. I find the following in a popular chap-book :—

" *Il Ragno Industrioso*. In the *Book of Dreams*, and in the works of the famous cabalists Rutilio Benicosa, Casamia, l'Indovino, Il Palmaverde, Nostradamus, and the ancient Sybils or Haruspices, we often find methods of divining the secret of getting numbers by the lottery. Among the many extraordinary experiments made, the most singular is that by means of the spider.

"Take one of these insects—let it be very large—and put it, without hurting it, in a little box, on the bottom of which are many small pieces of paper, numbered from one to ninety. Cover it with a transparent veil, and give the spider time to weave a web.

" Naturally the insect in going here and there will turn up certain numbers. These must be noted. Do this three times, and then let the spider go. Many have won lucky numbers in the lottery by means of this experiment."

It may be observed that it is necessary to the success of this *sortilege* that we let the spider go. So in several of the charms of MARCELLUS, the animal used in such spells must be dismissed in safety—*Ecce dimitto te vivam!*

The spider, it may be observed, can also be used for other divination as well as for lucky numbers in the lottery. Thus, if you write " Yes " or " No," she will turn up for you an affirmative or negative for any question, or select the names of friends or enemies, or pick out lucky days.

But there is an appalling and revolting side to the character of the spider. All the spinners whom we see are females. The male is a little insignificant creature, in no proportion as regards size or strength to his mate, who, indeed, very often devours him as if he were a midget. But he is impelled by an irresistible impulse to couple with her, and, when she consents, and the *liaison* is accomplished, he is eaten whole for dessert. Sometimes the Arachne eats a number of suitors before yielding ; so that every web is really a *Tour de Nesle.* There is a class of women in Paris—not unknown elsewhere—of any one of whom one may hear it said, in tribute to her irresistible sorcery of charms, "Elle a mangée sept hommes "—*i.e.*, ruined seven spendthrifts. Of whom the type is the spider.

Therefore the spider is revolting. She is poisonous, crafty, remorseless, a cannibal of her kind, and always horribly—morally—ugly. There is a very deep significance in the fact, which I speak of in another chapter, that there is some higher law than mere chance, or our own associations, in this making poisonous, repulsive, and discordant things show their nature by certain signs, or why sounds agree with the forms from which they came, and that there is something strangely human in the expression of not only flowers, but of innumerable phenomena. From which it may justly be inferred that there are in all objects certain phases of sensation, feeling, emotion, or a kind of thought, of which we have as yet no real conception. There are spirits in all things—but *how* we know not.

THE SPELL OF THE GREEN LIZARD

" An old lizard said to me, ' Nothing in this world ever goes backwards. All pushes ever onward—stones become plants, plants become animals, animals become human beings, and human beings gods.'

" ' And what becomes of the old gods ? '

" ' 'Twill all be arranged,' quoth the lizard."—HEINE's *Pictures of Travel*

Among his prescriptions for disorders of the eyes, MARCELLUS gives one to the effect that we should take a green lizard, blind it with a copper needle, and put it into a glass vase, with rings of gold or silver, iron, amber, or even copper—*aut etiam cupreis*—then plaster it up—*deinde vas gypsabis.* Open it on the fifth or seventh day, and you will find the lizard—*sanis luminibus*—with his eyes well again. Then you let him go away, but keep the rings and wear them, and touch the eyes with them ; but especially you must look sometimes through the hole or circle of the ring.[1]

When an old woman in Florence was asked if she knew this spell, she said " Yes," adding that it was, however imperfect, because the *incantation* was wanting. This she supplied in these words :—

" Quando la lucertola si leva del vaso e si manda via, si dice :—

> " ' Lucertola, va via !
> E il veleno portate lo via,
> Ma indietro non ti rivoltare,
> Che il mal d'occhi non mi debba ritornare."

In English :—

" ' When the lizard runs, say :—

> " ' Lizard, run away !
> Carry the poison (disease) away,
> And till thou comest again,
> May the trouble of my eyes never return ! ' "

There is very good reason to believe that this spell is old Roman-Etruscan. Firstly, there are other incantations in MARCELLUS, in which some animal is caught and made to bear a disorder, and then dismissed with an injunction. But, secondly, MARCELLUS gives another medical charm for liver complaint :—

" Take a green lizard—*et de acuta parte cannæ jecur ei tolle*—and put him in a red woollen or naturally black bag, and hang it on the part afflicted ; then let the lizard go ; but say to him : ' *Ecce dimitto te vivam, vide ut ego quemcunque hinc tetigero epar non doleat !* ' ('Behold, I send thee away alive ; see that I, whenever I touch this, may be free from pain in the liver.') "

All things considered, this is quite enough to form almost an identity with the Italian charm.

It is certain that by rings MARCELLUS here means also *beads.* What renders

[1] Mr. Neville told me the Cingalese kill a lizard over a slow fire, and the froth that runs from its eyes is a cure for sore eyes.—Note by MARY A. OWEN

this certain is, that he says some may be of *amber*. Now it is very remarkable that to this day, all over the world, amber beads are carried by people for weak eyes, and it is essential that they should be *looked through*, to strengthen the sight. I have a string of fifty-two amber beads, at least one hundred and fifty years old. There were twice as many, but the rest were given away, one by one, to people in Pennsylvania, suffering from their eyes. The old Etruscan spell of the lizard has been forgotten, save in Tuscany ; but the belief in the amber bead survives.

The connection of amber with the eyes is very ancient. It was supposed to be wept by the sun—*i.e.*, it came from the eyes of the Eye of the Universe. A later myth makes it come from the tears of the Heliades, who so regretted their brother Phaeton. Moore refers to this in his poem, " Farewell to thee, Araby's daughter."

Lizards are sometimes found with two tails, as is mentioned in MARYATT'S *Pasha with many Tales*. I find the following in my manuscript collection of Tuscan Folk-lore :—

> " If one can have a lizard with two tails, and will always carry it, it will be very fortunate—*porta una immensa fortuna*. It is sure that if he plays he can never lose ; *mai altro*—quite the contrary, he will always win, and be lucky in all things."

MARCELLUS gives another prescription relating to the lizard, as follows (cap. 29) :—

> " Lacertum viridem, quem, Græci σαῦρον vocant, capies per ejus oculos acum cupream cum licio quam longo volueris trajicies, perforatisque oculis eum ibidem loci ubi ceperas dimittes, ac tum filum præcantabis dicens :—
>
> > " ' Trebio, potnia, telapho.'
>
> " Hoc, ter dicens filum munditer recondes, cumque dolor colici alicujus urgebit, præcinges eum totum super umbilicum et ter dicas carmen supra scriptum."

In this the eyes of the lizard are blinded, as before, with a copper needle and thread, then the lizard is dismissed and the thread is enchanted with three magic words. The thread is then bound about the patient suffering from colic. What the three words mean I do not know. But the manifest conclusion is that the spell is of old Etruscan origin, and the modern Tuscan charm is, on the whole, identical with it.

MARCELLUS (cap. 23, p. 166) gives another charm with a green lizard :—

> " Lacerta viridis viva in ostio splenitei ante cubiculum ejus suspenditur, ita ut procedens et rediens eam semper manu sinistra et capite contingat, quo facto mire ad sanitatem proficiet."

That is, the lizard must be hung up alive in the door before the bed of the sufferer from the spleen, so that he may touch it while going out or in. " Which being done, wonderfully conduces to health."

The·same thing is done at present in Tuscany, but I was told that the chief condition is here wanting. It must be a lizard with *two tails*.

The reason why the lizard is connected with the sight and light is to be found in ancient symbolism. For it was believed that when the lizard became old and blind it went into the sunlight and recovered its sight. And as an old book on animals deduces, " Therefore man, who is blinded by sin, should turn to Christ who is the true Sun." For which reason RAPHAEL painted a lizard with the Virgin in the celebrated *Madonna della lucertola* (KUGLER, *Handbuch der Geschichte der Malerei*, 1837, vol. i., p. 248). It was also a type of divination as well as of light, whence it was a symbol of Apollo, the god of light. *Galeotes* (lizard), the Sicilian soothsayer, was begotten by Apollo on Themisto ($\theta\epsilon\mu\iota\sigma\tau\epsilon\iota\alpha$), or Prophecy (ÆLIAN, xii., 46 ; also CICERO, *De divinat*, i., 20). Hence the connection with amber, "the tears of the sun," and its use as a cure for the eyes.

It was because the lizard was anciently a symbol of heat and light that the salamander, which is a yellowish brown lizard, was supposed to live in fire. This was not, however, a common salamander, such as Heine, when a boy, once burned, but a very different and spiritual kind of creature, of the same form, which dwelt habitually in the flame, and such as was seen once by Benevenuto Cellini, who tells us that on the occasion his father gave him very solemnly a good whipping to make him remember it. Of which, as I have remarked in my translation of Heine's *Germany*,[1] the same flagellation to prevent him from lying would not have been misapplied.

As the lizard is such a bright, uncanny, lively, odd, and wild little creature, flitting like a green gold-spotted ray of light over grey rocks, as if endowed with strange intelligence, it is not remarkable that many have seen in it an elf which sometimes takes human form. Which came unto me in a waking dream as follows, as I watched them to-day in the garden at Via Reggio :—

" As I rode by the night o'er the brown heath bare,
In the bright moonlight stood a castle fair ;
Lords and ladies, great and small,
Were crowding in to a festival,
Grass in the wind a-waving.

---

[1] *Vide Germany*, by Heinrich Heine, translated, with notes, by Charles G. Leland. London : W. Heinemann. 1872

They bade me enter, and in I went,
I drank good wine to my heart's content,
I laughed and danced with ladies fair,
Ne'er in my life had I such cheer;
Grass in the wind a-waving.

When all at once I heard a cry:
Haro by yaro! Asleep fell I,
While the lady dancing by my side
Seemed like a lizard away to glide;
Grass in the wind a-waving.

I woke in the early morning still,
In an old grey ruin on a hill,
Over the rock and in the sun,
I saw a golden lizard run!
And grass in the wind a-waving!"

CHAPTER II

Birds and Treasures

" No one knows better than a bird of the air
Where treasures are concealed."

ARISTOPHANES, *The Birds*

T was an ancient belief in many countries that the birds knew all things, and, as OVID says, announce the will of the gods, because they are near them ; that is, they fly to heaven, or as SENECA expresses it, " Birds are inspired by the divinities." And it was especially an old Etrusco-Latin, as well as a Greek conviction, that they knew where treasure was concealed. Thus ARISTOPHANES in *The Birds* says, that—" When a man asks birds where precious metals are hidden, they always indicate the richest mines."

In relation to this I have, from Rocca Casciano, the following, which appears to be very old :—

" When one would find a treasure, he must take the door of the house.in which he dwells, and carry it forth into the fields by night, till he come under a tree.

" Then he must wait till many birds fly over him, and when they come he must throw down the door, making a great noise. Then the birds in fear will speak with a human voice—*colla una voce diranno dove e nascosto*—and tell where a treasure is buried."

So far as the birds are concerned this treasure-hunting is Etruscan and Greek. The mysterious connection of the door with finding treasures appears in other countries. Thus in GRIMM'S *Stories*, Stupid Catherine carries away the door from her house, and by means of it—that is to say, by throwing it down and thereby making a terrible noise—frightens away a band of thieves, who leave behind them their treasure. The same story is common in Italy, where it is told with very coarse incidents of a stupid youth.

The reader will find by careful study and comparison of the whole which I have given in this book, that these Romagnola traditions have a very archaic stamp, and do not seem to have borrowed from other sources, but, in perhaps all cases, to have been original. I have been very much astonished, indeed, to find how extremely ignorant my living authorities were of the traditions, popular mythology, and folk-lore of Southern Italy, as given in the collections of PITRÉ. There is no parallel case in Europe of people, speaking almost the same language and belonging to the same race, who have so little tradition in common as Tuscans and Neapolitans, or Sicilians.

There is in the folk-lore of La Romagna, as in the language of the people, something which is harsh, simple, and Northern—not exactly German or Scandinavian—but with traces, as it were, of some strange primeval race, like them and yet not the same. It may owe something to the Lombard, and possibly to the Celt, but, after all, these traditions and sorceries are neither Lombardic nor Celtic. What they seem to be by every analogy is Etruscan, allied to Sabine.

This finding a treasure by means of birds agrees wonderfully with the very ancient Latin legend of the seer ATTA NAVIUS, who, when a child in his Sabine home, kept swine. Once, while he slept, some of his herd wandered away, and on awaking he could not find them. At first he wept bitterly, being afraid of his father's anger, but, plucking up heart, he went to the chapel of the Lares, in the next vineyard, and prayed the guardian spirits that he might find his pigs, promising them if he did so, to offer them the largest bunch of grapes in the place. He found the pigs, but how was he to find the largest bunch of grapes? He watched for a flock of birds, and they led him to it. Then his father, knowing this, took him to town, and put him to school to the masters of divination and other learning. If we substitute for the largest bunch of grapes, a treasure, we have here the spirit or essence of the Tuscan tradition. Divination not only by the flight, but by the voices of birds, formed one of the most important elements of the old Etruscan soothsaying—the *augurium ex avium volatu vel garritu* being the second of the five principal classes.

The bird who specially indicates treasures by night in old Latin lore is the

Picus Martius, or great woodpecker. " He always appears," says PRELLER (*Myth.*, p. 298), "as a wood-bird and digger in forests, where he lives alone and digs and hews and knows all hidden secrets and treasures." His Umbrian name was *peiqu*, at present in Romagnola it is *piga*. His connection with the door appears to be this : ÆLIAN (*Hist. of An.*, i., 45) and PLINY (*Hist. Nat.*, x., 20) mention that if the hole or door of the woodpecker's nest in a tree be closed, the bird will bring an herb, which at once removes the impediment. If this herb be secured it will open any door. But I offer this only as a mere conjecture. In any case the mere coincidence is worth noting.

As in very early times, therefore, the red-headed woodpecker was regarded as a goblin, or a god, named Picus, who knew where treasures were hidden, and sometimes revealed them. It is probable that from this myth were derived the elves with red caps, who had the same attributes.

And if Picus was the origin of the red-cap goblin who is found all over Europe, and even among the Eastern Algonkin Indians of America (as Mikumwess), I also conjecture that research will yet show either that all the Teutonic or Northern polytheism or fairy mythology is either derived from an early Latin source, or else has common origin with it. But as the Latins and Etruscans had attained great culture while the Northern races were in a very barbarous state, I prefer the former theory. It is indeed beginning to be admitted that the Scandinavian mythology, far from being autochthonic, exhibits throughout traces of Latin influence.

THE SPELL OF THE FALLING STAR

" Such meteors, or falling stars, which men of yore could not explain, were held to be divine omens, or intimations of the desires of the gods, and according to Homer that one signified to the other that there should be war or peace."—FRIEDRICH (" Meteore "), *Symbolik der Natur*, p. 100.

All over the world people say in joke or earnest that if, when we see a meteor, or " a falling star," dart across the sky, and can utter a wish before it disappears, that wish will be granted. Among the old Norsemen such a line of headlong fire in the heaven was believed to be caused by a dragon flashing along afar, hence the frequent mention of the appearance of such beings. In the Medicine of MARCELLUS the sight of such a heavenly body is applied to working a celestial cure for lippitude, or blear eyes, as follows :—

" Ut omnino non lippias, cum stellam cadere vel transcurre videris, numera, et celeriter numera, donec se condat, tot enim annis, quot numerabis, non lippies."

("That your sight may never be dim, when you see a star fall or fly across the sky, count, and count quickly, ere it disappears, and so many numbers as you count, so many years will you be clear-sighted.")

In Tuscany, when you see a star fall—*quando si vede una stella chi cadde*—one should say :—

> " Non casca la stella
> Ma casca l'amante mio
> Che venga o di giorno,
> O di notte,
> O al punto di mezza notte,
> A battere alle porte di casa mia
> Che non possa vivere,
> Non possa stare,
> Finche alla porta di casa mia
> Non viene appichiare

> (" It is not the star which falls
> But my lover : may he fall
> 'Till he come by day or night,
> Or at midnight,
> To beat at my door.
> Nor may he live nor stand,
> Till he knocks at my door ! ")

Or else this for an enemy :—

> " Non casca la stella,
> Ma casca la maledizione
> Che di giorno e di notte
> Non faccio altro che maledire
> La maledizione che casca
> In nome di . . ."

> (" 'Tis not the star which falls,
> But my curse,
> That by night, or day,
> I do naught save curse,
> That the curse may fall
> On . . .") (Here the enemy is named.)

The conception that as a star falls from the sky, so may your enemy go downward headlong with your curse pursuing him, is brilliant, original, vindictive, and replete with " pure cussedness." I have no doubt that to a true believer and a "good hater" it must be an immense relief. It is suggestive of Lucifer, the Star of the Morning, plunging headlong to hell from the height of heaven, while an Arab sees in it a daring *djinn* who has attempted to scale the walls of paradise and been repulsed by the angels.

The Spell of the Acorns

" 'Men of yore devoured one another,' says Diodorus Siculus, 'but Jupiter forbade this, giving them instead acorns.' Hence these are called the daughters of the Oak, since they so resemble female heads with the hair bound in ancient fashion."—Preller

There is given by Marcellus (Grimm, p. 16; *M.*, c. 15, p. 111) a curious forward and backward song and ceremony to cure soreness of the tonsils. It is as follows :—

"Glandulas mane carminabis, si dies minuetur, si nox, ad vesperam, et digito medicinali, ac pollice continens eas, dices :—

> " Novem glandulæ sorores,
> Octo glandulæ sorores,
> Septem glandulæ sorores,
> Sex glandulæ sorores,
> Quinque glandulæ sorores,
> Quattuor glandulæ sorores,
> Tres glandulæ sorores,
> Duæ glandulæ sorores,
>   Una glandula soror.

> Novem fiunt glandulæ,
> Octo fiunt glandulæ,
> Septem fiunt glandulæ,
> Sex fiunt glandulæ,
> Quinque fiunt glandulæ,
> Quattuor fiunt glandulæ,
> Tres fiunt glandulæ,
> Duæ fiunt glandulæ,
> Una fit glandula,
>   Nulla fit glandula."

This is preceded by another charm, to which reference is made. The whole came to this, that the patient is to take nine acorns, either just before sunrise or sunset, and holding them (I think he here means counting them, one by one) with the middle finger and thumb, say :—

> " Nine little acorn sisters (or girls),
> Eight little acorn sisters,
> Seven little acorn sisters,"

and so on, diminishing to

> " One little acorn girl."

Then begin with " Nine little acorn sisters," and *count back* till you come to " Nulla fit glandula "—" And then there was no little acorn girl." I am sure that in its original form this was *Ten* little acorn girls, following the fingers. There is in America and England a child's "counting-out" song for a game which runs from ten little Indian boys to one, and then backwards.

This incantation is still used in Tuscany, though I could not learn that it is specially applied to the cure of the tonsils. But it was not limited even in the time of MARCELLUS to these. He himself gives (19, 20, GRIMM, p. 13) two other charms in which nine grains of barley are counted in nearly the same manner. And also a word (21, *Ibid*) to stop the flow of blood :—

> "Si cycuma, cucuma, ucuma,
> Cuma, ma, a.

Which is like another English nursery song :—

> " Constantinople, stantinople, tinople, nople, ople, *pull!*
> Pull, ople, nople, tinople, stantinople, Constantinople."

In which we have the counting or addition and subtraction in a different form. The spell or child's game as used in Tuscany is, however, applied to good luck, and runs as follows : Taking ten acorns, the actor sings :—

> " Tu lo sai la voglio fare,
> Per l'indietro io voglio mandare,
> La verita in mia mano la deve dare,
> Queste *diande* per l'indietro io contero
> Fino al uno io tornero.
> E se mai non sbagliero,
> La vittoria io la vincero.
> Adesso io incomincio
> Da uno, due, tre quattro,
> Cinque, sei, sette otto, nove e dieci
> Dieci, nove otto, sette,
> Sei, cinque, quattro, tre
> Due—uno !
> Senza mai sbagliare,
> La vittoria io la devo fare,
> E mai nel contare io sbagliero
> La vittoria io vincero."

Or in English :—

> " You know what I want to do.
> I will work it back for you,
> The truth shall be at my command.
> I will count these acorns in my hand ;
> There shall no error be.

> Thus I'll gain a victory,
> And so I now begin, you see:
> From one, two, three, four,
> Five, six, seven, eight, nine, ten.
> Ten, nine, eight, seven,
> Six, five, four, three,
> Two—one.
> So without the least mistake
> Now the victory I take.
> I have counted well and true,
> To me the victory is due!"

I was at first disposed to regard this as a mere counting forwards and backwards, or counting-out rhyme, as it is used, not having read it carefully. But on discovering that the word *diande*, which I did not know, was the Romagnola for *ghiande*, or acorns, I saw it was essentially the same with the incantation of Marcellus. I then learned that acorns were actually used in the count.

The idea which runs through the spells of Marcellus is that the success of the cure depends on the counter not making a mistake, and, in the modern Tuscan version, that if one undertakes anything, or wishes to know if he will succeed, he is to infer the result in like manner. It is very evident that, as the same principle was applied in different ways, there must have also been some *Hauptpunkt*, or head-central invocation by counting, to divine luck in general, and I hazard the conjecture that we have this transferred to us in the modern Italian spell. That is to say, that there was an Etruscan *chief* spell to divine whether good fortune would result from an undertaking—which spell was modified to apply to certain disorders, &c. And as divination as to the success of undertakings was the very beginning and formed the bulk of all Etrusco-Roman augury and rites, it would be very remarkable if this Italian spell should be the chief one, or nucleus of the rest. This is only conjecture, but I entertain no doubt that it is in any case as old as the time of Marcellus, and therefore in all probability Roman-Etruscan.

According to JOHANNES MEURSIUS (*De Ludis Græcorum*), there was among the Greeks a game with acorns called *Tropa*. The description of it is not given. But I conjecture that it was the same as that of the Italian which is at once a spell for good luck and also a child's counting-out game—the object being, as in " Peter Piper picked a peck of pickled peppers," to repeat a difficult formula rapidly without an error.

There is yet another species of divination relating to this nut. Take as many acorns as there are letters in any person's name, plant them, and if they all come up or grow well, he or she will prosper, or you will win his love.

The reader who is interested in counting-out rhymes will find much on the subject in the work of Carrington Bolton ; also in another recently published by D. Nutt, London, and in the *English-Folk-Rhymes*, by G. F. Northall (London : Kegan Paul, Trench, Trübner, and Co.). A vast amount of ancient erudition on the subject of divining by numbers and similar matters, may be found in a very rare work, of which I possess a copy, entitled, *Tractatus Philologicus de Sortitione Veterum, Hebræorum inprimis ex S. Scriptura Talmude*, &c., by MARTIN MAURITIUS. Basle, 1692. It does not seem to have been observed that the Sortes Virgilianæ were in the nature of, or allied to, counting-out rhymes. Mauritius quotes from the work of Rabbi Ben Ezra a curious tale of how the lives of certain men doomed to be cast into the sea were lost, and those of certain *Talmidim* saved by judiciously managing a counting-out song. There is a curious and rude old German version of this. The chapter is in connection with the one *De Sortibus poeticis*. Only counting out by numbers is described, but the counting by poetical lines is evident from the context. And it is evident that such counting out to save lives would be regarded as cabalistic or magical.

THE SPELL OF THE SWALLOW

" O rondinella bella, tu sei un' incantrice."
Canzoni Popolari d'Agrumi

MARCELLUS of Bordeaux, in treating of disorders of the eyes, informs us that by the aid of the *hirundo*, or swallow, all such trouble may be effectually averted— as follows :—

" Cum primum hirundinem audieris vel videris tacitus illico ad fontem decurres vel ad puteum, et inde aqua oculos fovebis et rogabis deum, et eo anno non lippias, doloremque omnem oculorum tuorum hirundines auferant."

Or in English :—

" When you hear or see the first swallow, go, without speaking, to the first well or fountain and there wash your eyes and pray God that that year they may not be dimmed, and so the swallows will carry away all trouble from them."

In Tuscany at the present day the sufferer does the same for sore eyes, and then repeats the following :—

" La prima rondinella di primaver' e arrivata
La buona fortuna mi ha portata
Ad una fonte sono andata
E gli occhi mi sono lavata,

> Che da tanto tempo ero amallata,
> E nessun medico mi e riuscito,
> Ma la prima rondinella che e arrivata
> Questa grazia me l'ha fatta
> Benedette siano sempre le belle,
> Le beate rondinelle !

> (" The first spring swallow I have seen,
> A lucky thing it was, I ween.
> I ran to where the fountain flies,
> And in its water washed my eyes,
> Which were so long my pain and grief,
> Yet no physician brought relief;
> Yet the first swallow which I see
> Has caused a happy cure to me.
> Blest may the swallows ever be ! "

It may be observed that this incantation contains *all* that is in the Roman prescription, and, what is more, supplies the *spoken* spell which is wanting in it. *Et rogabis Deum*—" And pray God "—is certainly an early Christian interpolation. In the Italian the swallow itself is invoked and thanked, which is in perfect keeping with the very ancient hymns, Greek and Latin, in which it is mentioned.

Marcellus also teaches us again that though " the first swallow does not make a summer " it rules the spring, whether it be of weather or water, and may thereby prevent toothache. For when you see it—as before—hold your tongue and " ad aquam nitidam accedes "—go to pure shining water, and dip your middle finger of the right hand in it and say :—

> " Hirundo tibi dico
> Quomodo hoc in rostro iterum non erit
> Sic mihi dentes non doleant toto anno."

> (" I say to thee, O swallow,
> As this will never be in thy beak,
> So may my teeth pain me no more for a year.")

" And by renewing this annually you may always have sound teeth." All of which is essentially identical with the modern Tuscan spell.

It is believed in Tuscany that if swallows make nests in a house it brings good fortune. *Ma guai a distruggerle—perche portarebbe molte disgrazie*—but beware of disturbing them, for it brings many troubles.

MARCELLUS gives another prescription for the eyes, as follows (p. 11, GRIMM) :—

"Si muleris saliva, quæ pueros, non puellas ediderit, et abstinuerit se pridie viro et cibis acrioribus, et imprimis si pura et nitida erit, angulos oculorum tetigeris, omnem acritudinem lippitudinis lenies, humoremque siccabis."

Which is, that if your eyes pain you, you must take the saliva of a woman who has given birth only to boys, not girls. And she must have abstained from sexual union and stimulating food for three days. Then if her saliva be bright and clear anoint your eyes with it and they will be cured.

In Italian the cure is as follows :—

"If a woman has given birth to a child of seven months, take her saliva and milk mixed and anoint the eyes with them, saying :—

> " ' Bagno gli occhi
> A questa donna,
> Non ne lo bagno
> Col mio sputo,
> Ma lo bagno
> Coll' innocenza
> E la purita,
> Del mio bambino.'

> (" ' I bathe my eyes
> From this woman
> Not with my saliva,
> But I bathe them
> With innocence,
> And the purity
> Of my child.')

" Then make a sign of the cross on the eyes, and say :—

> " ' Bendetta che tu sia !
> Per l'innocenza
> Del mio bambino,
> In tre giorni,
> Possa guarire ! '

> (' " Blest be thou !
> By the innocence
> Of my child,
> In three days
> May I recover ! ')

" Then spit thrice behind you. And this must be repeated three mornings fasting."

There is indeed some confusion in this, as I have given it. But it is clearly on the whole identical with the spell of Marcellus. In another prescription, (67, Grimm) Marcellus declares that " Mulier quæ geminos peperit, renes dolentes super calcet, continuo sanabit," if a woman who has borne twins will step on the reins when they pain it will cure them. " Also very obscurely in what seems to be a detached fragment to cure the gout "—Dices *illius* quem peperit *illa.*

> " Venenum veneno vincitur
> Salva jejuna vinci non potest.

" You must say of that which *she* has brought forth :—

> " ' Poison is conquered by poison,
> Fasting spittle cannot be conquered.'

" Say this thrice and spit every time on your soles (footprints) or of him who is to be cured."

Taking them altogether we may say the Roman and modern spells correspond very generally if not exactly in every detail.

There is also another Tuscan spell for sore eyes, which is as follows :—

" Take elder (*zanbuco*, i.e., *sambuco*) and boil it, and with it bathe the eyes, making thrice the sign of the cross, and say :—

> " ' Santa Lucia, Santa Lucia,
> Il mal degli occhi
> Gli vada via ! '

> (" ' Santa Lucia, to you I pray,
> May the pain in my eyes
> Be driven away ! ')

" But this must be done by a man or woman who is a seven-months' child."

All of these cures for the eyes refer in some way to a woman who has given birth to only boys or to a seven-months' child. There is yet another Tuscan remedy allied to these. To cure a pain in the ear go to a woman who is nursing a seven-months' child, and while the child sucks thrice, one should put three drops of her milk into the ear of the sufferer, and say :—

> " Le butto questo latte
> Perche il male del orecchia
> La possa passare ! "

To return to the swallow in Tuscany, the feathers of this bird are an amulet as follows :—

Quando si vuole una grazia o una fortuna, sono portati, legati con un nastro rosso—when one desires some favouring fortune they are bound up with a red ribbon and carried. And for this purpose they are also put into beds. There is a Roman ballad (Agrumi, Ital. pop. songs) in which the swallow is addressed as an enchantress.

> " O rondinella bella
> Tu sei un' incantrice ! "

The swallow is believed to be good for troubles of the eyes (as was the lizard), because it is, like it, an emblem of light, or sight. As it was the herald of spring and of sunshine it was naturally associated with clear vision. So through all nature ran the golden chain connecting all things in poetic vein.

MINOR CURES FROM MARCELLUS

(With their modern parallels)

MARCELLUS informs us (cap. 1, p. 35, GRIMM, p. 10) as follows, regarding headache :—

"Cum intrabis urbem quam libet, ante portam capillos qui in via jacebunt quot volueris collige, dicens : tecum ipse ad capitis dolorem te remedium tollere, et ex his unum capiti alligato, ceteros post tergum jacta, nec retro respice."

("When you enter any city, collect before the gate as many hairs as you will of any which may lie in the road, saying to yourself that you do this to remove your headache, and bind one of the hairs to your head. Throw the others away behind you and do not look back.")

On inquiry I was assured that this was known to-day in Tuscany, but I did not find any special variation from it except that *salt* should be thrown with the hair. And I incline to think that this was included in the ancient charm, but was not known to MARCELLUS. Salt was an essential part of all ancient offerings and sacrifices (MARK ix. 49). It was considered as binding and perfecting them.

Very much allied to this is the following, which is still in use :—

" Whenever hairs are found they should be thrown into the fire, the one who does this saying :—

> " ' Se sei anima buona
> Va in pace !
> Se sei una strega,
> Scoppia, che tuoi colpi
> Si sentono da lontano,
> E che il diavolo
> Si possa sentire
> Si possa scatenare
> Per venir' ti te appigliare ! '

> (" ' If thou art a good soul
> Go in peace !
> If thou art a witch
> May you burst so that the sound

> May be heard afar !
> May the devil note it
> And burst loose,
> So as to come and catch you.' ")

Of the use of human hair in spells to do harm I shall speak in another chapter.

MARCELLUS gives us (cap. 8, 67) a cure for the eyes which is peculiarly nasty though none the less curious for that :—

" Mel Atticum et stercus infantis, quod primum dimittit, statim ex lacte mulieris, quæ puerum allactat, permiscebis, et sic inunges ; sed prius eum qui curandus est, erectum ad scalam alligabis, quia tanta vis medicaminis est, ut eam nisi alligatus patienter ferre non possit, cujus beneficium tam præsens est, ut tertio die, abstersa omni macula, mirifice visum reddat incolumem."

(" Take Attic honey and the first fæces of a babe, mix it with the mother's milk and anoint (the eyes), but first tie the patient to the stairs (or a ladder) which is of such medical power, that unless he be so bound he cannot endure it, the benefit of which will be that on the third day, all stain being wiped away, the sight will be perfect.")

The binding to the ladder or stair is found in the following Tuscan spell :—

" If any one is bewitched, bind him, or his clothes (the latter are preferred) on a *scala* (stairs or ladder) —but it, or they, must be of wood ; then take a knife, and, while sharpening it, say :—

> " ' Non lego questa robba
> Ma lego la strega
> Che non abbia più bene ! ' "

(" ' I do not bind these things,
But I bind the witch
That she may no more have good luck ! ' ")

We have here only the binding to the ladder, but a part of one prescription or charm is often found in another, in MARCELLUS, as well as in the modern charms. In all these cures the ceremony and the incantation form by far the most important part, or the *sine qua non erit remedium*.

MARCELLUS (No. 30, cap. 14, p. 103) gives the following for the throat :—

" Picem mollem cerebro ejus impone, qui uvam dolebit et præcipue ut super limen stans superiori limiti ipsam picem capite suo adfigat."

(" Put a piece of soft pitch on the head of him who suffers from a sore throat, and especially see that he does this when standing on the outer edge of the threshold.")

In Tuscany much taking of magical medicine is done on the threshold ; it also plays a part in other sorcery. This is because it is the line or limit between the place inhabited and the outer life where spirits freely roam, it being an understood law of demonology that they cannot enter a room until called on. There are evidently, however, numerous exceptions to the rule, else we should have no hauntings of houses.

In chapter 19, page 130, MARCELLUS tells us that—

" Serpentis senectus, id est exuviæ licio alligatæ et vulso circumdatæ mire prosunt." That is, that "a serpent's skin bound to the girdle is of great assistance."

In the Romagna Toscana it is believed that if any one finds a serpent's skin he must say :—

> " Ho trovato la pelle
> Di questo serpente,
> Che possa portare
> La fortuna a me ;
> Non portero
> La pelle di serpente,
> Ma portero la buona fortuna,
> Che sia sempre in casa mia."

> (" I have found the skin
> Of this serpent ;
> May it bring
> Good luck to me !
> I will not carry
> The skin of the snake,
> But I will bear the good luck
> That it may ever be in my home ! ")

Out of the immense amount of learning which has been collected on the subject of serpent symbolism one thing is undeniable—that this creature was, among the Etruscans, Greeks, and Romans, a type of health, longevity, and fortune. And it is in this sense that it appears, both in the work of MARCELLUS and in this Tuscan incantation, as a cure or amulet. I conjecture that there was of yore an incantation pronounced on finding the skin which was unknown to the Roman physician. For a careful examination of all these prescriptions or charms, in any form, cannot fail to convince any one that the *words* were always a *sine qua non*, and in fact the most important part of all.

As a curious instance of serpent-lore still existing in the Romagna, I may mention that the picture of a snake is painted on the wall for good luck or to avert the *malocchio,* but it must always be with the head down and tail up.

MARCELLUS gives the following :—

" Si arista vel quælibet sordicula oculum fuerit ingressa obcluso alio oculo ipsoque qui dolet patefacto et digitis medicinali ac pollice leviter pertracto, ter singula despuens dices : *Os Gorgonis basio.* Hoc item carmen si ter novies dicatur etiam de faucibus hominis vel jumenti os aut si quid aliud hæserit, potenter eximit.

That is, that if a grain or mote be in one eye, close the other one, draw the middle finger over that which pains, and say, *" I kiss the Gorgon's face."* Which is repeated thrice, and the charm is so powerful that it will draw a bone from the throat of a man or of a mare.

In Italian they say :—

"If anything be in the eye or in the throat of man or beast spit thrice and say :—

"' O grande Serpente
Io ti baccio il volto ! '

("' O great Serpent
I kiss thy face ! ' ' ")

To which my informant added, " But you must *look on the ground* when you say this."

On referring to MARCELLUS afterwards I found that to remove a small irritated spot from the eye (*varulus*) you perform a ceremony which ends by touching the ground thrice and spitting. Of course touching the ground implies looking at it.

MARCELLUS gives as a cure for sore eyes :—

"Qui crebo lippitudinis vitio laborabit, millefolium herbam radicis vellat, et ex ea circulum facit, ut per illum aspiciat, et dicat ter, ' *excicum acriosos*,' et totiens ad os sibi circulum illum admoveat et per medium exspuat," &c.

Which is to the effect that the patient shall pull up a plant of millefoil or yarrow, make a ring of it and spit thrice through this ring. And further that the herb shall be planted again, and should it grow, the patient will recover.

In Tuscany there is for the same complaint a remedy which is perfectly in accordance with a portion of this. It is called *La Corona della Ruta*, or the Crown of Rue.

"When one suffers with sore eyes take a branch—*coccha*—of rue and tie it round in a wreath, *in forma di una corona*, with red ribbon. The patient should be in bed and not see the garland made ; it must be always prepared by a woman in another room, and it must not be seen by children or even by any animal, and she who binds it must say :—

"' Preparo questa corona
Per metterla sopra agli occhi
Di quella ammalata,
(O ammalato, che sia)
Che degli occhi possa guarire
E mal d'occhi non gli possa ritornare.'

("' I prepare this wreath,
To place it on the eyes
Of that sufferer,
That his sight I may restore,
And he may never suffer more ! ')

"And when she gives it to the invalid he must look through it three times, and say :—

> " ' Santa Lucia, Santa Lucia, Santa Lucia !
> Del mal d'occhio fatemi guarire ! ' "

"Then he must spit through it three times."

Which is, on the whole, very much the same as the old Roman-Etruscan formula.

Santa Lucia the modern Catholic saint of light, is probably the direct descendant of the Etruscan Losna, goddess of the moon, also of the sun. (*Vide* Losna.)

Our author recommends (cap. 14, ,p. 100; p. 14, GRIMM) that for the toothache one should carry "salis granum, panis micam, carbonen mortuum in phœnicio alligabis" ("A grain of salt, a crumb of bread, a dead coal tied in red cloth"). In Tuscany quite the same is made up, and borne as an amulet for health and good luck.

MARCELLUS also prescribes the use of earthworms—*lumbrici*, or the *vermis terrenus*—for local pains. In one of these he declares that the worms are to be put into a bucket or receptacle of wood—if possible, one hooped with iron—and water poured on them, which is to be drunk. In Tuscany this is the remedy :—

LOSNA

"For one suffering headache take earthworms, also a *litre* of spirits, and say :—

> " ' Lombrici che per la terra strisciate,
> Tutte le stregonerie le conoscete,
> Come pure conoscete
> Da me il buon piède ;
> Vi prego il buon piède di raccatare
> E dentro allo spirito lo potrete lasciare ! ' "

(" ' Earthworms who slip through earth below,
    Secrets of sorcery ye know,
    When *the good foot* doth o'er you tread,
    Or when it passes overhead,
    Transfer its power and its merit,
    Now I pray you to this spirit,
    To do such virtue as it may,
    And let this headache pass away ! ' ")

(The allusion to the *good foot* is to that of the sorcerers, or persons possessed of a peculiar power.)

" Then in the evening, before the patient goes to bed, he must bathe his head with the spirit, and say : —

" ' Mi bagno il capo
    Collo spirito di lombrici a fare
    Perche il mal di capo mi possa passare ! '

"·And the next morning the pain will have quite disappeared."

I nearly missed this, because my informant did not know the word *lombrici*, or earthworms, since in Romagnola they are called *ronbricati*. This very curious incantation explains what MARCELLUS does not—why earthworms are used. As *chthonic* creatures, or of darkness, they are supposed to be familiar with the secrets of the under-world. The allusion to this, and to the foot of the sorcerer renders it certain that this is an extremely ancient spell.

MARCELLUS also gives as a cure for headache :—" Hemicranium statem curant vermes terreni pari numero sinistra manu lecti, cum terra de limine eadem manu triti " (" Earthworms—an equal number gathered with the left hand, powdered with earth from the threshold.") This also indicates that, as in the modern recipe, the same remedy was used for the same disorder.

I have already alluded to an amulet given by the same writer, consisting of salt, bread, and a coal in a red bag, or cloth. In another (cap. 8, p. 63), he speaks of the special virtue of a cure made of *four* ingredients, " quia ex quatuor rebus constat ut quadriga equis constat, et celeres effectus habet, *barma* dicitur." I suspect that his salt, &c., in a red bag is imperfect or wanting, because, when the following was given to me in Italian, something was said about the value of *four* articles in it.

LE QUATTRO COSE DELLA BUONA FORTUNA

" The four things of good fortune. Take a little *red* bag, and sew it with red woollen thread—not with silk or cotton ; the bag, too, must be of woollen, and of coarse cloth, and while sewing it, sing :—

> " 'Chuco questo sacchetino,
> Per la buona fortuna di me,
> E della mia famiglia,
> E che ci tenga sempre lontano
> Dalle disgrazie come pure
> Dalle malattie ! ' "

"Then take a crumb (*midolla*) of bread, and a little coarse salt, a sprig of rue, and some cummin, and keep repeating, while making it up, the same charm. And when made, the charm must always be borne on the same person, by night as well as by day."

The translation of the incantation is as follows :—

> " This bag I sew for luck to me,
> And also for my family ;
> That it may keep by night or day,
> Troubles and illness far away ! "

LA FORMICOLA   THE ANT

Once when I read a certain prescription from MARCELLUS to a *strega*, she admired it very much, declaring that she had never heard it before, or anything like it.   It was the following :—

"Ad dolorem uvæ scribes in charta, et collo laborantis in linteolo suspendes :—

> " ' Formica sanguen non habet nec fel,
> Fuge uva ne cancer te comedat ! ' "

(" For one suffering from sore throat write on paper the following, and stick it on the ceiling :—

> " ' The ant has neither blood nor poison :
> Fly, O pain, lest the crab devour thee ! ' ")

"But," my informant added, "I know of a cure for which *ants* are used."   It was as follows :—

" When one spits blood, take ants and put them in some of the blood, and let it stand all night, and say over it :—

> " ' Butto queste formicole
> Dentro a questo sangue ;
> Che questo sangue
> Possano ripigliare.
> E a questo malatto
> La possano riportare,
> Che i suoi pulmoni
> Non si voglione guastare,
> E la ma malattia
> Avanti non possa più andare.' "

> (" ' I put these ants into this blood
> That *his* may be both well and good !
> That he his health may soon regain,
> And his lungs be sound and sain !
> May his trouble soon be o'er,
> And illness trouble him no more !' ")

MARCELLUS remarks that the ant is a bloodless animal, therefore it is used to stop bleeding according to a kind of rude and naïf homœopathy, which continually occurs in magical medicine. As regards my very indifferent translations into rhyme of these recipes, I beg leave to inform the reader that though not very good poetry, they will answer *every whit* as well as the originals to cure disorders if he wishes to try them ; yea, and that for this purpose they are just as effective as if they had been made by Lord TENNYSON himself.

VERBENA

MARCELLUS recommends *verbena* as a magical cure for a tumour. An authority in *stregoneria* hearing this, said : " I do not think it is used in *medicine*—but," she added with animation, " it is admirable in scorcery, and for a charm." Then she gave me the following, laying stress on the fact that it must be carried on the person :—

" *Verbena* is an herb which brings great good luck, and it must always be borne upon you. Especially note if an old woman wishes to sell you some, when she offers it you must never refuse, else she might curse you (*i.e.*, bewitch you). You must always buy some, and say :—

> " ' Non compro questa verbena perche e erba,
> Ma compro la fortuna che essa porta !' "

> (" ' I buy not this verbena as the herb which here I see,
> I buy it as the fortune which I trust 'twill prove to me !' ")

My witch was quite in the right when she declared that. Verbena was admirable in magic and for a charm. Had she known and read Latin she might have supported her assertion with a great array of classical authorities. However, she doubtless had a great many more ancestors than I ever had who could talk Latin, and perhaps the tradition came down in the family ; since she says they were all *stregoni*, or wizards and witches—always !

The Verbena was called *par éminence* the holy plant—*hiera botane*—by the Greeks, and it was regarded as holiest of all in sacrifices, where it was burned especially during invocations of spirits and predictions. It was the plant of Venus : it gave, as was believed, great power of procreation, and, above all others—as FRIEDRICH writes—drove away evil spirits, and destroyed witchcraft and all such influences. Ambassadors carried it as a symbol of peace. *"Semper e legatis unus utique Verbenarius loquitur"* ("One of a band of legates was called the Verbena-bearer ") (PLINY, *Nat. History*, xxii., 3).

" For there dwelleth in the Verbene a certaine *fata*, or faery, who bestoweth fortune on those invoking her." Think of this when you smell Verbena ! Also remember that if you take a bit of it from a church it will bring you good luck : " Ex ara hinc sume verbenas tibi atque eas substerne " (*Terentius, Andr.*, iv., 4).

Our author gives two remedies for *hordeolis oculorum*—" grains in the eyes "— for both of which he prescribes *nine grains of barley* to be treated in a magical manner—such as nipping off the points, one by one, and repeating a Greek incantation every time. In Tuscany I find the following for the same trouble, or "for the eyes ":—

" Take nine grains of barley, and put them in a black pot with nine flowers of elder and nine bits of rue. Boil them for a quarter of an hour, then let it cool till it is tepid. Then dip into it a piece of linen and lay it on the eyes of the patient, and then take the nine grains of barley and the elder flower and the rue, and lay them all on the cloth, and say :—

" ' Tutto questo l'ho fatto bollire
Per mettere sopra agli occhi
Di questo malato che con la grazia
Di Santa Lucia prima di tre giorni
Possa guarire ! ' "

It is worth observing that the modern method is seriously a good remedy (all except the nine grains of barley), while that of MARCELLUS is mere rubbish. For a very immoral bewitchment—" Si quem coire noles, fieri que cupies in usu venerio tardiorem—confestim enervabitur "—MARCELLUS prescribes nine grains of wheat. I should add that the English version of what may here be called the tin-pancation—as a black tin pan may be used—is as follows :—

" All of this I have had boiled
To put upon the eyes,
Of this poor man—Saint Lucy aid !
And on the third day, by thy aid,
He will in health arise ! '

Santa Lucia is the saint of light, therefore of sight. The two were identified in ancient Roman mythology.

There is a very great resemblance between the cat and the hare when skinned, also between their skins. This being admitted, with the addition that MARCELLUS gives several prescriptions in which cats, or the skins of animals, are employed, we may infer that the following is not without affinity to an Italian charm.

" Pellem leporis recentem in olla munda vel tegula ita cum lana sua combures, ut in tenuissimum pulverem redigere possis, quem cribratum in vaso nitido servabis inde cum opus fuerit tria cochlearia in potione dabis bibenda, quæ res sive calculos sinè vessicæ dolores continuo compescit."

Which is, that for the stone or pains in the bladder you should burn the fresh skin of a hare in a small pot or on a tile, so as to reduce it *to the finest powder*, which, when pulverised, you must keep in a clear (glass) vase, and give the patient three spoonfuls in a drink.

The Italian spell is to bewitch any one, or to do him harm :—

" When you would do evil to any one, kill a black cat, skin it and rub the skin (by burning is, I suppose, understood) to a very, very fine powder (*si trita fine fine*), and when it is triturated finely to a powder, mix with it pulverised horse-scrapings and pepper and earth, over which a toad has passed. And while taking this earth from under the toad, say :—

> " ' O rospo, rospo, che siei composto
>   Tutto di veleno, del tuo veleno
>   Lasciane sparso un poco sopra,
>   A questa terra che passo portarlo
>   A casa mia.

> (" ' Toad, all poison from thy birth !
>   Shed thy poison on this earth !
>   Give me of thy poison some,
>   That I may bear it to my home.')

" Then put all together in a small bag, and at the time of mixing say :—

> " ' Terra e polvere insieme
>   Lo riunite, e polvere di gatto
>   E la peggio, ma e la miglio,
>   E per me perche mi deve vendicare,
>   Polvere di pelle di gatto,
>   Con polvere di cavallo,
>   E pepe unito a terra di rospo,
>   Terra avvelenata e tutto
>   Un immischia che molte persone
>   Voglio rovinare che non abbiano
>   Più pace e ne bene, fino che
>   A me non si vengano
>   A racommandare, ed anche all'ora
>   Le concedero grazia se mi pare.' "

> (" ' Poisoned earth and powder fine
>   To the powdered cat I join,
>   'Tis the worst, and yet the best
>   For my vengeance—for the rest

Cat skin powdered ; naught is worse ;
With the scraping of a horse,
Pepper next, to make it good,
Earth well poisoned by a toad :
'Tis a mixture which, when done,
Will rack and ruin many a one,
And they shall know no good or peace,
Nor shall their sufferings ever cease,
Until they humbly come to me
And beg for mercy on their knees,
Which I *may* grant—if I should please.' ")

Se mi pare ! This was chanted *crescendo,* and when the witch came to the last word her face was infernal—not violent, but serpent-like ; horrible, yet cold. Does this remind the reader of a scene in SHAKESPEARE'S " Macbeth "? Or is the incantation like his ? Not to me, for his was *poetry* written for the stage, and this was reality—the witchcraft of old, old times—the spirit of the sorceress who would kill, the life of necromancy which is death.

I say truly that if I could write all that I have seen in exploring this Italian witchcraft, few indeed would believe me, and fewer still could understand it. For it all belongs to a world and a life of which no cultivated person, whom I ever met, has any comprehension, and for which he can certainly have no sympathy. When I reflect that GOETHE and HEINE and BYRON, and I know not how many more poets and great word-artists have travelled over Italy grasping eagerly at every scrap of magic and passion and human romance, I wonder *what* they would have thought or written had they known what was *living* among these people, deep in their hearts. We may read history for ever, but we can never learn from it, or from literature—till we get the key to it—what a strange race was this old Etrusco-Roman !

Under the ashes of Italy there is burning a fire of which only now and then a spark is seen, but it has never been extinguished any more than that of Vesuvius. Imagine an English or German peasant woman bursting out into such spasms of sorcery and poetry—I have known one in Italy, in reciting an incantation, to be seized with convulsions. And in all the people, low or high, there is a something which seems to be repressed—a genius as of stifled art, or magic power—a science which will yet be manifested when the time comes.

There is a very remarkable prescription in MARCELLUS his book, for a hip complaint.

It amounts to this : that the remedy must be given to the patient *super scabellum vel sellam ita ut pede uno quem dolet stans ad orientem versus potionem bibat, et cum biberit saltu desiliat, et ter uno pede saliat, et hoc per triduum faciat, confestim remedio gratulabitur.* That is—" Standing, on a little stool or chair, so that, one foot being forward, the patient facing the East drinks his medicine, and then jumps down, and hops three times on one foot, and so he will be well in three days' time." In another he prescribes a potion to be taken standing on one foot on the threshold. The chief elements of this gymnastic performance appear in the following Tuscan spell :—

" When one takes medicine, one should stand on a stool (*sgabello*), or on the threshold of a door, and utter :—

> " ' Prendo questa medicina
> Perche sono ammalato,
> Ma non sono ammalato
> Di fisico, ma da morale,
> Percio prendo questa medicina
> Sopra a questo sgabello
> Che mi possa guarire di questa
> Malattia, e mi voglia
> Dare·felicita e bene,
> Percio scendo da questo sgabello,
> E su questo piede sinistro,
> Sempre dallo sinistro piede,
> Per tre volte mi rigiro,
> E per tre volte io chiamo,
> Il gran Salvatore e se ne
> Non mi corrisponde allora,
> Mi rivolgero alle strege,
> Alle strege o ai stregoni.' "

> (" ' I this medicine am taking
> For a sad and serious illness,
> Yet the illness which I suffer
> Is of mind more than of body,
> And I therefore take my physic
> Standing on this stool and hoping
> It may soon relieve my troubles,
> Therefore from this stool descending,
> Now I'm on my left foot standing,
> Ever standing on my left foot,
> And three times I turn upon it,
> Three times calling the great Saviour,
> But if He should give no answer,
> Then I'll turn me to the witches,
> To the witches and the wizards.' ")

Which last lines indicate that devotion to the principle of having two strings to one's supernatural bow of faith which has enabled witchcraft to hold its own so well, that it is possible that the *stregone* may exist as long as the priest—which will not be long, to judge by the spirit which is growing up among the people. Once the *least* allusion reflecting on the clergy, within my own memory, was promptly punished and without mercy. Now, as I write, the last great caricature at every street-corner represents the departure of the Pope for ever with a gang of disreputable-looking attendants. It is accompanied with bitterest satire, and ends with the words, "*A good riddance to bad rubbish!*" *Eppur si muove.* I think that this incantation is essentially ancient, but very much modernised in form. The remedy is Roman, but it seems to be in a new bottle.

It is said by MARCELLUS (cap. 28, p. 201) that "*Corregia canina medius cingatur, qui dolebit ventrem, statimque remediabitur*" ("He who suffers from a pain in the stomach will be relieved should he girdle himself with a dog-leash") (that is, a strap of any kind). I rather wonder that GRIMM should have regarded this as superstition since it is a well-known fact that a girdle—*e.g.*, a Russian belt—really gives great relief for such suffering. However, if it was to be done specially with a *dog's*-leash, and no other, it was undoubtedly superstitious ; and that this was the case may be inferred from the following Tuscan formula :—

"Take a *funicella del cane*—a rope which binds a dog—and say :—

"'Prendo questa funicella,
Che il mio cane legava,
Attorno alla mia vita,
Me la voglio passare
Che il mio male di ventre
Al cane se ne possa andare,
Ed a me mai non possa ritornare.'"

("'I take the rope which held my hound,
Now round my life the cord is bound,
May that which makes my agony
Pass to the dog away from me,
And I no more a sufferer be!'")

This is quite after the style of several of MARCELLUS'S own prescriptions, in which he shows how a disorder can be transferred from a human being to an animal. As in the following (cap. 27, p. 190) :—

"Tormina patientibus multi ventrem viventis anatis adponunt ad firmantes, transire morbum ad anatem, eamque mori."

("To those suffering from a colic. Let them fasten a live duck to their stomachs, thus the disease will pass from the man to the duck, and the duck will die.")

This is found in Tuscany with the invariable musical accompaniment of an incantation :—

" When one suffers from a pain in the stomach take a duck, and the body of the bird must be placed against that of the invalid, and then say :—

> " ' Anatra ! Anatra !
> Che il male mio tu possa
> Pigliare, e di questo male
> Io ne possa guarire ;
> E tu di questa male
> Tu ne possa morire,
> Che a me questo male
> Non mi possa mai ritornare
> Fino che non torni
> Tu a risucitare ! ' "

> " ' Duck, duck, so may it be,
> That thou shalt take this pain from me !
> That the ill depart, and I
> Shall get well, while thou must die :
> And may I never feel the pain
> Till thou shalt have thy life again ! ' ")

Which was bad for the duck. However, this went for very little with a physician, one of whose most vaunted cures was to put a patient *in balneo repleta humano sanguine*—in a bath full of human blood. Such a bath of the blood of young children was once ordered for the Emperor Constantine, and because he, being moved by the cries and tears of their mothers, resolved not to take it, his extraordinary humanity was rewarded by a miraculous cure. As related by the early chroniclers, this seems to have been regarded—even by Christians—as a great act of mercy and magnanimity. It does not seem to be at all understood that for several centuries after the decay of the Roman power the world relapsed as regards barbarism and inhumanity, instead of advancing with Christianity as is popularly believed.

MARCELLUS gives the following as means by which fidelity may be secured in a woman :—

" Mulierum, quam tu habueris ut nunquam alius inire possit, facies hoc : lacertæ viridis vivæ sinistra manu caudem curtabis eamque vivum dimittes, caudem donec inmoriatur eadem palma clausam tenebis, et mulierem, verendaque ejus dum cum ea cois, tange."

The Tuscan recipe, though very different in details, is quite the same as regards the principal item, that is, the lizard caught with the left hand :—

" When a man wishes his wife to be faithful, he should take *sperma illius mulieris* and put it in a bottle, and then catch a lizard with the left hand, and put it in the same bottle, and cork both up very tightly, and say :—

> " ' Qui racchiudo la fedelta
> Di mia moglie che non possa
> Mai sfugirmi ! '

(" ' Here I put the fidelity
Of my wife, that she may be
Ever, ever true to me !')

" Then be careful not to lose the bottle, and always to keep it in the house."

I do not clearly understand for what complaint MARCELLUS means the following prescription—*nisi ad verrucas*—but I give it, according to GRIMM :—

" De tribus tumulis terræ, quos talpæ faciunt, ter sinistra manu quot adprehenderis tolles, hoc est novem pugnos plenos, et aceto addito, temperabis."

(" Take from three mole-hills three handfuls of earth thrice, that is, nine handfuls, and mix them with vinegar.")

The following is a Romagnola charm for bewitching or injuring any one :—

La Terra dei Mucchi delle Tarpe (*Talpi*).

" Take earth from three mole-hills and put it in a red bag, and while removing the earth say :—

> " ' O terra che di terra vi racatto,
> Sopra tre mucchi che dalle tarpe siete stati ammuchiati,
> E come avete ammuchiato questa terra
> Ammuchiate i dispiacere di quella famiglia
> Che non abbiano bene e ni pace
> E tutte le sfortune piombino sopra al suo capo !

(" ' Earth, O Earth, who long hast laid
On the hills which moles have made,
As they heaped thee, may there be
Evil heaped on this family !
And disaster fall like lead
Evermore upon its head ! ' ")

I could almost believe that MARCELLUS has misplaced this spell, in applying it to a cure. For, as my authority explained, " the mole lives in darkness, and, like the earthworm, is under the footprints of the *stregone*, or wizards, which give it power for good or evil according to their natures, but it is generally most powerful for bewitching." In saying which she gave in a few words a great amount of classic folk-lore unawares. FRIEDRICH (*Symbolik*, p. 386) writes on this as follows :—

" As the mole is subterranean he has a chthonic, demoniac reputation, as of one hostile to man, which is to be found in such old Roman beliefs as, ' If you throw a mole into a house the grandmother will die.' To this might be added several to the effect that by means of it disaster can be wrought to a family, especially to its head."[1]   It was of yore much used in sorcery.   Thus, according to PLINY (*Hist. Nat.*, xxx., 7) :—

" He who will swallow the heart of a mole, still quivering, will *receive* the gift of prophecy ; a mole's tooth pulled from the living animal cures toothache, its blood cures weakly persons."

I was not aware of this when the Tuscan spell was given to me, but I can now understand why so much stress was laid upon its force in magic.   It has its value as illustrating the recipe of MARCELLUS, but is much more interesting as setting forth the old Roman superstitions regarding the mole.   The very ancient use of pitch in superstitious practices appears in the following from MARCELLUS, which I here repeat for another illustration :—

" Picem mollem cerebro ejus impone, qui uvam dolebit et præcipue ut super limen stans superiori limiti ipsam picem capite suo adfigat."
(" Stick a piece of soft pitch to the head of a man suffering with sore throat, and this should by all means be done when he is standing on the threshold.")

In a Tuscan incantation to break love, pitch appears in its very ancient signification as an ingredient of witchcraft :—

" When you wish to prevent a young man from visiting a girl in any house, take shoemaker's wax (*pece da calzolai*) and four nails.   Make of these a cross, and put such crosses under the seats whereon the lover and maid sit.   And the end will be that they will quarrel, and he will no more come to the house."

The last spell, or recipe, of MARCELLUS is to cure the gout :—

" Carmen idioticum, quod lenire podagram dicitur sic : In manus tuas exspues, antequam a lecto terram contingas, et a summis talis et plantis ad summos digitos manus duces et dices :—

" ' Fuge, fuge, podagra, et omnibus nervorum dolor,
De pedibus meis et omnibus membris meis ! '

" Aut si alii præcantas, dices illius quem peperit illa :—

" ' Venenum veneno vincitur
Saliva jejuna vinci non potest.'

" Ter dices hæc et ad singulas plantas tuas, vel illius, cui medebere, spues."

This is, in brief, spit in your hands before rising in the morning, pass your hands from your soles to the ends of your fingers, and say :—

---

[1] *Die Zoologie der alten Römer und Griechen* (Gotha, 1856), p. 85

    " ' Fly, fly, O gout, and all my nervous pains
    From both my feet, nor linger in my veins ! '

" Or if you chant it for another, say of that which she bore ;—

    " ' Poison by poison is conquered,
    Fasting spittle cannot be conquered.'

" Say this thrice and spit on your soles, or on those of the one whom you would cure."

There is in Tuscany a very terrible illness, caused, as some say, by eating bad maize-meal, others attribute it to bad living and malaria. It is called *la pellagra*. As the name very much resembles *podagra*, or gout, I was told that the following was a cure for *pellagra*, to which my informant added, *anche per la gotta* —also for gout—which latter complaint I need not say is not so common among temperate peasants. *La pellagra* causes madness.

" Per guarire la gotta o la pellagra. To cure gout or *pellagra*. Take for three mornings a small boy (*bambino*) while fasting, and make him spit three times on the place where the gout shows itself, and while doing this let him say :—

    " ' Gotta, o gotta ! (*o pellagra !*)
    Va via dal mio piede,
    Il veleno vince il veleno,
    Come pure lo sputo
    Vince il veleno, e
    Lo sputo mio d'un bambino
    Innocente sara quello
    Che vincera la gotta maladetta,
    Che non torni mai più
    A fare capo sopra alla tua persona.'

    (" ' Gout, O gout, to thee I say,
    Go thou from my foot away !
    As poison conquers poison, see
    This infant's spittle conquers thee !
    That thou shalt ne'er return again,
    And give me any further pain ! ')

" Then the boy must spit behind him thrice, and repeat this for three mornings."

Of the one hundred medical spells described by MARCELLUS, and commented on by J. GRIMM, I have identified about *fifty*, with as many still in use in Tuscany. And if we consider that in this collection of the Roman physician there are a great many which run, so to speak, into one another, and how much there is in them all which is to be found in many of the modern Tuscan spells, such as the not looking behind, and spitting thrice, and, in fact, the whole system, spirit, and method of the cures, we should not be far from the truth in saying that probably all are still in existence, and that, beyond all question, a very great number, which were old in his day, are still extant. But a general consideration and comparison of all the ancient and modern examples given in this book will best enable the reader to judge of its value.

As a comment on this chapter Miss Mary A. Owen adds the following notes drawn from American negro sorcery :—

" Voodoo

"Voodoos warn against throwing hairs about, for if a bird gets a hair and weaves it into a nest the owner of the hair will have frightful headaches—nothing can cure until the hair is found and burned. Also, if a person gets the hair of another and introduces it into a slit in the bark of a growing tree, the unfortunate will go crazy as soon as the bark grows together over the hair." [Also Hungarian gypsy. C. G. L.]

"You may call a friend to your presence from the ends of the earth by putting four of your own hairs in a bottle of water, calling the bottle by the name of the one you wish to see, and placing it in the door you wish him to enter. Within four days (for in that time the hairs will have swelled into snakes) he must start towards you.

"The skin of the serpent worn around the waist cures rheumatism. The rattles worn in the hat cure headache and prevent sunstroke. The heart swallowed whole cures consumption.

"To cure sore eyes, bathe them in water containing the gall of a duck and a spoonful of syrup made of boiled water-melon juice.

"A black hen split open and placed on the body cures fevers and relieves the pain of cancer.

"The right fore-foot of a mole is a good-luck charm. The brains of a mole put in a black silk bag and tied round the neck of a babe will make it cut its teeth without pain or fever. If the gums of a teething child are rubbed with a mole's foot the teeth will at once appear.

"The brains of a rabbit tied in a black bag and rubbed on the child's gums will bring the teeth through, so also will a necklace of elder twigs.

"If a child under a year old is allowed to see itself in a looking-glass, it will cut its teeth 'hard'; but this may be prevented by tying a mole's foot above the glass."

The Three Wise Men of the East and the Witch Medals

> " Die heil'gen drei Kön'ge aus Morgenland
> Sie frugen in jedem Städtchen ;
> 'Wo geht der Weg nach Bethlehem,
> Ihr lieben Buben und Mädchen?' "
>
> HEINE, *Buch der Lieder*

There appeared in the *Gypsy-Lore Journal* of January, 1889, a very interesting article by DAVID MACKITCHIE, in which he discussed an old opinion that the Magi, or Three Kings of the East, were often held to be, as LONGFELLOW describes them, "the three gypsy kings, Gaspar, Melchoir, and Balthasar." This may have been a mere popular fancy ; but there is abundant evidence to prove that, whether of Indian or other Eastern blood, there was in all probability a great deal to connect them with gypsies as regards their lore.

If the three kings were Magi, or Wise Men from the East, we may conclude that they were of the Chaldæan, or Persian, order, of which there were many at a late date roaming about the Latin empire. They were all soothsayers, or diviners, and it was in this capacity that they appear in Bethlehem. That is, they were of the old Chaldæan-Accadian school of sorcery, which I believe to have possibly had a common Turanian origin with that of the Etruscans, which still survives but little changed in the sorceries of the Tuscan Romagna ; and both of these were the same with the Shaman magic of the pre-Aryan dwellers in India. Reduced to facts, it is more than merely possible that the "wisdom," or lore, of the three kings was "Gypsy" (that is, Indian or Persian), or perhaps Chaldee, in its origin, and that they were really itinerant diviners or soothsayers.

This is not much more than conjecture—albeit there are "guesses good and bad." But a very curious incident casts a strange side-light upon it. In Hungary I have known gypsies, when a child was very ill, to seek to cure it by hanging from its neck Maria Theresa dollars. In the Romagna of Tuscany there is an ancient belief that certain old Roman coins are a sure defence against witchcraft, especially for children. To combat this the priests have made certain medals, which, like the older articles, pass current under the name of witch-medals— " *medaglie delle streghe.*"

I noted down in conversation the following remarks in relation to them :—

" ' Quando si ha una medaglia delle streghe, e si mette questa medaglia al collo, con questa sara sempre libero delle streghe ' (' When one has a witch-medal, and wears it on the neck, one will be always free from witches ').

" These medals are put *chiefly on children*, but also on grown persons. And when putting one on, one should say :—

" ' *Metto questa medaglia per liberare liberamus delle streghe* ' (' I put on this medal to free—*liberamus*—from witches ')."

On asking if those who believed in "the old religion," or "witchcraft," put faith in the new witch-medals, I received an account which I did not note down, but which was to the effect that the Catholics believed in the *old* witch-coins, or in witchcraft—*avendone avuto multe cose giustificate*—"as many things had proved it to them." And that the believers in witchcraft accepted the new medals, exceptionally for certain reasons, as agreeing with sorcery. For " *si portano queste medaglie perche le tre rege sulla faccia erano stessi grande streghone* " ("They carried them because the three kings on them were themselves great wizards ").

I subsequently received some of these new medals. They are sold for a soldo,

or halfpenny, are octagonal, and made of brass, and bear on one side the three
kings worshipping the infant Jesus, and on the other the following inscription :—

S. 3. REGES
GASP. MEL. BALD.
ORATE PRO NOBIS
NUNC ET IN HORA
MORTIS NOSTRÆ.
AMEN.

The reputation of sorcery hung about the Magi, and the believers in witchcraft accepted them as friends.   It was a happy thought to put them on the
new witch-money—it was " acceptable to all parties."   I have, however, heard
from a Catholic, that this compromise of saints with the devil caused a
scandal among true believers.   It might be here remarked that this mysterious
group of the three magicians was by no means unknown long before in
different forms and under other names to both Christians and heathens, and
that in later lore the three fairies who appear at the birth of a child not only
present him with gifts but predict his future.   It is also noteworthy that
frankincense, which formed one of the gifts of the Magi, enters into the composition of all the modern witch-charms or fetish-bags of the Romagna—I myself
having been presented with one containing some—that myrrh is also one of these
magic medicines, and that if the offering to the infant Jesus had any meaning at
all, it was magical, and intended to avert sorcery and evil influences.   It may be
alleged that the Tuscans borrowed this use of incense from the rites of the
Roman Catholic Church ; but even Cardinal Newman himself would hardly have
denied that incense was used in sacred rites by the old Romans.   And I am
confident that a fair and full examination of all that I shall give, as regards this
Tuscan witch-lore, will convince any unprejudiced reader that it is of very great
antiquity.   For though superstitions spring up spontaneously and simultaneously,
everywhere and everywhen, yet this very fact, on due reflection, does but go the
further to prove, firstly, the vast probable antiquity of all widely-spread beliefs or
legends, and, secondly, the likelihood that they were *transmitted* from man to man,
since he who has the innate impulse to create will be the readiest to receive—a
great truth much ignored by those who incline to one side or the other, but
especially by those who believe there has been little or no "borrowing."   If
it be true that the use of frankincense as a "devil-driver" would occur *per se* and
naturally to an old Italian, or to a Hindoo, so much the greater is the probability

that if one brought it to the other, the other would accept it. Therefore, while we admit that instances of spontaneous creation of myths, legends, and customs, *may*, and do, take place, yet, when we consider how extensively men have travelled, even in prehistoric times—as is shown by jade relics—and with what incredible rapidity even a rumour will spread over an empire, and, finally, what a remarkable story-telling and myth-mongering creature man is, it becomes evident that all conjectures as to simultaneous creation from concurrent causes must be accepted with the greatest possible caution after the severest scrutiny. At present the popular tendency is to accept as self-evident—without proof—the slightest probability that a "use" (be it in any form) sprung up of itself from "like influences," while transmission is subjected to the severest criticism. Now, as transmission may, in millions of cases, have been due to wandering apostolic pilgrims, who took the whole world for a route, sailors, strays, and cast-aways—such as the Huron woman who was said to have been found in Tartary—it is a safe thing to challenge a proof which was perhaps buried for ever in the grave of some old vagabond thousands of years ago.

Myrrh, frankincense, and gold combined are an ancient and widely-spread gift for children. They were magical and luck-bringing among the Romans ; and whatever was connected with superstition, luck, and divination among them was of Etruscan origin, for their whole body of such beliefs had been derived from the fabled Tages.

There is another kind of witch-money which is very mysterious indeed. It is called La Sega delle Strege, or the Witches' Saw. I give a description of it, as taken down *verbatim* :—

"The *Sega della Strege* is a small coin which witches have. They go with this on Tuesdays or Fridays to the roads to cut or scrape the earth from footprints of people. With the coin they remove the earth, and with it they do great harm " (*i.e.*, to those people).

"The spell against the Saw of the Witches—*Sega mulega*—is mentioned in the song :—

"' Sega mulega stregone e strege di Gaeta,
Che filano la seta.'

"*Mulega* is a witches' word. It means the earth which they take with it from footprints. It signifies that it is not earth which they cut but a piece of flesh which will disappear from the soles of their feet.

" If any one suspects that he has been thus bewitched, let him stand quite naked and take a black or red ribbon. Then let him be measured with the ribbon, firstly, the entire extent of his outstretched arms, and then his height from head to foot.

This song of *Sega mulega* is a very common nursery rhyme, sung while making the " cat's cradle " with a twine, which suggests the measurement with the ribbon. But it is also closely allied to witchcraft even in this; for as the cord makes a coffin, or other figures, omens are drawn from it, as I had fully illustrated to me by seeing it done. It is a nursery rhyme now, but it was an incantation once; and a witch declared to me that, if properly understood, it is one now, and must be sung while divining with a cord. It is in full as follows :—

> " Sega mūlega, stregoni e streghe di Gaeta !
> Che filano la seta
> La seta ed il bombaggio ;
> Mi piace quel giovane
> Che sbatte le castagne
> L'isbatte tanto forte alle streghe,
> Fa tremare le porte ;
> Le porte sono d'argento,
> Che pesano cinque cento ;
> Cinque cento, cinquanta,
> La mia gallina canta——'
> ' Non era gallina che canta.'
> ' Ma e un gallo——' ' Non e un gallo che canta,
> Ma una strega senza fallo.'
> ' Se una strega é, una strega pur sia !
> Ma che il diavolo la porti via ! "

> (" *Sega mūlega !*
> Wizards and witches of Gaeta !
> Ye who spin silk and cotton—see !
> There is a youth who pleases me,
> He who is beating the chestnut tree :
> Beating the witches with terrible shocks,
> The gates are trembling at his knocks !
> The gates are of silver—five hundred they weigh,
> Five hundred——fifty—is it so ?
> Five hundred and fifty—— I hear my hen crow——
> ' But 'tis a cock ! ' ' No—a hen—without doubt,
> And, as surely, a witch, without.'
> ' If she's a witch, a witch let her be !
> But the devil may take her away for me ! ")

Whether this be a nursery song, or old incantation, there is certainly in it a wild uncanny " Northern " spirit, far surpassing that of the " *Ghurughiu* " witch-song which Goethe heard in Naples.

CHAPTER III

THE EXORCISM OF DEATH

"Begone, O Death! I fear thee not!"—*Song of the Reaper*, "*Des Knaben Wunderhorn*"

"Carmen autem evocat: orium idem tradit . . . qui pestem a suis aversam in hastes ferret."—LIVY, I. viii

HE following very singular and uncanny spell involves one of the deep secrets of the wise women which they do not make known. It is entirely heathen, there being no trace of Christianity in it, though it is used on an occasion when one would suppose that among Catholics all the appropriate rites of the Church would be employed. It turns upon the very ancient belief that death may be averted by an incantation pronounced by a sorceress, and it is very interesting in several respects, as showing the degree to which the old Etrusco-Roman sorcery still prevails in the rural districts of Tuscany —albeit there is no lack of it even within the shadow of the Duomo in Florence itself, as I well know.

I believe that I am not quite accurate when I call this " Etrusco-Roman." For in fact the religion, such as it is, which forms the *real* faith of the *strege* and their patrons, goes back to a time of which there is no record. The Græco-Roman polytheism died before Christianity arose ; before that was the Etruscan, Oscan, Sabine, or Umbrian, and long, long before these, the simple sorcery of the Tartar Shaman. And it is *this*, with more or less picked up, by the way, from Etruscans here and Romans there, but in the main just what it was thousands of years ago, which we have to-day. But to the spell :—

" When one is very ill in a house, and death is feared, go to a witch and say : ' I need a favour from thee ; death will not come to my *malato*—invalid.'

> " ' Al mio malato non voglia far venire,
> E sono venuto da te a sentire,
> Perche tu bene me lo possa dire.'

> (" ' Death will not take my friend away,
> Therefore tell me as well you may,
> What one must do, what one must say ? ')

" Then on the night when death is expected, the witch sleeps, and Death appears to her in a dream, and announces to her that on a certain day the invalid is destined for him, or will be in his power.

" Then on the night when Death comes for his victim, the witch takes a pumpkin and makes in it eyes and nose, and two holes, and puts in them two pods of beans, with the beans in them, to seem like horns. And when Death is expected, the witch makes the sign of the horns (*la iettatura*, called in Tuscany *le corne*), and—*si mette a scongiurare*—begins her incantation, thus :—

> " ' O spirito di Morte indegna,
> Da questa casa tu ne puoi andare,
> Questo malatto nella notte
> Tu non potrai pigliare,
> Perche le corne a iettatura
> Ti sono venuta a fare !
> E appena l'alba sara spuntata,
> Il ammalato più non ti sarai guadagnato
> E dalla morte verra liberato ! ' "

> (" ' Spirit of Death, to thee I say,
> Thou shalt not with thee bear away
> This suffering man, for at thee now
> The awful magic sign I throw ;

And when thou seest the morning dawn,
Without thy prey thou shalt be gone,
This time there'll be no gain for thee,
And from thy power he'll be free ! ' ")

This picture of the Witch defying Death is a very striking one, and it may be studied as a subject by an artist. I was assured that this is all kept a secret from the priests ; but that is the case with all the spells described in this book.

Ovid describes in detail a ceremony which is essentially the same. There was in Rome a feast of expiation to the Lemures, or spirits of death, which was observed on the 9th, 11th, and 13th of May, and its object was to conjure away death for the coming year.

" At midnight the father of the family walked barefooted through the house, making with his fingers the sign which spirits fear—*Signaque dat digitis, medio cum pollice junctis—occurrat tacito ne levis umbra sibi.* (That is, he made *le corne* or *la jettatura.*) Then he washed his hands with pure well-water—put *beans* into his mouth, and threw them about the house without looking behind him, saying nine times : ' These I give, and with these beans I redeem me and mine ! '

" Then he washed his hands again, and if he did this nine times, repeating, ' *Manes exite paterni !* ' he could look around, for then the ceremony was over."

The pumpkin-head is not mentioned here, but there are the beans and the *jettatura*. But Preller distinctly declares that with the course of time the ceremony of the Larvæ was more developed into one of terrible apparitions, bugbears, or bogeys. " They accompanied it with imitations of skeletons and ghastly figures." This identifies the Tuscan spell with the Roman ceremonies, for the pumpkin is evidently meant to represent a skull. Even in our times the hollow pumpkin, with a lamp on a pole, being supposed to look like a skull with fiery eyes, is well known to all rustics, and Brom Bones employs it in Washington Irving's Legend of Sleepy Hollow to frighten Ichabod Crane. This means that Death is frightened away by his own likeness. So among the Babylonian and Ninevite peoples, as may be read in the Chaldæan Magic of Lenormant, the great powers of evil among whom was Death, were more afraid of their own likenesses than of anything else, for which reason horrible figures were placed here and there to protect all houses. Mirrors are also a protection against demons. I have also no doubt that though there was really a fancy for the eccentric and odd in the Middle Age, still the true reason for multiplying grotesque goblins everywhere was due to a similar belief. There is a strange kind of homœopathy running through the lore of that time, a manifold application of *similia similibus curantur*, the killing of witchcraft by witchcraft, the driving out of devils by devils, the cure by the weapon which gave the wound, which came to perfection in

Paracelsus. This is not fortuitous, it occurs too frequently to be accidental or a result of correlative causes, and I believe that this primeval faith that Death was scared away by Death was the beginning of it.

I believe, in fact, that just as lions and monsters for the base of pillars can be traced back from Byzantine to Babylonian-Ninevite architecture, so the placing grotesque images of imps, demons, and goblins had a like origin in the same country, on the principle that the devil shuns his own likeness. It is certainly very distinctly preserved in this Tuscan Exorcism of Death. This belief explains the presence of such vast numbers in Christian churches of those diabolically odd figures which have so long been a puzzle to antiquarians. They were meant to banish devils.

The Spell of the Cradle

When I was born—it was in the city of Philadelphia—I had for nurse an old Dutch woman named VAN DER POEL, who was supposed to be something of a witch, or, like all old Dutch women, familiar with occult matters. One day I, the babe, was missing, as was my cradle. The house was searched in alarm, and at last I was found in my cradle in the garret. There were lighted candles round it, an open Bible and a plate of salt on me. I think there was a key or shears also, and money; but of this I am not certain. It was explained as a ceremony necessary to secure my success, or future happiness. Other and older printed authorities declare that it will cause the infant to rise in life, the going upstairs being symbolical of ascent; also that the person thus carried will become an adept in occult lore, or sorcery and magic. From the *Journal of American Folk-Lore*, June, 1892, I learn that among the descendants of German colonists in North Carolina "the first time a baby is taken out of its natal room it must be taken up" (stairs), "or it will not go to heaven. If the door of the room steps down . . . then the person carrying the baby must step on a chair or book with the baby in her arms" (N. C. Hoke).

On relating this to a Tuscan witch she at once recognised it as a well-known observance, and explained how it was carried out in the Romagna, as follows :—

" In the Romagne there are witches good and bad. When they are attached to any family or place, and know that a babe is born there, they enter the house as secretly as they can and take the cradle (*culla*) with the babe, and carry it up to the garret, or attic, that is, to the highest room under the roof. Then the witch takes the sack (*saconcini*) of the cradle, and lays the babe on it, and puts at its head coarse salt, and the Bible, opened, is put at the feet. And then four gold chains and four gold rings are put, one in every corner of the bed, and two lighted candles are placed at the babe's head. Then with the chains the bed is hung to the rafters (*sospesi al palco*), with the child in it, and the witch repeats :—

> " ' Io ho fatto questo
> Non per interesse mia,
> Sola per l'amore che porto
> A questa famiglia che per quanto
> Sono gran di richezza,
> Ma che il suo figlio più grande
> Possa venire di talento,
> E se lo ho messo sospeso
> Cosi in alto lo ho messo,
> Perche col suo talento possa venire
> La persona più alta
> E più importante di questo mondo.' "

> (" ' This for myself I have not done,
> But for love to this little one,
> Not because his family
> Great or wealthy chance to be.
> But that he may rise, have I
> Brought him to this room so high ;
> Thus may he by talents thrive,
> And be the greatest man alive ! ' ")

Truly a kind wish, and if it always took effect there would be no lack of talent in the world. In the Italian ceremony the benevolent witch must, after repeating the invocation, depart without looking behind her, and not return to the house that day, which latter condition is of ancient Latin origin. This incantation was repeated in prose, not sung.

DIVINATION WITH LEAD

The custom of divining by means of melted tin or lead dropped into water is, as FRIEDRICH remarks, of great antiquity, as may be inferred from the fact that it has long been known to every race acquainted with these metals. The ceremony consists of melting the lead (wax was also used among the Latins), dropping it into water, and inferring future events from its shapes. Then these were taken to bed by the person for whom the oracle was destined, when, by the influence of the image, a dream would confirm what its appearance predicted. It is barely possible that it might have entered into the heads of people in different countries to divine by the shapes which melted metal would assume, but that they should all conceive taking it to bed " to dream on " is inconceivably less probable than that it was transmitted in superstitious times from race to race. This theory of sporadic or independent invention of myths, customs, and superstitions has been carried of late to such extravagance, that if we accept it all we must believe that barbarous man, long before he had thought of anything else, developed all alone, wherever he existed, all the folk-lore which we now have, and that he zealously confined it to his own race, wherever he went! For the ideas which " naturally occur " to savages and peasants are very few indeed, as those know who have lived among them, and as is proved by those of the Romagna, who seem to have no superstitions which are not as old as the days of the Romans.

Their manner of divination by means of melted lead is as follows : It is of some importance, because it is not only elaborate, but, as can be shown by analogy, it is very ancient in every detail :—

"You must take three seeds of a rose, three leaves of nettle, two leaves of rue, and three seeds of cummin. Put all these together. Then take lead, and at midnight light two tallow candles, binding them with a (red) ribbon. Then take a plate, put the lead and the herbs on it, and the herbs last, that is to say, put the plate on the fire, and when the lead is melted put the herbs on it. Then pour the lead into water, and see what forms it takes.

"Should it take the form of a river (*fiume*), it is a bad sign. But this may be used to throw into the house of an enemy to do him evil.

"If the lead can be thrown into running water, and if it take the form of a baptismal font (*fonte*), it is a very good omen, and should be kept in a red bag, and this must be bound to the frame of the bed, or, better still, be put into the bed, care being taken that no one touches it.

" When the lead and the herbs are put into the plate one should say :—

> " ' Lo faccio per vedere
> Se verra la fortuna
> (O sfortuna) in casa mia.' "

> (" ' This I do that I may see
> If good (or bad) luck will come to me ! ' ")

I have another description of this ceremony, which is more in detail :—

" Melt the lead and put the seeds of roses, leaves of rue, and three seeds of cummin on it. At midnight light two candles connected with a red ribbon. When melted, hold the plate out of a window, saying :—

> " ' O strege, strege !
> Che la granata non potete vedere
> Io ve la levo per farvi piacere
> O strege, che di Venerdi
> Siete beate,
> Queste grazie me potete fare,
> E questa grazia mi farete
> Se volete,
> Se questa gra(zia) voi mi fate,
> Che il mio piombo mi faccia la forma
> Diu na fonte . . . significa

Anderanno bene le cose mieie,
Si il piombo fa la forma
Di un fiume e segno
Che le cose vanno molto male.'

(" ' O witches, witches !
Who cannot bear to see a broom,
I have removed it to please you !
O witches, who are happy on Friday,
Do me this favour ; ye can if you will !
That my lead may take the form of a font,
Which is a sign that all will go well;
But should it be a river, 'tis a sign
That no good fortune now is mine.' ")

This was chanted so irregularly and so mingled with ordinary conversation that I could not clearly distinguish between the spell and the explanation. Then my informant resumed as follows :—

"Put the font into a red bag, and throw this into the house of one to whom you wish good luck, and say :—

" ' Non vi butto il piombo,
Ma la felicita
Che venga in casa vostra ! '

(" ' It is not lead which here I throw,
But happiness,
That it into your house may go ! ')

"But to harm an enemy, throw the *river* into his house, and say :—

" ' Non butto il piombo
Ma la sfortuna,
Che vengha in chasa tua,
Che tu non possa avere
Pace ne bene ! '

(" ' 'Tis not lead which here I throw,
But evil fate, that ye may know,
E'er the spell of fate be o'er,
Peace and fortune never more ! ')

"If the lead forms a river, or the bad sign, to avert it, put the lead on the chimney-piece or in some corner, and put on the fire some of the herb which is called, in Romagnola *felchsa*, in Italian *frecce* (fern). It is a plant which causes great suffering to witches. And while it is burning say :—

" ' Bruccio questa robba,
Perche voi altre streghe maladette
Non potete avere mai bene,
Perche io vi cerchato una fortuna
Che non me l'avete voluta dare ! ' "

("'This plant upon the coals I burn
To do ye witches an evil turn.
May every evil come to ye.
I asked a favour, and I see
That none from you has come to me!'")

I believe that this formula ot mixing the lead with the ashes of the herbs and seeds is the true ancient Roman-Etruscan one, because rue, nettles, cummin, and rose-seed entered into the oldest incantations with which we are acquainted. But what makes the ceremony complete and most curious is the burning the *fern leaves* to destroy the influence of the witches. It was specially explained to me that it was very powerful against all sorcery and evil influences, and in every way a mysterious and strange herb. Of it FRIEDRICH says :—

"There are very many associations of sorcery, marvels, and superstitions connected with this plant, most of which are kept secret. . . . The scale-fern is especially regarded by the people with great respect, because many virtues are attributed to it—especially as a power against evil spirits. Its roots are used in invoking those which are good or evil. The five scales on the stalk, which are supposed to resemble a hand, are called the hand of luck, or John's hand, and are carried as a protection against misfortune or sorcery."

Should the lead and ashes, &c., simply amalgamate into one piece, it has no special meaning.

Divination with lead means the making of forms or figures by the aid of incantations, and it is therefore closely allied to the same by dropping the white of an egg into water, and judging from the shapes which it assumes what the future will be as regards a question asked. This is world-old and world-wide, but in Tuscany it is practised as follows :—

"Take a glass of water at midnight, exactly. Let fall into it the white of an egg, and say :—

"'Faccio quest' uovo,
Perche che tu maladetta strega
La fortuna tu possa darmi
Un spiegazione
Sopra questo uovo,
Te lo lascio fuori di finestra
Venti quattro ore
Che tu abbia il tempo
Di farmi vedere
La mia fortuna!'

("'I show this egg, curst witch, to thee,
That I in turn my fate may see.
For a day at thy command,
On the window it shall stand,
That my fortune I may know :
That it shall my future show!')

" After twenty-four hours consider it closely.   If it shall have taken the form of a burying-ground, it means a death in the family ; if it show a church and a priest giving the benediction, it means a wedding. Stars presage happiness.   And if the lineaments of any person can be traced, it means good fortune from that particular person."

The witches who attend to the egg-prophecies must be a singularly amiable class of ladies.   They are addressed with a curse, and then modestly requested to take the trouble to arrange a prediction !

DIVINATION BY OIL

" Est enim evangelium signum pacis et saluberrimum OLEUM gratiæ et misericordiæ divinæ."— COCQUIUS, *Histor. ac contemplatio sacra Plantarum.*   Vlissing, 1664.

There are in the streets of Florence, not far from the Signoria, houses which were, possibly, old in the time of Dante—who knows ?—or who knows the age of anything in this land where relics of even prehistoric culture abound, and nothing seems so strange as the new ?   Into one of these houses I entered—into total darkness—felt my way upstairs to an invisible door—knocked, and entered a large room only divided from another by a large ancient arch.   There was but a half-light from a single window, and the whole formed a very Rembrandt-like picture. At the table sat the fortune-teller, and before her was a glass of water into which, with strange gestures while uttering incantations, she was dropping oil from a bottle.

" *Che fai*—what art thou doing, daughter of a thousand witches ? "

" I am making an *incantesimo*—an incantation—with oil.   Do you want to learn how to do it ? "

Yes, I wanted to learn.   I knew that the divination by oil was prohibited by law and gospel, church and state, even in the edicts of Charlemagne, and that it was in all times one of the *secreta rariora* which the witches kept for special occasions.   The author of the *Trinum Magicum, sive Secretorum Magicorum Opus*, published in 1611, tell us: *"Aliqui itidem aquam in vitreum catinum effundunt, oleique guttulam admiscent et sic in aqua mira se cernere posse putant."*   In English : " Some again pour water into a glass basin, mixing therewith a drop of oil, and so think they see marvellous things in the water."   Which was all he knew about it, since if he could have told more he would assuredly have done so.

The whole oracle was, however, duly, sincerely, and thoroughly consulted in my presence, and it runneth thus, as I wrote it down, step by step :—

" Take the flask with oil—a small one—make with it thrice the sign of the cross on the head and face, saying :—

" ' In nome del cielo,
    Delle stelle e della luna,
    Mi levo questo malocchio (o altra cosa),
    Per mia maggior fortuna ! '

(" ' In the name of heaven,
    Of the stars and moon,
    I pass away this trouble
    For better luck and soon ! ')

" Then with the same bottle or vial, make three crosses with the right hand over the glass of water, exactly from side to side, also making the *corna* or *jettatura* with the forefinger and little finger of the left hand extended, and the middle and ring-finger closed, or held by the thumb. And these extended fingers rest on the edge of the tumbler.

" While doing this the *strega* repeats :—

" ' Befania !   Befania !   Befania !
    Chi mi ha dato il malocchio,
    Me lo porte via ! '

(" ' Befania, Befania, Befania !
    Thou who didst cause this trouble,
    Bear it away from me ! ')

" Then pour in, or let fall, very carefully, three drops of oil. If they combine at once, it is a good sign, or an affirmative to any question. If you wish to know whether you are to find what you seek, or meet a friend, or anything of the kind, all will go as you desire. But if the three drops remain apart it is a bad or negative sign.

" Then to thoroughly explore all the chances, this ceremony is renewed three times. And every time throw the water and oil into the street, or a court. Should a man be the first to pass, all will yet go well. If a woman, the omens are still unfavourable. And then once more make the *castagna* or chestnut, the sign of the thumb between the fore and middle fingers, which is far more potent than the *corna*" (even the early Roman writers call it terrible) ; "note that this also is on the edge of the glass, with the left hand, while with the right the oil is dropped skilfully so as to make a cross of oil, or spots of oil across the water (which has been renewed). Then cross the head and face three times with the oil, repeating the Befania invocation three times as before." (All of this was done with incredible quickness.)

" And if, after all, the oracle is unpropitious, drop into the glass about a teaspoonful of salt, and repeat the formula of ' Befania.' Should the oil turn of a whitish colour, this is a sign that the Befania relents and that all may yet go well."

But if she be deaf to every spell, nor heed the sacred salt, then drop into the glass a hot coal—the last desperate resource of diabolical recklessness.

" Flectere si nequeo superbos Acheronta movebo."

This mixes the oil and water despite of all the devils. And this done you go forth with the fierce, proud feeling that though every omen is against you you are to prevail by a strong will. But ere departing there is still something to be done. You express your gratitude to the Spirit of the Fire, which is short but extremely heathen, and I have no doubt very ancient :—

" O fuoco benedetto,
   Chi brucia immensamente,
   E bruce tutte le gente,
   Ti prego di brucciare
   Questo malocchio,
   E chi me l'ha dato ! "

(" O blessed Fire,
   Thou who burnest so immensely,
   Thou who warmest all mankind,
   I pray thee to burn
   This evil spell,
   And the one who smote me with it ! ")

Then, as in old Latin rites, the coal and all must be thrown into a running stream, and you depart without looking behind you. " Fers cineris Amarilli foras, rivoque fluenti, transque caput jace, ne respexeris." The reader will find by comparison that this charm has much in common with the Divination by Ashes.

I must confess that I greatly admire this species of divination, and have perfect faith in the last, or hot coal, portion of it. The witch had by her side a *scaldino*—an earthenware brazier in the form of a basket—just as her ancestresses always had in the days of VIRGIL, and perhaps long before the time of TARQUIN, and when the coal went hissing into the oil and water her face had the beautiful expression of a sorceress defying a fiend. It was a fine picture, and a great artist would have appreciated the flashing black eyes under a thicket of tangled hair— and my mind darted from the witch of Vesuvius to VIRGIL and APULEIUS and THEOCRITUS—who had all seen the same antique and terrible face—doubtless in the *orgasme* of the hot coal !

Other oracles and incantations " say their say," give you a " yes " or " no," and are done with it. But in *this* you begin amiably and smoothly with the oil, and a gentle, if heathen, incantation to the planets. You give Fate every chance, and are prodigal with magical courtesies, or ceremonies. But you do not give it up should the reply be unfavourable. Not at all. You proceed to the greater piquancy of salt. Salt is polite too—but there is an intimation in it that there is an iron hand under your velvet glove—that you mean business and will see the thing out. And then—salt failing—comes the red-hot coal. Should the sky fall you will hold it up with your spear, and defy the devil. In other words, that which was to have been, may be *compelled* to take another course by means of persevering in enchantments. Which corresponds to prayer and penance—in all religions whatever—all of which teach that the future may be changed or formed to suit those who are " good."

It may not have occurred to many readers to reflect that what all such divinations as this are equivalent to, is *prayer*, accompanied by formalities. When religious people—as is very often done in America—hold meetings to pray for a certain object or purpose, it is quite the same as if they divined with oil and salt and invoked Befania. In the year 1859, when THEODORE PARKER was extremely obnoxious to the rigidly orthodox of all sects, a number of very Presbyterian pious ladies held meetings for the purpose of praying that he might be taken away from this life; and his death, soon after, was attributed to the fervency of their zeal. No secret was made of this—it was boasted of in religious newspapers. I was at the time editor of *Vanity Fair* in New York, a lady wrote a poem gracefully satirising this Voodoo work, and I drew for it an illustration, which I published. I do not see wherein this piously praying a man to death differs from the very wickedest witchcraft described in this book.

Every effort to beg or force from the Unknown or Supernatural certain knowledge or favours, be it by prayer, fasting, incantation, or ceremonies, is *sorcery*—call it by what name we will. From the beginning of time men have tortured and put one another to death for employing different methods of conjura-tion, the Catholic has burned and imprisoned and made miserable to death literally millions, the Mahometan and Brahmin and mild Buddhist have all done their best in the same work—and not one of them has ever reflected that they were all only shades or clouds of the same primeval witch and devil's darkness.

There is a rising light which will in time dissipate it all. This is the sun of science. And on every side we hear petitions that the majority of men shall still be kept in the old darkness, somewhere or in some way. "There *must* be a religion—what would the *multitude* do but for a religion?" (I never met, by the way, in all my life a man who really considered *himself* as belonging to "the multi-tude.") Or, "Would you take from man his tenderest belief—from the little child its faith in angels and a God, &c?" To which the answer is plain and clear—which is, that if the parents know enough to be exemplarily honest in all their mutual dealings, and how to teach the child to be likewise, the proper form for instinctive sentiment of any kind will never be wanting; for it is in humanity.

There is another method of using oil, not for divination or warring on witches, but to bewitch, that is to fascinate men. It consists in stealing from a church some of the oil of baptism, if you can get it—if not, that which is blessed and put into the lamps before the Virgin or saints will do quite as well. And if a girl anoints her lips with it, the man who kisses her

> "Will be seized with a wild, strange love;
> He'll heed not the dark world beneath him,
> He'll heed not the heaven above."

No—all and everything will be lost in a delirium of devotion to the *demoiselle à l'huile* before him, compared to whom the best sardine is as nothing. He must have her without regard to expense. Now as it is the great end and aim of all Italian (and much English) woman-nature and life, to produce such feelings in men, it is not remarkable that this oil-stealing is carried on to a great extent. It is a very ancient, unholy custom, and is regarded as being to the last degree sacrilegious by the priests, who look upon all kinds of magic and sorcery—save their own—as doubly damnable. PAULUS GRILLANDUS who, in his time, as he proudly informs us, ordered the torture and burning alive of hundreds of heretics and witches, tells the following tale, *apropos* of naughty girls who steal the holy wafer to make love-charms. In his work, dated 1547, he relates that :—

" It is not now a year ago since I saw and examined two shameless and lewd women (*due impudice mulieres*) at Rome, who were held captive by the Reverend lord *locum tenens* of the Reverend D. Vicarii Papæ "—(GRILLANDUS was " in society " about that time and wished to show his skill)—" and by *examining*" —(this kind of examining meant rack and red-hot pincers)—" I found they had taken the oil of baptism, and anointed their lips while speaking these words : *abrenuncio tibi ;* which being done, if they kissed men, these would love them. But despite all their craft, they atoned for their crime by suffering the extreme of condign punishment."

This means, darkly, something worse than rack and burning alive, or *convicta et combusta*, for to this holy griller, GRILLANDUS, such punishment was a mere common-place.

However, in spite of church and stake, girls in Italy have kept on doing it— *i.e.*, stealing oil—and no great wonder either, since the fear of torture and the certainty of hell everlasting would never prevent any true daughter of Eve from doing anything which would attract admiration. And this is the way it is now worked, as described to me by one who was familiar with the process :—

" When a woman wishes to inspire sincere love in any man, she should go into church while the priests and women are singing the benediction, and from a lamp burning before a male saint (*pure che non sia una santa*), take from it three drops of oil, which must be blessed, but only with the forefinger, and put them in a little dish or plate (*piattino*), and say :—

" ' Non prendo questo oglio
Ma prendo la benedizione
Da questo santo . . .
(*Secondo il nome del santo*)
Perche questa benedizione
Vada sempre al mio amore,
Che non possa partirsi mai
Da questo mio cuore ! ' "

(" 'I take not oil for my affliction,
But I take the benediction
From this saint . . . (the name is here given)
That it may move the man I love,
And that he may ne'er depart
While he lives from this my heart !' ")

Then the little dish should be carried home and very carefully hidden so that no one may see it, and for three Fridays in succession the lips must be anointed with the oil.   And, kissing her lover on the lips, the girl must say :—

" Io ti baccio e ti baccio sinceramente,
E sempre nascosto delle gente,
Io ti baccio di vero cuore,
E ti baccio di vero amore,
E questo santo . . . mi vorra aiutare
Che tu pure tu mi possa amare,
E presto tu mi voglia sposare."

(" I kiss thee, love, and most sincerely,
In secret, for I love thee dearly,
I kiss thee from my very heart,
I kiss thee, dear, with truest love,
And may Saint . . . for his part,
The witness be my truth to prove
That thou mine own shalt ever be,
And that, ere long, thou'lt marry me ! ")

For doing and saying which trifling thing young girls were torn with red-hot pincers, their joints pulled out of socket by the rack, hot oil poured all over them (*vide* HORST, *Dæmonomagia*, SPRENGER, &c.), and then were *burned alive*.   That is, at Rome before the Pope, by his order, when the Roman Church was in the full plenitude of its power, *infallible* wisdom, and Christian philanthropy, light, and sweetness, meekness, and mercy.

I believe that this modern Italian ceremony gives the whole truth, and all the veritable details of the oil-stealing.   I do not believe that any such words as *abrenuncio tibi* were ever uttered.   The priests in their accusations always declare that the witches were always renouncing and denouncing Christianity, but of all this there is hardly a trace in the practices of the witches, as truly set forth by themselves ; and considering how they were treated, it is wonderful that they did *not* abuse it on all occasions.   The object of stealing the oil was to get the mysterious occult virtue or power of the benediction uttered by the priest, else why would it be stolen at all, and what sense would there be to take it while denying its power ?   True, there is not much sense of any kind in the whole proceeding, be it on the part of priest or witch, but what there is is with the woman, who wished for nothing cruel or inhuman, but only to get a sweetheart.

It is not magic, or sorcery, or witchcraft, when a *priest* pronounces an idiotic incantation or spell or benediction over oil, to burn before a lamp, or touch up a sinner with it on his death-bed. But if a girl takes a few drops of this same enchanted liquid to attract a lover it is a crime—deadly mortal sin, &c.

It is related that during the first occupation of Paris by the allied army, the Cossacks not only drank the oil of the street lamps, but that in the plenitude of their impiety they even drained to the dregs all which was in those of the churches. Now, if stealing only three drops of the *oleum benedictum* by a foolish young girl deserved all the tortures of the Sacred Inquisition—and after that a passage "through flames material and temporal unto flames immaterial and eternal"— what *should* have been decreed to a dirty, bristling savage, sinful-with-all-the-sins, heretic of a Cossack who "topped off" the whole lamp? Imagination shrinks appalled before such tremendous wickedness. When you have sent your milliner, or servant-maid, or "female," to the Byss of the Abyss (as Jacob Böhme calls it), of the hell of hells, what *can* you do with the *greater* malefactor? Let us reflect!

And a strange moral lurks behind it all. I, reader, have been—and for that matter thou with me in the spirit—in an unholy conventicle of witches where, according to the general testimony of all the great and wise and good men living two hundred years ago, Satan himself was present glowering over us who were—

> " Seeking awfully by night
> An infernal base delight."

And we performed ceremonies which are distinctly described as damnable by all the great authorities of both churches, Catholic or Protestant—authorities, mind you, such as Luther—who are yet to-day absolutely believed in, and deferred to. Yea, with this oil, and coal, and hot water, and church-lamp business we damned ourselves outside of all redemption, through all the colours of the rainbow from A to &c. Behold, O reader, what I went through for thy sake! "Matter of breviary," quoth Friar John.

PYROMANCY AND INCENSE

"Das Feuer ist heilig, und wird göttlich verehrt weil es ein reines Element ist, und deshalb mussten seine Priesterinnen auch reine Jungfrauen sein."—"Das Feuer," J. B. Friedrich, *Symbolik der Natur*, p. 60.

"Sic in igne præter alia elementa, sacra omnia insistebant, quod is, crecto proximus coelo sit."—*Polydore Virgil de Inv. Rerum.*

The author of the *Trinum Magicum* (1611), referring to old Roman divination, describes minutely that by fire. He tells us that :—

" There is also *Pyromantia*, in which powdered resin was thrown into the flames. If the flame rose in one, it was a good sign ; if lambent and divided, unfortunate ; if in three points, a glorious *eventum* or result ; if much dispersed, an ill death ; if crackling or snapping, misfortune ; if it was very suddenly extinguished, great danger."

Resin here includes or means frankincense.

The identity of the modern pyromancy in Tuscany with that of the old Roman, whether it be by observation of flame, or by putting grain, frankincense, or poppy leaves on coals, is very remarkable. They were narrated to me as follows :—

FLAME

" Let the wood be lighted, and if in doing this the fire ignites with difficulty, or makes ugly (*brutte*) or little flames, it is a bad sign, either as regards events or what we may have in our mind. In the Romagna the old men say if you would know how a thing will turn out, you must study the fire attentively. If it burns well, all will go well ; and if ill, they will end badly.[1]

" If it burn with *one* flame clear and fine, it is a sign of good fortune. Several flames, or now on one side and then on the other, with a snapping, mean that relations or friends will soon come to visit you.

" And before consulting the fire, if you wish to get very decided omens, repeat this :—

     " ' Fuoco, Fuoco benedetto !
        Alla casa mia fortuna aspetto,
        E sempre a te vengo sperare
        Che l'augurio di buono,
        Fortuna tu mi voglio dare ! '

     (" ' Fire, Fire, blessed Fire !
        Unto fortune I aspire,
        So I hope that I may see
        That thou still wilt truly be
        A fortune-giver unto me ! ')

"And coloured or varied flames are like broken ones."

This recalls, and that very vividly, a passage from the *Œdipus* of SENECA :—

    " *Tir.*   Quid flamma ? largus jamne comprehendit dapes ?
     Man.   Subito repulsit lumen, et subito occidit.
     Tir.   Utrumne clarus ignis, et nitidus stetit,
          Rectusque purum verticem coelo tulit,

---

[1] " The Voodoo thinks that if you have any kind of burning wood before you, and there is snapping and crackling, it indicates a serious quarrel. If a coal or spark flies towards you it is a very serious matter indeed. To avert the threatened trouble run at once to the fire and spit in it."—Note by MARY A. OWEN

Et summam in auras fusus explicant comam ?
An latera circumserpit incertus viæ.
Et fluctuante turbidus fumo labat ?
Man. Non una facies mobilis flamma fuit,
Imbrifera quales implicat varios sibi
Iris colores, parte quæ magna poli
Curvatæ picto nunciat nimbos sinu.
Quis desit illi quisue sit dubites color :
Cæmlea fulvis mista oberravit notis
Sanguinea rursus, ultimum in tenebras abit
Sed ecce pugnax ignis in partes duas
Discedit—
Immugit aris ignis et trepidant foci."

This corresponds accurately to the modern omens and incantation.

GRAIN ON COALS

"There was," observes the author of *Trinum Magicum,* "another kind of Captromancy. For either grains of sesame or of black poppy were thrown on hot coals, and from the smoke rising from them omens were drawn, as DION CASSIUS observes." In Tuscany the divination is now as follows :—

"Take from the crop a few grains (*chicchi*), lay them on the coals, and if they burst or pop well (*scoppira*), it is a sign that the crop for the next year will be a good one. And if they do not burst it will be bad. And poppies are used—but I know nothing about that."

This is perhaps the real method anciently followed.

Anciently wheat or barley, or poppy-pods were used, but as it was found out in later times that Indian corn, or maize, exploded or "popped" better, it has been substituted. The following is a more detailed account of this augury :—

"Take some grains of *gran Turco*—maize—and put them on a plate, and that on the fire at midnight and say :—

" ' Metto questo gran Turco,
Quanti diavoli siete
Vi scongiuro che mi dite :
O mi fate sapere,
Se il mio amore
Oggi mi viene vedere ;
Mi amore mi ama,
Mi vuol benee mi sposerá,
Questo gran Turco tre cambiamenti,
Tre cambiamenti mi fara :
Se mi ama il gran Turco
Fara la forma di un cuore,

> Se mi sposera fara la forma,
> La forma di un fiore ;
> Ma si non mi ama,
> Fate diavoli maladetti
> Che il gran Turco non faccia forma
> Ne di cuore, e ne di fiori ! ' "

(" ' I put this corn, devils, to see,
However many ye may be,
I conjure you that you may tell
Me if my lover loves me well ;
So make him come this afternoon,
And if he means to wed me soon :
Therefore I pray you make
This corn a certain form to take—
Should the grain be like a heart,
He from me will never part ;
Should the shape be like a flower,
Soon will come the nuptial hour ;
If he love me not at all,
Then the devil take it all !
If he love not, let there be
Neither flower nor heart for me ! ' ")

INCENSE ON COALS

This is used to ascertain who has bewitched any one or to remove the evil spell.

"Take a *scaldino* (a receptacle of glazed crockery like a basket in form), with charcoal glowing hot, and then take incense and *cummin*, and put them on the coals. Then with a large knife in the left hand, the *scaldino* being held in the right, go into all the rooms and above and below the bed, pronouncing all the time the benediction. And with this knife stir the contents. And as the cummin and incense burn, repeat :—

> " ' Non buco questo incenso,
> Ma buco il corpo, l'anima,
> E tutti i sentimenti
> Del corpo di quella infame,
> (O del infamo),
> Che mi ha messa
> La mala fortuna
> In casa mia ! '

(" ' I do not pierce (or stir) the incense,
But I pierce the body, the soul,
And all the feelings
Of the body of the wretch
Who has put bad fortune
Into my home ! ')

" When all the incense is burned, put into the scaldino a leaf of yellow paper (always yellow), and two nails tied in the form of a cross. If you do not know who has done the harm, throw the incense and coals into a running stream or into a river. But if you suspect any person, you have the scaldino and nails carried into his or her house and hide it under the roof where it cannot be found. Do not forget to have in it the crossed nails. Then the guilty person will be compelled, or impelled, to undo the harm or spell ; she or he will have no rest till this be done."

It is understood in this that to succeed the incense must burn freely. In the old Roman oracles ("huc illud pertinere puto de Nymphæ o prope Apolloniam") the incense was taken, the prayer or incantation uttered, and the incense thrown on the fire. If it was all burned the omen was favourable, also if it snapped out of the fire and burned, or the flame followed it, all was still well. This did not apply to probabilities of death or marriage—*morte nuptiisque exceptis.*

Though different as to the method and objects, there is quite enough in common between the ancient and modern ceremony to warrant the conclusion that the latter was derived from an old Roman source.

There is also another very interesting and evidently very ancient incantation with burning incense, intended to remove an evil of any kind, or to invoke good fortune from the mysterious witch known as the Befania.

" Take frankincense, both of the best and the inferior kind, also cummin seed. Have ready a new scaldino, which is kept only for this purpose.

" And should it happen that affairs of any kind go badly, fill the scaldino (or earthen fire-dish) with glowing coals, then take three pinches of best incense and three of the second quality, and put them all *in fila*, in a row, on the threshold of the door. Then take the rest of your incense and the cummin, and put it into the burning coal, and carry it about, and wave it over the bed and in every corner, saying :—

> " ' In nome del cielo !
> Delle stelle e della luna !
> Mi levo questo mal d'occhio
> Per mia maggior' fortuna !
> Befania ! Befania ! Befania !
> Che mi date mal d'occhio maladetta sia
> Befania ! Befania ! Befania !
> Chi mi ha dato il maldocchio
> Me lo porta via
> E maggior fortuna
> Mi venga in casa mia !

> (" ' In the name of heaven
> And of the stars and moon,
> May this trouble change
> To better fortune soon !
> Befania ! Befania ! Befania !

> Should this deed be thine ;
> Befania ! Befania ! Befania !
> Take it away, bring luck, I pray,
> Into this house of mine ! ')

"Then when all is consumed in the scaldino, light the little piles of incense on the threshold of the door, and go over it three times, and spit behind you over your shoulder three times, and say :—

> " ' Befania ! Befania ! Befania !
> Chi me ha dato il maldocchio !
> Me lo porta via ! '

> (" ' Befania ! Befania !
> Befania ! I say,
> Since thou gavest this bad luck,
> Carry it away ! ')

"Then pass thrice backwards and forwards before the fire, spitting over the left shoulder, and repeating the same incantation."

There is in Tuscany a spell against gossips, backbiters, slanderers, and spreaders of evil reports. It is as follows :—

"Against people who chatter evil against us (*le persone chi ciarlano sul nostro conto*), take incense with the two fingers and the thumb (*con tre dita*) and put it on the threshold of the door and at the window, put a distaff and a spindle with the weight (*penzoloni*) hanging down, and then set fire to the incense, and say :—

> " ' Incenso, Incenso !
> Che bene tu possa bruciare !
> E coso possono bruciare
> Le male lingue che ciarlano,
> Tanto di me, e appena
> Tu sarai bruciato,
> La rocca e il fuso
> Dalla finestra me ne andero a levare
> E anche quelle voglio bruciare,
> E cosi bruciare, e cosi bruciare,
> Pure quelle male lingue
> E di me non tornerrano più a ciarlare,
> Fino che la rocca e il fuso
> Come prima non tornera, questo come prima,
> Non potra mai tornare ;
> E le linguaccie indegne
> Male di me non più potrano parlare !
> E cosi bruciare, e cosi bruciare,' " &c.

> (" ' Incense, Incense !
> Mayst thou burn well !
> And so may burn, and so may burn
> The tongues who speak ill of me !

Thou shalt be burnt,
Then will I take from the window
The distaff and spindle,
Them too will I burn,
And so may burn, and so may burn,
Those evil tongues ; may they ne'er return
Unto their gossip till the distaff
And spindle turn as once before !
May neither turn again !
And so may the vile, unworthy tongues
Never speak ill of me again.
And so may burn,' " &c.)

There is a certain classic Latin air in this invocation, a rude strength and an ingenious expression in *tornerano*—turning and returning—as applied to the spinning and the tongues, which is really poetical. But what is most interesting in it is its similarity to an incantation described by OVID. An old woman, he tells us, conjures as follows to protect all present against slanderous tongues and the evil eye. First she takes with three fingers three pinches of incense, and puts these under the threshold in a mouse-hole. Then, while murmuring incantations, she wraps woollen thread round a *reel* of dark colour, while moving seven beans in her mouth. Finally she takes the head of a fish called *mana* (*anima*) smeared with pitch and penetrated with a bronze needle, sews up its mouth, and dries it by a fire into which she pours some wine, and drinks the rest of it with the girls present. This is the version of PRELLER, but from one line I understand that the reel means distaff, spindle, and the leaden *penzolono*. " Tum cantata ligat cum fascio licia *plumbo*."

PRELLER suggests *rhombo* for *plumbo*, but the weight is generally of lead. However, all things considered, it is pretty clear that in both ceremonies we have three pinches of incense, with the distaff and spindle—all against slanderers.

The distaff and spindle formed an important part of classic magic, and as PRELLER remarks, " Spinning and turning round belong in their nature to sorcery." There is a curious illustration of this in the following Romagnola recipe for constructing a magical scarecrow :—

" TO KEEP GOBLINS AND FAIRIES FROM STEALING FRUIT

" Take red rags, and with them, and with a distaff and spindle, make an image like a little old woman. Put two of these in the field or vineyard. Then put two brooms to make a cross, and say :—

" ' Se e uno spirito a fare,
Che la frutta mi viene a sinpare,
O tu vecchia me li vorrai discacciare,

Se poi fossero strege ho granate,
Che in croce vi ho messo, mandate
Indietro tutte le strege e stregoni,
Che non vengono a mangiarmi i pomi ! ' ' "

("' If thou, goblin, art a fairy,
Who hast stol'n my fruit—beware ye !
The old woman there shall scare ye !
Or should they perchance be witches,
There's a cross of broomsticks, which is
Powerful, and with them grapples
When they come a-stealing apples.' ")

Should the reader think there is a ring of HERRICK in this, he may also remark that it is fully as apparent in the Italian as in my translation.

It is believed in the North that a witch can be discovered by means of fire. WOLF (*Deutsche Mährchen und Sagen*) relates that when the children of a peasant are bewitched, a fire is made. Should the flames unite and form one—just as in the Italian incantation—the first person who enters the house will be the witch.

" Little Lady Rosy-hood
In the fire-place lives ;
Eating only coal and wood,
Heat to all she gives.
Bobbing up and dancing,
Merry all the day,
But when the wood is ashes,
Then she no longer flashes,
And in smoke she flies away."

THE SPELL OF THE LAMP

" At the festival of the great mother of all life, Neith, the Egyptians burned lamps in which were oil and salt—and this signified the new life of the year. For salt symbolised the creation of life, and the light that it came forth from darkness into existence ; therefore this did well suit that festival."—FRIEDRICH, *Symbolik der Natur.*

The picturesque Italian lamp, consisting of a long upright brass rod, up and down which slides the cup with generally three wicks, the rod being supported on a base, is of Roman origin, and well known to all travellers. It is used in magic as follows, when a babe is bewitched, to find out who has laid a spell on it :—

" Take a *lampada, detta lucerna,* such a lamp as is called a *lucerna,* and having lighted all three of its wicks put it on a square table with a sharpened knife and three pins.

" Then at midnight, seated in a chair by the table, make the sign of the *jettatura* (*le corne*). And, wishing to know the name of the person who has bewitched anybody, you go to sleep, and it will be revealed to you in a dream. But first repeat the following :—

" ' Mary, blessed Virgin, if the illness of this child (or other person) comes from any illness, come to me in sleep. Mary, blessed Virgin, I commend myself to you to do me the favour that he may soon recover. But if he be bewitched by any one, then, oh devil unchained from hell, extinguish one of these lamps and make me to know who was the cause of this illness, and if it be a witch that I may know her name, and that I may find her in the form of a cat, and her life at longest may last only three days.'

" And this being done the one bewitched will recover in three days, and not be so afflicted again."

This singular mixture of invocation to the Virgin and the devil was further confused, apparently by the narrator's imperfect memory of the incantation.

There is another method of using the lamp, by which names are given or signs indicated by the lights going out, each light being first named or numbered. This leaves the snuff of the wick smouldering, and magic used this also in incantations. Thus Marcellus gives the following (94, GRIMM, p. 25) :—

"Si quem coire noles, fierique cupies in usu venerio tardiorem, de lucerna quæ sponte exstinguetur, fungos adhuc viventes in potione ejus exstingue, bibendamque inscio trade : confestim enervabitur."

Which is to the effect that to deprive a man of his virile power you must give him wine to drink in which the glowing snuff of a wick has been extinguished.

In Tuscany there is the following, used for any illness : —

" When any one is ill, let a lamp be placed in his room, one burning oil, and small (*una lucernina sempre se e possibile*), and when it goes, or burns, out, take the long, round snuff (*moccolaia*) and put it into wine, and give this to the invalid to drink. Should he drink it voluntarily he will get well, if he refuse it it is a sign that he will not recover."

It is here understood that the snuff is put into the wine without the knowledge of the patient. I should add to this that every lamp is supposed to have its peculiar spirit, who may be invoked. That is to say, if you buy one of these antiquely formed lamps—though any old Roman lamp will answer the purpose—and pronounce over it in faith and seriousness an invocation to a spirit—or what is better, get some old woman who practises sorcery to do so for you, with incense—then you will have by you a household spirit, elf, or fairy, who may be consulted in many ways. And as people say in England that á fire, with its life-like moving flames, is " company," so the Italian girl, as she sits and sews, finds a fairy companion in the mysterious and silent, yet animated light of the lamp. Which wick-fire seemed so mysterious to the Rosicrucian Lord Blaize that he wrote a book on it, and on the blessed secrets of salt, in which book the Clothes-Philosophy of *Sartor Resartus* was clearly anticipated. If you want such a triple lamp, reader, you must buy an *old* one, and it will cost from three to five francs.

CHAPTER IV

EVIL INCANTATIONS

HERE exist among the Tuscan witches a very great number of spells, the object of which is to injure or even kill enemies, and there is reason to believe that these are the most ancient of all. For the further we go back behind the genial embodiment of the forces of Nature and Polytheism the darker and more vindictive does sorcery become. This may be tested by races still existent. For just as the babe in the womb is said to pass through the stages corresponding to those of lower forms of animals, to the higher, so we may see the primitive or prehistoric man more or less modified by soil or climate, in the Fuegian, Papuan, or Australian, and specially in the African races. Among all these the horrible old witchcraft, which aims far more at death and injury and revenge than at doing good, predominates over benevolence. And that there should still be so much of it, employing the earliest known forms of sorcery, in Italy, is an almost conclusive proof of its antiquity. As animals must destroy life before they can enjoy it, so man seems in his animal stage to have found his first great pleasure in injuring or killing others.

It is perfectly true that races in a low or primitive state of society, even if separate and without intercourse, would, under similar conditions, develop the same superstitions or myths. But it does not follow from this that there has been no " borrowing " or tradition. On the contrary, an impartial examination of *all* such folk-lore with the most scrupulous comparative analysis, shows that there has been an immense, if often mysterious, amount of transmission, and that the theory of innate ideas—or what amounts to the same thing—must be very sparingly exercised.

It may, however, certainly be conceded that the Romagnola spells did not grow of themselves of late years, but really sprang from ancient sources. For those who now hold them live in the same country as the Etruscans or old Latins, who were their progenitors, and as they retain innumerable customs of their ancestors—as recorded by classic writers—none but the most captious critic can be disposed to contest closely the possibility of their having inherited their superstitions.

I have such a number of these spells to do harm that I can give only a few of them. The first is as follows. It is from a large manuscript collection made for me by an expert. It was taken from the archives of the witches, that is to say copied, as were many of these recipes from others which are jealously preserved from publicity, as the wise woman naturally prefers to impart her wisdom *viva voce*. The " evil " in this case was naïvely explained as that which was done to the man's mistress by withdrawing his love !

"To do an evil—*per fare una malia*—so that a man may be drawn from loving another woman, and only be attached to his wife—take three Indian chestnuts or wild horse-chestnuts (*marroni d'Indi, marroni selvatici*) and powder them fine, as *fine as possible*." (Marcellus lays stress on the same trituration.) "Then take a new earthen pot, and put into it the powder, and mix with it three drops of the husband's blood, or of the woman whom he loves, and put this blood with the rest, and, if it be possible, add to this as much more blood of either as can be obtained, and to this a half *litre* of spirits (a full pint) and some water, and boil it in a *bagno maria* (*balneum Mariæ*), that is, the pot in another pot of water, and when it shall have boiled for a quarter of an hour, put the pot under the bed, and then at midnight, the wife, should leave the bed and bathe the head of the husband a little, in the form of a cross, also bathe *sotto negli in testicoli*, and say :—

> " ' Non bagno te, bagno il tuo cuore,
>   Che sempre più tu mi possa amare,
>   E più tu non mi possa lasciare,
>   E con altre donne tu non possa andare,
>   E quell' affare
>   Con altre donne non ti si possa alzare.'

> (" ' I bathe not thee, I bathe thy heart,
>   That thy love from me may ne'er depart!
>   That thou shalt to me be true for aye !
>   Nor with other women go thy way,
>   Nor deal with them, be it as it may.')

" And this must be done for seven nights, thrice in a night.   Then throw the pot and all its contents into a running stream, saying :—

> " ' Butto via questo pento',
>   E butto via il pensiero
>   Del mio marito per altre,
>   E che porti tutto l'amore
>   A me che io pure tanto l'amo.'

> (" ' Now I cast this pot away,
>   With my husband's thought to stray,
>   To others' love that I may see
>   Him true, as I shall ever be !')

" And having thrown it into the water, walk away without looking behind you, and for three days after do not pass by that place."

" Rivoque fluenti—jace ne respexeris "—" by the running water—look not back again."   This portion is as old as the days of VIRGIL, and I doubt not that the whole spell was ancient in his time.

The next is entitled, " TO INJURE AN ENEMY " :—

" To make a man or woman suffer, take a peppercorn and a [illegible], such as is found in the fields, and boil it with the hair of the man or woman and repeat :—

> " ' Non faccio bollire questi capelli,
>   Ma faccio bollire questa robba,
>   Unita a l'anima e il cuore
>   Di quello che non possa più vivere,
>   E non possa più stare,
>   In mezzo alle strege
>   Tu ti debbi sempre trovare !'

> (" ' I do not boil the hair alone,
>   But all these things together thrown,
>   With his heart and soul that he,
>   May perish and for ever be
>   Only in witches' company.' ")

The success of such charms depends chiefly on the seriousness or earnestness with which they are pronounced. When the witch utters them for herself or for another, she does it with an air of terrible vindictiveness, such as would cause any one to shudder. In a community where everybody is very superstitious, and where even the established religion earnestly teaches the terrors of exorcism and excommunication and the virtues of amulets, it is to be expected that the ignorant will also dread the same in another kind of sorcery. Therefore if a man believes that he has been or is to be Voodooed, be it by priest or witch, he is in mortal terror ; nay, he may even die of apprehension.

Another charm is as follows :—

" *Take a toad.* Obtain some of the hairs of your victim. Tie them to the left leg of the toad, and put the animal into a covered pot. As it suffers the enemy will suffer, when it dies he will die. But if he is only to suffer and not die, remove the hair from the leg of the toad and let it go."

To torture an animal and cause its sufferings to pass by means of spells to a human being is common in witchcraft. Such is the following :—

" To put misfortune (*il male auguro*) into a house, so that all things may go wrong, take a black cat and cut away all its skin, for so much as it suffers so much will the person suffer whom you would bewitch.[1] And etting the cat go, say :—

> " ' Ti ho tagliato il pelo,
> Perche tu mandi alla malora.'

> (" ' I have cut the skin from thee
> That thou shalt carry misery—to——.')

" Then name the one whom you wish to suffer. Then take the skin or hair, with nettles, skins of Indian figs with the prickles, powdered horse-scrapings, pepper, wild chestnuts, carrots, and garlic, and with these the hairs of the person, and pulverise all very finely (*fine, fine, che sia possibile*). Then take linseed and hemp-seed, seeds of melons and pumpkins, and put them all in a black glazed pot, which place on the hole of a privy. Then take two candles tied with black and red thread, and let it remain for three days, first lighting the candles, and as soon as they are burned out renew them. And when three days are passed, then, exactly at midnight, put the pot on the fire, and say :—

> " ' Non faccio bollire questa pentola,
> Ma faccio bollire il corpo e l'anima
> Di. . . .'

> (" ' It is not this pot which I boil,
> But I boil the body and soul
> Of. . . .')

---

[1] A bad trick has its power greatly increased if the materials (red clover, sulphur, pounded glass, and red flannel, or the red seeds of the Indian turnip) are tied up in a bit of skin torn from the haunch of a live cat.— M. A. OWEN

"This liquid is then put into a small bottle, and thrown into the house of the one to whom you wish harm, and from that time that person will have no peace."

This amiable *pot-pourri* is interesting from the character of its ingredients, all of which are found in the ancient recipes for injuring enemies. Thus carrots as a species of *rapum, rapa,* or *raphanus,* by name are allied to *rabio, rabo, ραπιω,* to quarrel. "Whence it is," says FRIEDRICH, "a symbol of discord." There is much curious tradition showing its connection with evil and evil spirits.

A short and simple method of setting people by the ears is to buy some of the herb known as *discordia :* "And when you wish for a vendetta" (no uncommon want in Italy), "throw it into a house, and say :—

> "'Non butto questo pezzo di roba,
> Ma butto la discordia,
> Che non possia dare più
> Pace in questa casa!'"

("'It is not this thing which I throw,
But discord, that they ne'er may know
Peace in this house—so let it go!'")

Also the following :—

"For an Enemy. Take salt and pepper and put it into his clothing, or in his house, and say :—

> "'Vi metto questo pepe,
> E questo sale,
> Che in vita vostra
> Pace e felicita
> Non vi possa dare.'"

("'I put this pepper on you,
And this salt thereto,
That peace and happiness
You never more may know.'")

Pepper is supposed to cause ill-feeling and promote quarrels. "Les anciens livres des songes," says DE GUBERNATIS (*Mythologie des Plantes,* vol. ii.), "prétendent que le poivre vu en songe est de mauvais augure, et une source des querelles dans la maison et dehors, et toutes sortes de déplaisirs."

I have two spells for bewitching people on their wedding-day, so that they may be utterly miserable, and never agree. One is as follows :—

"If you desire that a woman shall never find happiness in marriage, take on the wedding-day an orange flower, and put into it a little fine salt, pepper, and cummin, with *sconcordia (discordia),* and attach this to the bride's back, saying :—

" ' Tu sia maladetta !
   Tu non possa avere
   Un giorno di pace'!
   E quando vai
   Inginnochiarte
   Avanti l'altare,
   Tu possa essere gia pentiti
   Del passa che tu fai ! '

(" ' Be thou accursed !
   Mayst thou never know
   A single day of peace !
   And even when thou dost go
   To kneel before the altar,
   Mayst thou feel forsaken,
   And bitterly regret
   The step which thou hast taken ! ' ")

In another, *si deve prendere del sangue menstruale chi viene alla donna*, mixed with rue and cummin, boil all in pure water, and make it into comfits. Give these to the bride and groom on their wedding-day. And while preparing the comfits, repeat :—

" Faccio queste confette,
   Per che portano
   La maledizione,
   E la scomunica,
   Ai due spose !
   (E pronunciaro qui loro nome),
   Che non possono vivere uniti !
   Tutti giorni possono leticare !
   E uniti un anno
   Non possono stare !
   Questa e la contezza
   Che se devono dare.
   Basta ! "

(" I make these comfits, may they bear
   Deep affliction, malediction,
   Here upon this married pair !
   (Here the names are given)
   May they never be united !
   May they quarrel every day !
   May their marriage bond be slighted
   Ere a year has passed away !
   This shall be the life between them,
   Let that life be as it may !
   Enough ! ")

Which last word is doubtless repeated by the reader. I have more of these spells of black witchcraft too abominable to repeat, therefore I am glad that my limits forbid me to give further cursing. Very nearly allied to these spells are those levelled against witches, and others intended to bring faithless lovers, male or female, back to their forsaken ones.

The malediction is the mainstay of witchcraft. BROWNING has made his Spanish monk say :—

> " If hate killed men, Brother Laurence,
> God's blood could not mine kill you ! "

The *strege* believe, however, as do all among whom they live, that concentrated, intense venomous hatred, or *will*, allied to spells *can* kill. And there are many who, believing themselves to be thus hated, do die. And when the hate has really been awakened by a deep wrong, be it from conscience or the mysterious working of destiny, and causes beyond our ken, it is wonderful to see how often the arrow strikes—sooner or later ! Believe in *nothing* if thou wilt, neither in the heaven above or in the earth below, but " cast up the account of Orcus—the account thereof cast up," and if there is one on earth whom thou hast deeply, deliberately *wronged*, thou shalt find thy Nemesis. " Dread him whom thou hast struck."

There is a generally prevailing popular opinion carefully inculcated by teachers of religion, to the effect that the man who seeks for revenge is always *entirely* in the wrong. This is, in spirit, allied to the republican doctrine that the minority have no rights—or simply *væ victis !* It was all very pretty in a rough past, but at present it cannot be denied that our laws, legal or social—as religion has made them—protect us only against the *gross* outrages, such as are incident to a state beyond which we have passed. For a very great proportion of the bitterest and most biting injuries which the cultivated man can endure there is no legal or social punishment whatever. This, like the precept to endure all wrongs patiently— or to turn the other cheek—is against human nature and justice. It might possibly be enforced in a monastery, but it is inapplicable to life in general. And thus it is that the witch, the Shaman, and the lawyer and priest get a living. There would be fewer of them if we had less exalted ideals. If we were to sell all we have and give it to the poor, we should, so far from doing any good, build up an immense army of beggars, and the general application of the principle of turning the other cheek to be smitten, would simply develop bullying, cruelty and smiting, beyond all toleration. It was indeed very extensively preached by monks during the Middle Ages, with the result of creating more cruelty, torture, and outrage than had ever before been known in any civilised countries. In due proportion, or rather out of all proportion, to meek virgins, Beato Angelicos, and illimitable saintly charities, were the squeezings of the last farthing from peasants, rapine, torture and murder. The ideal of excess in goodness produced its natural result in excess of evil. The softer the light the blacker the shadows, and it is a rule, with little exception, that in galleries where Angelicos and Memlings, and all such works of "ineffable sweetness" and divine tenderness abound, there too we find revolting pictures of breaking on the wheel, flaying alive, scalding, disjointing, and roasting, executed with a genial strength which shows that such subjects were dear to the hearts of all in those days. One of the most horrible inventions of legal mediæval torture was in the likeness of the blessed Virgin.

THE SPELL OF THE HOLY STONE AND THE SALAGRANA

" Look through a holy stone
And see the fairies pass.
O a violet blue
Is a fairy shoe !
Blue violets in the grass."

The reader is probably aware that if he be at the bottom of a deep uncovered well he can see the stars at noonday. Or that if he look through a long tube he can distinguish objects more clearly—for it is not generally known that all the properties of a telescope are not entirely in the glasses. Nay, even a small roll of cardboard like a funnel helps us to see pictures in a gallery. And if we only look through our hand in a cylinder, or shade our eyes, or draw the lids together, we, by keeping off the "side-lights," improve our vision. The reader who wishes to preserve his sight unimpaired should never read by night facing a light. Then he will have a double strain on the eyes, one from the light, and one from the type. Let him read with his back to all light.

It was the discovery of this principle that led to an old belief that by looking through certain consecrated rings, or stones with holes in them, or a wreath of verbena, one could improve the sight, or see things invisible at ordinary times. How far the imagination aided in this with people who habitually " see visions and dream dreams" I cannot say. But the ceremony by which it is effected in Tuscany is as follows :—

" To see spirits, take a stone from the sea, one which has a hole in it, *un buco tondo*—a round hole—then go to a burying-ground, and, standing at a little distance from it, close one eye, and, looking at the cemetery with the other, through the stone, repeat :—

> " ' In nome di San Pietro,
> E di San Biagio !
> Fate che da questa pietra
> Io possa vedere che forma
> Fanno gli spiriti.'

" Then repeat a *de profundis* thus :—

> " ' De profundis clamao,
> In te Domine, Domine !
> Et Domine, et fiantatis,
> Bugsein et regina materna,
> Edognis Domine ! '

English :—

> " ' In the name of great Saint Peter
> And for Saint Blasius' sake,
> By this stone I fain would see,
> What form the spirits take ! '

" Then you may see by means of that stone the spirits which have no peace, all in flame, *chaminare in persona chome quando erano vivi*—wandering in such forms as they were when alive—some like priests in white or black garments, some in black, some as friars or an old woman with a torch in her hand. And of these are many who, being avaricious in their life, left behind them hidden treasures, the thought of which gives them no rest.

" Then if any one who is bold and brave, will, while they are talking among themselves, speak out and say, ' If in the name of God you would be at rest (*salvo*) tell me where your treasure is, and what I must do to obtain it, so shall ye be saved ! '

" Then if he be poor and would be rich, it is enough that he have no fear to do this thing, and this is an easy way to become wealthy."

Truly, "easy enough if it be true"—and I would remark by the way that the old woman with the torch in her hand is a classical character. But there is much strange lore as regards stones with holes in them which is worth studying. It begins apparently in India. There are found by the river Gundak in Nepaul, stones called *Salagrama*, which are regarded as very sacred.[1] Once when Vishnu the Preserver was followed by Shiva the Destroyer he implored the aid of Maia (Illusion or Glamour) who turned him to a stone. Through this stone, Shiva, in the form of a worm, bored his way. But Vishnu escaped, and when he had resumed his form he commanded that this stone of delusion (*sala-maya*) should be worshipped. As they are found by Salipura or Salagra, they receive their name from the latter. They are generally about the size of an orange, and are really a kind of ammonite.

---

[1] NORK, *Etymologisch-symbolisch, Mythologisches Realwörterbuch*, vol. iv., p. 198. WILFORD, *Asiatic Researches*, vol. xiv., p. 413. FRIEDRICH, *Symb. der Natur*, p. 124. TEMME, *Volksagen v. Pommern und Rogen*, p. 125. Also a monograph pamphlet by G. OPPERT.

In the later Edda we read that Odin once, in order to steal the mead of poetry, turned himself into a worm and went his way through a hole in a rock. Hence all stones with holes in them were called Odin-stones, or, in England, holy-stones. There are many superstitions attached to them, as is well known to every one who is at all familiar with British folk-lore, but what is most important is the fact that as an amulet against witchcraft or nightmare, and in being lucky-stones, they correspond exactly to the Salagrama stones of India. I know of a family in Yorkshire which has a stone in the shape of a harp with a hole in it, which always hangs behind the front door of their house. What is to be specially noted in the Hindu myth is a principle which appears very strongly in the Norse and Algonkin mythologies. This is that of Maïa, or Glamour, or Illusion. Thor is fooled by it when he goes to Jötunheim ; it plays all the time like summer-lightning through the midnight mysteries of Norse tradition ; even Oddo the monk in his life of King Olof declares that all the incredible marvels narrated in the old legends were due to it. It is quite as clearly enounced and illustrated in the Algonkin sagas which were in all probability directly derived from the Norsemen.

It is therefore interesting to know that this reverence for the holed or holy worm-stones is found in a very peculiar form in Tuscany. Once I had sent to me from the Romagna as a remarkable gift from the witch-company, a stone, which I was assured had been, I may say, worshipped for a very long time. That it had been really reverenced was evident in its being surrounded by the little ornaments of coloured bread-paste, &c., which we often see on images of saints and the infant Jesus. It was a piece of stalagmite full of cavities. I have since seen such stones for sale in a curiosity-shop at a price out of all proportion to their value, because they were amulets, and again I found one which had been evidently carried and lost.

Flints with holes in them, as well as ammonites, are common in England, but not at all in Italy, therefore the stalagmite has been substituted.

I conjecture, without proof, that the English saying, " He can see through a mill-stone as far as any man " really had its origin in the belief that by looking through the hole in a mill-stone the sight was improved. As every mill-stone has a hole through it there is not much sense in the literal acceptation of the proverb. But if looking through the hole improved the sight, then he whose sight was most improved would see furthest.

Since writing the foregoing I have learned much which is very curious relating to the stalagmites which are regarded with such reverence in Tuscany. I had found one in the street which, on being examined by experts, was pronounced to be an undoubted excellent amulet. But to make it all right it was re-consecrated in a proper manner by having the appropriate incantation pronounced over it, and by its being put into a red bag with cummin. But what was my astonishment to learn that the proper name for such a stone is a *Salagrana*, which certainly very much resembles the Indian word Salagrama. I was particular in my inquiry from many persons, and received the following statement in relation to it :—

" *Salagrana* is a stone which much resembles in form a sponge. It is called a stone, but is not stone, for it is the dung of the animals called *ronbrigoli* (*lombrici*, or earthworms), which only eat earth and throw up little hills which take the form of a stone, or rather of a sponge, which petrify. They are commonly found in grottoes. They keep away witches. One should make a small red bag, and put the *salagrana* in it and with it gold and silver and a little handful of *concordia* (an herb), and this sack must be kept a secret from everybody. And first say :—

" ' Questo sacchetino bello e preparato
Mi e stato regolato,
E sempro lo voglio conservare
Perche voi altre strege indegne.
Non mi potete ammaliare,
Perche nella pietra che contiene,
Il mio sacchetino sono tante grane,
Che non potete arrivare
A contare ;
E contiene pure tanti buchi
Che non vi fanno vacare,
La soglio dell uscio
E cosi la malia
Non mi potete dare,
Altro che fortuna in casa mia
Non mi puo restare,
Fortuna d'interesse come pure d'amore,
Tutta quella che mi richiede il cuore ! ' "

(" ' Here the bag I hold and see,
Bag presented unto me,
That no wicked witch may come
To do me evil in my home.
In the stone which it contains,
Are so many veins and grains,
That no witch can count them all,
And so many fissures small,
That she cannot cross the door
And do me evil any more ;
May I have good luck and love,
Which I prize all things above ! ' ")

The exact resemblance of the stalagmite to the heap of an earthworm is remarkable, and it was very natural that it should be supposed they were thus made. But curious as is the coincidence of *salagrana* and *salagrama*, there is something far more interesting in the incantation. This is the passage which declares that " there are so many grains that no witch can count them all," and " so many holes that she cannot cross the door." This involves a very ancient and mysterious belief that when a witch is confronted with a great number of seeds or grains, she can go no further in her work till she has counted them every one. Thus all the world over—as among the negroes in America—it is believed that if a man is hag-ridden, he must put a great number of small grains of some kind in the form of a cross about his bed. Then the witch coming cannot get to him till she has counted every one. And in the *Arabian Nights' Entertainment*, Amina the ghost must eat her rice, grain by grain, with a bodkin.

A traveller in Persia has observed that the patterns of carpets are made intricate, so that the evil eye, resting on them and following the design, loses its power. This was the *motive* of all the interlaces of Celtic and Norse designs. When the witch sees the salagrana her glance is at once bewildered with its holes and veins. As I have elsewhere remarked, the herb *rosalaccio*—not the corn-poppy, but a kind of small house-leek, otherwise called Rice of the Goddess of the Four Winds—derives its name from looking ere it unfolds, like confused grains of *rice*, and when a witch sees it she cannot enter till she has counted them, which is impossible ; therefore it is used to protect rooms from witchcraft. The reader cannot fail to observe that this recalls the story of Amina and also the salagrana. That " the Tuscan word may have come from the gypsies " is a suggestion by Senator D. Comparetti.

In addition to the resemblance of the words salagrana and salagrama we have the very curious fact that the former is believed, though erroneously, to be made by worms, while the holes in the latter, according to the tradition, were made by a worm. Thus, quite apart from the similarity of names, we have the far more singular coincidence of worm-stones worshipped in both India and Italy. The Italian salagrana has not *always*, literally, holes in it, but it presents that granulated hole-like or corrugated appearance which is supposed to bewilder the evil eye.[1]

The Spell of the Shell and the Tone of the Stone

> " Shake one and it awakens, then apply
> Its polished lips to your attentive ear,
> And it remembers its august abodes,
> And murmurs as the ocean murmurs there."

[1] This chapter on the salagrana, somewhat extended, was read as a paper before the Oriental Congress in London, 1891

" Fingebantur autem ille cecinisse ; ut est in veteri epigrammate de cantu Sirenum.

" Quod tuba, quod litui quod cornua rauca quarantur
Quodque leves calami quod suavis cantat."
JOHANNES PRÆTORIUS 1665

Few persons are aware of the ease with which the ear may be trained to apparently conduce imaginary sounds to the perceptive faculty. The fairy who supplies us with images by means of hearing must be a very credulous little lady, and easily imposed upon. If we only *believe*, and have our attention called to any continuous sound, we can imagine that we hear words in it, and if the reader will experiment for himself he will be astonished at the success of the trial. Thus, if an audible draught of wind be blowing and six persons in a room hear it, and five of them converse together to the effect that they can distinguish in the sound certain words, they can bring the sixth to firmly believe that he also hears them.

The gypsies in Hungary (*vide Gypsy Sorcery*) believe, or make others believe, that by listening to a shell words may be heard. The dupe hears the sound which is always heard in a large shell. Then he is blindfolded, and a shell substituted which has a hole at one end, to which a long tube is attached. Through this the gypsy speaks. One of these shells with the tube attached was shown to me by a gypsy woman near Budapest

Very closely allied to this telephone-tube is the following, which I learned from a Tuscan witch :—

" For the shell you take a thread or cord which is tied to a tree, it must be three or five *braccie* in length, or more, but always in uneven number, and an end is tied to a shell, and you say :—

" ' O Spirito della Conchiglia !
Una cosa a te vengo demandare,
Purche tu mi possa dare
Soddisfazione si questa grazia
Che io desidero,
Tu mi farai,
Da questa conchiglia
Al mio orecchio
Tre cose mi farai sentire :
Gallo cantare,
Cane abbiare,
E gatto miolare.
Si queste tre cose io sentiro,
E segno che la grazia
Che io desidero,
Sicuro io avro.' "

" ' O Spirit of the Shell !
A favour I desire,
I pray thee give to me
The thing which I require,
And in this thy shell,
Which I hold to my ear,
There are three sounds, and one
Of them I fain would hear:
The crow of a cock,
A dog barking for me,
The mew of a cat ;
If one of the three
I shall clearly hear, 'twill be a sign
That what I seek shall ere long be mine ! ' ")

This is obscure, but one thing is clear—that the cord is a telephonic line used to convey the voice of the sorceress, just as it is carried through the tube. So they work the oracle.

In a little work called *Il Libretto di Stregonerie,* printed in Florence—"The Book of Witchcraft"—I find another method of divining by sound, or really by auricular deception. It is called *L'amante nel pozzo,* or—

" The Lover in the Well.

" Take a stone of rather large size, as round as you can get it, and go by night to a covered well; it is best if it were in the middle of some field or garden. And just as the clock strikes one, cast the stone, *con gran fracasso*—with as much noise as you can make—into the water.

" Then listen with care to hear the sound produced by the fall of the stone. Although it may be a little obscure or confused, and not always very intelligible, yet with a little patience and attention one can detect in the sound which the stone makes in the water the name of the person whom one is to marry, or else an answer to any question."

From a much better—that is, from a living—authority, I learn that this charm may be so executed as to injure an enemy. Go to a running river, and cast in the stone as violently and spitefully as you can, saying :—

" Non butto questa pietra,
Ma butto il bene e la fortuna
Della persona . . . che il bene
Gli vada nell'acqua corrente
E cosi non abbia più bene."

(" It is not a stone which I throw,
But all the fortune here below
Of (here the name) as the waters flow
And as they roll from this river's shore,
May his happiness pass for evermore ! ")

There was an ancient way of divining by means of stones thrown into water, but it appealed to the sight, and not to the ear. The author of the *Tractatus Magicus* (1611) gives it without reference, but his authorities are almost all from classic writers.

"Variæ ejus sunt species divinationis per aquas . . . alia conjectis in aquam stativam tribus lapillis et observatis gyris, qui trifariam invicem implexi circa lapillas sumitur."

That is, throw three pebbles into the water, and judge from the rings which they make how matters will go. Which I have done with only this conclusion : that the circles are much like men's reputations for deeds which are very great—it may be at first in one place, whence they soon vanish—spreading afar, but growing thinner as they spread. Yes, yes :—

"Glory is like a circle in the water."

It was anciently believed that all stones had in them a voice which could be drawn out in different ways. In an interesting article on Divination in the *St. James's Gazette*, February 27, 1886, which I have elsewhere cited, I find the following :—

"We have it on the distinguished authority of many sixteenth and seventeenth-century magicians that Helenus predicted the fall of Troy by the form of divination known as "Lithomancy." During the night a number of stones were washed by torchlight at a spring, and it was essential to the success of the experiment that the person handling them should be veiled. Several prayers having been recited and numerous genuflexions made, the stones, in tones sweet and low, gave answer to the question that had been put."

Truly there are sermons in stones, and a legend tells us that they know a good sermon when they hear one. An Irish saint, who was blind, was once induced by a mischievous boy to preach to a multitude of cobble-stones, and when he ended all the *lapides* cried "*Amen !*"

THE SPELL OF THE SNAIL

Snails were regarded from very ancient times as mysterious creatures. For as they leave a slimy trail behind them, it was supposed that they also left in it their life. So in Psalm lviii. 8, it is said of unjust judges : "As a snail which melteth, let every one of them pass away." As the slug or shell-less snail quite disappears when salt is put on it, they naturally appeared to be diabolical, because devils cannot endure salt. And there is a very ancient species of divination, which consisted in putting snails near sticks and in judging from the one which they ascended how an affair would result. For *quas esse androgynas putat* Herodotus, they are hermaphrodites — *therefore* capable of determining double or doubtful events.

This old divination by snails still exists in Tuscany. It is as follows :—

"To determine if a lover be faithful take a *chiocciola* or *lumaca* (*lumaca*, snail or slug), such as are in gardens, and which leave a streak as of silver behind them.

"Take one of these and a vase, and much ivy and vine leaves and calamint, and arrange the vase on a tree like an umbrella (reversed ?), and within it put two portraits—that of the lover and of the lady—that is, of the one whom he is supposed to woo—one on one side of the vase, one on the other, and cover it with a white cloth, and put within the snail, and leave it there for three days, having first said :—

> " ' In nome del Padre,
>   E del Figlio,
>   E dello spirito maligno,
>   Che mi possa dire la verita,
>   Se il mio marito (o amante)
>   A una altra donna ? '

> (" ' In the name of the Father,
>   And of the Son,
>   And of the Evil Spirit,
>   May they declare to me the truth
>   If my husband or lover
>   Has another love ? ')

"Then after three days examine whether the snail has gone to the picture of the man or the woman. And if it be on the former, he is true ; but if on the woman, it is a sign that he is unfaithful."

IL CANTO DEL GALLO

One day I asked one of the wise women if she thought there had been much change of late years among the *contadini* as regarded education and new ideas. She replied :—

"*Da vero*, Signore, it is not now as it was with all these old affairs. Things go better perhaps with the *contadini*, but they *are* getting new ideas and hardly know what to think. If anything went wrong once, it was always a *malocchio*—there was bad fortune put upon them and they conjured it away. And there were always good signs—if a cock crowed it was a good omen. Then they said : *quando il gallo canto* :—

> " ' O bel gallo—tu che canti
>   La mattina allo spuntar del alba !
>   Canta in cortesia,
>   La buona fortuna per casa mia ! '

("'Beautiful cock, who dost sing
    In the morning at day-spring,
    Sing now, I pray to thee,
    Good luck to mine and me!'")

The witch was right in saying, or in meaning to say, that these omens were once very serious matters which entered into every phase of life. And cock-crowing was a very cheering and important omen to all Christians. Thus the Reverend Georgius STRIGENITIUS, who was *Pfarrherr Superintendens, Thumprediger* and Assessor of the Churfurstliche Sachsische Consistorii at Meissen, in the seventeeth century, preached in his *Gallinacio,* or sermon, on the crowing of the cock of the high priest in Jerusalem, as follows :—

" Other birds serve mankind with their song only for joy and merriment. But the domestic cock helps housekeeping and other work, so that it shall not be neglected."

And the ancient bishop Ambrosius (l. 5, *Hexam.,* c. 24) tells us in soft Latin which is almost a song : " Est galli suavis in noctibus, nec solum suavis sed etiam utilis. . . . Hoc canente lutro suas relinquit insidias. Hoc ipso Lucifer excitatus oritur, cœlumque illuminat."

With much more which I thus translate :—

" It is a pleasant thing to hear the cock
    Crow in the night, and, what is better still,
    The sound is profitable unto man :
    For as a trusty watchman he awakes
    And cheers the sorrowful and troubled soul,
    And tells the weary wanderer on his way
    So much of night is gone. And when he crows
    The thief alarmed ceases his evil work,
    And with that sound the Morning Star awakes
    And spreads his brilliant light o'er all the sky
    In ruddy glory. Then the mariner
    Is glad at heart, and sings because he knows
    That as the day comes on the wind abates,
    And the wild sea grows calm ; and when he crows
    The pious man at once begins his prayers,
    And earnest scholars turn them to their books—
    Legendi quoque munus instaurat—
    Because the light has come and they can read ;
    And when the cock crowed thrice Saint Peter saw
    How great his sin had been—which he before
    Had twice denied. And when he crows,
    Hope wakes in every heart—the invalid

> Ægris levatur incommodum, he
> Picks up a heart ; the sorely wounded man
> Feels less pain in his wounds—and for a time
> The burning agonies of fever cease."

It is a good sign when cocks crow often through the night.[1]   Which the Bœotians knew (PLINY, l. 10, c. 25), and it inspired them so much that they conquered the Spartans.   "For when the cock is beaten he does not crow."   Which JOHANNES PRÆTORIUS declares is a fond and vain thing whereat all the people should say " Tush ! ", because Moses forbade the Jews to give heed to, or divine by, the songs of birds : recalling a passage in one of Lever's novels, in which the hero is fined at Trinity College, Dublin, for keeping " singing birds "—the birds in question being *game-cocks*.   However, we may still believe with SHAKESPEARE that on Christmas Eve :—

> " The bird of dawning singeth all night long."

But good Ambrosius, as his writings show, was far more familiar with the New Testament than with the Old.   However, the Jews made an exception in favour of the cock, since in the Talmud it is said that when it crows one should say, " Blessed be the Eternal One who has given unto the cock understanding to know day from night."   And, as FRIEDRICH sagaciously remarks, " Because they had no watches in those days, therefore in every house they kept a cock."

Which reminds me of a dream which I once actually had in Brighton in the year 1871.   I beheld in a vision a certain man, and he said unto me, " In the ancient times men knew the hour only by the crowing of cocks, now they ascertain it by mechanical means."   To which I, scornful that he should tell me such a well-known thing as if I were a child, replied, "Yes—I see.   Now we ask what o'clock it is—then they inquired what *o'cock* it was."   And in great joy I awoke.

Apropos of this wondrous dream I will narrate another, which is even stranger.   It was in this city of Florence, in the month of January, 1891. I thought I was in a brilliant French circle of a century ago, whose *coryphée* was a witty and beautiful duchess.   One gets into good society in dreams.   And there was present a gentleman who was far from being clever, but whose son, who was not only witty himself but the cause of wit in others, inspired him

---

[1] It is a very bad omen if you hear a cock crow before midnight.   It betokens unpleasant surprises before the next night, so say all negroes.—Note by MARY A. OWEN

by a suggestion to say a very good thing. Whereupon our hostess, with exquisite piquancy, said to the young man, " Mais Monsieur, voila une merveille sans pareille—vous avez absolument fecondé votre père ! "

It haunted me that this dream (which I recalled as distinctly when I awoke as if it had been printed) was directly derived from, and suggested by, what was previously written by me on cocks and magic, but I could not at first make out the connection, when all at once it occurred to me, that in ancient days it sometimes happened that a cock, inspired by a demon, laid an egg from which was hatched a basilisk—a creature of terrible brilliancy—*i.e.*, a *bon mot*—thus he was *feconde* : and it was *this* which the duchess (who had probably been talking with Saint Germain) had in her mind.

For, as Lactantius observes (I have a copy of his works—edition Geneva, 1613—which I bought for threepence from the wheelbarrow before mentioned), the demons, who are neither angels nor men, are intelligent beings—*peritos ac rerum scios.* " They invented astrology and Etruscan divination, augury, oracles, magic, mythology, and moreover taught men how to make ornate and feigned images of exquisite beauty of kings long passed away, and endowed them with other names." Hence temples and new images again—*hinc templa devoventur et vovæ imagines consecrantur*—therefore it must have been easy for them to make a basilisk, or a joke. Then they rose to be gods, as they had once been men. Which is the doctrine of Euhemerus of Messina, which pervades all this Romagnola mythology.

> " As cocks were eggs in earlier humble state,
> So gods were men, though now they be so great."

" Namque Deus, Dæmon et heros, unus idemque erat rudibus hominibus "— God, devil, and hero were all the same thing to the rude men of yore, as Elias Schedius declares.

Divination was naturally enough attached—perhaps without much tradition— to a bird which so mysteriously knew the time of day or night.

A writer in the *St. James's Gazette* (February 17, 1886) once set this forth " fully and finely " as follows :—

" Divination is among the most ancient of the black arts, and for ages it was one of the most popular. Of the scores of divinatory processes known to the mediæval magicians the divining-rod is almost the only one which remains in use among civilised peoples. It is by no means the most interesting and curious ; and, as so much has been written upon this method of finding water, it may well give place here to the description of some more uncanny fashions of divination. Some of these forgotten rites date from the formulation of cabalism ; others were invented by the wizards of the golden days of magic. They were of all sorts : simple, fantastic, revolting. The secrets of the future and the history of the past could alike be laid bare by the order in which a cock pecked up a given number of grains of wheat, by writing the name of a suspected person upon an onion, by the flickerings of the flame of a lamp, by the movement or non-movement of the jaws of an ass while it was being roasted, and in a vast number of more unholy ways.

" Divination by the cock (in mystic language 'Alectryomancy') was a favourite method of ascertaining the name of a person—whether it was that of a thief, an enemy, a successor, or a future husband or wife. When either the sun or the moon was in Aries, there were scattered upon the floor of an enclosed space as many heaps of grains of wheat as there are letters in the alphabet—a few grains to each heap. While this was being done the verse commencing 'Ecce enim veritatem' was said. Then a young cock, perfectly white, was taken, and its claws cut off. The claws were wrapped in a small piece of parchment from the lamb, upon which two Hebrew words were inscribed, and then swallowed by the cock—when, it is to be presumed, he was hungry enough to commence his repast in this unusual fashion. Holding the cock in his hands, the sorcerer recited the conjuration : ' O Deus creator omnium, qui firmamentum pulchritudine stellarum formasti, constituens eas in signa et tempora, infunde virtutem tuam operibus nostris, ut per opus in eis consequentur effectum. Amen." Then the cock was set down in front of the heaps of grain while the two verses from the Psalms, beginning ' Domine, dilexi decorem ' were repeated. A careful note was made of the letter attributed to each heap as the cock pecked it up, particular record being kept of any unfinished heap to which he returned, by reason of the frequent recurrence of the same letter in proper names. The letters thus indicated spelled the name required. The Emperor Valens is said to have employed this method to ascertain the name of his successor. The letters were Theod. ; and surely enough he was succeeded by Theodosius the Great."

There is a survival of this in Italy, which has passed to London ; I refer to divination by means of little trained birds, who pick out fortunes, or printed predictions, for a penny.

DIVINATION WITH ASHES

" Solet etiam divinatio interdum ex cineribus fieri."—*Tractatus Magicus*, 1611

This is extremely interesting from its great antiquity, being mentioned in many works. Of it the author of the *Trinum Magicum*, referring apparently to DION CASSIUS, says :—

" And they were accustomed to divine sometimes with the ashes from the sacrifices. And to this day there is a trace of it, when that which is to be divined is written on the ashes with the finger or with a stick. Then the ashes are stirred by the fresh breeze, and one looks for the letters which they form by being moved. Or if *three maids* wish to learn which of them shall be married to a man, then they draw three lines in the ashes. He commands each one to choose a line (*sulcum*) and to turn her back so as not to see the lines, which meanwhile another indicates with the tongs, until one of them shall have chosen the same furrow three times, and when that one chooses his, she will be his future wife."

The Tuscan rite as taught me is as follows :—

" Take a goblet or cup full of pure water (hot) and three chairs in which three girls or women of the same age must sit. Each must take a pinch of salt and put it into the boiling water all together or at once. The one whose salt dissolves first will be the most fortunate. Then each must take a little bag of red woollen stuff full of ashes which have been very finely sifted ; let them sit with the cup in the middle, all three clad in black with black veils, and each has a sacred wafer which is marked with a cup.

" And to obtain these the three women go to church and partake of the communion, and when the priest gives them the consecrated wafer to put in their mouths they must slip it into their hands without the priest's knowing it. Then as these three wafers are marked with a cup, therefore it is not necessary to bless them, but two must be marked with special marks or pictures as of a heart or flower, that they may be known ; thus over the cup they make with a pin's point the heart or flower.

"Then each throws her ashes with the wafer into the boiling water and says, or one says :—

> "'Non butto la cenere,
> Ma butto l'ostia,
> Non butto l'ostia,
> Ma butto il corpo e l'anima
> (Secondo la persona che vuole nominare).
> Che non n'abbia più pace,
> E ne bene, fino che questa cosa
> Non ho ottenuto per bene.'

> ("'I do not throw the ashes,
> But I throw the wafer.
> I do not throw the wafer,
> But I throw the body and soul of . . .
> (Here the person is named)
> That he may no more have peace or happiness
> Until I have obtained this my desire !'[1])

"Then they must place their hands behind them and make the sign of the *castagna*, and not turn round to see the cup for a quarter of an hour ; and when they at last look they will see whether the wafers are floating on the surface. In this case they will all three have obtained their wish, and if only one swims, then the one whose it is will be favoured ; but if none float, no favour will be granted. *Allora se ne vada senza mai voltarsi indietro*—then they go without looking behind them."

This agrees with the ancient ceremony in this—that there are ashes used by three women, who go away without turning round. The whole is finally thrown into a running stream. In which we have a souvenir of VIRGIL and of THEOCRITUS.

> "Hinc cineres sub primum sideris ortum,
> Colligat, et fluvii ferat ad vada proxima vivi
> Una ministrarum, venitque ad flabra secundi
> Spurgat arenosis petris
> Namque ipsa retrorsum
> Respiciens properé redeat."

What renders this Tuscan incantation even more interesting is that it is the only complete account which I have ever met with of the manner in which the witches of the Middle Ages used the consecrated wafer in their sorcery. PAULUS GRILLANDUS, in his work *De Sortilegiis*, speaks of it with great horror, and tells us that it was specially used by women for love-spells. "In istis etiam

---

[1] *I.e.*, his love

sortilegiis ad amorem : ut plurimum admiscentur sacramenta ecclesiarum, sicut est hostia consecrata " (PAULUS GRILLANDUS, *Tractatus de Hæreticis et Sortilegiis* (Lyons, 1547), lib. ii., fol. 20, 21). GRILLANDUS had several cases of the the kind ; one of a priest "who took the *sacratissimam hostiam ipsam*—the very most sacred host itself, uttering as incantation—*verba satis turpia atque nephandaque hic referre non expediat* ("words utterly vile and wicked which it is not expedient to introduce here "). I have no doubt that these " nephanda," or wicked words, were the same which are given in the Italian incantation. "Nephanda " abundantly proves that if GRILLANDUS would not give his readers bad spells he certainly did not object to let them have bad spelling. His witches sometimes wrote "horrible words" with blood on the wafers ; at other times they powdered and administered them in wine. It is very remarkable that he—fully believing that such use of the wafer was a great sin—should publish the fact. He indeed tells us in one case he did not see or *perceive* any effect from it—which looks as if he had tried it ; but believers in magic might very well say that it was possible the party acted on did not " manifest " in his presence. Or did he publish the peculiar particulars hoping to make business ? Sometimes witches strew ashes on people and so cause terrible cutaneous disorders. While reading the proofs of this work in Homburg les Bains, I met with a very old blind man who was very well related to several professors, &c., though he had been only a poor carpenter ; and he told me that the witches, from a peculiar kind of coal-pebbles, prepared *ashes* which they strewed on their victims, and that he had thus suffered for six years. " Many people," he said, " ridicule this, but it is true."

Ashes in ancient symbolism signified that which is dead and past, or gone into oblivion. *Pulvis et umbra sumus.* It is remarkable that among the old Slavonians there was a divination by means of ashes which was much like the Roman. Women sat round the hearth and drew lines at random in the ashes. Then these were counted, and if the number of lines was even, the omen was fortunate (SCHWENK, *Mythologie der Slaven*, p. 24). Nearly the same oracle is still consulted in Poland. Ashes are strewn on the floor around the bed of an invalid, and a " wise woman" predicts from the lines whether the patient will recover" (GRIMM, *Deutsche Mythologie*, vol. ii., p. 1117).

Apropos of ashes and of the dead, I may here mention that in the year 1855 a German in Pennsylvania burned the body of his wife—which act was generally bitterly reprobated as heathenish, vile, revolting, and unchristian by the press. I, however, wrote in the Philadelphia *Evening Bulletin* an editorial article defending the German, and declaring that it would be an excellent thing for public health—as well as for the interests of the coal trade—should the practice of burning the dead become general. It would probably extinguish cholera and yellow fever for ever. These remarks of mine were considered at the time as very bold, even in the United States, where freedom of expression is not unusual. I do not know positively that I was the first person to advocate cremation in modern times, but I believe that I may claim to have been at least one of its *Vorgänger*, or pioneers.

CHAPTER V

THE AMETHYST

" The February-born will find
  Sincerity and peace of mind,
  Freedom from passion and from care,
  If they the *Amethyst* will wear."

Birthday Mottoes

" L'Amethiste a un lustre violet rouge, et est ainsi nommé, comme n'estant yure, aussi il resiste à l'yuronguerie . . . et profite aussi à ceux qui se veulent addonner à l'estude."—JEAN BAPTISTA PORTA, *De la Magie Naturelle.*

I ONCE knew a young Frenchman who affirmed that he was the only man living who knew the ancient language of Carthage—or some such town—which he had recovered from its ancient monuments. " So you really can read ancient Phœnician ! " I exclaimed in admiration. " *Mais, Monsieur,*" was the reply. " *Je le parle.*" " And with whom do you talk it ? " I inquired. And he replied, " *Monsieur, je fais des monologues.*"

I often feel as regards all this old Etrusco-Roman folk-lore as if I had rediscovered or dug up and deciphered it, like a forgotten tongue and after all were, with my Frenchman, the only soul on earth who knew the long-buried language or cared for it, and that when I speak of it must do so *en monologue.* And there is a charm and a solemn beauty in the spiritual or wizard language of the olden time ; and no wonder, for there was an era when it moved the world, and oracles spoke in it, and grand religions lived in it, and with them lived, in all their deep faith and many-hued gleams of glory, the Etruscan and the Roman.

And when I now and then find a flower of early faith still growing under the vile broad-leafing rank weeds which have covered all this antique garden, my heart leaps up and I begin to soliloquise even as I am doing now. What moved me to it was this: There is a lady in Florence to whom a nun, to whom she had been kind, sent three singular stones for a gift of gratitude, saying that she had nought else to give. As soon as I beheld them I saw that they were amulets, probably given up by some sinful penitent believer in witchcraft to a father-confessor. One was an amethyst, of no great value as a gem, but about two and a half inches in length, which has been, I think, originally a *celt*, and has at some later time had its edge ground off. It was probably of earliest ages; then carried by some old Roman, and so lost and found till it was given to me for a Christmas present in a red silk bag, December 25, 1891. Of the other two stones, one was a *salagrana* and the second a piece of antimony.

Everybody knows that the amethyst derives its name from its anti-vinous properties; for if you bear one you cannot be injured by wine. This I knew, and nothing more, till I carried the stone to my sybil and asked for a professional opinion on it. And it came in a form which subsequently startled me. I noticed as a very remarkable thing that, though she made no mention of it, she seemed to regard the stone as something personally known to her, at least by report, and that she studied it with great respect. It occurred at once to me that it was some *very* famous fetish which had long been lost, but of which the tradition had been preserved, like the black Voodoo stones of America. And I am now more convinced of it than ever.

"That is a magnificent amulet," she said, as if surprised, "very ancient and beautiful. This *pietra avvinata* — this stone mixed with wine (wine-stone)— buried and disinterred many years, must be carried to cause a good memory. Should any one wish to intoxicate you to betray you (*per farci qualche tradimento*), if you wear it he will not succeed. Wear it always at your side, and say:—

" ' Pietra che da qualche stregone o strega
    Tu sei certo stato sotterato,
    Perche la fortuna ad altri non hai voluto lasciare ;
    Ma si vede che tu ne sei pentita
    Ed hai voluto nelle mie mani farla ricapitare
    Ed io sapro bene conservarla
    E sempre al mio fianco portarla.
    Ti scongiuro o pietra !

    Scongiuro questa pietra che sempre fortuna mi voglia portare
    E da ogni male mi voglia liberare'
    Specialmente dai nemichi che volessero farmi
    Qualche traditimento
    Questa pietra mi possa liberare
    E se mi volessero ubbriachare,

O con vino o con liquore,
Questo pezzo di pietra avinato sara sempre
Il mio stregone liberatore !
Ti scongiuro o pietra ! ' "

(" ' Stone, who by some wizard or some witch
Hast certainly been buried long ago,
Because thou wouldst not bring good luck to others,
Now it is plain that thou hast repented,
And hast wished to recall it unto me ;
And I know right well how to preserve it,
And I ever by my side will bear it.
I conjure thee, O stone !

I conjure this stone to ever bring me fortune !
And that it may free me from all evil.
Specially from foes who fain would cause me
Some deceit.
May this stone free me !
Should any wish to intoxicate me
With wine, or other liquor,
This piece of wine-stone shall ever be
My wizard, freeing me from it !
I conjure thee, O stone ! ' ' ")

Now I knew that the amethyst was esteemed of old to be infallible against intoxication, or, as Baptista Porta saith : " *L'amethiste attaché au col sur la bouche du ventricule (al fianco) deliure de l'yurongnerie.*" But I did not know that it was " good for the memory," by which my witch meant, in her simple way, as I found, also intellect and intelligence. The belief of the fortune-teller very evidently was that this famous amulet—of which there was a tradition—had been buried by or with its owner, long ago, in order that others should not inherit it, but that it had by wizard influences been brought to light again, especially for me.

I have by me about two dozen books, but was not aware that among them I possessed a treatise—*De Gemmis*—by Franciscus Rueus, printed at Frankfort in 1608. It had escaped me, being bound up at the end of *De Miraculis Occultis*, by Levinus Lemnius. And turning over my small library, hoping against hope to find something to confirm this connection of the amethyst with intellect, I found that I, by mere chance, had just the very book of all books in the world which I required. For in it there is a chapter—xi., *De Amethysto*—in which it is said to not only protect against intoxication, but to stimulate genius—even as the witch had declared. " Addunt et alii malas illum arcere cogitationes, et præcox felixque ingenium efficere " (" It drives away bad thoughts, and confers ripe and happy genius "). And it also brings luck ; but here Rueus remembers himself, and declares that he will not impart the heathenish and unchristian superstitions which are reported of it—as I have done.

All of which reminds me of a story of my early days. When I was a small boy in Philadelphia, I had a Quaker schoolmaster, named Jacob Pierce, who delivered to us lectures on mineralogy, and encouraged us to make collections, giving us on every Saturday " specimens " as rewards of good conduct—in which distribution I, to my shame be it said, rarely had the first or any other choice (though it once happened to me that the rejected corner-stone which fell to my lot was the very gem of all). Being therefore a zealous mineralogist, it befell that one day on the wharf I found in the discarded ballast of stones brought by a vessel from Tampa Bay, Florida, many *ammonites*, among which was one which had been converted to pure chalcedony from its surroundings. With overloaded pockets I went into the office of a certain broker and banker, who, having examined my find with his friends, pronounced it to be " nothing but common oyster-shells and such-like rubbish." And after I had with pains investigated my three amulet-stones, I was told that they were in all likelihood only three common mineralogical specimens which the nun had picked up—which may, of course, be true—Italian nuns and their poor retainers being, as is well known, universally addicted to science in general and geology in particular.

The specimen prize which I got from my teacher was an amethyst, which I " traded " with another boy for an air-balloon, which caught fire while I was inflating it, and so perished. *Dii avertite omen !* and grant that this my amethyst-balloon of a book may soar to the skies—without burning my fingers!

May I add that the Rabbis called the amethyst *achlamah*, from *chalam*, to dream ; for they believed that it attracted to its wearer marvellous dreams. And Saint Isidore compared it to the Trinity, because it hath in it three colours : firstly, *purple*, which is imperial, and denotes God the Father and Ruler of the world ; that of *violet*, or humility (God the Son in His lowliness among men); and that of *rose*, which is expressive of love and of the Holy Spirit (*vide* Picinelli, *Mundus Symbolic*, p. 684).

Among the Egyptians the amethyst corresponded to the Zodiacal sign of the Goat (Kircher, *Œdip-Ægypt*, ii., p. 2). And as the goat was an enemy to vines, so the amethyst was a foe to wine.

Apropos of which citations I must, in frankness and simple honesty, remark that if there be here and there in this book some slight show of erudition—which I doubt not provokes the gently-pitying smile of many a learned folk-lorist—it is chiefly due to the girl with the wheelbarrow from whom I purchase antique lore, parchment-bound, at from a penny to threepence (this latter in cases of great temptation) the volume. This I take home and perfectly master, which accounts for these learned extracts. That is the way it is done. Then there is my tobacconist, who has for months past wrapped up cigars for me in leaves of the old *Encyclopædie Française;* or from a Latin folio of legal lore, to which I am greatly indebted. And on another occasion, when I bought two Etruscan vases for seven francs, I induced the dealer to throw in the work of Marsilius Ficinus on the Neo Platonists Iamblichus, &c. (Lyons, 1577), which edition I had been after for many a long year. And as it included the *Pimander,* &c., of Hermes Trismegistus (which work I copied entirely in my sixteenth year, not being able to buy it) you may judge if I was glad to get it!

The Spell of the Black Hen

" When thy black hen dies, thank God,
  Else thoud'st been lying 'neath the sod."

" When a black hen over a miser flies
  Soon after that the miser dies."
                                        German Proverbs

In the year 1886 there was found in the belfry of a church in England a curious object of which all that could be learned at first was from the authority of an old woman and that it was called a witch's ladder. An engraving of it was published in the *Folk-Lore Journal,* and several contributors soon explained its use. It consisted of a cord tied in knots at regular intervals, and in every knot the feather of a fowl had been inserted.

I was in Italy when I saw this engraving, and read that the real nature of the object had not been ascertained. I remarked that I would soon find it out, which I did, and that most unexpectedly. For by mere chance, the very first Italian woman with whom I conversed, being asked if she knew any stories about witches, began with the following :—

" Si. There was in Florence four years ago a child which was bewitched. It pined away. The parents took it to all the shrines in vain, and it died.

" Some time after something hard was felt in the bed on which the child had slept. They opened the bed and found what is called a *guirlanda delle strege,* or witches' garland. It is made by taking a cord and tying knots in it. While doing this pluck feathers one by one from a living hen, and stick them into the knots, uttering a malediction with every one. There was also found in the bed the figure of a hen made of stuff (cotton or the like)."

The next day I showed the woman the engraving of the witch-ladder in the *Folk-Lore Journal.* She was astonished, and said, " Why that is *la guirlanda delle strege* which I described yesterday." I did not pay any attention at the time to what was said of the image of a cock or hen being found with the knotted cord, but I have since ascertained that it formed the most important part of the whole incantation.

This is the spell of *Il Pollo nero*, or the Black Hen. It is as follows:—

" To bewitch one till he die: Take a black hen and pluck from it every feather; and this done, keep them all carefully, so that not one be lost. With these you may do any evil to grown people or children.

" Take the hairs of the person, or else the stockings, and those not clean, for there must be in them his or her perspiration. Then with black and red thread sew the stockings across one another. And if you have the hairs of the person, make of them a *guirlanda unita con stoppa*—a cord spun with flax or hemp—then take the feathers and *si cuopre questa robba* you cover (or work up) this thing in the form of a hen, and, taking the feathers, work or weave them with black and red thread into the covering of the hen, and put black pins in the form of a cross into the hen. It must then be hidden in the mattress or straw bed of the one whom you wish to bewitch, and say:—

" ' Questo pollo e maladetto,
E maladetto sia tutte
Le maledizioni la portate via,
Dal fondo del inferno,
Ma ora per una ora,
Le coma gliele voglio fare,
Che la maledizione la possa lasciare,
Et te (*il nome*) te la possa portare
Tu non abbia più pace!
E ne giorno e ne notte!
Fino che la strègeria
Che ti io ho fatto
Non ti vengo a levare!' "

(" ' This hen is accursed,
And cursed be all!
May the curses carry him away
Curses from the depths of hell
Now, for an hour
I would give him horns,
May the curse leave them on him!
And thou (the name) mayst thou bear them,
And have no more peace
Neither by day or night,
Until the bewitchment
Which I have wrought
Be removed by me!' "

THE COUNTER-CHARM.—"To remove this bewitchment you must open the mattress and find the hen and wreath, and throw all that holds it into running water.

" And then take the person bewitched, man, woman, or child, *che sia*, as it may be, and carry him or her into a church while a baptism is going on, and say:—

" 'In nome di Gesu, di Giuseppe,
E di Maria la benedizione
Di quel bambino benedisca
L'anima mia ! '

" This the one who is bewitched must say, but if it be a child who cannot speak, then the person who carries it must say :—

" ' In the name of Jesus and of Joseph,
And of Mary, may the blessing
Of that infant also bless
The soul of this child ! '

" Then carry it to some place near and bathe it in holy water."

This spell is considered as very terrible, and I had some difficulty in getting it. There is much curious lore connected with it, and there is every reason to believe that it is extremely ancient. In the museum (archæological) of Geneva, among the very old relics from Lacustrine dwellings, there is one of a hen, flat, knitted or felted from black hair or wool, or both. I copied it with some care, and my witch authority in Florence at once declared it to be a black hen made for magic. As it was found in water it may have been thrown there to destroy the spell, as the counter-charm prescribes. And that it is very ancient is effectively proved by the fact that other objects of the same material, and of the stone age, were found with it. This is presumptive evidence that the spell belongs to pre-historic or neolithic times.

The black hen, being an object of great fear and reverence, was worshipped by the Wends. From them it passed as a crest to the house of Henneberg (*vide* the *Symbolik* of FRIEDRICH) and to the quarterings of the Prince of Wales (*Puck*, 3 vols., 1852, by Dr. Bell). The gypsies in Hungary, to effect a certain cure, apply the body of a black hen to the sufferer, pronouncing an incantation. In Roumania when a Jewish girl has an *affaire du cœur* with the devil—or possibly with a devil of a fellow—the result is a black hen. But what is very nearly connected with this is the following : In Wallachia if a man has been robbed he goes to some sorcerer to take up "the black fast" against him. To do this the wizard must, in company with a black hen, fast for nine Fridays. Then the thief will either bring back the plunder or die. Mrs. Gerard, who gives this account, says nothing of what the ceremonies are attendant on the charm. I have no doubt that if we had the whole we should find that the Italian ceremony requires the nine Fridays' fast, and that the Wallachian Transylvanian spell is directed against any enemy, as well as a thief (*vide Gypsy Sorcery*, by CHARLES G. LELAND).

One of these Italian witch-garlands was exhibited by Mr. Tylor at the Folk-Lore Congress in 1891, and I have another which was given to me for a Christmas present. It is in a box covered with red flannel. In the box was a sprig of thorn leaves. The wreath had been completed by attaching it to a small *Japanese* cock made of feathers.

I have found in a number of works on folk-lore and superstitions such a number of spells and incantations, of which the black hen forms the chief item, that I find it impossible to include them within the limits of this work. I may mention, however, that when I was a boy in Philadelphia, in America, once hearing that a whole dead chicken, quite dried up, had been found in a feather bed.

As feathers for beds are always picked over, I have little doubt that this object had been put into the bed by some black person as a Voodoo charm.

The Spell of the Bell

" Much the witches fear the spell,
  When by night they hear a bell ;
  Off they fly, over the sky,
  When they hear *dondo, dondo, dondo !* "

Romagnola Song

The chief, if not the only use of bells in ancient days was to drive away demons, or dispel evil in every form ; and it is very evident that they were introduced to Christian churches far more for this purpose than to call to prayer. For, as in Ireland, the church bells were generally of the size and shape of the average cow-bell of America, making no more noise than the latter. There was found not many years ago in Rome a *tintinnabulum,* or little bell of silver bearing magical characters, the purport of which was to avert the evil eye. I have a facsimile of this presented by the late Sir Patrick Colquhoun. And also a very small bronze Etruscan (or Roman, according to Professor Milani) bell found at Chiusi—resting on my paper as I write—and what an aid it would be here an it could speak all that it e'er has seen !

These little square old bronze Roman bells with round corners are much prized among the peasantry for amulets. In the mountain land they are always kept in one of the two small cupboards, or recesses, on either side of the chimney-piece. I have a quaint little song in the Bolognese-Romagnola dialect, setting forth the fear of the witches when they hear at twilight-tide " those evening bells."

The following from Volterra, which is given word for word, sets forth the

manner in which the old campanologistic faith has been preserved to the present
day :—

" The little bell (*campanello*) is held of great esteem in the Romagna, as well as in Volterra, as a *jettatura*,
or sign against witches.   When one goes out of an evening he should carry one in his pocket—*ma pero bisogna
che sia di bronzo e quadrato*—but it should be of bronze, and four-cornered ; and while going along the bell
jingles in the pocket ; but because it sounds there the ring is indistinct, and the witches cannot count the
strokes of the clapper (*quante volte il pallino batte*), and are thus obliged to fly, and cannot approach the bearer
nor do him harm.

" Then putting it into the recess, or small cupboard by the chimney-piece (*buco del cammino*), repeat
this incantation :—

> " ' Metto nel buco del cammino,
> Questo campanello per tenere lontano
> Pluto e le sue compagne,
> Che in questa casa non si possino presentare ;

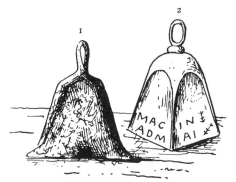

I.—ETRUSCAN BRONZE BELL, FROM CHINUSI, WORN AS AN AMULET
(In possession of the writer)   2.—OLD ROMAN MAGIC BELL

> Ne in forma di cane e ne di gatto,
> Ne di topo, ne di civetta,
> Ne di serpe, e ne di cornacchia,
> Quando alla mia casa si vengano
> A presenta questa campano suonare
> E tutti maligni si possino allontanare.' "

> (" ' In this corner of the cupboard,
> I put this bell to drive afar
> Pluto and his company,
> That in this house they' may not come,
> Neither in form of dog or cat,
> Nor of mole, nor of an owl,
> Nor of serpent, nor of crow !
> Should they come into my home,
> May the bell ringing drive the wretches away ! ' ")

Pluto—not Satan—here appears as leader of the witches. I have observed that the further we get from the Romagnola mountains into the plains, the more do the Roman gods appear. The shoemaker who gave this incantation had, however, some tincture of letters, having studied and read. Pluto may be a survival, but he is gently doubtful. But as I would not deprive a dying god of his very last chance for life on earth, I add that subsequent inquiry removed this dire suspicion. Pluto still lives. It may be noted here, by the way, that the belief that bells ring of themselves, and that chains rattle, to announce the presence of spirits, is of old Roman origin, as I find confirmed by Maffei in his *Magica Distrutta*—a work in which the author rides full tilt at the windmill of sorcery, utterly annihilating it, but never perceiving that he also destroys with the same lance another black spectre known as *la Santa Fede Cattolica*, or *La Chiesa Apostolica*, all of whose marvels and miracles came out of the same old tub. Think of this, O friend, when, in some darkened and gloomy hour, you are in church and hear the *padre* ring his little bell, and let a happy thrill of heathenism pass at the sound through your heart !

Not only bells, but trumpets and cymbals were used to drive away demons— which reminds me that few know whence came the idea of the last trump at the Day of Judgment—

> " Tuba mirum spargens sonum,
> Per sepulchras regionum,
> Cogens omnes ante thronum."

It is the great blast to be blown at the death-bed of a dying world, and was derived from a heathen source, as is set forth in the following passage from the same *Arte Magica Distrutta* of Maffei (1757) :—

" There was a strange religious ceremony which the Gentiles observed when dying. This was to play during the last agony on the horn, or trumpet, or instruments of metal, and of great noise. The motive to this was doubtless the belief that it drove away *larve* (demons) which, as it was believed, hated the sound of metal, which vulgar opinion is set forth by Lucian in *Philops*. The *Dire* were witches who flew through the air, concerning the driving away of whom by noise Pliny writes (l. 28, c. 2). Eusebius tells us that demons were driven away by the sound of *timpans*."

[*Timpani* are tambourines, and it is an awfully curious thing, by the way, that when bees swarmed these *timpans* were anciently used, and that *tin pans* are now beaten in their stead.]

That bells have souls, wills, and ways of their own is apparent from the number of marvellous instances recorded of their having rung of themselves without any human aid—as they did at the death of Von Rodenstein—albeit

Prætorius, who devotes several pages to this important subject in his marvellous and rare *Glückskopf* (1669), suggests that it may have been done by a *Poltergeist*, which is a spirit much given to noise and mischief, and which makes its appearance, in my belief, very often in the form of a medical student, but always as a youth.

Remains to be remarked that the little bronze bell is supposed to be a fairy lady—as her form suggests—and is the more human as having a voice. Which fancy did not escape the monks, who addressed them as saints, as you may read in the chapter on Bells in Southey's "Doctor" :—

> "Bellula bella, mî puella :
> Tu me corde tenes ! "

THE SPELL OF THE BOILING CLOTHES

The reader must not suppose that the charms, incantations, and devilments of different kinds which are here solemnly confided to him, are known to the multitude. Many have, it is true, leaked out ; but most of them are secrets rich and rare, treasured up among the elect who, dying, leave them as a rich legacy unto their issue. This was recalled to me by a curious incident alluded to in the preface. Firstly, I pray you read the following, as taken down four years ago— in 1888—from a witch :—

" *Quando si ha uno bambino stregato* (" When a babe is bewitched,"). Take the clothes of the child, and put them in a pot to boil at midnight. All the garments must go in, with shoes and stockings. Then take a new and very large knife, and sharpen it at a table, and say, sticking it in the table :—

> " ' Non infilo questo coltello
> Ma infilo la maladetta strega
> Che non viene ! Che non viene !
> Non possa resistere
> Sinquando in mio bambino
> Il salute non lo fa ritornare ! '

> (" ' I do not sharpen this knife,
> I whet the accursed witch,
> That she cannot resist coming
> Until unto my child
> She again restores health ! ')

" Then the witch will appear at the window—it may be at the door—in the form of a cat, or dog, or some form or spectre. But be in no fear, for these are but shifting forms (*forme cambiate*), and do not take the knife from the table nor let the clothes cease to boil till three o'clock.

" And being by this charm compelled to come and obey, the witch will remove the illness from the child."

In the *Secolo* of Milan, which has by far the most extensive circulation of any journal in Italy, there appeared, March 3, 1891, the following account of a serious and very singular disturbance :—

" A Mediæval Scene at Porta Ticinese

" We seem to dream, and yet this which we relate occurred yesterday morning here in Milan, and it is true in every one of its startling and shocking details.

" In the Via Ripa Porta Ticinese, No. 61, in a modest room on the fourth floor, dwelt the family of a journeyman varnisher, Malaterra Franciosi and his wife, Virginia, aged twenty-five, a glove-maker, with two children, one of which has been ill for a month with some unknown, obstinate, and strange disorder.

" A neighbour of the Franciosis, a woman who pretended to some knowledge of medicine, declared that the child was bewitched ; that it would be quite useless to have recourse to physicians and priests, and that the only way to cure it would be to discover the sorceress who had made the mischief. But how was it to be done ?

" The woman, as a great secret, after much entreaty from the Franciosis, taught them how it was to be done by putting the clothes of the child into a pot with water and boiling them. She declared that at the instant of the boiling, the witch would be drawn to the place by an irresistible diabolical force, and thus compelled to make herself known. This was done, and the clothes put in the pot and the pot on the fire.

" By mere chance, just as the water began to boil, a woman entered. This was one Angela Micheletti, thirty-four years of age, seven months gone with child. She was the wife of a labourer. Being a friend of the Franciosis, and on her way with a pair of wooden shoes to have them mended, she dropped in to inquire as to the health of the child.

" At seeing her the mother screamed ' *Dalli alla strega !* ' (' Give it to the witch !') La Micheletti, thinking that her friend had gone mad, tried to calm her, but the other, more exasperated, howled with all her force, ' *Aiuto! La strega !* ' (' Help ! the witch !') La Micheletti fled into the street.

" In an instant a great crowd had assembled, who, hearing the cry and accusation, all set upon La Micheletti as if she had been a mad dog, *per lacerarla à brani*—seeking to tear her to pieces. So she fled, pursued by the mad mob, crying, ' *Dalli alla strega !* ' The poor creature, more dead than alive, took refuge in the church of Santa Maria del Naviglio, but the crowd rushed in, and while she knelt before the grand altar, raising her hands in supplication, weeping and screaming for mercy, her hair was literally torn from her head and divided among the women who attacked her, and then she was very cruelly beaten. The *parocco*, or parish priest, tried to shield her, but in vain, and he himself escaped narrowly from being knocked down.

" The poor victim was then carried, amid all abuses and curses, from the church, and haled along to the room of the Franciosis. Here was another savage scene. La Micheletti being required to disenchant the child, to which she replied asserting her innocence of all such evil, and received howls, curses, and blows.

" Finally the Delegate, Sig. Omodeo, succeeded, with some military police and with great trouble, in dispersing the mob. Then the woman Franciosi, convinced too late of her unpardonable folly, fell on her knees before La Micheletti exclaiming, ' I am not to blame ; I was advised to do so by another—I was blinded by love of my child !'

" In the afternoon the poor Micheletti, accompanied by her husband and Sig. Omodeo, was taken home in a brougham and put to bed. This morning she was better but still trembling from her terrible experience. The sad impression of this savage mediæval scene will long be remembered in the suburb of Porta Ticinese.

" The women who tore the hair from the head of La Micheletti, went to their homes and burned it, pronouncing incantations, and than ran to the room of the Franciosis to see if the child was cured. And as they declared they had found it somewhat better, they cried, ' *Ecco se non è vero ch'è stata stregata !* ' (' See now, if it is not true that she is a witch !') "

Sometimes gloves or stockings alone are boiled for certain peculiar " points " in bewitching. Of the burning of hair to remove bewitchment I have elsewhere spoken. But the real moral meaning of this horrible story will not appear at once as it should to every reader. It is this: It was all very well for the *parocco*, or parish priest, to try to shield the woman at the altar, &c., but had that priest ever in all his life once told the people that there is no such thing as witchcraft, and that it is all delusion? Did any priest in Italy, or any of the Catholic teachers whose duty it is to enlighten their flocks, ever tell them plainly that there is no such thing as sorcery. No ; of course not. For that would be to attract doubts as to the truth of their own peculiar sorts of sorcery, incantation, and magic—just as the small American boy, who, when informed by his father that there was no such Christmas spirit as Santa Claus, asked reproachfully, " And have you been playing it off on me in the same way about Jesus too ? "

The Church at Rome does not deny the existence of modern witchcraft and sorcery. There are three, and I know not how many more, Roman Catholic books written to prove that all the mighty miracles of modern spiritualists, such as carrying cigarettes to secret places, playing banjoes in the dark, and bringing penny bouquets from Paradise, are all done by the devil, and these books have been licensed and approved by the Pope. Can anybody imagine that if these Milanese had been Protestants they would have acted as they did ? By their fruits shall ye know them !

Now in all such superstition Milan is as light to darkness compared to our Florence, and Florence in this respect is the same in relation to the Toscana Romagna.

I have also from Peppino, the youth frequently alluded to, a long and detailed account as to how quite recently, a child which was dying in the village of Premilcore in the Romagna Toscana, was saved by boiling its clothes and saying :—

> " Diavoli tutti
> Del inferno scatenatevi,
> Tutti e fate venire,
> La strega del mio bambino,
> In mia presenza. Sia ! "

Then the witch appeared, and by casting the usual *gomitolo*, or skein, into the air, the child was cured. Then the witch was taken by two other witches into the fields and rolled unmercifully over the ground till she lost all her power of witchcraft.

RING SORCERY

"A droite l'anneau presage
Prompt et heureux mariage,
A gauche il figure :
Abandon, rupture."

Le Jeu de Cartes de Mlle. Lenormand

Divination by means of rings was well known to the early Romans, and is thus described (*Trac. Magicus*, p. 92) : "Dactylomantia divinat annulis ad certam cœli posituram constructis vel incantamentis, et super tripodem ad certa verba motis" ("Dactylomancy is divining by means of rings made at certain planetary conjunctions, or with incantations, and moved on the tripod with certain words"). For tripod read tambourine, and for rings any small objects, and we shall have one of the most ancient forms of divination in existence. These small objects are, among the Hungarian gypsies, seeds of the deadly thorn-apple; in Lapland, the small image of a frog.

In modern Italy there is another kind of ring prophecy. It is, however, very ancient, and is known in many countries. Take a bowl, or vase, or cylinder, divide its inner edge into so many parts as there are letters of the alphabet.

Take a gold, or any other ring, and let it be consecrated. (*Consacrasi l'anello prima dell operazione.*) Then tie a thread to it and hold the end of the thread in the right hand and a sprig of verbena in the left. Let the ring hang in the cylinder. According to one authority the thread should be wrapped round the thumb and pass over the pulse so as to secure the right vibration. Then ask a question and the ring will begin to swing, and strike on the letters and spell out the reply.

As I have said, this is a very ancient species of prediction or invocation. It is the same in principle with the planchette, but requires only one operator. It may be observed that when the person who holds the thread is deeply in earnest, or believing, and has prepared himself to work the oracle by serious reflection, the replies spelled out are often very remarkable, not to say startling, and whether produced by involuntary mental action or by external causes, they are in most cases curious. I have met with the assertion that by means of the thread and ring one can always ascertain exactly what o'clock it is when the edge of the cup is divided in twelve parts. " How would it be where.the day is divided into *twenty-four* hours ? " It would be just the same, and true answers would be often given, because the action is *subjective*, or comes from the operator.

Another variety of this kind of divination is to place an evenly balanced rod, or needle like that of a mariner's compass, on a pivot, in the centre of a plate. Around the edge, in circles, are letters and numbers. This is a kind of roulette. Give the bar a turn and when it ceases revolving observe the letter or number opposite which it stops.

Again, take a round, flat surface, say a wooden plate surrounded by a border half an inch in height. This surface is covered with numbers and letters. Then take a ring and spin it as one spins a coin. We draw conclusions from the letters, &c., on which it falls.

Apropos of roulette and the ancients there is at Homburg les Bains a collection of ancient Roman remains, and in an adjoining room the roulette table which was last used in 1871. Two or three of the average class of English, or American, tourists, being shown through the collection, cried, on seeing the wheel, " And is *that* old Roman, and did the Romans play roulette ! How interesting ! " For the truth of which I vouch " with both hands," having heard it.

An ancient ring which has been long worn is said to be the best for divination. I have one of silver with the image of a toad cut in hæmatite in it, about four hundred years old, which has, I doubt not, been frequently tried in spells. Also a silver and enamel messenger ring which once belonged to King Roger of Sicily, which, if it could tell all it ever witnessed, might describe the story of Schiller's Diver.

AMULETS, OMENS AND SMALL SORCERIES

I include in this chapter certain odds and ends of folk-lore which are not without interest. The first which I shall give is *the pine-cone.*

" Take a pine-cone, after all the *pinoli* (nuts or seeds) have been removed. Then on every scale, or within it between the scales, put a *lupine* (dry). Then take a flower-pot and fill it with fine earth, and plant the cone in it quite covered with earth or buried. Put it out in the air, and water it like any flower. Should it grow well and look prettily it is a sign that all things will go well with you. But its growing badly is a bad sign. But you must always keep it by you to secure the good luck, and even carry it with you when you travel. And to maintain the principle (*bisogna tenere la sistema*) you should plant a new cone every year."

American young ladies have a somewhat similar oracle in the sweet potato which also makes a very pretty fortune-teller. If it flowers or leaves well, it is a sign that the owner will be magnificently dressed on her wedding-day, and have a grand *festa*, which, I suppose, will be "in all the papers." *Apropos* of this very small gardening, it may be mentioned that since Roman times, and perhaps much earlier, the planting of cress, mustard, or seeds of any sort to divine luck by their growth, has been common in all countries. One very easy form is as follows : If you keep a bird—say a canary—get an empty box, a raisin box, eighteen inches or two feet in length, fill it with earth and hang the cage over it. Throw into the earth the cleanings of the cage and a few canary or hemp seeds. These will soon grow, and when sprouting or about an inch high will be devoured by the bird with avidity. This is very lucky for the canary.

Very old keys are good amulets for luck. They may be carried in the pocket or hung up by a red ribbon in the room. And it is very lucky to find one. While picking it up you should say :—

> "Non prendo questo chiave l'ho trovato·
> E lo porto con me, ma non porto
> La chiave pero la fortuna
> Che sia sempre appresso di me.

> ("'Tis not a key which I have found
> Nor one which I shall bear around,
> But fortune which I trust will be,
> Ever my friend and near to me.)

"And this may be said for anything else which is found."

The special meaning of the key is success with women, the word key (*chiave*) being applied to the virile organ, and *chiavare*, "to key" to the act of copulation. Its general signification as an omen is success in your next undertaking. Thus to dream of a key or see one is a good sign :—

> "La clef près de ta main
> Annonce qu' à la fin
> Tu auras du succès
> Dans tes derniers projets."

If you blow or whistle in a key, especially an old one, it will call to you spirits or fairies, who will be favourable to you and aid you, in love above all things.

We can divine with keys in several ways. By locking a padlock when a couple are married, one can stop all intimacy between them. But it is with the sieve that Master Key becomes a great sorcerer, as was once set forth in the *St. James's Gazette* :—

" Methods of discovering the names of thieves and the whereabouts of stolen goods were endless ; and many an old hag, down almost to our own time, has driven a profitable trade with 'infallible' means of divination as old as the fire-worshippers. The formulæ most frequently used for these purposes were known as 'the key' and 'the sieve.' The name of the suspected person was written upon a piece of paper placed around a key ; the key was tied to a volume of Scripture, and the whole suspended by a cord spun for the purpose, from the finger of a young unmarried woman. Three times she repeated in a low voice the verse 'Exurge, Domine'; and if at the words moved the key and the book turned, the guilt of the suspect was proved. If neither of them moved his innocence was clear. Divination by the sieve was long in high favour, for this was deemed to be the most certain of all methods. Hence, says Erasmus, the proverb 'To divine with the sieve'—to express the certainty of a thing. A sieve was suspended from a pair of scissors held by two assistants. The operator, having pronounced the name of the suspected person, repeated a shibboleth consisting of six words—*dies, mies, jesquet, benedoe, fet, dowina*—' which neither he or his assistants understood.' If the person whose name was mentioned were guilty, the six magical words 'compelled the demon to make the sieve spin round.' Pierre D'Abanne—the author of a most entertaining manuscript work on the elements of magic, preserved in the Bibliothèque de l'Arsenal[1]—recounts that he used this method three times with the most complete success, and then gave it up ; fearing that the demon, in revenge for having been compelled to tell the truth three times in succession to one man—greatly, no doubt, to his chargin, since he is by nature a liar—would draw his tormentor into toils from which there would be no escape.

Never pass by a coin, however trifling ; should you let it lie your luck will pass to the person who finds and takes it. But on picking it up repeat the same lines.

" To know the future or how any event will end, or what your luck will be in a lottery: Take a dry poppy-pod, make a hole in it, shake out the seed and place in it a paper on which your question is written. Then put it beneath your pillow and repeat :—

> " ' In nome del cielo, delle stelle, della luna,
> Fate mi face il sogno secondo . . . (le mie intenzione). ' "

> (" ' In the name of heaven the stars and the moon !
> May I dream and that full soon,
> If this I see . . . (here repeat your wish).' ")

The poppy was not only sacred to the god of dreams and of sleep, but owing to the immense number of its seeds was a type of fertility and wealth. Hence the gilt poppy-heads, so commonly seen in the apothecaries' windows, which are or were originally amulets to bring money.

Another amulet allied to dreaming is made by taking twigs or bits of small boughs from an oak-tree (in England of mountain-ash). Bind two of these so as to make a cross, or lay them across one another on the table, or stand, by your bed, and repeat before going to sleep :—

> " Non metto questa quercia,
> Ma metto la fortuna,
> Che non possa abbandonar'
> Mai la casa mia."

---

[1] It has been several times published ; the last edition is by Scheibele of Stuttgart (in his *Kloster*).

("'Tis not oak which here I place,
But good fortune—by its grace
May it never pass away,
But ever in my dwelling stay.")

The sticks should be bound with red ribbon (woollen), and the cross thus formed and spelled becomes an amulet which may be hung up to bring good luck or drive away misfortune.

Whenever one puts on a new garment, he or she should repeat this spell :—

"Porto questo vestito
Per maggior fortuna
Sia maladetto, maladetto sia !
Chi cerca nella mia vita
Di portar qualche malia !"

("This coat I wear, this garment bear,
To bring good luck to me ;
If any man begrudge that luck,
May he accursed be !")

Should you find, or pick up, or even see any object, you may divine by it what is to happen. Thus if the first bit of ribbon, or string, or cloth which you find is of any colour, especially if it be new and fresh, it will portend :—

Red (especially scarlet)—Good fortune, prosperity, successful love.

Yellow—Jealousy ; according to some, gold.

Grey—Peace, calm, content.

Silver—Disquiet, disturbance, passion, pain.

Gold—Fortune, prosperity, gain, intelligence.

Black—Vexation, discontent, trouble.

Orange—Misfortune.

The belief in the magic virtue of red, especially of red wool, is as general in Italy as it is ancient. As it is the colour of the blood and of fire, it is sacred to life and heat. So a red ribbon or cloth hung from a window or over a bed brings luck.

" When one sees a very fine large butterfly, catch it as carefully as you can without hurting it, and look under its wings, for there you may often find characters which indicate winning numbers in the lottery, or Yes or No to a question. Then let it go again, for your luck will depend on not injuring it. And this is the case with serpents or any animals which are marked, for there is writing in all things if we can but read it."

To find a horse-shoe is as lucky in Tuscany as it is elsewhere. Hay is also luck-bringing. If you find a horse-shoe, make a red bag and put the horse-shoe into it with hay, and it will be an admirable amulet. It is to be kept always in the bed.

"If a youth loves a maid he will do much to win her affections should he give her *amorino*, that is mignonette."

In this case we can infer that *nomen est omen.*

Shoes or gloves when boiled in water yield a liquid which if not palatable is however of great use in witchcraft, though I am not informed as to the exact manner in which this *soupe au shoe* is served up.[1]

When children see a *lucciola*, a fire-fly, they sing a strange little song which is also an incantation for luck :—

> "Lucciola ! Lucciola !
> Viene a gara !
> Mette la briglia
> A la cavalla,
> Mette la briglia
> Al figluolo del re,
> Che la fortuna
> Venga con me,
> Luciola mia
> Viene da me !"

> ("Fire-fly ! O Fire-fly !
> Enter the course ;
> Come, put the bridle
> Now on the horse !
> Come, put the bridle
> On the king's son,
> So that good fortune
> By me may be won !
> Fire-fly ! O Fire-fly
> Make it my own !")

When a woman has a sore throat (*effeto di lu gola abassata*), she must take her own apron and measure or fold it in a cross thrice (*misuararla in croce*), for three mornings in succession. Then when she has done this she must, before eating, put three pins crossed with a sharpened knife stuck into the table and say :—

> "Diavolo, vi discongiuro !
> In carne ed ossa,

---

[1] In Voodoo if a woman gets another's shoes which have just been taken off, and takes off her own and laces them inside the other pair, and so leaves them till morning, the man is sure to fall in love with her.—Note by MARY A. OWEN

Si questa donna e stregata
Questa strega tenerla stregata,
Più non possa,
Sinoquando questa donna non guarira
Questo coltello del tavola non sortira
E cosi la strega più pace non avra'!"

("Devil, I conjure thee alone,
In flesh and in bone!
If this woman bewitched be,
The witch at once shall set her free!
Till she's freed from all her pain
The knife i' the table shall remain,
And the witch shall feel the knife
In her soul and in her life!")

This is interesting as indicating the Shamanism according to which every pain or the least disorder is supposed to be caused by sorcery—a doctrine which exists in full force in another form known as Prayers for the Sick.

Egg-shells are witches' goblets for drinking. Therefore lest they use them for such, one should after eating an egg break the shell to fragments, and throw them into a running stream and say:—

"Se sei una strega
Va al diavolo,
Che tu porta via
Assieme coll' acqua corsia!"

("If thou art a witch,
Go, O devil's daughter!
And be borne away
On the running water!")

It is commonly said that—

"Spilling or dropping wine
Is a very lucky sign;
But spilling or dropping oil,
Much good luck will spoil."

However, when the wine upsets, some think it is witch-work, and so they put the palm of the hand in the wine, and then strike it on the forehead and say, making the sign of the cross:—

> " In nome del cielo,
>> Delle stelle e della luna !
>> A chi me ha dato il malaugurio,
>> Me lascia la buona fortuna ! "

> (" In the name of heaven,
>> Of the stars and moon ;
>> May the one who gave misfortune,
>> Bring me better luck and soon ! ")

But that, *vin repandu porte bonheur*, is a very old belief. It forms the theme of an old Norman-French *fabliau*. There is a very curious custom observed in La Romagna, which was thus described :—

" When it has not rained for a long time and the fields are dry, they take stones and roll them through the field and say :—

> " ' Queste pietre voglio rullare,
>> Ma non rullo le pietre,
>> Rullo le pietre, rullo l'acqua
>> Che in terra possa venire,
>> Ed i campi mi possa umidire,
>> E cosi buona raccolta possa venire ! ' "

> (" ' I wish indeed to roll this stone,
>> And yet it is not it alone,
>> I roll the stone that water may
>> Come in these fields so dry to-day,
>> And water well the thirsty field,
>> So that it may good harvest yield ! ' ")

PRELLER states (*Rom. Myth.*, p. 312) that in the temple of Mars there was kept a great stone cylinder which, when there was a great drought, was rolled by his priests through the town. And we know that such an application of similar stones was common in Italy in dry seasons, especially in the country. And LABEO in his work on the Etruscan books of ritual, writes : " Fibræ jecoris sandaracei coloris dum fuerint, manales tunc vertere opus, est petras, id est quas solebant antiqui in modum cylindrorum per limites trahere pro pluviæ commutanda inopia." Traces of the custom are found in other countries.

As among the Romans, the picture of a bunch of grapes, rudely painted, is placed in vineyards in Northern Italy, as an amulet to secure a good crop.

There are many curious ideas current as to old Roman and Etruscan relics, which are, however, generally supposed to be connected with ancient sorcery. On this subject I obtained the following very curious information :—

" When a woman is *incinta*, or *enceinte*, she should not look at animals, and especially beware seeing those figures depicted or set forth in bronze, leather, or cloth, which are half animals and half men, with heads like goats and legs of Christians (*col capo di capra, e le gambe di Cristiano*), or faces with the legs of devils, like those of a horse (*i.e.*, Pan and the sylvan gods).

" If a woman at such a time looks at these it may easily happen that she will have a son like them, for it may come to pass in such cases that he will be born in similar form and so easily become a wizard. "

That is, the old latent sorcery will pass to the child and be developed in it. The images here referred to are mostly the old Roman bronze figures of rural deities or *lares*, which are so frequently found in *schiavi*, or excavations. Among these are many *ex voto* offèrings, the same in nature with the little figures of wax so common in Catholic churches. It is worth observing that the ancients went to much greater expense in such marks of gratitude for divine aid than do modern Catholic Christians. Bronze was dearer then than wax is now, but it was quite as freely employed by the faithful.

Certain spells are used in Tuscany with a double meaning, that is to say, they are employed either to injure a certain person, or else to defeat an evil witch, or to break a spell or cure a disease. Among these are the following : A plant or herb, having had an incantation pronounced over it (nearly the same in form with several which I have given) is left to wither, the belief being that, as it fades, the person or disease or enchantment will slowly die or vanish. Again, an apple is cut to pieces— a common form of magic—or an orange or lemon is stuck full of pins and left to dry up, with the same consequences. Also a stick is broken, which is similarly a formula known in the West where it has become a legal form, or else a piece of woollen felted or woven cloth is pulled apart. All of these spells are very ancient and may be found in certain conjurations, given in Lenormant's *Magie Chaldaïenne*, for which they were translated from Accadian cylinders. The author remarks that while pronouncing them the operator had to perform certain conjurations resembling those described in the *Pharmaceutria* of Theocritus and in Virgil's VIII. the Eclogue, which are also essentially those now in use. The Assyrian incantations are as follows :—

I

As this plant withers, so shall also the spell !
The burning fire shall devour it !
It shall not be arranged on the lines of a vine arbour ;
it shall not be trained into an orchard, an . . . ;
the earth shall not receive its root ;
its fruit shall not grow, and the sun shall not smile upon it ;
it shall not be offered at the festivals of kings and gods !
The man who has cast the evil fate, his wife,
the violent operation, the finger pointing, the written spell, the curses, the sins,

the evil that is in my body, in my flesh, in my bruises,
may [all that] be withered like this plant!
May the burning fire devour it this day!
May the evil fate depart and may I behold the light again!

II

As this fruit is divided into pieces, so shall also the spell be!
The burning fire shall devour it;
it shall not return to the supporting branch from which it is cut off;
it shall not be offered at the festivals of kings or gods!
The man who has cast the evil fate, his wife,
the violent operation [*i.e.*, evil invocation], the finger pointing, the written spell, the curses, the sins,
the evil that is in my body, in my flesh, in my bruises,
may all [that] be divided in pieces like this fruit!
May the burning fire devour it this day!
May the evil fate depart, and may I behold the light again!

III

As this twig is plucked up and broken in pieces, so shall also the spell be,
The burning fire shall devour it!
its fibres shall not again unite themselves to the trunk;
it shall not arrive at a perfect state of splendour!
The man who has cast the evil fate, his wife,
the violent operation, the pointing with the finger, the written spell, the curses, the sins,
The evil which is in my body, in my flesh, in my bruises,
may [all that] be broken in pieces and plucked up like this twig!
May the burning fire devour it this day!
May the evil fate depart, and may I behold the light again!

IV

As this wool is rent so also shall the spell be,
The burning fire shall devour it!
It shall not return to the back of its sheep;
it shall not be offered for the garments of kings and gods!
The man who has cast the evil fate, his wife,
the evil spell, the finger pointing, the written spells, the curses, the sins,
the evil which is in my body, in my flesh, in my bruises,
may all [that] be rent like this wool!
May the burning fire devour it this day!
May the evil fate depart, and may I behold the light again!

Like unto this are two other incantations, one applied to rending a banner, the other to tearing up a piece of frilled stuff. I call attention to the fact that these are so strikingly like the modern Tuscan both as regards subject, spirit, and general treatment, that the burden of disproof in reference to a common origin should in common sense fall on the sceptic. These Chaldæan cylinders speak of seventy-seven fevers—*i.e.*, all diseases—as coming from the seven primary demons of disease. The Bogomile Slavonian heretics of the fourteenth century also recognised the seventy-seven fevers and had an exorcism for them.   And in an old German spell current in Pennsylvania we have as a cure for fever the following :—

"Good-morning, dear Thursday !   Take away from —— the seventy-seven fevers !   O thou dear Lord Christ, take them away from him. . . ."

In the Chaldæan incantation against the plague (*i.e.*, the seventy-seven personified) the operator must turn his face towards the setting sun.   In the German spell he must not speak to any one till after sunrise, which involves the same idea.

It is very remarkable that all over the world a black pebble of kidney shape is supposed to be one of the most powerful of amulets.   At the Folk-Lore Congress of 1891, such stones were exhibited from widely different countries.   I myself possess one which was brought from Missouri and presented to me by Miss Mary A. Owen, to which most extraordinary value and reverence was attached by the black Voodoos and their disciples.   It had been kept with the most jealous care for many generations in the families of these sorcerers, and came originally from Africa.   To become an ordinary Voodoo, the postulant must fast and watch, undergo revolting penances, and cultivate " power " and " will " all his life.   But the possession of an authenticated " cunjerin'," or conjuring-stone, renders all this unnecessary, the owner by the mere act of possession becomes a grand past-master Voodoo, or *multote*, and requires no further initiation.   Even the chief black sorcerer in Missouri, or the king, has never been able to get one.[1] It would be useless to attempt to palm off a similar black pebble for a real one, since it is said that there are in all North America only six—or rather five, mine being one of the half-dozen—and their possessors are all well known, as is every mark in the stones.   Black believers have been known to make a pilgrimage of a thousand miles to be touched with this marvellous stone—or to hold it in the hand.   I hold it in my left hand as I write, mildly trusting that I may thereby charm, or at least interest thee, O reader.   It must, like all Voodoo amulets, be carried in a wrapping, or a bag, which may be closed by wrapping a string round it, which must not, however, be tied, as that would prevent the free egress or ingress of the spirit which dwells in it.   Once a week it should be dipped in, or touched with, whiskey, but I am assured that *eau de Cologne* will answer just as well, which it surely ought to do, since the recipe for it was given by an angel to Saint Elizabeth of Hungary.

---

[1] This remarkable man who was known as " King Alexander " died while this work was being printed.

LEAD AND ANTIMONY

"Talismani erano pietre, o gemme co *pezzetti di metallo* . . . in forza di quale si credeva avessero straordinarie virtú, e singolari, ma la frequenza loro, e il credito venne da' Gnostici, e da Basilidiano, de quali assai parla nel suo libro, santo Ireneo."—*Arte Magica Distrutta*, MAFFEI, 1757

"Non solùm verò in plantis quæ vestigium habent vitæ, sed etiam in lapidibus aspicere licet, imitationem et participationem, quandam luminum supernorum."—*Proclus de Sacrificio et Magia* (Interpre MARSILIO FICINO), LUGDUNI, 1577

A piece of lead ore is supposed to possess peculiar virtue as an amulet against *malocchio,* or to bring luck. Of these I have seen three, two of which I possess, with the invocation which must be pronounced when one is tied up in the usual red woollen bag. Far more potent, however, are the old Roman sling-stones, or pointed slugs of lead, of which such numbers are everywhere found, and of which I have two, which I bought for a half-franc each, as talismans for the evil eye. But more effective still is a lump of crude antimony. This is supposed

ROMAN SLING-STONE

to also contain zinc and copper, which give it great power. For these I have also the *scongiurazioni,* which are as follows. I believe them, however, to be imperfectly recalled :—

" Antimonio che sei di zingo e di rame :
Il più potente ti tengo sempre con me,
Perche tu mi alontani le cattive gente,
Da me alontanera,
E la buona fortuna a me attirerai ! "

(" Antimony, who art of zinc and copper!
Thou most powerful, I keep thee ever by me,
That thou mayest banish from me evil people,
And bring good luck to me.")

That for lead was obtained for me, written in the following words, *verb. et lit.* :—

" Antimogno che di piombo sei
Non ai la stessa forza della zingo e rame,
Ma prestati per la forza che tu ai
Tutte le chattive persone da me alontanerai
Ela buona fortuna mi attirerai ! "

("Thou antimony, who art lead,
Not having the force of zinc and copper,
But grant that by the power which thou hast,
That thou wilt keep all evil people from me!")

It will be observed that in both of these invocations great stress is laid on the virtue of *copper*, which is probably derived from the old Roman religious feeling regarding it, as the "body" of bronze. But after much weary inquiry, owing to the difficulty which my informant had to put her ideas into form, I elicited these ideas : " The metals have all their occult virtues and their light—that is, their lustre—when broken ; deep in the earth, and in darkness, this light still shines in itself; it is a light dreaded by evil beings. Copper and gold have the reddest light ; this is the most genial, or luck-bringing ; and copper is supposed to form part of antimony. Antimony is stronger than lead, because it consists of three metals, or rather always has in it copper and lead."

There is strong confirmation of this theory in Cardanus (*De Rerum Varietate*, xvi., 8, 9) and Peter of Arles (*Sympathia septem metallorum et septem selectorum lapidum ad planetas.* Paris, 1711), or as it is set forth by Nork in his *Etymologisch-symbolisch-mythologisches Realwörterbuch* :—

" What the stars are in the nightly heaven, that are the gleaming metals in the dark abyss of the earth, therefore it is intelligible that those earthly gatherers of light should be associated with the heavenly ones, and as the worship of light was concentrated in the sun and planets, so unto every leading planet there was assigned a glittering metal according to its degree of radiance."

This is also curious since it suggests the source whence Novalis drew his famed simile that miners are inverted astrologers, reading in the earth the past, just as other seers read in the heavens the future. And it seemed to linger quaintly in the fancy that copper and antimony and lead have all their "light" and magic mystic power.

A few days ago I bought in an old shop an amulet of lead ore in which a piece of copper was embedded. This was, as the American negroes say, " a mighty strong cunjerin' stone." So I purchased it for a franc—the bargain including two little old bronze Etruscan images, one of Aplu and the other of god Nosoo, or the *deus incognitus*.

Apropos of this shop, it was one where the *prezzi fissi* principle was carried out, that is, of fixed prices marked on the wares. This does not mean at all in Italy that a dealer will not take less, but that he binds himself not to take any *more*. The price is convenient as giving a basis for a bargain. Its being "fixed," according to the Italian idea, is that the piece of paper marked is "*fisso*," *i.e.*, fixed, or stuck on the article indicated. Now this young man had the first volume of the *Museum Etruscum* of Antonio F. Gori, 1737, marked "ten francs," but seeing that I wanted it he offered it for eight.

"Throw in that fourteenth-century Virgin on a panel, with a gold background," I said, "and it's a bargain."

So the Madonna was thrown in in a hurry—she was really well worth about tenpence—and we were all satisfied.

This was indeed—as the French advertisement in a shop for the sale of Roman Catholic "idolatries" announced—"une Vièrge d'occasion." I may here mention that these are the only kind of pictures which I ever buy; in which I very much resemble a young gentleman of my acquaintance who only admires ladies with large fortunes. All of his madonnas, like mine, have gold backgrounds.

The picture was fearfully dilapidated, but with *gesso* and gouache colours, and white of eggs, and gum, and gold, I restored it so that it seems better than new for it looks every whit of its four hundred and fifty years, or even older. But then the surroundings are favourable to such work—for Florence is a famous place for rehabilitating damaged Virgins—and I have heard some marvellous stories about such *rifatture*—which I omit for want of space.

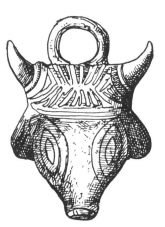

BRONZE ETRUSCAN AMULET AGAINST THE EVIL EYE
(In possession of the Author)

INDEX OF SUBJECTS AND AUTHORITIES